NEGOTIATING RITES

OXFORD RITUAL STUDIES SERIES

Series Editors

Ronald Grimes, Radboud University Nijmegen

Ute Hüsken, University of Oslo

Eric Venbrux, Radboud University Nijmegen

THE PROBLEM OF RITUAL EFFICACY

Edited by William S. Sax, Johannes Quack, and Jan Weinhold

PERFORMING THE REFORMATION

Public Ritual in the City of Luther

Barry Stephenson

RITUAL, MEDIA, AND CONFLICT

Edited by Ronald L. Grimes, Ute Hüsken, Udo Simon, and Eric Venbrux

KNOWING BODY, MOVING MIND

Ritualizing and Learning in Two Buddhist Centers in Toronto

Patricia Q. Campbell

NEGOTIATING RITES

Edited by Ute Hüsken and Frank Neubert

Negotiating Rites

Edited by Ute Hüsken
Frank Neubert

OXFORD
UNIVERSITY PRESS

OXFORD
UNIVERSITY PRESS

Oxford University Press, Inc., publishes works that further
Oxford University's objective of excellence
in research, scholarship, and education.

Oxford New York
Auckland Cape Town Dar es Salaam Hong Kong Karachi
Kuala Lumpur Madrid Melbourne Mexico City Nairobi
New Delhi Shanghai Taipei Toronto

With offices in
Argentina Austria Brazil Chile Czech Republic France Greece
Guatemala Hungary Italy Japan Poland Portugal Singapore
South Korea Switzerland Thailand Turkey Ukraine Vietnam

Published by Oxford University Press, Inc.
198 Madison Avenue, New York, New York 10016

www.oup.com

Library of Congress Cataloging-in-Publication Data

Negotiating rites / edited by Ute Hüsken and Frank Neubert.
p. cm.
Includes bibliographical references and index.
ISBN 978-0-19-981229-5 (hardcover : alk. paper)—ISBN 978-0-19-981231-8 (pbk. : alk. paper)
1. Ritual. 2. Negotiation—Religious aspects. I. Hüsken, Ute. II. Neubert, Frank.
BL600.N44 2011
203'.8—dc22 2011006732

1 2 3 4 5 6 7 8 9

Printed in the United States of America
on acid-free paper

Contents

Contributors

Mikael Aktor is an associate professor at the University of Southern Denmark, where he teaches the history of religions and Sanskrit. His research has focused on Classical Indian law, modern global Buddhism, and Hindu ritual and temple sculpture.

Nikki Bado is associate Professor of Religious Studies at Iowa State. She has written two books: *Coming to the Edge of the Circle: A Wiccan Initiation Ritual* and *Toying with God: The World of Religious Games and Dolls*, with Rebecca S. Norris. Bado is co-editor of the Equinox book series on Contemporary and Historical Paganism and serves on the board of the *Journal of Magic, Ritual, and Witchcraft*. She is currently a Visiting Research Fellow at the Nanzan Institute for Religion and Culture in Nagoya, Japan.

Patricia Q. Campbell is a scholar of contemporary western Buddhism and ritual studies. She is currently teaching in the areas of ritual studies and East Asian religions at Mount Allison University in New Brunswick, Canada. She has published ethnographic studies of western Buddhists in Canada and is the author of *Knowing Body, Moving Mind*, a study of ritual and learning in western Buddhism, which is forthcoming from Oxford University Press.

Magnus Echtler teaches African religions at the University of Bayreuth. He has been working on rituals of popular Islam in Zanzibar, religious video films in Nigeria, and most recently on African Initiated Churches in South Africa.

Amy Holmes-Tagchungdarpa is an assistant professor in the Department of History at the University of Alabama. She is the author of *The Social Life of Tibetan Biography: Textuality, Community and Authority in the Lineage of Tokden Shakya Shri* (forthcoming) and essays on Tibetan, Chinese, and Himalayan social and cultural history. She received her PhD at the Australian National University.

Ute Hüsken is a professor of Sanskrit at Oslo University. She was educated as an Indian and Tibetan studies scholar and as a cultural anthropologist in Göttingen

(Germany). Hüsken was a member of the Dynamics of Ritual collaborative research center at the University of Heidelberg (Germany) and is co-chair of the Ritual Studies Group (American Academy of Religion). Together with Ronald L. Grimes (Canada and the Netherlands) and Eric Venbrux (the Netherlands) she initiated the new Oxford University Press series Oxford Ritual Studies, of which she is co-editor.

Petra Kieffer-Pülz studied Indology, Tibetology, and classical and Near Eastern archaeology at the universities of Basel and Bern in Switzerland and Berlin and Göttingen in Germany. She received her MA and her PhD from Göttingen University. She was a research assistant at the Sanskrit-Wörterbuch der Turfan-Funde (Academy of Sciences, Göttingen) and was employed at Martin Luther University in Halle-Wittenberg with the German Research Foundation project Die Gaṇṭhipadas in der Vajirabuddhiṭīkā (The Gaṇṭhipadas in the Vajirabuddhiṭīkā). She currently works on the German Research Foundation project Wissenschaftliches Pāli (Scholastic Pali) at the Academy of Sciences and Literature in Mainz. She has published on the Buddhist traditions of India and Sri Lanka, with a focus on Buddhist law.

Shari Rochelle Lash is a graduate of the Religion and Culture Master of Arts Program at Wlifrid Laurier University. She is currently assistant to the senior rabbi at Temple Sinai Congregation of Toronto, presently the only large synagogue in Canada with a constitutional policy that includes officiation at same-sex marriage ceremonies. A portion of Lash's research, "Struggling with Tradition: Making Room for Same-Sex Marriage in a Liberal Jewish Context," is published in the "Wedding Realities" issue of *Ethnologies* (2006).

Erik de Maaker is a lecturer and researcher at the Institute for Cultural Anthropology and Development Sociology of Leiden University in the Netherlands. He studied anthropology in Amsterdam and Leiden and wrote "Negotiating Life: Garo Death Rituals and the Transformation of Society," a PhD dissertation on the mortuary rituals of a community in upland northeastern India. De Maaker was a postdoctoral research fellow at Radboud University Nijmegen, where he conducted research on contemporary mortuary practices in the Netherlands. His present research in South Asia focuses on the material and ritual dimensions of religious practices and the politicization of ethnicity and indigenous identity. Using qualitative research methods along with video and photography, one of his specialties is visual anthropology. He has produced several ethnographic films and DVDs, among them *Teyyam: The Annual Visit of the God Vishnumurti* and *Ashes of Life, the Annual Rituals of Laboya*. Among his published essays are "From the Songsarek Faith to Christianity: Religious Change and Cultural Continuity in West Garo Hills" in the journal *South Asia*.

Kathryn McClymond is an associate professor and chair of the Department of Religious Studies at Georgia State University. She is a comparative historian of religion, with a special emphasis on ritual. Her first book, *Beyond Sacred Violence:*

A Comparative Study of Sacrifice, argued against prevailing conceptions of sacrifice as a violent, destructive activity. This book won the Georgia Author of the Year Award in 2009. McClymond is currently working on a book project for Oxford University Press on ritual disruption and its significance for ritual theory.

Christian Meyer is an assistant professor in Sinology at the University of Leipzig. He has been a visiting scholar at Academia Sinica (Taipei) and the Department of Cultural and Religious Studies at the Chinese University of Hong Kong and is a research fellow at the Institute of Sino-Christian Studies in Hong Kong. He is the author of *Ritendiskussionen am Hof der nördlichen Song-Dynastie 1034–1093* (2008) and is currently writing a book on the adoption of the discipline of religious studies in Republican China (1912–49).

Frank Neubert is an assistant professor for the study of religions at Universität Bern, Switzerland. His research focuses on modern forms of Hindu religions in India and globally, as well as on processes of cultural transfer. He recently published *Krishnabewusstsein: Die International Society for Krishna Consciousness, ISKCON* (2010).

Grant Potts is an associate professor of religion at Austin Community College in Texas and teaches in Religious Studies and University Programs at St. Edward's University.

Ulrike Schröder is a senior scientist at the University of Heidelberg's Department for the History of Religion and Intercultural Theology, where she researches the discourse on ritual transformation processes since the eighteenth century in the South Indian context and its consequences for theory formation in religious studies and ritual science. Her most recent publication is Ritual, Caste and Religion in Colonial South India (ed. together with Michael Bergunder and Heiko Frese, 2010).

Barry Stephenson holds a PhD in religious studies from the University of Calgary, Canada. His research deals with religion and literature, the arts, and ritual studies. He is the author of *Veneration and Revolt: Hermann Hesse and Swabian Pietism* (2009) and several essays on ritual and performance. A co-chair of the steering committee of the Ritual Studies Group of the American Academy of Religion, Stephenson is an independent scholar and university lecturer in religious studies. *Performing the Reformation: Public Ritual in the City of Luther*, a study of Luther-themed festivity and pilgrimage in Wittenberg, Germany, was published by Oxford University Press (2010).

Annette Wilke is a professor of the study of religion and head of the Department of the Study of Religion (Allgemeine Religionswissenschaft) at the University of Muenster, Germany. Besides systematic studies in religion, her major fields of research are Hindu traditions (devotional, Tantric, and Vedantic), goddess worship, and the Tamil Hindu diaspora in Germany. Her most recent publication is *Sound and Communication: An Aesthetic Cultural History of Sanskrit Hinduism* (2011).

Introduction

Ute Hüsken and Frank Neubert

RITUAL AND NEGOTIATION: PRELIMINARY REFLECTIONS

IN COMMON UNDERSTANDING, but also in scholarly discourse, ritual has long been seen as an undisputed and indisputable part of (especially religious) tradition, performed over and over in the same ways—stable in form, meaningless, preconceived, and with the aim of creating harmony and enabling a tradition's survival. While these are certainly valid perspectives on rituals, a close look at ritual actions and texts shows that these assumptions can be seriously challenged. Not only are rituals frequently disputed; they also constitute a field in which vital and sometimes even violent negotiations take place. Negotiations—understood here as processes of interaction during which differing positions are debated and/or acted out—are ubiquitous in ritual contexts, either in relation to the ritual itself or in relation to the realm beyond any given ritual performance.[1]

We argue in this volume that a central feature of ritual is its embeddedness in negotiation processes, and that life beyond the ritual frame often is negotiated in the field of rituals. It is exactly this point of view that opens up fruitful new perspectives on ritual procedures, on the interactions that constitute these procedures, and on the contexts in which they are embedded. By explicitly addressing and theorizing about the relevance of negotiation in the world of ritual, the essays in this volume hopefully will induce scholars and students alike to think differently and to find new starting points for more nuanced discussions.

This interdisciplinary endeavor thus aims at filling a serious gap in scholarly thinking and discourse about ritual. Ronald L. Grimes initiated explicit discussions on the interrelation of conflict, critique, and ritual with his pathbreaking works on ritual criticism in the 1980s,[2] but so far no works have exclusively analyzed the interrelationship between ritual and notions of negotiation. This is exactly what this volume does.[3] Although several publications deal with important aspects of conflicts within and about rituals,[4] the related negotiations have been addressed only implicitly. This also holds true for treatments of the theoretical foundation of ritual studies, such as *Theorizing Rituals: Issues, Topics, Approaches, Concepts,* edited by Jens Kreinath, Jan Snoek, and Michael Stausberg. This publication of the Dynamics of Ritual Collaborative Research Center at the University of Heidelberg (Germany) presents valuable new suggestions for defining ritual as well as detailed analyses of varying approaches to ritual. Yet the defining aspect of conflict and related negotiations are addressed in various articles only as asides.

Negotiation in fact has become a key concept in the cultural and social disciplines in the past several decades.[5] Competition, contestation, change, and conflict have become central areas of social theorizing, and the question of how the social is negotiated clearly has gained urgency in a rapidly globalizing world. The increasing fluidity of boundaries, the discovery of the social life of events and even of material objects, the contestation of values and meanings in the context of growing mobility of social actors and their networks, and many other issues became prominent with increasing globalization, all of them involving a form of negotiation. In this volume the notion of negotiation is applied to ritual settings in order to deepen our understanding of how the poles of stability/change, structure/performance, and tradition/innovation are mediated in social encounters. At least two important discussions prepared the ground for this book: a mature debate on the performativity of ritual, and reflections on culture as process and negotiation. Both approaches are foundational for the investigation of activities that we would call "negotiation" in relation to rituals, emphasizing the fluidity and processual character of social interaction rather than its stable characteristics. We consider the concept of negotiation a fruitful tool for analysis, especially when applied to the study of ritual, because "ritual" can be seen as a mode of participation in social activity,[6] which is itself fluid and therefore always contested, challenged, and negotiated. When talking about negotiations and ritual it is essential to be explicit about one's understanding of negotiation as well as one's notion of ritual. There is no lack of definitions of ritual, and no two definitions are alike.[7] If anything, there is an increased tendency among scholars to avoid the term "ritual" altogether in favor of "ritualization,"[8] "public events," or broader notions such as "religious practice." Moreover some of the traditions discussed here do not even have an indigenous equivalent to the modern Western understanding of "ritual."[9] The contributors to this volume represent diverse academic disciplines (Indology, religious studies, social anthropology, Asian history, Sinology). They do not attempt to agree on one uniform definition and understanding of ritual, a term implicitly influenced by a particular religious worldview. Nevertheless the diverse uses of the term in this collection are conceptually connected by the relevance of a varying number of the characteristics attributed to ritual in standard definitions: as repetitive, formally stylized behavior based on scripts or models that is perceived as different from everyday behavior, separated through a (cognitive) frame; invested with meaning that is not necessarily immediately connected to the action performed; referring to and making use of symbols; consisting of building blocks; being traditionally sanctioned; taking place at specific places and/or times; rehearsed, structured, patterned, ordered, sequenced, and rule-governed. This plurality of characteristics makes it possible to see the ritual dimensions not only of a wide range of events, but also of discourses about events, performances, or actions that some might call ritual, others not. Thus the rituals or ritualized behavior investigated in the following case studies represent a broad spectrum, such as worship (*pūjā*) in a Tibetan Buddhist tradition practiced in Canada (Campbell), animist mortuary rituals in northern India (de Maaker), a New Year's festival in Swahili society (Echtler), atonement rituals (*prāyaścitta*) in ancient Indian texts (Aktor, McClymond), rituals of Tibetan "Treasure revealers" (Holmes-Tagchungdarpa), initiation rituals in Tibetan Buddhism (Hüsken and Kieffer-Pülz) and in Wiccan religion in the United States (Bado), Jewish same-sex wedding rituals in the United States and Canada (Lash), rites connected to imperial power in eleventh-century China (Meyer), festivities remembering Martin Luther in the former East Germany (Stephenson), "hook-swinging" ritual as viewed by colonial, Brahmanic, and subaltern actors in South India (Schröder), the historical development of the interpretation of Indian Tantric rites (Wilke), and scholarly discourse on ritual (Potts). Not only are the actions and corresponding discourses diverse, but also the materials that form the basis of the individual case studies; some contributors use texts, some analyze ritual performances, others use both textual analysis and qualitative field study.[10]

As with "ritual," we decided to work with a very broad concept of "negotiation" in this volume. Negotiations take place on all levels of human activity; they are expressed by a wide variety of actions and discourse and in all shades of intensity. As negotiations take different forms, there is no single definition that is clear-cut and convincing, as the contributions to this volume show. Accordingly in many cases other terms could easily replace "negotiation" as it is used here. The processes called "negotiations" here range from mere interactions, textual reinterpretations, discussions aimed at achieving an agreement or a uniform tradition, to violent fights. In this volume we started from a tentative definition of negotiation as "any process of interaction during which differing positions are explicitly or implicitly debated and/or acted out." Consequently what unites the diverse (and markedly different) understandings and uses of this term here is the open eye for processes that originate in disagreement and that at the same time aim at a certain form of agreement, even though such agreement might not actually be achieved. It becomes clear that rituals are not stable entities, but ways humans deal with one another. The investigation of social reality reveals that rituals are indispensible in situations of crisis and conflict. They provide a frame and a means to socialize, especially in times of change—that is, in situations that are seen as a chance and as a threat at the same time. Finally, rituals provide opportunities for what might be labeled "proxy negotiations" when disagreements in other fields of social interaction are debated and acted out via rituals or negotiation about rituals.

Disagreement and conflict—the very foundation of negotiation as we understand it here—trigger activity and critical thinking. Whereas explicit differences of opinion create reflexivity and awareness of one's own and others' positions, implicit and presumed or imputed disagreement stimulates different modes of action.[11] This volume is based on the insight that negotiations pervade human social life and are an essential ground for social life.[12] Rituals as modes of social action are no exception. The negotiations initiated by disagreement and conflict on the correct performance or meaning of rituals—understood as modes of action—shape and reshape rituals and consequently discourse on rituals. However, negotiations are not only about change and stability in ritual, but also about change and stability maintained or created by ritual. Analyzing these negotiations thus helps identify which issues matter and what exactly is at stake; while the dynamic aspects of ritual are revealed, its crucial features also come to the fore.

PARTICIPATION, SUBVERSION, AND CONTEXTUALIZATION

Three major themes emerge from the analyses presented in the essays assembled in this volume. First, *participation* comes to be regarded as central to negotiations around ritual, both as negotiated participation in ritual and as participation in the negotiations about rituals. Second, the disagreements and conflicts that are the basis of processes of negotiation seem to be caused by *subversion* of ritual prescriptions, ritual roles, and power relations surrounding the ritual performances. Third, the concept of negotiation helps to more thoroughly *contextualize* both ritual prescriptions and concrete ritual performances.

Participation proves to be central to several of these investigative essays. While participation in ritual is often mainly understood as "deep participation," and as such is characterized by deep attention, deep commitment, and intensity, all of which go hand-in-hand with a (perceived) loss of individual agency,[13] what becomes clear in this collection is that participation must be understood in a broader sense to include any mode of attending to (or refusing to attend to) a ritual. This breadth implies varying levels of intensity in different roles and in different states of awareness of one's own participation and its implications.

While all our contributors address the issue of participation at least implicitly, those engaged in qualitative field studies identify participation both as a means of investigation and as an important aspect of negotiation processes taking place in and around ritual. In some rituals or ritual systems participation or attendance is an integral means of making statements, of creating, maintaining, or changing relationships (de Maaker, Holmes-Tagchungdarpa). However, it seems that here participation points to the importance of the agency of one's role in ritual, not to individual agency; awareness of the agency involved on the part of participants is therefore largely irrelevant. Thus in de Maaker's case study the negotiation of social relationships occurs by means of participating or refusing to participate in the postmortem gift exchanges in Garo society. A range of options, including the obligation to and the freedom not to participate, allows people to negotiate between distinct interests and to readjust the social network. Through their mode of participation people simultaneously negotiate the relationship between their "House" and that of the deceased. The public's participatory role is also underscored by Holmes-Tagchungdarpa, who argues that public consumption (communalization) of a Tibetan ritual tradition is crucial to its success or failure. The practicing community can either verify or refuse to verify the lineage (that is, the teaching, the teacher, and the practice) through community participation in initiation rituals. Thus different social groups play a key part in negotiating the lineage's authenticity.

Participation, both its frequency and its repetition, is an important mode of gradually becoming an insider when it comes to internalizing "foreign" or "new" rituals. Thereby one not only learns the practices but also makes sense of them (Bado, Campbell). Looking at ritual practice opens our eyes to the importance of the body as a learning agent. It elucidates how participation is learned or enacted by means of the body. Here the performance approaches to ritual prove especially helpful, wherein ritual action, enacted either visibly or in imagination (Wilke), is seen as action of the body, thus dissolving the Cartesian mind-body distinction. This is also confirmed by Seligman et al., whose investigation of Confucian and Jewish texts brought to light that ritual action "trains the most basic impulses, so that the inner comes to reflect the outer, and not the other way round."[14] This body-centered perspective on participation is very much in accordance with Schieffelin's interpretation of participation as a state of body-and-mind "that privileges resonance, identification, and engagement," a fundamental aspect not only of ritual but also of everyday life.[15] Campbell thus describes how individual participants in Buddhist rituals of worship negotiate the ritual's meaning in relation to their own worldviews through participation. The tradition in its Canadian form privileges participation in the service over apprehending the ritual's meanings. Familiarity is gradually achieved by means of repeated attendance. Consequently a variety of meanings and purposes is attributed to the ritual by the practitioners. With time and repetition, interpretations of the ritual that were initially personal and subjective are worked out. Visualizations (also formalized ritual actions), however, a common practice in Tantric Buddhism, cannot be "properly performed" without some preknowledge of what is to be visualized, and so some instruction is required. Bado argues that initiation into Wicca religion is largely somatic training, achieved through physical participation in rites. The gradually developed "body-in-practice" is an acting and learning agent, and so the awareness of ritual practice, as a step-by-step process, recedes into the background as the ritual action is incorporated by the novice, and the tradition is thus made his or her own. In any case a closer look at the way people acquire the knowledge of and about ritual and how it should be performed or presented also helps us understand the deeply felt and sometimes even violent quarrels over ownership, performance, and rights to certain ritual traditions.

In some case studies the negotiations are explicitly focused on the mode of participation. Here the critical questions are Who participates in what role? and What are the limits of stretching, interpreting, and redefining ritual roles? (Hüsken and Kieffer-Pülz, Lash). In these case studies disagreement and the subsequent negotiation processes regarding the modes of attending evoke awareness of participation. The mode of participation seems to be determined largely by the position one holds in relation to performing the rite, but also by one's initial mind-set and expectations. By contrasting American and Canadian Jewish same-sex marriages, Lash clearly shows how the legal status in the two countries affects the mode of participation: in the United States, where same-sex marriages are not legally acknowledged, the rites are performed as rites of resistance, whereas in Canada, Jewish same-sex marriages are performed as rites expressing conformity with Jewish tradition. Hüsken and Kieffer-Pülz show how the perspectives of (potential) participants in Tibetan Buddhist initiation rituals from different cultural backgrounds (Himalayan and Western Buddhists) collide on how female ordination should be performed. Here the issue is not only who participates and how, but also who participates in what role in the negotiation processes; in short, negotiations are about performances rather than strictly about meaning.[16]

When an entire ritual tradition is in question, participating and performing can become a means of *subversion* (Schröder). Thus Schröder focuses on ritual as a discursive formation in which aspects of ritual action and their discursive context merge, providing a dynamic resource for the negotiation of social and religious identity. In her case study from India the lower castes' participation in the ritual is clearly a form of resistance to the normative power of colonial rule, thereby subverting the ruling norms by articulating and acting out alternative positions. By contrast the upper castes attempt to disengage from the "uncivilized lower classes of society" and thus refuse participation in terms of active local support as well as in general public discourse, thereby also making a strong statement about their status.

As Schröder's case study shows, the term "negotiation" implies tension between change and stability, but it also draws attention to subversion and transgression of idealized standards or a seemingly stable hierarchical order. In other words the rules of ritual performance are sometimes, willingly or not, transgressed.[17] This fact necessitates negotiations about whether, and how, to make good on such transgressions. Schröder's essay shows how specific performances take place and are labeled as rituals in order to subvert both traditional religious and sociopolitical hierarchies by explicitly transgressing rules. Echtler's case study is an impressive confirmation of the well-known thesis that rituals serve as a frame for transgressions of social norms and values. These transgressions are a means to negotiate and stabilize social relationships. Viewed from another angle, the transgressions contribute to the formation and maintenance of personal and collective identities. Both Schröder and Echtler show how subdivisions of society (i.e., non-Brahmans, and young men and women, respectively) use ritual transgression to affirm their identity to themselves and to "the other."

On an individual level, life cycle rituals and initiations serve to change individual identities. So discussions on the ritual form and textual basis of the ordination procedures for Tibetan Buddhist nuns implicitly affect their specific role in present-day Tibetan Buddhist groups as well as their immediate contemporary context (Hüsken and Kieffer-Pülz). The same principle holds true for Jewish same-sex weddings (Lash); the ceremonial performance can be used to show that the couple is a "normal wed[ded] couple" by enacting traditional parts of wedding ceremonies, or the performance can demonstrate that a same-sex wedding is something special, that it stands apart from heterosexual weddings, simply by transgressing or subverting traditional forms.

All the features of *negotiating rites* described in this volume's essays indicate that close attention must be paid to *contextualization* when analyzing rituals. Schröder and Meyer, for example, show that the rituals they analyze cannot be properly understood without reference to the power structures in which participants, performers, and observers are entangled. Even in cases where negotiations are not part of the ritual performance itself, it is clear that negotiations are nevertheless a necessary and unavoidable precondition of ritual performance. If there were no differences or ambiguities to be negotiated, there might not be a necessity to perform rituals at all. Or as Seligman et al. state, "Ritual and ritualistic behavior are not so much events as ways of negotiating our very existence in the world," and ritual provides the central space for playing out the constant tension between tradition and creativity.[18] The close relationship between the two again raises the question of ritual and context for which Don Handelman uses the metaphor of the "Moebius band":

> The idea of the Moebius surface (or ring) is used to argue for a frame that relates to the problematic of being inside and outside the frame, as a function (to a degree) of the organization of the frame itself. The ritual frame opens to the outside while enabling itself to be practiced as relatively closed. Through such framing, the outside is taken inside and integrated with the ritual. No less, the inside is taken outside of itself and thereby made part of the frame. Therefore, the frame is "in process" within itself, and in an ongoing relationship to its inside and to its outside. The topology of the Moebius ring constitutes a single surface both external and internal, outside and inside itself. The Moebius surface is twisted on itself so that the inside of the surface turns into its own outside, its outside into its inside. If the Moebius form is conceptualized as a frame, then this framing is inherently dynamic, relating exterior to interior, interior to exterior. Changing and recursive, the Moebius frame enables exterior and interior to interpenetrate, while keeping them separate.[19]

The negotiated aspects of social life in connection with ritual performances demonstrate the interpenetration of ritual (traditionally "inside the frame") and context ("outside"). While it seems that, within the frame of ritual, negotiation of social relationships comes to a halt, the results or decisions enacted in rituals become subject to new negotiations right after the performance or even within the frame itself as it opens toward the "outside." The performative frame of ritual thus only ideally excludes "worldly matters" from its realm.

THE VOLUME

The contributions to this volume are arranged according to three interrelated variations by which the relationship of ritual and negotiation as described above can be understood.

(1) Sharing a World
   - a In the eyes of many participants and insiders to a tradition, rituals negotiate their relationship with what is perceived to be the transcendent (gods, ghosts, ancestors, etc.).
   - b In the eyes of observers and participants, rites negotiate the relationships of participants among each other and with outsiders.

(2) Getting It Straight
The performance, meaning, structure, and contents of rituals are matters of constant negotiation among participants, specialists, and outsiders. In fact negotiations of rituals and their "proper performance" have often been reasons for tensions and even schisms within religious movements.

(3) Meanings and Values of "Ritual"
The notion of ritual and the classification of certain performances, actions, and events as "rituals" or "not rituals"[20] is a matter of constant negotiation among practitioners and scholars and between those two groups. "Ritual" is a term that implicitly carries a variety of meanings and values.

While most of the authors in this volume deal with negotiation processes intrinsic to traditions, others address the question of what happens to rituals when they change over time and thus adapt to shifting contextual circumstances, or when different cultures claim to "share" a ritual. Yet one field that urgently calls for attention in this respect is not dealt with here, namely rites of negotiation. Because our focus is on ritual, we do not deal with the question of why processes of negotiations, such as peace negotiations, tend to take ritual form.[21] Clearly ritual negotiates the social since it is a mode of participating in social reality, even if it might be argued that "the distinctive efficacy of ritual does not reside in its ability to provide answers to problems raised by social life."[22] However, the issue of how and why negotiations are ritualized, and the related important question as to how this knowledge can be used to make these negotiations successful in different cultural and global contexts, requires thorough dialogue and interaction with political and economic researchers and their respective institutions, which calls for a book of its own. The present volume, with its emphasis on negotiations in and about rituals, may be seen as an initial step to trigger further research in this area.

Divergent as the topics and methods may seem, the following essays are connected by the notion of negotiation that conveys insight into the socially embedded and constructed nature of what is called ritual.

Part 1: Sharing a World

This group of essays analyzes the role of ritual in living, establishing, and maintaining different kinds of social relationships. As we stated earlier, rites serve as a mode of negotiation in all kinds of social conflict. Thus negotiation, the ritual forms it may take, and the rituals that end negotiation processes enable the people in a given society to "share their world" by diminishing conflict and disagreement in a ritually legitimized manner.

Often rituals end negotiation processes and performatively enact the results of the foregoing negotiations. This is the main topic of "Negotiating Karma: Penance in the Classical Indian Law Books." By analyzing rites of penance and expiation (*prāyaścitta*) as described in ancient Indian law texts (*dharmaśāstra*), Mikael Aktor takes a close look at the modes of negotiation connected with such rites. Whereas the ritual performance itself remains rather stable, he shows how a number of negotiations take place in the context of the rituals. First, penance rites are embedded in the constant negotiation of religious values, such as the interpretation of *karma* and the cycle of rebirth. Second, specific actions are subject to different evaluations; therefore whether a penance is necessary (and if so which one is appropriate) must be negotiated. Third, pragmatic concerns lead to negotiations regarding how to apply or interpret certain rules laid down in the law texts. Aktor concludes that in his case studies "negotiations surround the ritual proper, but they can never be located in it." Instead the performance of a ritual enacts the results of the foregone negotiations and thus affirms them in a socially legible way by imposing a ritually legitimized authority. Thus Aktor sees rituals as both instruments of and subject to politics, but never as politics itself.

Erik de Maaker details the negotiations surrounding death rites among the Garo, a tribe in the hills north of India's border with Bangladesh. "Negotiations at Death: Assessing Gifts, Mothers, and Marriages" addresses the importance of participation in death rituals in the assessment and reinterpretation of social relationships with special reference to the processes of gift exchange after a person's death. This ritualized gift exchange, he concludes, allows for negotiations of closeness and distance among the concerned "Houses."

Magnus Echtler adopts a different perspective in analyzing the negotiation of gender roles in Swahili society. "'The Clitoris Is Indeed Your Sweet': Negotiating Gender Roles in the Ritual Setting of the Swahili New Year's Festival" demonstrates how one form of transgression in the district of Makunduchi, ritual fighting among young men, is replaced by another, namely highly obscene songs that address the relationships between young men and women and consciously subvert the rules governing such relationships in everyday life. Echtler identifies these songs and their ritualized performance as "liminal transgressions" that define and stabilize social relationships far beyond their immediate performance context.

Analyzing festivities remembering Martin Luther in the reformer's hometown of Wittenberg, Barry Stephenson in "Ritual Negotiations in Lutherland" shows how performance sequences from street theater to liturgy manifest different ways of negotiating social status and relations. He reveals how the revival of the carnivalesque after the breakdown of East Germany proves to be a powerful mode of coping with or criticizing the political setting, indicating "the health of democratic processes." He also argues that ritualized mimetic behavior, which is characteristic of the carnivalesque, creates ambiguity that allows for creative negotiations of social identity.

Christian Meyer's "Negotiating Rites in Imperial China: The Case of Northern Song Court Ritual Debates from 1034 to 1093" demonstrates the influence of scholars and officials on imperial ritual performance. Although major rituals were performed only personally by the emperor himself, as ritual experts the scholars were powerful participants in the court debates on ritual. Meyer shows that the negotiation of ritual performance played a crucial role in negotiating power. Because the concept of *li* (ritual) always included the idea of hierarchy, the rituals' performances served as instruments and demonstrations of imperial power, and so these rituals became a major medium in power struggles. Accordingly debates about how to perform imperial court rituals, especially which music should be played, were in effect not only negotiations of power between scholar-officials and ruler, but also served as a means of strengthening one's party in the factional struggles.

Part 2: Getting It Straight

In many cases negotiations evolve around the question of how certain rites must or must not be performed. Questions of "correct" performance at times also lead to schisms within traditions. The essays in this section analyze debates on these aspects of rituals that are usually labeled as "formality."

The scholar and Wicca practitioner Nikki Bado explores the role of the body as the site of interaction and negotiation with the sacred in "Performing the Ancient Ones: *The Body-in-Practice* as the Ground of Ritualized Negotiation." Bado argues that initiation into the Wicca religion by way of somatic training "is embedded in a long and complex multidirectional process of increasingly somatic practice." In this process the "natural body" is made into a "body-in-practice," based on a particular mode of perception. In the course of initiation the body is increasingly involved as an acting agent, thus becoming the "knower" of the skills necessary for successful ritual work. Through the gradual integration of the body as a learning agent, the learner first "discovers and [then] creates meaning through bodily engagement, through sensual and participatory conversation and intimate interaction." The physical body thus "emerges as equally important to belief or intellectual knowledge." Religion as disembodied belief is thus transformed into religion as embodied practice. The author's use of the Japanese philosopher Yuasa Yasuo is especially enlightening, as he not only shows how somatic practices turn into learned responses that become habits, but also suggests that spiritual development occurs in a similar fashion.

"Negotiating Tantra and Veda in the *Paraśurāma-Kalpa* Tradition" deals with the discursive sublimation of Tantric rites (including the use of alcohol, meat, bodily fluids, and sexual intercourse) within the Hindu Kaula Śrīvidyā tradition as it emerges from the mediaeval Sanskrit ritual manual *Paraśurāma-Kalpasūtra*. Annette Wilke shows how the text makes use of the body and sensuality at the same time that it refutes a Veda/Tantra opposition, thus reworking hierarchies, power structures, and definitions of orthodoxy. Merging body and mind in this text is a "soteriological program." The Tantrics' "body laboratory," Wilke concedes, does emphasize interiority and bodylessness, but at the same time it includes corporal experience. This strategy keeps the ritual intact yet purged of all "impurities," thereby helping to spread the Tantric tradition even in orthodox Brahman circles. Wilke concludes that the imaginary and the virtual "become so prominent that finally only metonymy and metaphor are left—remarkably without substantially endangering the ritual."

"Same-Sex Weddings in Canada: Rituals of Resistance or Rituals of Conformity?" shows that legal status clearly influences a ritual's meaning, performance, and function. Shari Rochelle Lash argues that in the United States, where same-sex marriage is not uniformly legalized, such weddings serve as rituals of resistance in both form and content, whereas in Canada the accepted legal status of same-sex marriage leads to nuptials that conform to their counterparts, in this case traditional Jewish weddings.

"The Social Element of Visionary Revelation: Public Rites as a Means of Negotiating Authenticity in Tibetan Buddhist Visionary Lineages" examines the crucial place of rituals in establishing the religious role of a *Gter-ston*, a "Treasure revealer," that is, someone who discovers religious texts called "Treasures" in Tibetan Buddhism. What does one have to do in order to be recognized as a legitimate Treasure revealer? Amy Holmes-Tagchungdarpa argues that such a recognition is established by a highly formalized procedure. By participating in the rituals discovered in the Treasures and promulgated by the revealers, believers support and thereby help to establish or maintain the legitimacy and authenticity of a revealed text, its corresponding practice, and, significantly, its discoverer.

In "Negotiating Ritual Repair: The *prāyaścitta* Material in the Baudhāyana Śrauta Sūtra" Kathryn McClymond examines intrinsic ritual measures in the Brahmanic Indian ritual system of the Baudhāyana tradition aimed at preventing evil consequences that arise from breaching ritual rules. McClymond shows that it is precisely these "atonement rituals" that allow for stretching the rules, while simultaneously reminding the performers of the "ideal" procedures, thus keeping the rather conservative ritual system intact and alive.

Part 3: Meanings and Values of Ritual

The essays in this section concentrate on rituals and the negotiations about their meanings and their "ritualness."

Ulrike Schröder analyzes asymmetric power relations in the colonial context of nineteenth-century South India. "Hook-Swinging in South India: Negotiating the Subaltern Space within a Colonial Society" examines archival material that reveals how officials dealt with the crucial question of whether certain practices were "religious" or "nonreligious," "ritual" or "custom." Formal recognition as a religion or as religious ritual by colonial authorities safeguarded a given practice from direct colonial influence; conversely a practice that was explicitly denied such a label was subject to restriction, prohibition, and even criminal prosecution. Schröder also offers insight into the use of such discourses by subaltern actors as a means of subversion and resistance to both colonial superstructures and suppression in traditional social hierarchies. Thus the practitioners of so-called hook-swinging festivals in South India—rituals during which practitioners willingly have themselves suspended on hooks driven through the flesh of the back in worship of the goddess—petitioned for official recognition of their practices as religious rituals, and in order to achieve this made changes in the performances.

"Negotiating Meaning and Enactment in a Buddhist Ritual" explores the ways a religiously and culturally Tibetan ritual tradition is interpreted by Western practitioners in Toronto. Patricia Q. Campbell argues that, although the meaning and function of the ritual may differ among performers, its enactment serves as the unifying element. Moreover she argues that attendance precedes understanding. Yet while diverse meanings are not mutually exclusive, there are limits, Campbell argues, to attending a ritual without being able to attribute meaning to it. In this context she reflects fruitfully on ritual action that takes place exclusively in the mind (thereby conceptualizing the mind as part of the body).

"Ordination into the Buddhist Saṅgha as an Initiation Ritual and as a Legal Procedure" analyzes negotiations surrounding recent attempts to establish a female ordination line in the Tibetan Buddhist tradition. Ute Hüsken and Petra Kieffer-Pülz show how the conflicting agendas of the agents involved determine their respective views of the ritual of ordination as a Buddhist nun: whereas for the "Western nuns" ordination is seen as a legal procedure (their main concern is to find a "legally valid" way to perform these ordinations), for the "Himalayan nuns" the procedure constitutes a transformative ritual of initiation with long-lasting effects that tie the nun to her teacher. The question of whether and how such an ordination should be performed therefore is evaluated entirely differently by the members of the two groups.

Not only the diverging interpretations of what a ritual means, but also differing approaches to a discursive understanding of the meaning of the term "ritual" are negotiated when it comes to the "meaning of ritual." "Negotiating the Social in the Ritual Theory of Victor Turner and Roy Rappaport" offers a metatheoretical approach by reflecting on the terminology used by theoreticians of ritual in negotiating basic academic concepts. Grant Potts highlights the fact that the notion of ritual itself is a scholarly construction; as such it is a highly negotiated concept. On the one hand, scholars try to agree on the usage of the term "ritual," while on the other hand negotiating the relationship of ritual to the obscure notion of "the social." Narrating a history of the idea that rituals are constituent facts in negotiations of social relationships, Potts analyzes scholarly discourse on ritual.

CONCLUDING REFLECTIONS

The comparative reflections on negotiations gathered in this volume highlight those issues that are usually at work behind the scenes. Conflicts that require negotiations in order to reconcile diverging agendas make the crucial issues evident both to observers and participants, especially when diverse perspectives and their agents confront one other. Because disagreement—the engine that drives negotiations—triggers and initiates activity and thinking about possible ways of reconciliation, it also creates reflection, reflexivity, and awareness of one's own and others' positions. However, when the disagreement is more implicit, simmering below the surface, it may also instigate unreflected action. As it is, disagreement and efforts to solve the ensuing problems decisively shape ritual and lead to ritual creativity. Several of the case studies in this volume clearly demonstrate that rituals are also a means of expressing and enacting subversion and resistance to dominant discourses. They are strategically used to make unpopular or uncomfortable statements and to reverse existing hierarchies. The analysis of negotiations therefore contextualizes rituals; rituals cannot fruitfully be treated if they are detached from their contexts and their contextual negotiations, especially since rituals also frequently enact the results of completed or ongoing negotiations. By so doing rituals express newly formed or altered social relationships (as in marriages, initiations, or healing rituals)[23] that result from the foregoing negotiations. In other words, "ritual continually renegotiates boundaries, living with their instability and vulnerable nature."[24] This volume shows that the boundaries of ritual are continually renegotiated as well. It is precisely the process of negotiation that highlights the oscillating mutual influence of rites, boundaries, and structures.

Notes

The idea for this volume was born at a conference held by the Dynamics of Ritual Collaborative Research Center at the University of Heidelberg, when the editors realized that many contributions to the conference referred to the notion of "negotiation" in relation to the analysis of rituals. The exchange on the topic and the copy editing by Susan Scott was made possible through generous funding by the Deutsche Forschungsgemeinschaft (German Research Council) and the University of Oslo.

1. On form, see, for example, Gladigow, "Sequenzierung von Riten und die Ordnung der Rituale," 57–76. The main proponent of the theory of meaninglessness is Frits Staal; see "The Meaninglessness of Ritual," 2–22, and *Rules without Meaning.* For a critique see Michaels, "Le rituel pour le rituel' oder wie sinnlos sind Rituale?," 23–47, and "Ritual and Meaning," 247–61.

On preconception, see, for example, Rappaport, *Ritual and Religion in the Making of Humanity.* Rappaport interprets rituals as formalized action perceived as not encoded by the actual performers (see especially 32–33).

On harmony, see Radcliffe-Brown, "Religion and Society," 153–77.

A classic of social-functionalist approaches to ritual is Victor Turner's *The Ritual Process: Structure and Antistructure.* In addition Bruce Lincoln presents a functional analysis of myth's and ritual's roles in creating and maintaining social stability based on Durkheimian notions in *Discourse and the Construction of Society.*

2. See Grimes, "Infelicitous Performances and Ritual Criticism," 103–22; "Ritual Criticism and Reflexivity in Fieldwork," 217–39; and *Ritual Criticism.* Other works dealing with instances of negotiation and ritual criticism include Schieffelin, "On Failure and Performance," 59–89; Howe, "Risk, Ritual and Performance," 63–79.

3. Closest to taking up this question is a volume edited by Ute Hüsken on ritual mistakes and failure, *When Rituals Go Wrong.*

4. See, for example, Rao, "Regeln in Bewegung"; Wolf, "Kosmologie in Verhandlung"; Schnepel, "Der Körper im 'Tanz der Strafe' in Orissa." The volume *Discourse in Ritual Studies*, edited by Hans Schildermann, deals with the possibility of changing diverse aspects of rituals and performances, change here implying that these aspects are made "more suitable" from the view of both practitioners and "customers." The volume *The Power of Discourse in Ritual Performance*, edited by Ulrich Demmer and Martin Gaenszle, asks questions regarding discourse on ritual and deals with different sorts of negotiation on the practitioners' level as well as on a theoretical and metatheoretical level. However, theorizing about the interrelation between ritual and the processes of negotiation is missing. *Social Performance: Symbolic Action, Cultural Pragmatic and Ritual*, edited by Jeffrey C. Alexander, Bernhard Giesen, and Jason L. Mast, deals more explicitly with negotiations of and around what the authors call "social performances," of which ritual is a special form. The authors include in their study all kinds of historical and modern performative acts, including both singular events and regularly held social rituals, to show the influence of these events on social reality.

5. See, for example, Byron and Kockel, *Negotiating Culture;* Festenstein, *Negotiating Diversity;* Pottier, *Negotiating Local Knowledge;* Karsten, *Negotiating History and Culture.* On negotiation in the context of ritual studies, see, for example, Rao, *Negotiating the Divine;* Roberts, "Toasting Uyghurstan," 147–79; De Pee, *Negotiating Marriage;* Guinn, *Protecting Jerusalem's Holy Sites.* A search of the Karlsruher Virtueller Katalog (kvk) for titles including "negotiating" resulted in 1,904 entries in the Library of Congress (www.ubka.uni-karlsruhe.de/kvk.html, accessed December 17, 2009).

6. See Houseman, "An Upside-down Perspective on Ritual, Media and Conflict," 2.

7. See, for example, Snoek, "Defining 'Rituals,'" 3–14.

8. For a critique directed toward the usefulness of "ritualization," see Houseman, "An Upside-down Perspective on Ritual, Media and Conflict."

9. See Stausberg, "'Ritual': A Lexicographic Survey of Some Related Terms from an Emic Perspective," 51–100; see also Meyer's contribution in this volume.

10. The authors in this volume who deal with ritual texts suggest that, frequently, scripts (here written texts) for rituals are *pre*-scripts; in other words, they do not necessarily represent actual practice but rather idealized versions of rites, versions that still have to be adapted to the actual local, historical, and social setting. (On the relation between performance and script, see Snoek's attempt to define ritual in "Defining 'Rituals,'" 11–14.) Moreover Schröder points to the fact that in the case of India, an orientalist assumption that texts form the basis of a religion created the hegemony of religious texts over practices, and Hüsken and Kieffer-Pülz examine negotiations that try to harmonize the performance and textual aspects of a Buddhist initiation ritual. Authors dealing with rites they have personally encountered are explicit about their position; indeed the scholarly perspective is regarded as one of many possible views on rituals (see especially Potts; Hüsken and Kieffer-Pülz), since the entire analytical process benefits from the engagement with practitioners and critics.

11. In *Ritual and Its Consequences: An Essay on the Limits of Sincerity* Seligman et al. rightly point out that ritual is "not necessarily—or even not primarily—something one thinks about" (25). They argue that ritual is an unreflected mode of action, whereas "sincerity" is their label for pure reflection.

12. In some strands of sociological theory "negotiation" plays a prominent role in the conceptualization of society. Thus, for example, in social exchange theory the term is used quite narrowly to denote processes similar to marketplace activity, "in which people are guided by what they stand to gain and lose from others" (Macionis and Plummer, *Sociology,* 28). Symbolic interactionism, as another example, deals with social interaction and the negotiation of meaning and identity as means of the constant re-creation of society understood as a constantly ongoing process.

13. See Schieffelin, "Participation," 621.

14. See Seligman et al., *Ritual and Its Consequences,* 35ff.

15. See Schieffelin, "Participation," 615–20.

16. See Seligman et al., *Ritual and Its Consequences,* 51.

17. For examples of such willing or inadvertent transgressions and ritual modes of "dealing" with them, see the essays in Hüsken, *When Rituals Go Wrong.* The notion of transgression is also a topic of Aktor's and McClymond's contributions to the present volume.

18. Seligman et al., *Ritual and Its Consequences,* 8, 37.

19. Handelman, "Framing," 571–82.

20. See Neubert, "Ritualkritik, Ritualdiskurs und Meditationspraxis," 411–39, for an analysis of a debate in which the question of the ritualness of certain practices is at stake.

21. Other examples are negotiations of marriage alliances, especially in the Indian context, and negotiations in the wide sphere of economy.

22. Houseman, "An Upside-down Perspective on Ritual, Media and Conflict," 2.

23. See, for example, Sax, "Heilen Rituale?," 213–15.

24. Seligman et al., *Ritual and Its Consequences,* 9.

Bibliography

Alexander, Jeffrey C., Bernhard Giesen, and Jason L. Mast, eds. *Social Performance: Symbolic Action, Cultural Pragmatic and Ritual.* Cambridge: Cambridge University Press, 2006.

Byron, Reginald, and Ulrich Kockel, eds. *Negotiating Culture: Moving, Mixing and Memory in Contemporary Europe.* Berlin: Lit, 2006.

Demmer, Ulrich, and Martin Gaenszle, eds. *The Power of Discourse in Ritual Performance.* Münster: Lit, 2007.

De Pee, Christian. *Negotiating Marriage: Weddings, Text, and Ritual in Song and Yuan Dynasty China (10th through 14th Centuries).* Ann Arbor: University of Michigan Press, 1998.

Festenstein, Mathew. *Negotiating Diversity: Culture, Deliberation, Trust.* Cambridge, UK: Polity Press, 2005.

Gladigow, Burkhard. "Sequenzierung von Riten und die Ordnung der Rituale." In *Zoroastrian Rituals in Context,* ed. Michael Stausberg, 57–76. Studies in the History of Religions 102. Leiden: Brill, 2004.

Grimes, Ronald L. "Infelicitous Performances and Ritual Criticism." *Semeia* 43 (1988): 103–22.

———. *Ritual Criticism: Case Studies in Its Practice, Essays on Its Theory.* Studies in Comparative Religion 10. Columbia: University of South Carolina Press, 1990.

———. "Ritual Criticism and Reflexivity in Fieldwork." *Journal of Ritual Studies* 2 (1988): 217–39.

Guinn, David E. *Protecting Jerusalem's Holy Sites: A Strategy for Negotiating a Sacred Peace*. Cambridge: Cambridge University Press, 2006.

Handelman, Don. "Framing." In *Theorizing Rituals*, ed. Jens Kreinath, Jan Snoek, and Michael Stausberg, 571–82. Numen Book Series Studies in the History of Religions 144–1. Leiden: Brill, 2006.

Houseman, Michael. "An Upside-Down Perspective on Ritual, Media and Conflict." In *Ritual, Media, and Conflict*, ed. Ronald L. Grimes, Ute Hüsken, Udo Simon, and Eric Venbrux. Oxford Ritual Studies Series. New York: Oxford University Press, 2010.

Howe, Leo. "Risk, Ritual and Performance." *Journal of the Royal Anthropological Institute* 6, no. 1 (2000): 63–79.

Hüsken, Ute, ed. *When Rituals Go Wrong: Mistakes, Failure, and the Dynamics of Ritual*. Numen Book Series 115. Leiden: Brill, 2007.

Karsten, Fritz. *Negotiating History and Culture: Transculturation in Contemporary Native American Indian Fiction*. Frankfurt: Lang, 2000.

Lincoln, Bruce. *Discourse and the Construction of Society: Comparative Study of Myth, Ritual, and Classification*. New York: Oxford University Press, 1989.

Macionis, John J., and Ken Plummer. *Sociology: A Global Introduction*. Essex: Pearson Education, 2005.

Michaels, Axel. "Ritual and Meaning." In *Theorizing Rituals*, ed. Jens Kreinath, Jan Snoek, and Michael Stausberg, 247–61. Numen Book Series Studies in the History of Religions 144–1. Leiden: Brill, 2006.

———. "'Le rituel pour le rituel' oder wie sinnlos sind Rituale?" In *Rituale heute: Theorien-Kontroversen-Entwürfe*, ed. Corina Caduff and Joanna Pfaff-Czarnecka, 23–47. Berlin: Dietrich Reimer, 1999.

Neubert, Frank. "Ritualkritik, Ritualdiskurs und Meditationspraxis: Das Beispiel von Vipassanā nach S. N. Goenka im 'Westen.'" *Numen* 55 (2008): 411–39.

Pottier, Johan, ed. *Negotiating Local Knowledge: Power and Identity in Development*. London: Pluto, 2003.

Radcliffe-Brown, R. "Religion and Society." In *Structure and Function in Primitive Society*, 153–77. New York: Free Press, 1965.

Rao, Ursula. *Negotiating the Divine: Temple Religion and Temple Politics in Contemporary Urban India*. Delhi: Manohar, 2003.

———. "Regeln in Bewegung." In *Im Rausch des Rituals: Gestaltung und Transformation der Wirklichkeit in körperlicher Performanz*, ed. Ursula Rao and Klaus-Peter Köpping. Münster: Lit, 2000.

Rappaport, Roy A. *Ritual and Religion in the Making of Humanity*. Cambridge: Cambridge University Press, 1999.

Roberts, Sean R. "Toasting Uyghurstan: Negotiating Stateless Nationalism in Transnational Ritual Space." In *Contesting Rituals: Islam and Practices of Identity-Making*, ed. Pamela J. Stewart and Andrew Strathern, 147–79. Durham, NC: Carolina Academic Press, 2005.

Sax, William S. "Heilen Rituale?" In *Die neue Kraft der Rituale*, ed. Axel Michaels, 213–15. Heidelberg: Universitätsverlag Winter, 2007.

Schieffelin, Edward L. "On Failure and Performance: Throwing the Medium Out of the Séance." In *The Performance of Healing*, ed. Carol Laderman and Marina Roseman, 59–89. New York: Routledge, 1996.

———. "Participation." In *Theorizing Rituals*, ed. Jens Kreinath, Jan Snoek, and Michael Stausberg, 615–26. Numen Book Series Studies in the History of Religions 144–1. Leiden: Brill, 2006.

Schildermann, Hans, ed. *Discourse in Ritual Studies*. Leiden: Brill, 2007.

Schnepel, Burkhard. "Der Körper im 'Tanz der Strafe' in Orissa." In *Im Rausch des Rituals: Gestaltung und Transformation der Wirklichkeit in körperlicher Performanz*, ed. Ursula Rao and Klaus-Peter Köpping. Münster: Lit, 2000.

Seligman, Adam B., et al., eds. *Ritual and Its Consequences: An Essay on the Limits of Sincerity*. New York: Oxford University Press, 2008.

Snoek, Jan. "Defining 'Rituals.'" In *Theorizing Rituals*, ed. Jens Kreinath, Jan Snoek, and Michael Stausberg, 3–14. Numen Book Series Studies in the History of Religions 144–1. Leiden: Brill, 2006.

Staal, Frits. "The Meaninglessness of Ritual." *Numen* 26, no. 1 (1979): 2–22.

———. *Rules without Meaning: Ritual, Mantras and the Human Sciences*. New York: Lang, 1989.

Stausberg, Michael, ed. "'Ritual': A Lexicographic Survey of Some Related Terms from an Emic Perspective." In *Theorizing Rituals*, ed. Jens Kreinath, Jan Snoek, and Michael Stausberg, 51–100. Numen Book Series Studies in the History of Religions 144–1. Leiden: Brill, 2006.

Turner, Victor. *The Ritual Process: Structure and Antistructure*. New York: Aldine, 1982.

Wolf, Silke. "Kosmologie in Verhandlung." In *Im Rausch des Rituals: Gestaltung und Transformation der Wirklichkeit in körperlicher Performanz*, ed. Ursula Rao and Klaus-Peter Köpping. Münster: Lit, 2000.

PART ONE

Sharing a World

1

Negotiating Karma

PENANCE IN THE CLASSICAL INDIAN LAW BOOKS

Mikael Aktor

RITUALS OF PENANCE ARE PERFORMED to redeem the negative soteriological consequences of sinful acts. Through fulfillment of the observance of penance, the sinner is released from such consequences and resumes a neutral state. In Hinduism such rituals are known as *prāyaścittas*. This, however, was not the original meaning of this word. In the Ritual Sūtras the term *prāyaścitta* referred to certain reparation rituals that were designed to nullify the effects of ritual errors committed during a primary ritual performance: "ritual gone wrong."[1] But in the later Dharma literature, the *dharmaśāstra*, the term took on an extended meaning. In this literature, whose purpose is to lay down general duties for all classes (*varṇa*) and castes (*jāti*) in an ideal society ruled by a Hindu king,[2] the same term refers to penitential rites performed for the purpose of removing the personal karmic effects of all kinds of transgression (*pātaka*). The variety of these penances is as wide as that of the transgressions possible, ranging from simply a short glance at the sun to get rid of the bad effect of having looked at an Untouchable (*caṇḍāla*) to elaborate rituals lasting twelve years to remove the evil karma of having killed a Brahman.[3]

This development in the scope of the term *prāyaścitta* corresponds to a broadening of the very notion of ritual. Whereas the Ritual Sūtras deal with domestic or public performances involving one or more sacrificial fires, the assistance of one or several priests, Vedic mantras, and so on, the Dharma literature treats all kinds of daily activities in the life of a "twice-born" man but applies consequences to these everyday acts that make them work like rituals. "Twice-born" here refers to a member of one of the three upper classes, *brāhmaṇa* (priests, scholars), *kṣatriya* (nobility, warriors), and *vaiśya* (landowners, merchants); the fourth class, *śūdra* (workers, artisans), did not belong in this category as they were not entitled to Vedic initiation, understood as a second birth. These everyday acts, such as eating, hygiene, sex, work, and economic transactions, are dealt with in the Dharma literature from an ideal point of view; that is, they are prescribed rather than described. And it is the prescriptive quality (*vidhi*) that is crucial for their karmic effect. Because they have been prescribed in sacred texts (*smṛti*) supposedly composed by Vedic seers,[4] to follow the prescriptions is an act of *dharma* and therefore involves good karma; consequently to ignore the prescriptions is *adharma* and involves bad karma.

In the Dharma literature ordinary daily activities are dealt with in terms of the same logic by which rituals are analyzed in the Mīmāṃsā philosophy of Vedic ritual, and it is in this sense that it is relevant to characterize these prescriptions as a ritualization of everyday life. Mīmāṃsā philosophy, it must be noted, had a strong influence on the Dharma literature, even in its early stages.[5] In the view of this philosophy the reason even ordinary acts produce karma—that is, have effects that will ripen in future lives—is the same as that which connects a Vedic sacrifice and the prospect of going to heaven after death or of any other benefits in future lives. Both are grounded in the special force called *apūrva*. According to the Mīmāṃsā view of Kumārila, *apūrva* is "that particular 'potency' that gathers and stores the efficacy of the Vedic rituals and makes it possible for transitory sacrificial performances to have lasting effects in the distant future."[6] This force is postulated as a necessary consequence of Vedic rules (*vidhi*). The idea behind the rule that "he who desires Heaven, should perform a sacrifice" (*svargakāmo yajeta*), for instance, would be meaningless if such a transcendent connection did not exist, and since the Vedas are accepted as the ultimate authority, this connection must necessarily exist.[7] The same goes for transgressions. What accounts for the unlucky karmic results in any future birth that are caused by a wicked act in the present life is not the instrumental act itself but the transgression of a negative rule such as that prohibiting the killing of a Brahman.[8]

In the same way that *prāyaścittas* function as apotropaic rites that prevent errors done in Vedic ritual performances from creating negative consequences for the sacrificer, so *prāyaścittas* as penances prevent the bad karma of all kinds of misdeeds from bearing unlucky fruit for the person who committed the immoral acts.

In what follows I want to suggest how this development of the scope of *prāyaścitta* is related to a development of the idea of karma itself in the transition from late to post-Vedic literature. From this point of view penance in the Dharma literature negotiates the earlier soteriology of the Upaniṣadic doctrine of karma. Further I want to examine other levels of negotiation that are involved in these penances. For instance, there is a debate in the Dharma literature about what kind of misdeeds can be atoned for by penance and about the social effects of atonement itself. But before going into these matters it is necessary to explicate critically both the notion of ritual and that of ritual negotiation.

NEGOTIATING RITUALS

What is ritual? And in what sense, if any, can ritual properly be characterized as a negotiating activity? The following discussion is based on the premise that negotiation necessarily involves an open-ended situation, a situation that in principle may turn either way. This must be specified in order to delimit this aspect of ritual from the much broader idea that rituals are very often employed as an exercise of power. Rituals uphold or change power relations in the social sphere, or they assert a power over aspects of reality. But does this involve negotiation? Or does it not rather present the object to be transformed or renewed with a fait accompli?

FUNCTION AND ORIGIN OF RITUAL: THE MEMORIES OF REAL CONFLICTS

Acknowledging the dramatic character of rituals is a good place to start. Rituals enact ideal situations. But they do so against the possibility of defeat or meaninglessness inherent in real situations. They lay claim in advance to what is hoped for, and they assign meaning and importance to impermanence and change. In dramatizing such claims rituals might be seen as negotiating the realities of life. According to one theory of ritual, this confrontation with reality is the very origin of ritual activity. Walter Burkert suggests in his works on Greek myth and ritual that both the act of demonstrating one's own power and that of dealing with the stronger power of others are fundamental to ritual in its earliest developments. Thus carrying or spreading branches—or straw, in an Indian ritual context—is seen as an invitation to sit down and therefore as an expression of appeasement. "He who rests on a *stibás* [a bed of branches in Greek cults] gives up all tension and aggressiveness." In a similar vein offerings of first fruits are seen in the context of anxiety. As an animal may have to abandon its kill when attacked by a stronger one, so "[I]n human societies . . . demonstrative abandoning or giving away will secure some empty space for the possessor of goods, to prevent the clash of greediness." The same type of explanation applies to animal sacrifices, which are analyzed in the context of the hunt as a "giving back" (i.e., the animal returned to a supernatural power), and for a later stage in this cultural evolution, in the context of animal husbandry, as a "giving away" (what is owned).[9] What necessitates the ritual in all these examples is the idea of an unequal power relation, in which symbolic acts are performed to avert the dangerous possibility of a violent confrontation, although the real dangers of social confrontation have been projected on a mythical level of supernatural beings through the ritual process. In this way Burkert highlights both the basic power struggles that are the sources of human ritual behavior and the social economy that makes symbolic activities important as a means of averting destructive social conflicts.

There are two basic premises in Burkert's argument. One is the validity of the macrohistorical perspective of human and even animal evolution. In this perspective the communicative function of ritual is not attributed to a referential relation to verbal concepts but has its source in a cultural sign system far more archaic than its "latest invention, verbalized speech." In defining ritual he looks even further back in evolution to ethology. With reference to Konrad Lorenz's famous graylags, which assure each other of their solidarity by the display of common aggression against a nonexistent interloper, Burkert defines ritual as "*action redirected for demonstration*."[10] An element of action is taken out if its normal context and used as a communicative device. Rituals consist, then, of a large number of everyday acts, such as cleaning oneself, preparing food, eating, drinking, consuming drugs, making love, and greeting or fighting others. But the ritual context manipulates the normal rationale of these activities to add to them a communicative character. The communion wafer, for instance, hardly serves as a solid meal, but its communicative quality nevertheless presupposes a basic experience of hunger and nutrition.

The other premise of Burkert's theory is the idea that in a ritual semiotics, in contrast to linguistic semiotics, signs are not arbitrary. Rather there will be a metonymic relation between the ritual *signifiant* and *signifié*.[11] No one would raise his clenched fist as a sign of submission or throw himself to the ground as a sign of aggression.[12] In principle the communicative value of the ritual sign lies therefore in the fact that everyone knows the normal context from which it is redirected. No matter how much ritual actions are diverted from their original contexts and overlaid with mythological and theological concepts, it is worth considering the phenomenology and the semantics of the original situation in the analysis of a given ritual, as will be demonstrated in the discussion of penance below.

From the perspective of Walter Burkert, then, ritual might be seen as a negotiating activity, at least in the sense that it has evolved originally from an awareness of potentially lethal conflicts that need to be averted. In most religious rituals, however, the superior power of the conflict has been projected onto a level of superhuman beings who, just like the nonexistent interloper among Lorenz's graylags, become nonexistent partners in communication in rituals marking a change or renewal of existing relations within the social group itself, or even of relations with the universe.

FORMAL CHARACTERISTICS OF RITUAL: ASSERTING IDEAL SITUATIONS

But can these ritual performances really be categorized as acts of negotiation? Would "assertion" be a more accurate term? One way to distinguish negotiation of power from assertion of power could be to discriminate between the formal and the contextual perspectives of ritual. While rituals may be born out of the need to handle real conflicts in real contexts, their overt formal characteristics seem to hide such origins. Instead rituals design situations that circumvent the real conflicts between partners by insisting on ideal relations between them. They present, so to speak, the partner with an offer that cannot be refused. Gift exchange is a well-known example of a simple ritual relation that can accomplish this. Because the obligation lies with the recipient not only to reciprocate a gift that has been received but also, equally powerfully, to accept the gift in the first place, gift exchange can work as a powerful means of forcing binding relations on others.[13] But in real contexts the rules are often bent and the power relations thereby distorted, or, in terms of this discussion, negotiated.[14]

The Danish scholar of ritual Jørgen Podemann Sørensen has worked to refine an analysis of ritual that is restricted to its merely formal aspect. By making this restriction he has been able to offer a general description of how ritual asserts its ideal intentions as if in fact accomplished. The point of departure is Hubert and Mauss's definition that rites are "actes traditionnels d'une efficacité *sui generis*."[15] Ritual efficacy is further characterized as a matter of rhetoric. This is done in order to distinguish between "the formal efficacy of ritual rhetoric and the actual role of ritual in shaping a culturally postulated social world." Indeed "one of the points of speaking of the rhetoric of ritual is to single out exactly those formal features of ritual texts and actions that postulate efficacy." The rhetoric of ritual is first of all characterized as a rhetoric that situates the speech and the actions of the ritual in a *privileged position*, in which "to say or otherwise signify something is also to do it."[16] This position is dramatized in various ways: as the speech of gods or forefathers, as the actions of mythical exemplars, as a regression to a critical transformative state. But in its most general analysis the privileged position of ritual is reduced to an abstract point zero, a ritually postulated "state of not yet being" in which anything can be transformed, and which therefore becomes a source of all ritual efficacy.[17]

Sørensen's analysis of the formal aspect of ritual shows that the notion of negotiation is alien to the ritual proper as this is described, for instance, in a prescriptive ritual manual. Such texts give the impression that there is nothing to negotiate, since rituals are designed with respect to accomplishing exactly what they intend. They assert their ideal ends without discussion. It is only when the perspective is broadened to include the contexts surrounding the ritual proper that the notion of negotiation makes any sense. There are many such contexts. The actual design of the ritual in prescriptive texts may have a prehistory of considerations in relation to contemporary social, religious, and political practice; rituals may be the result of interpretation of earlier practices and doctrines; each performance of the ritual may take place in a specific context and may be a scene for variation, improvisation, adjustment, even protest related to this context; scholastic debates within a group of ritual specialists may in time result in various changes to, instructions for, and comments on the prescriptions that redefine the application, context, and importance of the ritual; and so on. Thus we might say that negotiations surround the ritual proper, but they can never be located in it. Formally even a change or variation of ritual is a new "ritual proper," but seen in context, change can be a statement of negotiation.

PERFORMATIVE ASPECTS OF RITUAL: NEGOTIATING THE RITUAL ASSERTIONS

Catherine Bell has shown how ritual negotiation takes place in ritual performances. The notion of performance, in turn, only makes sense in actual historical or ethnographic contexts, just like the notion of *parole* in linguistics. As an example Bell cites an almost trivial daily offering of incense to ancestors and deities that is expected to be performed twice a day by the senior woman of the house in a Chinese home. Although the ceremony allows little room for personal variation, "by virtue of small emphases in the performance, the woman's routine will evoke her obedience to lineage demands, her prestige in a partnership with that lineage, a deep devotion to a deity in contrast to token respect to the ancestors, fears about grandchildren, or a socialist impatience with superstitious nonsense." Thus a performance approach to ritual

> is alert to the micropolitics that are always involved in these routine acts, the ways in which people manipulate traditions and conventions to construct an empowering understanding of their present situation. For example, the daily incense offering has been called an "act of obeisance" of junior to senior, living to dead, woman to male lineage. . . . Although offerings to her husband's ancestral lineage are a significant part of the marriage ritual, a woman usually assumes the daily routine of tending the altar when the ancestors on the altar have become the kin of her own children. And such duties inevitably involve a negotiation of power. For example, her care of these nonblood kin is thought to have important consequences for the well-being of the family, and there is some suggestion that her role in this activity could be used to make her influence felt.[18]

The preceding discussions suggest that the notion of negotiation makes sense only in certain contexts, and therefore I think analysts ought to exercise some caution in applying the term. Even in contexts where negotiation might in fact take place, the word "negotiation" is often too weak an expression of what is transpiring. Negotiation implies a kind of civilized diplomacy that in many situations is an understatement of the actual conflict. In such cases "struggle" or "confrontation" may be more appropriate words.

PENANCE IN THE DHARMA LITERATURE

Penance (*prāyaścitta*) forms one of the major subjects of the Hindu Dharma literature, and is to be distinguished from punishment (*daṇḍa*) in several respects. In general within the penal system the focus is on the object of a crime, that is, on the victim and the harm suffered by him, while within the penitential system it is on the subject of the crime, that is, on the perpetrator and the karmic harm he has done to himself. The initiative and obligation to punish criminals lie with the king, whereas the initiative to undergo a penance is with the perpetrator, who, in severe cases, must approach a council of Brahmans to have the penance fixed. Nevertheless the king is responsible for ensuring that the transgression is in fact atoned for. In addition to major penances there are smaller observances, such as sipping water, bathing, or glancing at the sun for a moment. These rites, which are prescribed as purifications for all sorts of minor breaches, are also classified as penances but are undertaken by the transgressor himself without involving the council. Much in the texts indicates that the ideas and interests of the two institutions are not absolutely separate. For instance, the death penalty is also regarded as a penance in some contexts, and although a sinner is expected to engage in the penitential process by his own initiative, there is also strong public pressure, expressed in the rule that those committing serious sins who refuse to undergo penance should be excommunicated from their caste communities.[19]

The purpose of penance is clearly soteriological. The locus classicus is found in the Mānava Dharmaśāstra: "In this way, as a result of the remnants of their past deeds, are born individuals despised by good people: the mentally retarded, the mute, the blind, and the deaf, as well as those who are deformed. Therefore, one should always do penances to purify oneself; for individuals whose sins have not been expiated are born with detestable characteristics."[20] Doing penance means, then, that the evil karma of a transgression is completely destroyed. According to Parāśarasmṛti, "Like water on a stone is cleaned away by wind and sun, so the misdeed of a person disappears after the penance has been decided by the council of Brahmins. It does not go to him who performs the penance; it does not go to the council; it is eradicated like water by wind and sun."[21] This effect is obtained by a combination of four types of activity: the recitation of sacred texts, austerity, sacrifice, and the giving of gifts. Austerity takes the form of sexual abstinence, cold baths, wearing wet cloths, standing all day and sitting all night (alternatively, sleeping on the floor), and fasting.[22] The last type of hardship is particularly prominent, and many penances are distinguished by their special manner of fasting. The following are examples.[23]

The Arduous Penance (kṛcchra), also known as the Prajāpati Penance (prājāpatya)
: A fast for twelve days. For nine days the penitent eats only one meal a day: the first three days in the morning, the next three days in the evening, and the following three days only if it can be obtained from others without asking. The last three days he observes a complete fast.

The Very Arduous Penance (atikṛcchra)
: Like the former, but instead of one meal, only one morsel of food is allowed for the first nine days.

The Penance beyond the Very Arduous Penance (kṛcchrātikṛcchra)
: Like the Arduous Penance, but instead of any solid food, the penitent drinks only water. In some texts this is prolonged for twenty-one or twenty-four days.

The Hot Arduous Penance (taptakṛcchra)
: Like the Arduous penances, but solid food is replaced by hot water, hot milk, and hot butter during the respective three-day periods where any food is allowed.

The Children's Arduous Penance (bālakṛcchra)
: The three-day periods of the Arduous Penance are reduced to one day each. Thus the fast lasts only four days.

The Lunar Penance (cāndrāyaṇa)
A fast lasting one month, during which the intake of food is decreased and increased gradually by one morsel of food according to the course of the moon, with fifteen morsels on the day of the full moon and complete fast on the day of the new moon. As with the Arduous Penance, several variations are mentioned.

The Parāka Penance
This is a complete fast for twelve days.

The Sāṃtapana Penance
A penance lasting two days, during which the penitent subsists by ingesting small amounts of the five products of the cow (*pañcagavya,* i.e., milk, curd, ghee, urine, and dung), together with a decoction of the sacred Kuśa grass for one day and fasts on the second day. Extended version of the penance lasting for seven, fifteen, or twenty-one days are also mentioned.

The Cow Urine and Barley Penance (gomūtrayāvaka)
A cow is fed with barley grains, which are collected from its dung and subsequently boiled in cow urine. The penitent subsists by eating the boiled grains for one or more days.

The One Meal Penance (ekabhakta)
Subsisting by eating one meal a day for one month.

During all these observances the penitent lives according to an ascetic regimen of sexual abstinence, cold baths, quiet recitations from sacred texts, offerings, and the aforementioned forms of austerity.

The effects of performing the penances come to light through an analysis of the consequences of not performing them. In general these consequences can be categorized under four headings:

1. Social and economic isolation: a ban on economic transactions with the sinner until the transgression is atoned for by penance.[24]
2. Disease and bodily disabilities in the present or in future lives.[25]
3. An interim period between death and new birth in one of many hells.[26]
4. Rebirth in a low caste or in lower life forms.[27]

There are several different criteria involved in these discussions, such as the seriousness of the sin and whether it was committed deliberately or unknowingly. Thus Mādhavācārya, the author of the mid-fourteenth-century *Parāśaramādhavīya*, accounts for several of these criteria in his conclusion to these discussions. If a sin is committed unintentionally, the penances that are performed will both avert hell and free the sinner of social and economic isolation. But if the sin was committed intentionally, he must perform double the amount of the penance that is performed for unintentional sins, and even then he can free himself only from the social and economic isolation; he cannot avoid an unpleasant sojourn in hell. It is possible for such a deliberate sinner to avoid hell only if the penance implies his own death, which may be the case in the most severe sins, such as killing a Brahman, having sex with an elder's wife, or (for a Brahman) drinking liquor.[28]

Obviously there is both an inner, *karmic*, and an outer, social aspect to these consequences. The motivation for observing penances is not only a matter of one's own fear of karmic retribution, but perhaps more a matter of avoiding social ostracism. Interestingly this ostracism is enforced only when the sin is publicly known. If not, the sinner, if he is a Brahman of high learning and Vedic training, has the option of performing secret penances.[29] In particular these are distinguished from ordinary penances in that the sinner does not approach the council.[30] Instead he performs large amounts of quiet recitation together with various exercises in austerity, often in combination with breathing exercises (*prāṇāyāma*), which are not part of the public penances prescribed by the council but are possibly considered a particularly potent, virtuoso means of purification.[31]

THE DOUBLE SIGNIFICANCE OF PENANCE

Considering the various elements of these penances, they seem to have a double significance. Like other ritual elements they are both symbol and phenomenon. The symbolic aspect is expressed or implied in public, textual prescriptions and exegetical articulations, whereas the phenomenal aspect is mostly silent but is nevertheless an important and necessary part of the ritual efficacy of these rites. In the case of penance this dichotomy is especially clear, and the two aspects are almost polarized. On the one hand, these elements—austerity, dietary ingredients, decoctions, and so on—are loaded with symbolic reference to a positive, sacred sphere. On the other hand, they often involve a negative reality of unpleasant, painful, and humiliating experiences. According to the *Parāśarasmṛti*, a Brahman woman who has had sexual contact with a low-caste man (but has not become pregnant) must perform a penance lasting seven days succeeded by a One Meal fast until she has her next menstruation. First she must proclaim her sin openly before ten (male) Brahmans. Then she is made to stand in a well or a pit (*kūpa*) filled with a mixture of cow dung, water, and mud up to her neck for twenty-four hours. The next day she shaves her head and eats a meal of barley porridge, then she fasts for another three days and stays in water for one day in the same pit as before. After that she must drink a decoction prepared from the Śaṃkhapuṣpī plant (*canscora decussata*), some gold, and the five products of the cow. During the whole period, including the One Meal fast, she must not enter the house. At the end, to mark her recovered purity, she serves a meal to the Brahmans (probably the ten in the council) and donates two cows as a fee.[32]

Cow dung and urine are two of the five holy products of the cow. As essences of "cowness" they symbolize purity. Edward Harper's notion of "respect pollution" applies in this context. Human feces and urine are highly polluting, but the cow in itself is so pure that even its dung and urine are pure to humans, who express this relation by using these ingredients as ritual purgatives.[33] But all this is purely symbolic, and it would be a misunderstanding to overlook the disgust naturally felt when being submerged in cow dung and mud or when eating barley boiled in cow urine. Having prescribed another penance, which involves eating a mixture of barley, cow urine, milk, curd, and ghee, *Parāśarasmṛti* stresses that the penitent "should not eat this with a feeling of disgust, nor as if it were food left over by others or spoiled by worms," thus acknowledging the phenomenal aspects of these elements.[34] Surely a phenomenological awareness is an important element in any analysis of ritual. In this case it also confirms Burkert's idea of the ritual sign as nonarbitrary. However much ritual elements like cow dung, urine, the cutting off of a married woman's hair, and segregation are loaded with symbolism—that is, are assigned semiotic functions as arbitrary signifiers (in line with Durkheim's idea that anything in the world can be made a reference to the sacred)[35]—they are deliberately applied in these rituals by virtue of the force of their specific phenomenal, humiliating, unpleasant, or painful qualities. They mold sinners into humble penitents not merely conceptually but by experience.[36]

SIN AND EXPIATION

Robert Hertz's posthumous, unfinished study of sin and expiation contains interesting observations that add to the understanding of the Indian *prāyaścittas* as described above. Like Mauss in relation to gift exchange, Hertz wanted to be able to define the general inner logic of a transcultural social phenomenon on the basis of a comparative study. His argument is in two parts: in order to define expiation he must first define sin. Starting from the biblical parable of the prodigal son, on the surface a dialogue between two agents, God and a sinner, Hertz points out that when the father's pardon has the capacity of annulling the curse on the son, this is because both agree in attributing a sacramental power to this act of pardon. How else can an already accomplished act be made virtually undone? This shows that after all the two actors are not on the stage alone: "Ils obéiraient l'un et l'autre, dans une large mesure, à des représentations et à des sentiments que la société leur a suggérés."[37] Society is the third actor, and sin is not merely an inner, private issue. It is objective.

However, the objectivity of sin does not operate independently of a given belief system. Without faith in the belief system that defines certain acts as sin, these acts are not necessarily felt as such.[38] This observation seems to be confirmed by the universal idea that expiation requires first of all open confession. By confessing the sin to other members of the religious community, the particular belief system is acknowledged, and the healing, which otherwise would be in vain and inefficient, can take place, itself being part of the system.

What about the secret penances mentioned earlier? These seem to be evidence against Hertz's idea of the objectivity of sin. Hertz did not include Indian material in his study, but given the sinner's faith in the belief system, he insists that whether or not the sinner is able to keep his sin a secret, he will feel miserable and morally excommunicated. Thus sin destroys the sinner by manipulating his integrity, while expiation can save him.[39]

According to Hertz the force of sin and expiation lies in their sacred character. A sacred force has been transgressed by the sin and has to strike back unless the sinner shows open remorse by undergoing various kinds of suffering, which substitute for the sacrifice that alone has the needed renewing and creative potential to transform the destructive force. This eventually brings about the pardon that is able to remove the sin without destroying the sinner. In one of Hertz's reports of his teaching in 1908–9, quoted by Mauss as further evidence, this line of thinking is particularly clear: "La transgression d'un tabou altère, dans leur être, les pouvoirs protégés par le tabou, en même temps qu'elle voue le transgresseur à la mort. Cet état funeste dure aussi longtemps que la causé initiale n'a pas été abolie soit par la peine, soit par le pardon. Le pardon est une destruction de la faute sans destruction du coupable."[40]

Thus the power that has been violated is also the power that brings about the destruction—or the healing, if the violator is prepared to make the sacrifice of penance. This logic may also indicate how Hertz would have elaborated on "l'ascétisme pénitentiel" that was meant to be taken up in section 3 of the third part of the study, according to his note from January 1913.[41] At least it is understood that Hertz would have interpreted the penitential asceticism in terms of sacrifice.

It is interesting to think forward from Hertz's place in the history of religious scholarship. With Mary Douglas's *Purity and Danger*,[42] the notions of sin and expiation took a sociological and structuralist turn compared to Hertz's much stronger focus on religious and ritual logic. Louis Dumont belonged to the same trend as Douglas with his interpretation of purity in the Indian context as a matter of hierarchical social relations. Even though these new directions had a basis in the same Durkheimian sociology to which Hertz belonged, they reduced the sacred character of society to merely a matter of relationships between social agents, thereby underplaying the religious powers within given belief systems to which Hertz attributed the dynamic force of sin and expiation. It is possible by a Dumontian logic to explain, for instance, the penal rule that a Brahman who has had sex with a Śūdra woman must be fined five hundred copper coins, but he is fined one thousand coins if he had sex with a woman of even lower caste.[43] But the same logic cannot explain why the rule is different in a penitential context, where the same Brahman who has had sex with a Śūdra woman must live on alms and make recitations of sacred mantras every day for three years in order to regain his original purity.[44] In other words, Dumont's reasoning does not explain the difference between the penal and the penitential contexts and why it should be necessary to have both a penalty and a penance for the same offence. According to Hertz, however, the difference lies in the force protected by the religious taboo that motivates the penance (but not the penalty), that is the sacredness of the Brahman based on his appropriation of the Veda and not merely his position in the social structure. This force turns into the bad karma of his act, and if he does not undergo the prescribed penance it will make him suffer in other ways during future lives. It is the interpretation of this force, karma, that the Indian penitential system negotiates.

PENANCE AS NEGOTIATING RITUALS

There are at least four ways to see penance as negotiating rituals. First, the whole idea of removing bad karma by performing penance tacitly negotiates central aspects of the Upaniṣadic doctrines of karma and rebirth. Second, the process of deciding appropriate penances negotiates alternative interpretations of the situation and, by extension, its possible relations of power. Third, the learned authors of commentaries and digests negotiate the traditions left to them, for instance when sorting out contradictory rules in the Sūtras and Smṛtis. Fourth, these authors also negotiate the rules in relation to pragmatic concerns, sometimes bending them to bring them in line with contemporary interests. Here I focus on the first type and offer brief summaries of the others.

Negotiating Karma

The eschatology of the early Upaniṣads as articulated in the doctrine of the five fires and the two paths after cremation, the path leading to the gods and the path leading to the fathers,[45] reflects a changing view of life in a society bound by kinship. There are other, perhaps older formulations of karma and rebirth in the early Upaniṣads that merely connect the acts of one life with the conditions of the next without any link to the knowledge of the five fires and the cosmology of the two paths.[46] But the two-path doctrine is particularly telling with respect to the social contexts of the conflict between ritualists and antiritualists that lies behind these eschatological developments. The doctrine envisages two structurally opposite scenarios for a person after cremation. One, the path leading to the gods, is the path followed by those who live "in the wilderness," probably a topographic metaphor of a group of religious virtuosi characterized by their emphasis on an esoteric knowledge of ritual rather than on the performance of ritual and by a renunciate, ascetic lifestyle. Their path, which follows the bright elements of fire and continues along the fortnight of the waxing moon and the six months when the sun moves north, terminates in the worlds of Brahman, from whence the ascetics will never return again to a life on earth.[47] The other, the path leading to the fathers, is the path followed by those living "in villages" who perform (rather than meditate on) rituals and donate gifts. As a structural contrast to the former group, the "villagers" represent an orthodox ritualism centered on kinship ideals. Their path, which follows the dark elements of fire and continues along the fortnight of the waning moon and the six months when the sun moves south, leads to the heavenly world of the fathers, but it never ends. Instead these sacrificers are reborn on earth according to the acts of their former life, and they will go on circling "around in the same way" in this circuit, this *saṃsāra*, as long as they do not renounce the life of the village and acquire esoteric knowledge.[48]

This coherent doctrine of life and death neither emerged all of a sudden, nor was it a result of a linear process. Rather certain lines of thinking gradually became prominent among a variegated repertoire of afterlife ideas. In older layers of the Ṛgveda such ideas are not very frequent at all. There are, however, references to "fathers," to some kind of dark netherworld, and to an afterlife in heaven. In the youngest, tenth book of the Ṛgveda the fathers are clearly situated in heaven.[49] In the Brāhmaṇa layer of the Vedic corpus we hear of an immortal afterlife as fathers in heaven, but also of "redeath" (*punarmṛtyu*), that is, the conflicting idea that even ancestors would die again if they did not perform the right sacrifices during their life on earth, in particular the prestigious ritual of the Fire Altar (*agnicayana*). Both these ideas are ritualistic; that is, in both cases immortal life in heaven depends on ritual performances during life on earth.[50]

The two-path eschatology of the Bṛhadāraṇyaka and Chāndogya Upaniṣads represents a critique of this ritualistic ideal. Not only are the renouncers associated with bright qualities whereas the villagers all travel along the dark path, but the former are also secured a final release, whereas the orthodox villagers must return to a precarious life on earth again and again. The ancestors' heavenly world is reduced to a short visit stripped of soteriological value, and so this image of the closed *saṃsāric* circuit is a clear expression of the negative view taken by the renouncers of the traditional life cycle of birth, initiation, marriage, sacrifices, sons, and cremation. Salvation is no longer associated with the family and its immortality through the world of the fathers. By distributing a person's future births across *separate* families, places, and even life forms, the doctrine of karma and rebirth effectively broke the kinship continuity of the old soteriology.

The clear structural opposition of the imagery and cosmology of the path to the gods and the path to the fathers indicates a strong division between ritualists and antiritualists. The point of view of these Upaniṣadic pericopes is that of the latter, the new spiritual elite. Having renounced the world, they are close to final release. In contrast they depict the villagers' life as a gloomy path leading nowhere other than in continuously turning circles.

This clear antiritualistic orientation is absent in the law literature that started to emerge in the early post-Vedic period.[51] In an attempt to formulate an inclusive code of conduct for the whole of society, ascetic norms were nevertheless incorporated in a comprehensive scheme dominated by a traditional kinship-based ethos. This in turn became proportionately contradictory, or rather compartmental, with different, specific rules dependent on social class (*varṇa*) and personal stage of life (*āśrama*). However, due to the undeniable influence of the renouncer movements, the Buddhist in particular, the doctrine of karma and rebirth had become universal. But in order to oppose these successful movements and to accommodate to traditional family values, the law books, the literature of the traditionalist Brahman environment, offered new interpretations of this originally antiritualistic teaching.[52] These interpretations took the sting out of the Upaniṣadic *saṃsāra* doctrine by putting a stronger emphasis on a code of conduct that would lead to a good birth rather than on the goal of final release.

Āpastambadharmasūtra, the oldest of the law texts according to Patrick Olivelle, states, "People of all classes enjoy supreme and boundless happiness when they follow the Laws specific to them. Then, upon a man's return to earth, by virtue of the residue of his merits he obtains a high birth, a beautiful body, a fine complexion, strength, intelligence, wisdom, wealth, and an inclination to follow the Law. So, going around like a wheel, he remains happy in both worlds."[53] But the same logic holds for sinners. Those who break the law are born as Untouchable castes, having first spent their "sojourn in the next world living in an interminable hell."[54] As explicitly argued later in Manu's law book and mentioned earlier, this is the very raison d'être of penance. By performing penance these unlucky consequences can be averted.

Āpastambadharmasūtra also explicitly rejects the ideals of antiritualism and renunciation. First, the renunciate ideal is presented by quoting two verses "from a Purāṇa" that paraphrase the two-path doctrine:

> The eighty thousand seers who desired offspring went along the sun's southern course. They obtained cremation grounds.
>
> The eighty thousand seers who did not desire offspring went along the sun's northern course. They, indeed, attained immortality.[55]

The renunciate ideal of these verses is then rejected by the argument that the Vedas, which are the ultimate authority, prescribe sacrifices that necessarily involve the participation of the wife.[56] Further, and as a comment to the notion of immortality in the second verse, the text also quotes the Taittirīya Brāhmaṇa: "In your offspring you are born again. That, O mortal, is your immortality."[57] When sons perform the prescribed rites they increase the heavenly life of their ancestors. Eventually these ancestors dwell in heaven until the next destruction of the world. At the subsequent creation they serve as the surviving seed of coming generations, according to another Purāṇic verse quoted in the text.[58]

Behind these reinterpretations and the institution of penance connected with them lies a reorientation of values. In contrast to the Upaniṣadic antiritualists, who understood the bondage of the villagers as a cycle of karma and rebirth that they themselves knew how to break out of, the law books acknowledge that life in the world inevitably involves karma, but then offer the possibility of averting the feared results by penitential rituals. Consequently the law's view on transgressions is pragmatic: everyone commits errors; the point is to know how to avert their karmic results. This attitude is clearly expressed in typical formulations like this one (on unlawful food): "Such food should not be eaten. In any case of eating it, however, a penance has to be observed."[59]

Negotiating Transgressions

In the case of severe transgressions the sinner is urged to approach a council of Brahmans who will decide the proper penance. It is obvious that in the process of making this decision various criteria will be involved in a negotiation of different, perhaps conflicting considerations. Unfortunately the Dharma literature itself does not record actual council negotiations. However, a few medieval inscriptions give an impression of how these were conducted in certain cases. Even though the actual case did not involve a decision regarding penance but was about settling a conflict of status and rights between two groups of professionals, it shows that a decision was arrived at only after careful considerations with reference to both classical law books and examination of the claims by the parties involved.[60] The work of the council, then, was precisely to negotiate the options of a given case. Although classical law texts attempted to correlate specific transgressions with specific penances, there was room for many negotiable criteria. Was the incident deliberate or unintentional? Were the circumstances normal or unusually stressful? And so on. Eventually the penance that was decided would reflect these negotiations.

Negotiating Tradition

The criteria involved in the decisions of the council were also used by the commentators as a way of sorting contradictory rules in the law books, thus giving priority to one rule over another. The basic assumption was that Smṛtis have authority in all matters not dealt with explicitly in the Vedas. Therefore a contradictory Smṛti rule could not just be rejected but would have to be assigned a certain context in which it was valid. This gives the commentators the opportunity both to preserve the idea that the rules are all equally valid and to place them in order of priority. In particular this technique is used as a way of grading rules that apply different degrees of penance for the same transgression. We have already seen this in the example of how Mādhvācārya, the commentator on Parāśarasmṛti, dealt with conflicting rules about penance for cardinal sins (*mahāpātaka*), that is, killing a Brahman, (for a Brahman) drinking liquor, and so on, some of which demanded a penance that ultimately involves the death of the sinner while others did not. Mādhvācārya was able to do that by applying the distinction between intentional and unintentional sin.[61]

One transgression that generated a particularly wide variety of rules concerns a man who has sex with an Untouchable woman. For this Parāśarasmṛti prescribes the double observance of the Arduous Penance in the event of the man being a Brahman. If he is from any of the lower classes, the observance is less severe.[62] So the rule in the Smṛti text is already differentiated, but Mādhavācārya then goes on to compare a multitude of rules for similar transgressions in other Smṛtis, and for each rule prescribing a penance that is different from the one in Parāśarasmṛti he points out a particular context. The criteria are intention (intentional or unintentional), frequency (once or repeatedly for a shorter or longer period), consummation (whether the intercourse was interrupted or consummated, the latter being worse), and pregnancy (whether or not the woman becomes pregnant, the former being worse). With the aid of these different criteria it is possible for Mādhavācārya to sort a large number of rules that prescribe different penances for the same transgression, ranging from one Hot Arduous penance (for an unintentional, single, and interrupted sexual intercourse) to committing suicide (for intentional, consummated sexual relations over a period of one year).[63]

But even using this technique there are rules that commentators would not want to allow or assign any valid context. Such rules can be declared obsolete or, as they were literally labeled, "rules that are forbidden in the present Kali age" (*kalivarjya*). According to the doctrine of the four ages, since creation there has been a decline of virtue and human spiritual capacity, and we now live in the most degraded age, the Kali age. In this age certain controversial rules are bracketed out, the idea being that humans no longer possess the prerequisites for these rules, and thus it was possible for commentators to make adjustments according to historical changes without denying the ancient authority of Smṛti.[64] For instance there is a rule that shortens the period of Untouchability for those in whose immediate family someone has recently died. Generally they remain untouchable and unfit for serving meals to others for a period lasting ten, twelve, fifteen, or thirty days, respectively, for the four classes from Brahman to Śūdra. But some rules declare them already touchable after four, six, eight, or ten days when the bones of the deceased have been collected from the cremation pyre. These rules are declared forbidden in the Kali age by Mādhavācārya and in other texts.[65] Interestingly P. V. Kane, the compiler of a huge work on the Dharma literature that no student of that literature can ignore, rightly referred to the concept of rules forbidden in the Kali age in a passage criticizing what some would now call the "Orientalist" idea of the "unchanging East." Notably Kane did this several decades before Edward Said's and Ronald Inden's works emerged.[66]

Negotiating Ideals

There are certain ideal rules that simply are not realizable from the point of view of practical social reality. I shall mention one example, again referring to Mādhavācārya's discussion of penance in case of intentional transgressions. This is Mādhavācārya's conclusion that it is possible to atone even for deliberate sins, but that such a sinner will be released only from the social and economic isolation imposed on every transgressor of serious sins, not from hell or a low rebirth. This may sound like a noble solution after all, since nobody is totally lost. However, if we consider the medieval discussions among commentators about the right of ownership, we will understand that the purpose of the text is not directed so much toward the sinner as toward the learned Brahmans with whom he might have made transactions. To receive goods from a sinner implies, according to ideal rules, both that the receiver incurs sin through the transaction and that the transaction itself, including the ownership of what has been transacted, should rightly be regarded as void. We find, for instance, a rule in Manu's law book urging the receiver of wealth acquired through a "reprehensible activity" to give away that wealth.[67] The commentators understand this as referring to accepting wealth from unlawful givers, a category that includes people whose transgressions have not been atoned for.[68] This interpretation is in line with the subsequent verses, which prescribe a penance for accepting such gifts.[69] However, if the sinner expiates his sin by observing a penance, no one should avoid doing business with such a man.[70] Yājñavalkya's law book extended this latter principle to transactions even with deliberate sinners; if such a person expiates his sin, he is at least one with whom others can do business (*vyavahārya*).[71] But because other texts express the view that it should not be possible to atone for deliberate sins at all, Vijñāneśvara, the commentator on that text, had to address these other texts, creating a possible space for them as well as for Yājñavalkya's rule, thus anticipating Mādhavācārya's later discussion.[72]

The detailed elaborations of these discussions confirm Derrett's assumption that the textual restrictions on transactions "might affect considerable sums of money, or tracts of land."[73] By maintaining that penance makes it possible to deal lawfully with a deliberate sinner, this hindrance is partly removed. But not fully. If the sinner is indifferent to ideas of a ripening karma in some future life, the problem remains. After all, who knows what sins people have committed in secret without bothering about penance? Do transactions made with such individuals become void if the truth is revealed some day? This and similar problems led to the view that property is basically a worldly matter irrespective of the moral status of the person from whom it is obtained. The argument, developed fully by Vijñāśvara, is essentially that although the receiver undoubtedly incurs a sin by receiving wealth from a sinner and therefore has to undergo a penance, he nevertheless owns what he had received, since the transaction itself is not invalidated.[74]

CONCLUSIONS

To see ritual issues from the perspective of negotiation is enlightening because it draws attention to the politics of ritual, which are in many ways often overlooked and which show how rituals are engaged in order to establish or change power relations. However, precision is needed in such analysis. Ritual action presupposes an authority ostensibly rooted in some extraordinary source of power. Since this is taken for granted in the ritual enactment itself, arguments are not needed. Therefore negotiation is not located *in* ritual but around it. It is only in relation to a ritual's actual contexts that the negotiation procedures become visible. In terms of methodology, it is only from a historical, sociological, or similarly contextual perspective that rituals become visible as statements vis-à-vis other statements. From the noncontextualizing perspective of a phenomenology of religion, where the focus is on the formal or structural aspects of the ritual logic itself, the notion of negotiation is not relevant precisely because it is misrecognized by the very logic of ritual. Rituals may be antagonistic, displaying, for instance, threatening behavior, but in doing so they insist on only one particular power configuration. They do not recognize that the outcome of the real conflict may in fact turn either way. They do not subscribe to that open-endedness that must be a criterion of negotiation.

Penance in the Indian law literature serves as a particularly telling example of a type of ritual in which various negotiations can be discerned at several contextual levels. First of all, penance as an opportunity to avert the karma of wrong or immoral acts involved a critique of the Upaniṣadic, antiritualistic eschatology. In the Upaniṣads this eschatology was formulated as an opposition between a closed cycle of rebirths and the vision of final release. This eschatology was reinterpreted in the law literature in accordance with its own ritualistic and family-oriented position. Thus the institution of penance was developed as a technique that made it possible both to be involved in the world and at the same time to control the karma naturally generated by a worldly lifestyle—by mixing and transacting with many different people, for instance. Penance even made room for severe transgressions. These penances were both a personal technique of karma control and a set of sanctions enforcing social norms on the wrongdoers. As such these rituals were far from being merely symbolic forms of manipulation. They subjected the sinner to elements that involved deprivation, pain, humiliation, and disgust. But they also involved visions of purification and sanctity. All in all, such rituals had elements that contained considerable power to discipline and mold a humble penitent.

Notes

1. See Kathryn McClymond's chapter in this book.

2. MDhŚ 1.2; ĀDhS 2.2.8–9 and parallels. In general *dharmaśāstra* texts do not speak of castes, but either of classes (*varṇa*, i.e., *brāḥmaṇa*, *kṣatriya*, *vaiśya*, and *śūdra*) or mixed castes (*varṇasaṃkara* or, as in this verse, *antaraprabhavāḥ*, "those born in between"), the idea being that castes are derived from former sexual relations across the classes.

3. ĀDhS 2.2.8-9 and parallels; GDhS 22.4 and parallels.

4. Aktor, "*Smṛtis* and *Jātis,*" 260–67.

5. Olivelle, *Language, Texts, and Society,* 159.

6. Halbfass, *Tradition and Reflection,* 301–2.

7. Ibid., 303. See also Kane, *History of Dharmaśāstra,* 5:1210–12.

8. Halbfass, *Tradition and Reflection,* 306; Kane, *History of Dharmaśāstra,* 4:68.

9. Burkert, *Structure and History in Greek Mythology and Ritual,* 44, 53, 54–56.

10. Ibid., 48, 37.

11. Ibid., 48.

12. Burkert, "Glaube und Verhalten," 98.

13. Mauss, *The Gift,* 10–11.

14. Bourdieu, *Outline of a Theory of Practice,* 4–9.

15. Hubert and Mauss quoted in Sørensen, "The Rhetoric of Ritual," 149.

16. Sørensen, "The Rhetoric of Ritual," 149, 151–52; Sørensen, "Efficacy," 531.

17. Sørensen, "The Rhetoric of Ritual," 158.

18. Bell, "Performance," 215, 217.

19. Lingat, *The Classical Law of India,* 63–64, 232–37; Kane, *History of Dharmaśāstra,* 4:68–76. On the rule that excommunication is applicable only when sinners refuse to undergo a penance, see HaGDhS 20.1; MeMDhŚ 11.181; VijYS 3.194.

20. MDhŚ 11.53–54.

21. PS 2.8.9–10; excerpts from PS and MāPS in this article are translated by the author.

22. GDhS 19.11, 15 and parallels.

23. Different law books contain lists of various lengths. See, for instance, BDhS 4.5–6 (where these observances are used not to atone for particular sins, but as a preparation (restraints, *yantra*) to the Gaṇa ritual series of offerings and recitations) or MDhŚ 11.212–22. For more complete lists, see Kane, *History of Dharmaśāstra,* 4:130–52; Gampert, *Die Sühnezeremonien in der altindischen Rechtsliteratur*, 47–61.

24. MDhŚ 11.190; YS/VijYS 3.226; MāPS 2.8.1.

25. MDhŚ 11.48–54.

26. E.g. MDhŚ 12.54.

27. MDhŚ 12.55–81.

28. MDhŚ 11.74, 92, 104–5. Mādhavācārya's discussion is in MāPS 2.8.1. It is translated and discussed in Aktor, *Ritualisation and Segregation,* chapter 7.

29. For example, GDhS 24.1; MDhŚ 11.227; Kane, *History of Dharmaśāstra,* 4:125–26; Derrett, *Religion, Law and the State in India,* 83.

30. YS 3.301.

31. MDhŚ 2.83; 6.70–71. Breath control is by definition performed together with the quiet recitation of very central mantras and the syllable "OM"; see Olivelle's note to MDhŚ 6.70 in *Manu's Code of Law,* 291.

32. PS/MāPS 2.10.17–22; Aktor, "Untouchables, Women and Territories," 148–51; see also Aktor, *Ritualisation and Segregation,* chapter 6.

33. Harper, "Ritual Pollution as an Integrator of Caste and Religion," 182. Harper understands cow dung and urine as relatively pure or impure in the sense that, although purifying for humans, they are never used to wash or to bathe images of gods.

34. PS/MāPS 2.6.38b. This instruction is part of a series of rituals that are performed in order to purify a house that has been polluted by the stay of a low-caste person. See Aktor, *Ritualisation and Segregation,* chapter 6.

35. Durkheim, *The Elementary Forms of Religious Life*, 36.

36. Compare as a parallel Talal Asad's critique of a symbolist approach to ritual and his analysis of penance in medieval Europe in *Genealogies of Religion,* 34–39, 97–103.

37. Hertz, *Le péché et l'expiation dans les sociétés primitives,* 14.

38. Ibid., 46.

39. Ibid., 20.

40. Ibid., 56.

41. Ibid., 58.

42. Douglas, *Purity and Danger.*

43. MDhŚ 8.385.

44. MDhŚ 11.179.

45. BĀU 6.2 and ChU 5.3–10.

46. BĀU 3.2.13, 4.4.5–7. P. V. Kane thinks that these two passages are the earliest statements of the origin of the doctrine of karma and rebirth (*History of Dharmaśāstra,* 5:1547, 1551).

47. BĀU 6.2.15.

48. BĀU 6.2.16; ChU 5.10.3.

49. Bodewitz, "Life after Death in the Ṛgvedasaṃhitā," 31–35.

50. Bodewitz, "Redeath and Its Relation to Rebirth and Release," 30, 40–46.

51. Probably not earlier than the third century BCE, according to Patrick Olivelle in *Language, Texts, and Society,* 153, 165.

52. For a detailed study of the emergence of the Dharma literature and its dependence of Buddhism and Jainism, see Olivelle's three essays in *Language, Texts, and Society,* 121–77.

53. ĀDhS 2.2.2–3; Olivelle, *Dharmasūtras,* 8–9.

54. ĀDhS 2.2.5–7.

55. ĀDhS 2.23.4–5.

56. ĀDhS 2.23.10.

57. Taittirīya Brāhmaṇa 1.5.5.6; ĀDhS 2.24.1.

58. ĀDhS 2.24.3–6.

59. MāPS 2.11.47c–50b, p. 449.

60. The case is described in Derrett, *Essays in Classical and Modern Hindu Law,* 86–110, and by Derrett in Lingat, *The Classical Law of India,* 273–74.

61. MāPS 2.1.8.

62. This is in line with the general rule that Brahmans must pay more penance than people from lower classes for equal sins. For this and similar rules that differentiate between sinners of different classes, see Aktor, "The 'Grammar of Defilement' Revisited," 17–24.

63. MāPS 2.10.8. The text is translated and discussed in Aktor, *Ritualisation and Segregation,* chapter 5.

64. Lingat, *The Classical Law of India,* 180–95.

65. MāPS 1.1.34, p. 136; Kane, *History of Dharmaśāstra,* 3:929–30, 951. See also 3:930–68 for a list of *kalivarjyas*.

66. Kane, *History of Dharmaśāstra,* 3:967 (Kane's five volumes were originally published between 1930 and 1962); Said, *Orientalism;* Inden, *Imagining India.*

67. MDhŚ 11.194.

68. VS 57.4–5.

69. MDhŚ 11.195–97.

70. MDhŚ 11.190c–d.

71. YS 3.226.

72. Vijñāneśvara's *Mitākṣarā* is dated 1120–25, about two hundred years earlier than Mādhavācārya's *Parāśaramādhavīya*, according to Derrett, *Dharmaśāstra and Juridical Literature,* 50, 54.

73. Derrett, "The Development of the Concept of Property in India c. A.D. 800–1800," 44.

74. VijYS introducing YS 2.114, pp. 266–67; Derrett, *Religion, Law and the State in India,* 122–47. See also Kane, *History of Dharmaśāstra,* 3:548–52.

Abbreviations

ĀDhS: Āpastambadharmasūtra; see Olivelle, *Dharmasūtras,* 20–115.

BĀU: Bṛhadāraṇyaka Upaniṣad; see Olivelle, *The Early Upaniṣads,* 29–165.

BDhS: Baudhāyanadharmasūtra; see Olivelle, *Dharmasūtras,* 191–345.

ChU: Chāndogya Upaniṣad; see Olivelle, *The Early Upaniṣads,* 166–287.

GDhS: Gautamadharmasūtra; see Olivelle, *Dharmasūtras,* 116–89.

HaGDhS: Haradatta's commentary on GDhS, entitled *Mitākṣarā;* see Pāṇḍeya, *Gautamadharmasūtra.*

MāPS: Mādhavācārya's commentary on PS, entitled *Parāśaramādhavīya;* see Islāmapurkar, *Parāśara Dharma Saṃhitā or Parāśara Smṛti.*

MDhŚ: Mānavadharmaśāstra; see Olivelle, *Manu's Code of Law*.

MeMDhŚ: Medhātithi's commentary on MDhŚ, entitled *Manubhāṣya;* see Jhā, *Manusmṛti with the Commentary of Medhātithi*.

PS: Parāśarasmṛti; see Islāmapurkar, *Parāśara Dharma Saṃhitā or Parāśara Smṛti*.

VijYS: Vijñāneśvara's commentary on Yājñavalkyasmṛti, entitled *Mitākṣarā;* see Pāṇḍeya, *Yājñavalkyasmṛti of Yogīshwara Yājñavalkya*.

VS: Viṣṇusmṛti; see Jolly, *Viṣṇusmṛti*.

YS: Yājñavalkyasmṛti; see Stenzler, *Yājñavalkya's Gesetzbuch*.

Bibliography

Aktor, Mikael. "The 'Grammar of Defilement' Revisited: Comparing Rules of *Prāyaścitta* with Rules of *Āśauca*." *Indologica Taurinensia* 33 (2007): 13–32.

———. *Ritualisation and Segregation: The Untouchability Complex in Indian Dharma Literature with Special Reference to Parāśarasmṛti and Parāśaramādhavīya*. Vol. 9 of *Corpus Iuris Sanscriticum et fontes iuris Asiae Meridianae et Centralis*, ed. Oscar Botto. Turin: CESMEO, 2008.

———. "*Smṛtis* and *Jātis*: The Ritualisation of Time and the Continuity of the Past." In *Invoking the Past: The Uses of History in South Asia*, ed. Daud Ali, 258–79. New Delhi: Oxford University Press, 1999.

———. "Untouchables, Women and Territories: Rituals of Lordship in the Parāśara Smṛti." In *Invented Identities: The Interplay of Gender, Religion and Politics in India*, ed. Julia Leslie and Mary McGee, 133–56. New Delhi: Oxford University Press, 2000.

Asad, Talal. *Genealogies of Religion: Discipline and Reasons of Power in Christianity and Islam*. Baltimore: Johns Hopkins University Press, 1993.

Bell, Catherine. "Performance." In *Critical Terms for Religious Studies*, ed. Mark C. Taylor, 205–24. Chicago: University of Chicago Press, 1998.

Bodewitz, Henk W. "Life after Death in the Ṛgvedasaṃhitā." *Wiener Zeitschrift für die Kunde Südasiens* 38 (1994): 23–41.

Bodewitz, Henk W. "Redeath and Its Relation to Rebirth and Release." *Studien zur Indologie und Iranistik* 20 (1996): 27–46.

Bourdieu, Pierre. *Outline of a Theory of Practice*. 1972. Cambridge: Cambridge University Press, 1993.

Burkert, Walter. "Glaube und Verhalten: Zeichengehalt und Wirkungsmacht von Opferritualen." In *Le sacrifice dans l'antiquité*, ed. Jean Rudhardt and Olivier Reverdin, 91–125. Geneva: Fondation Hardt, 1981.

———. *Structure and History in Greek Mythology and Ritual*. Berkeley: University of California Press, 1979.

Derrett, J. Duncan M. "The Development of the Concept of Property in India c. A.D. 800–1800." *Zeitschrift für vergleichende Rechtswissenschaft* 64 (1962): 15–130.

———. *Dharmaśāstra and Juridical Literature*. Part of vol. 4 of *A History of Indian Literature*, ed. Jan Gonda. Wiesbaden: Otto Harrassowitz, 1973.

———. *Essays in Classical and Modern Hindu Law*. Vol. 1. Leiden: Brill, 1976.

———. *Religion, Law and the State in India*. London: Faber and Faber, 1968.

Douglas, Mary. *Purity and Danger: An Analysis of Concepts of Pollution and Taboo*. London: Routledge & Kegan Paul, 1966.

Durkheim, Émile. *The Elementary Forms of Religious Life*. 1912. Abridged ed. Ed. Mark S. Cladis. Trans. Carol Cosman. Oxford: Oxford University Press, 2001.

Gampert, Wilhelm. *Die Sühnezeremonien in der altindischen Rechtsliteratur*. Vol. 6 of *Monografie Archivu Orientálního—Studies, Texts and Translations*. Prague: Orientální Ústav, 1939.

Halbfass, Wilhelm. *Tradition and Reflection: Explorations in Indian Thought*. Albany: State University of New York Press, 1991.

Harper, Edward B. "Ritual Pollution as an Integrator of Caste and Religion." In *Religion in South Asia*, ed. Edward B. Harper, 151–96. Seattle: University of Washington Press, 1964.

Hertz, Robert. *Le péché et l'expiation dans les sociétés primitives*. 1922. Paris: Editions Jean-Michel Place, 1988.

Inden, Ronald. *Imagining India*. Oxford: Blackwell, 1990.

Islāmapurkar, Vāman Śāstri. *Parāśara Dharma Saṃhitā or Parāśara Smṛti, with the Commentary of Sāyaṇa Mādhavācārya*. 3 vols. Mumbai: Department of Public Instruction, 1893–99.

Jhā, Gaṅgānātha. *Manusmṛti with the Commentary of Medhātithi*. 3 vols. Kolkata: Asiatic Society of Bengal, 1932–39.

Jolly, Julius. *Viṣṇusmṛti (the Institutes of Viṣṇu), Together with Extracts from the Sanskrit Commentary of Nandapaṇḍita Called Vaijayanti*. 1881. Varanasi: Chowkhamba, 1962.

Kane, Pandurang Vaman. *History of Dharmaśāstra (Ancient and Mediæval Religious and Civil Law)*. 1930–62. 5 vols. 2nd ed. Pune: Bhandarkar Oriental Research Institute, 1968–77.

Lingat, Robert. *The Classical Law of India*. 1967. Delhi: Munshiram Manoharlal, 1993.

Mauss, Marcel. *The Gift: Forms and Functions of Exchange in Archaic Societies*. 1925. London: Cohen & West, 1969.

Olivelle, Patrick. *Dharmasūtras—The Law Codes of Āpastamba, Gautama, Baudhāyana, and Vasiṣṭha: Annotated Text and Translation*. Delhi: Motilal Banarsidass, 2000.

———. *The Early Upaniṣads: Annotated Text and Translation*. New York: Oxford University Press, 1998.

———. *Language, Texts, and Society: Explorations in Ancient Indian Culture and Religion*. Florence: Firenze University Press, 2005.

———. *Manu's Code of Law: A Critical Edition and Translation of the Mānava-Dharmaśāstra*. Oxford: Oxford University Press, 2005.

Pāṇḍeya, Umeśa Candra. *Gautamadharmasūtra, with the Commentary of Haradatta*. Varanasi: Chowkhamba, 1966.

———. *Yājñavalkyasmṛti of Yogīshwara Yājñavalkya, with the Mitākṣarā Commentary of Vijñāneshwar*. Varanasi: Chowkhamba, 1967.

Said, Edward W. *Orientalism*. New York: Pantheon Books, 1978.

Sørensen, Jørgen Podemann. "Efficacy." In *Theorizing Ritual*, ed. Jens Kreinath, Jan Snoek, and Michael Stausberg, 523–31. Leiden: Brill, 2006.

———. "The Rhetoric of Ritual." In *Ritualistics*, vol. 18 of *Scripta Instituti Donneriani Aboensis*, ed. Tore Ahlbäck, 149–61. Åbo: Donner Institute for Research in Religious and Cultural History, 2003.

Stenzler, Adolf Friedrich. *Yājñavalkya's Gesetzbuch: Sanskrit und Deutsch*. 1849. Osnabrück: Biblio Verlag, 1970.

2

Negotiations at Death

ASSESSING GIFTS, MOTHERS, AND MARRIAGES

Erik de Maaker

ONE EARLY MORNING, not very long after I had become a temporary resident of the village of Sadolpara, India,[1] someone informed me that Gujak had died. Gujak was an old woman and an important kinsperson for many of the people living there. Her death had no fewer than fifty men and women from Sadolpara change their routine for the day. That day they did not work their fields, as they had intended to do. Rather they attended the funeral of Gujak, which was held in the neighboring village of Chibonggre.

In the hours following Gujak's death more than a hundred people gathered near and inside the house in which she had lived. They came from villages in the vicinity of Chibonggre (such as Sadolpara) and from Chibonggre itself. About half of the participants were women, and each of them carried a heavy basket on a thumb line, filled with gifts for the deceased Gujak and her close relatives. Some of these baskets contained a vessel of rice beer, others had uncooked rice, and in addition to that there were food items such as tea, sugar, and biscuits. People arrived in groups, each of which organized around someone who considered himself or herself a close relative of Gujak. Some of the parties drove one or two cows, which, similar to the other gifts, were at once a gift for the deceased Gujak as well as for the people with whom Gujak had lived.

Once most of the guests had arrived, close relatives of Gujak offered to certain persons small sums of money, and in a few cases also heirloom objects such as a gong or a sword. The gongs and swords were usually accepted, but this did not necessarily hold for the monetary gifts. Some people who initially refused the money that was offered to them accepted it once the amount had been increased. Other people persisted in their refusal, as if acceptance of a gift would have had undesirable consequences. Why were some people reluctant to accept the gifts offered to them? And alternatively, why did the representatives of the deceased Gujak make such great efforts to have the gifts accepted?

It has long been recognized that rituals of death serve various ends at once. Death rituals organize the disposal of the corpse. But with the removal of the dead body, the bereaved are provided with a way to come to terms with the loss they are facing.[2] The conduct of a death ritual confirms the end of a life, but at the same time most death rituals include references to a new presence for the deceased, for instance in an afterlife. Such a continued presence can allow for the dead to serve as a source of vitality, essential to the continued existence and rejuvenation of the larger social and cosmological units that people identify with.[3] As Hertz noted, death then marks a transformation from one state to the other, rather than being perceived as just the end of life. Hertz analyzed secondary burials among the Ngaju Dayak of Kalimantan and the Berawan of Madagascar.[4] He noted that both first and secondary burials marked transitions in the state of the deceased. This led him to distinguish between the biological death of a person and his or her "social" death. Biological death occurs at once; that is, a person is either dead or alive. In contrast social death involves a process that extends over a long stretch of time, allowing for the bereaved to adjust to the gap in the social network that death has created.[5] Processes like these also operate in South Asia, as has for instance been shown by Randeria.[6]

The impact that a death has on the social relationships that people maintain depends on several factors, such as the roles that the deceased fulfilled, the assets that he or she controlled, and the expectations that people held about him or her. Obviously, then, the death of an old person will have quite a different impact than the death of someone who has just been born. In Sadolpara and surroundings, most property and land titles were vested with specific kinship titles, whereas property privately "owned" by individuals played a relatively unimportant role. Swidden cultivation had continued to be the dominant mode of agriculture. Fields were created in the jungle, worked for one or two years, and then abandoned. People's ability to claim a patch of forest to make a swidden rested on their membership in a specific kin group and was not defined in terms of individually held title. Although there was certainly a tendency to move toward sedentary plantation agriculture, this was a fairly recent development, and most social arrangements continued to proceed from the idea that people held claims that defined rights within a larger body of communal property.

Kinship, then, was the key terminology that people used to frame the social relationships that they maintained among one another. Given the significance attributed to membership in lineages and clans, any one Garo could frame his or her relationship to any other Garo in kin terms. Yet this omnipresence of kin ties created the need to emphasize certain kin ties over others, particularly those that were in one way or the other deemed of strategic importance. This made people's involvement with the death rituals socially significant since these were prime occasions, perhaps even the most important occasion at which people had the possibility to express kin relationships.

This happened in terms of presence at a funeral, the nature and value of gifts provided, and one's willingness to accept gifts offered by the bereaved. These gifts were significant in the way they referred to preceding gifts and the commitments they implied for the future. Therefore the transfer of gifts was seldom straightforward, but subject to extensive negotiations. Garo death rituals do not just serve to express social relationships, but actually produce "social order," as Bloch and Parry have argued.[7] After all, participation in death rituals makes visible the relationships that people maintain and acknowledge toward the deceased and his or her close relatives. In this sense Garo death rituals allow, and at the same time demand, that people "share a world" with each other, as pointed out in the introduction to this volume.

In this essay I analyze the choices that participants in Garo death rituals make with respect to gifts transferred, or that are *expected* to be transferred.[8] Accepting a gift is never "free."[9] Acceptance acknowledges or traces a relationship and creates an obligation for the future. This is in line with Mauss's argument that gifts are embedded in networks of reciprocation.[10] Far from limiting this reciprocation to physical objects, it also encompasses immaterial returns such as obligations, honor, and respect. So how are the various gifts that are offered at Garo mortuary rituals perceived by those who participate? What obligations do they create? To what extent does the transfer of gifts reflect an" intentionality" on the part of the giver,[11] and does it allow people to negotiate between distinct interests?

Garo death rituals include many elements that people consider "traditional." That is, people maintain that these elements were part of the rituals in the past as well. Garos talk about the past as "the time of the grandfathers and grandmothers" (*atchu-ambini somai*), linking it explicitly to the ideas and practices of earlier generations. People interpret and summarize such past practices as "custom" (*niam*), a notion that they frequently call upon to legitimize their decisions. Custom does not present itself as a set of rigid rules—although notably older ethnographies have a tendency to present it as such[12]—but rather as a series of principles. This even though interpretations of custom vary with the role that people assume at a funeral, and certain acts or interpretations that are appreciated from one perspective may be understood rather differently when people consider these in another manner. What authority is being attributed to custom? Are the death rites only facilitating negotiations between participants, or do the rituals themselves become subject to negotiation as well?

GARO DEATH RITUALS

In the hill area where Sadolpara and Chibonggre are located, most of the residents are Garos. From colonial days onward the Indian state has classified the Garo as a "tribal" community.[13] This classification is based on linguistic, social, and cultural criteria. Garos speak a language that belongs to the Tibeto Burman family of languages, trace matrilineal kinship, and distinguish themselves also in religious terms from neighboring communities. Their "tribal" status has contributed to the creation of the Garo Hills

District Council (GHDC), a body that administers the western part of Meghalaya state. The GHDC administers Garo personal law as well as the ownership and use of communally held lands. In India preferential discrimination applies to people from "tribal" communities. In the case of the Garo this results in benefits such as exemption from income tax, the allocation of a fixed share of state-level government jobs, and reserved seats in educational institutions and political bodies.

Before the inclusion of the Garo Hills into the colonial state, all Garos were adherents of the Garo community religion. With the colonial administrators, Australian and North American missionaries arrived. Although Christianity arrived in the Garo Hills by the middle of the nineteenth century, it took a long time before it gained popular ground. Only in the 1970s and 1980s, due to the gradual spread of elementary education as well as proselytizing drives initiated by the urban middle class, did the majority of the Garos convert to Christianity.[14] Consequently many people from the older generations have grown up within the community religion, and even for young Garos the concepts that are central to the religion have continued to be an important element of their idea worlds.

At the time I did my main fieldwork the Garo community religion had become marginalized throughout much of the Garo Hills. Only in some rural areas (which included Sadolpara and Chibonggre) had people resisted conversion. Nevertheless even such places had sizable Christian minorities, and death rites performed for deceased practitioners of the community religion always involved at least a couple of Christian participants as well. Christians participated in such death rituals, but refrained from those elements of the rituals that in one way or the other referred to the Garo community religion.[15]

Perceptions of death depend on ideas about the constitution of the person. This constitution defines his or her life and consequently the nature of death. According to the Garo community religion, when a person dies, his *janggi,* or soul (often equated with wind or breath), is believed to detach from his body. With this detachment the *janggi* transforms into a *mi•mang.* The living are expected to guide such a soul to the afterworld. This guidance is a matter of respect for the deceased person. It is also important for the living that the souls of the dead become located in the afterworld, since a soul that does not detach from its earlier existence can become a hazard. Such a soul is likely to roam around, desperately, and may harm people who are alive.

A dead body represents *marang,* a kind of death pollution that poses a threat to life (in other contexts distinct meanings can be attributed to *marang*). To contain this *marang* the corpse should be disposed of rapidly, preferably on the same day that the death occurred. Until a couple of decades ago all corpses were disposed off through cremation. Nowadays burial has become the standard. People say that they prefer to bury rather than to cremate because a burial takes much less time and is easier to arrange. The increasing popularity of burial is probably due to Christian practices since Christians always bury.

Although eschatology plays an important role in death rites, I will focus primarily on the social consequences of Garo death rituals. I start by addressing the manner in which social relationships are perceived and organized in Garo villages. From there I proceed to discuss the transformations that the mortuary rituals effectuate.

THE INHERITANCE OF KIN TIES

People who participate in Garo death rituals act in many ways as representatives of "Houses." A Garo House is a unit of belonging as well as a unit of property.[16] A House encompasses a husband and his wife, as well as unmarried children and (at times) unmarried brothers and sisters of the wife. Among the assets of a House are the house building, a granary, implements, food stocks, seed grains, and the crops that stand in the fields. The House also includes cattle, heirlooms (jewelry, gongs, weapons, and drums that derive from time immemorial), as well as titles to land.

A House, with all its possessions, rights, and obligations, is counted in with the *ba•saa*, or "localized matrilineage," of the wife.[17] The husband, who will usually belong by birth to a distinct localized matrilineage and clan, is considered the "head" (*skutong*) of the House.[18] Upon marriage the husband becomes an affine to the localized matrilineage of his wife. As such he can act, and is at times expected to act, on behalf of her kin group. At the same time a married man continues to relate to the localized matrilineage in which he was born; he is regarded as a custodian of the Houses of his "mothers," as well as of his other female matrilineal relatives.

A marriage arranged on the authority of the larger kin groups of the groom and the bride draws both these kin groups into a marriage alliance. Such an *a•kim* alliance demands that upon death of either the husband or his wife, his or her respective localized matrilineage is obliged to arrange a new spouse for the widower or widow. This principle of replacement was explained to me with reference to the position of a woman who had recently lost her husband: "They were married by *du•sia* [the term used to indicate a proper marriage]. Because the man died before the woman, the kin group of the man incurred a debt. This required them to send a person. . . . Had the woman died first, the *a•kim* debt would have been with the kin group of the woman. . . . To provide an heir in place of the deceased person is said to be fulfillment of *a•kim*." Such replacement of a deceased person is described as "to put back" (*datanga*) or "to give instead" (*on•songa*).

An *a•kim* debt (*gru*) implies an exclusive relationship between the localized matrilineage of the deceased person and the House that he or she lived in. It is therefore obligatory for this localized matrilineage to redeem the debt, and it has an exclusive right to do so. Unless the localized matrilineage of the dead person does not object, he or she should not be replaced by someone who belongs to another localized matrilineage.

A couple can anticipate *a•kim* replacement by designating a daughter as the heiress (*nokkrom*) to her mother. She is then "the one kept for the House" (*nok donggipa*). Often, but not necessarily, this is the youngest daughter. If there is no daughter in the House, or none of the daughters wants to become the heiress, a young sister of the wife who is willing to assume this role can be adopted. In any case the heiress should marry by *du•sia* a matrilineal nephew of her father, a cross-cousin. This is ideally a biological nephew, but a son of any classificatory sister of the father is acceptable, as long as she belongs to his localized matrilineage. The father of this girl is then a biological or classificatory matrilineal uncle of the groom. Once married to the heiress, the nephew becomes the heir to his uncle and father-in-law. Consequently Houses are perceived as a continuation from mother to daughter, as well as from uncle to nephew.

This continuity is essential: only if deceased spouses are replaced can Houses continue to exist. Ideally a deceased person should be replaced at the death ritual itself. If this is not feasible because there is no heir or heiress and no other candidate can be arranged at that time, both parties involved in the marriage alliance should at least express their commitment to the alliance and their intent to realize the replacement in the weeks or months to follow.

One consequence of the replacement of deceased spouses and the continuation of Houses is that everyone continues to have classificatory fathers, mothers, and grandparents. A daughter who replaces her deceased mother becomes the mother and stepmother (*ama-ma•de*) of the children of her House and a grandmother (*ambi*) to its grandchildren. The heir of a deceased man becomes father and stepfather (*apa-awang*) to the children of his House and a grandfather (*atchu*) to its grandchildren.

Each successive couple that lives in a House represents a generation (*chasong* or *wa•pak*). A House that counts many generations (*nok bibol,* or" trunk House") tends to have many "branch Houses" (*bipek*), each of which may in turn have other branch Houses. The hierarchy that is perceived among Houses belonging to a single localized matrilineage is modeled on mother-daughter ties. Between foundresses of a single generation the ranking is based on birth order. The hierarchy among Houses is absolute as long as it refers to those at the top and bottom of the hierarchy. But in relation to Houses that are ranked somewhere in the middle the hierarchy is relatively open to interpretation, and there are many instances when people maintain conflicting interpretations of the seniority attributed to certain Houses.

In addition people do not have absolute measures for the valuation of kin ties. Instead the assessment of such ties depends on the extent to which kin serve to channel support and facilitate economic cooperation and, last but certainly not least, the significance attributed to them in the context of mortuary rituals.

ASSESSING THE IMPORTANCE OF A DECEASED PERSON

People can participate in a Garo death ritual in different ways. This involves three distinct categories of relatedness to the deceased and the House to which he or she belonged. The first category consists of people posing as representatives of the House of the deceased; they identify with the localized matrilineage of the female side of the House (the deceased wife, or the widow) and are normally close relatives of the deceased. A second category involves representatives of Houses that relate matrilineally to the deceased (if a married woman has died, this second category can merge with the first category). The third category comprises the deceased's in-laws. It often happens that people at a single funeral act on behalf of more than one category. This notably holds for married men. Such a man can act on behalf of the localized matrilineage in which he was born, but he can also act on behalf of the localized matrilineage of his wife.

People's responsibilities at a funeral vary with the category they belong to or identify with. People positioned as representatives of a House in which a death has occurred have to make many decisions that influence the scale of the funeral. How valuable will the cloth be that is used to cover the corpse as it is laid out? Will heirlooms such as jewelry, gongs, and swords be offered as gifts to the people attending? And if so, how many? Will the dead body be buried or cremated? If the corpse is to be buried, as is normally the case, should the coffin be made of split bamboo or of much more costly wooden planks?

Of great consequence to the scale of a funeral are the decisions regarding who to inform about a death that has occurred. Depending on the importance attributed to the deceased, people will either limit such an announcement to people from the village in which the death has occurred, or spread the news to relatives and in-laws living in neighboring and distant villages as well. It is critical to make a correct assessment: if the circle of invitees is too small, those who have been omitted may be offended; if the circle is too large, people may feel obliged to attend the funeral of a person who is insignificant to them.

People who are notified about a death also have to decide whether or not to attend the particular mortuary ritual. Here the assessment of their relationship to the deceased person is critical: the closer the relationship, the more difficult to opt out of attending a funeral; the more distant the relationship is perceived to be, the more doubtful whether attendance is desirable. If people agree to attend a mortuary ritual they then have to decide about the kind and value of the gifts to take to the House of the deceased. Some gifts are not costly, but their presentation is compulsory. Most significant among these nonvaluable gifts are a handful of rice on the ear and unginned cotton wool, both of which are said to be seed grains for use by the deceased person in the afterworld. Other gifts, such as paper money and animals such as cows or pigs, can have much greater value.

Gifts such as money and a cow or a pig are given to the deceased as well as his or her relatives. In the latter sense they are gifts to help (*abisi*) the living. All animals that are given to the deceased have to be slaughtered at the time of the funeral. Their killing, it is said, allows these animals to accompany the deceased to the afterworld. At the same time their meat becomes available as food. Most of it is cooked into a meat curry; served with rice, this allows the representatives of the House of the deceased to provide a meal to the people attending the funeral. The deceased receives the smoked spleen of each of the cows. The money that is offered to the deceased can be shared out as gifts by the representatives of his or her House.

The extent to which people provide money and animals to help is an indicator of the significance they attribute to the deceased and the House to which he or she belonged.

The nearer a relationship is perceived to be, the greater the value of the help offered. In this way the offering of gifts allows people to make a statement about the relationship between their House and that of the deceased. Likewise offering a nonvaluable gift or failing to give a cow when one was expected can be taken as an indicator that this relationship is attributed less prominence than is expected by the other side.

DEFINING AND RANKING THE MOTHERS

Once most of the people have arrived at a funeral, the representatives of the House of the deceased are expected to offer countergifts to the people attending. One of these countergifts is *ma•gual*, a gift for the Houses of the mothers of the deceased person. *Ma•gual* first and foremost refers to heirlooms such as brass gongs, jewelry, or swords. However, heirlooms are costly and scarce and therefore often substituted with money.[19] Heirlooms are said to exist from time immemorial; according to oral history, the founders of villages such as Sadolpara brought the first heirloom objects with them from their village of origin. Some people even suggest that the heirlooms derive from Tibet, the place where the Garo forefathers presumably originated.[20]

In any case heirlooms are typically acquired by Houses as *ma•gual*. When a member of a House dies, that House can offer the heirlooms it has obtained as *ma•gual* to other Houses.[21] An heirloom that is offered as *ma•gual* is said to represent the bones (*greng*) of the deceased person at whose mortuary ritual the object is being offered. "It is like [the] bone of my younger brother" (*angni angjongni greng*), a woman said about a gong. She had received the gong as *ma•gual* at the death of a man who was like a younger brother to her. The gong, she said, would help her "to remember him." A gong offered at a mortuary ritual is associated with the person who died. This exchange overrules the association of the gong with the previous deceased person. People do not remember the history of an heirloom, but by transferring an heirloom at successive mortuary rituals it becomes associated with a cumulative number of dead. Except for the most recent, all these dead are anonymous.[22]

The representatives of the House of a dead man or woman are obliged to offer *ma•gual* to all the Houses of his or her mothers who are represented at the mortuary ritual. The Houses of close mothers of the dead person should be offered the most substantial *ma•gual*. Distant mothers can be satisfied with *ma•gual* that has a lower value.[23]

A House that accepts *ma•gual* formally acknowledges a filial relationship with the person who died. Conversely the refusal of *ma•gual* implies that a House rejects this kind of a relationship. For instance, when someone refused to accept *ma•gual* at the mortuary ritual of a woman, the person who offered the gift said, "If you act like this [refusing *ma•gual*], she won't have mother and father." Moreover the refusal of *ma•gual* by the House of the proposed recipient can be taken to express rejection of its relationship with the larger localized matrilineage of the House that offers it. When a representative of a House in which a death had occurred was confronted with many people who refused to take *ma•gual*, he said, "Why is none of you respecting us? . . . Aren't you considering us your grandchildren?" The man positioned himself as a representative of the localized matrilineage of the House in which the death had occurred, while he considered those to whom he offered *ma•gual* to be members of a larger group as well.

The representatives of the House in which death has occurred offer *ma•gual* to all eligible Houses. People say that the order of offering should reflect the ranking of the Houses in relation to the person who has died. The House of the "biggest grandmother" (*ambi dal•gipa*) of the deceased should be offered first, and then, in order of decreasing importance, the Houses of grandmothers, mother's elder sisters, mothers, mother's younger sisters, own elder sisters, younger sisters and nieces. It is compulsory that the ranking is respected, at least when it involves the Houses that are attributed the greatest seniority in relation to the deceased person. This offers the representatives of these most senior Houses an opportunity to formulate certain claims, as is clear in the following extract from my fieldnotes.

> At the mortuary ritual of Sisi, the representatives of her House could not offer *ma•gual* until a man named Rengteng had arrived. He was considered Sisi's "biggest grandfather" (*atchu dal•gipa*), as he was the head of the House that was most apical to that of Sisi.[24] Soon after his arrival, Rengteng was offered a *narikki sil* gong. This kind of gong has relatively little value. He politely refused it saying, "It is not necessary to give anything to me." Rengteng knew that no one else would be offered *ma•gual* until he had accepted it. The representatives of the House of Sisi rightly understood his refusal as a request for a more valuable gift. They offered him a more precious *kasamati* gong, which Rengteng readily accepted.

If a House of a close mother of the dead man or woman is represented at his or her mortuary ritual, it has to accept *ma•gual*. A refusal of *ma•gual* by the representatives of such a House, as happened with Rengteng, is a concealed demand to the House of the dead person to provide a more valuable gift.

Contrary to people who demand substantial *ma•gual* there are also people who are reluctant, if not unwilling, to accept it. They belong primarily to the Houses of more distant mothers. The representatives of the House of the deceased person will always offer money, never an heirloom, as *ma•gual* to these Houses. A monetary gift usually consists of several bills of small denominations. By adding or removing bills from the bundle, the value of such a gift can easily be adjusted. The representatives of the House of the deceased person should try to convince people representing Houses of distant mothers to accept a gift that is offered. Often they try to enforce acceptance by slipping the rolled up paper money into a pocket or under the collar of the proposed recipient. Normally such a person will try to avoid this kind of gesture, and tussling and scuffling results. The outcome of such an engagement cannot be predicted. Only gradually, in the course of the encounter, does it become clear whether the proposed recipient continues to refuse the offered *ma•gual* or can be convinced to accept it. Another extract from my fieldnotes:

> Rengji belonged to the localized matrilineage of the deceased Nagal. She had given twenty rupees to help the close relatives of Nagal. This was a modest amount, considering that four Houses had offered cows, and many others large sums of money. Rengji sat at the side of the gazebo in front of Nagal's house. A brother of Nagal walked up to Rengji and showed her some folded notes. He said, "Take this grandma, take this. . . . How can you refuse it, that would not be in accordance with custom." Rengji did not react. The brother slipped the folded notes under Rengji's dress. Wiljeng (an in-law to Nagal) [said], "Even if you take this, we are not free. If you refuse it, we are also not free." Rengji unfolded the notes and counted them. The brother [said], "To you, a gong should have been given. If we had one, if we had been able to give . . . a *narikki sil* [certain type of gong] would have been given." He stepped backwards, which made it more difficult for Rengji to return the money, and said, "This is just a little bit." The brother said to Rengji, "She [Nagal] is your grandchild." Wiljeng added, "Are we asking you to take from a stranger? She [Nagal] is like someone of your own House."

At this mortuary ritual the men offering *ma•gual* argued that the deceased Nagal was a "grandchild" of the proposed recipient Rengji, even "like someone of [her] own House." The men made statements that stressed Rengji's importance. Nagal's brother claimed that Rengji should actually have been given a gong ("if we would have had"). Saying, "Even if you take this, we are not free," one of the men claimed that the *ma•gual* offered was not substantial enough for a person as important as Rengji. But, he added, if she rejected it they "are also not free." He suggested that the representatives of the House of Nagal were obliged to make her accept *ma•gual*. Because they could not offer her more (or so he claimed), he argued that she should accept whatever was being offered, and in the end Rengji agreed to accept the *ma•gual*.

The representatives of the House of the deceased person have to make extensive efforts to convince people like Rengji to accept *ma•gual*, to ensure that as many Houses as possible acknowledge the deceased person as one of them. Most efforts need to be made toward Houses of which it is not certain, at least beforehand, whether they are willing to accept it or not. The men in charge of offering *ma•gual* humble the House of the deceased, arguing that it lacks the means to provide gifts that are substantial enough for the status of the persons being offered *ma•gual*. These men, it is important to understand, are expected to make such efforts; if they fail to be persuasive toward such Houses, their failure is likely to be understood as an unwillingness to offer *ma•gual*. And unwillingness to share with one's relatives would be shameful, damaging not only the reputation of the House of the deceased person but also the reputation of the larger localized matrilineage to which that House belongs.

If people like Rengji refuse the *ma•gual* that is offered to them, they are likely to justify doing so by underplaying the gifts to help that they themselves have made to the House of the deceased person. It is shameful to accept *ma•gual* if one has provided insufficient help. A woman who was offered *ma•gual* replied, "If I am not able to help you, but accept a gift, how can that be in compliance with custom?" A man refused *ma•gual* with the words: "I couldn't give anything, so how can I accept it? I won't take it. It would be shameful." However, refusing *ma•gual* implies rejecting one's relationship to the person who died. People can resolve this dilemma by accepting a smaller amount of money than that which the House of the deceased offers. That way people acknowledge their relationship to the deceased while avoiding the impression that they regard their own gifts to help as sufficient.

Representatives of Houses that relate only very distantly to the person who died can still qualify for *ma•gual*. Such Houses are not expected to accept the *ma•gual* that is offered to them, and the representatives of the House in which the death has occurred do not press hard for it. Although offering *ma•gual* to such a House categorizes the House as that of a mother to the deceased, the expected refusal of the gift emphasizes that this relationship is very distant indeed.

Whenever the representatives of the House of the deceased make an attempt to offer *ma•gual*, they have to assess the distance of the relationship between the deceased and the person to which they are offering the gift. Depending on this assessment they decide whether it is compulsory for a House to accept *ma•gual*, whether it is acceptable if the person refuses, and even whether it is expected that the person will refuse. The assessment of the relationship depends on many factors, and for the men who distribute *ma•gual* it is not always clear to which category a House belongs. At a mortuary ritual one of the men responsible for the distribution of *ma•gual* said about a woman, "The one who refused, will she come back and remind us of our duty?" People who qualify for *ma•gual* similarly have to assess their relationship to the person who died. Apart from the gifts to help, people must choose between demanding more valuable *ma•gual* than that which is offered, accepting less than what is presented to them, or refusing to take any of it at all.

A House that qualifies as that of a "mother" of a deceased person who was married assumes responsibility for the replacement of that deceased person. The need for replacement derives from the existence of an *a•kim* alliance relationship, but it is unlikely that replacement will actually occur unless the House of the deceased person offers *ma•gual*. Regarding a House that had provided a person to replace a deceased woman someone said, "They [her matrilineal relatives] have chosen to get her married, they have kept the gongs." If Houses accept *ma•gual* but fail to provide someone to replace the deceased person, people say that "*ma•gual* is forgotten" (*ma•gual guala*). *Ma•gual* is perceived as a gift to the source from which the deceased person originated. Given that *ma•gual* represents the bones of the deceased person, it involves the symbolic return of a nonputrefying part of his or her corpse to the Houses of origin. Simultaneously *ma•gual* is a gift in exchange for the person who replaces the deceased person.

So there is a relationship between the gifts to help that are offered to the House of the deceased and the *ma•gual* gifts that the representatives of the deceased offer to Houses that qualify as mothers of the deceased. In the value and kind of gifts exchanged the relationship between the Houses concerned is assessed, expressed, and negotiated. Likewise the kind of effort that is made to find a suitable replacement for the deceased person is an indicator of the closeness or nearness of that relationship.

CONCLUSION

What can an analysis of Garo funerals teach us about the capacity of these rituals to negotiate relationships among people and Houses as well as with the dead? The funeral of Gujak described earlier was attended by a large number of people because to her House was attributed considerable apicality. The House had existed for several generations and was embedded in an extensive network of kin ties. In their decision to attend the funeral, and in the kind of gifts they brought with them, people acknowledged the deceased Gujak. At the same time they showed their support for the relatives of Gujak and their commitment to the continuation of her House. In their acceptance or refusal of the countergifts that were offered by close relatives of Gujak, the recipients expressed the relative importance of the deceased for their House. For those who represented the House of Gujak, the order in which Houses were approached for the acceptance of countergifts, and the kind of effort that was made to have them accept these, indicated the status of these Houses relative to hers. Expressing relationships vis-à-vis the deceased Gujak thus conjoined with the assessment of the hierarchical relationships that Houses traced among each other.

Garo mortuary rituals thus allow, and under certain circumstances demand, that people assess and negotiate the importance of a person who died, his or her relatives and in-laws, and the Houses these people belong to. This assessment primarily takes place in the offering, refusal, and acceptance of gifts. All these gifts relate in one way or the other to the deceased person. The gifts provided by people who attend a funeral boost the prestige of the soul of the deceased person in the afterworld. The countergifts that are offered by the representatives of the House of the deceased person are associated with nonputrefying parts of the corpse, as well as with the corpses of innumerable preceding dead.

Among the Garo kinship serves as an idiom for interpreting and shaping social ties between people and the Houses they belong to. Garos can trace matrilineal or affinal kin ties (often both) to virtually any other Garo. Within this broad field of kin relationships, kin ties tend to gain weight when they are substantiated. One way to achieve this is the transfer of gifts at mortuary rituals. As I have shown, such gifts imply an acknowledgment of the deceased, as well as the House that he or she belonged to. Accepting gifts obliges the recipient to reciprocate in some way. In addition, when a gift is accepted the giver is obliged to accept future gifts from the recipient. The offering and acceptance of gifts at Garo mortuary rituals thus creates a context in which people try to tempt each other to engage in obligations or to reciprocate these. Relationships that are acknowledged should yield, in the sense that the Houses involved are expected to honor the recipients in the context of a future death ritual. Acknowledging relationships that are deemed important results in Houses sustaining and building prestige. Offering and receiving gifts at funerals thus plays an important part in sorting out the relationships that Houses maintain among each other. Negotiation plays a role in the choices that are made regarding the relationships that people deem more important and the ones that they consider of less relevance. This informs the kind of effort that people make to offer gifts and their willingness to accept them.

There is also scope for negotiation beyond the confines of the rituals. People accept "custom" as the general organizing principle. Yet interpretations of custom are situational, and the distinct interpretations of what is appropriate action in the context of a ritual results in the mortuary rituals as such becoming subject to negotiation as well. After all, people can challenge the importance that custom attributes to the death rituals. They may refrain from attending (where the general opinion is that they should do so), arguing that according to their interpretation of custom their absence would not harm the relationships at stake. Such denial of the importance of the mortuary rituals is relatively rare. Most people consider such a position inappropriate and disrespectful. This negotiation of custom contributes to the authority of the death ritual as an arena which allows for the assessment and substantiation of social relationships.

Notes

1. From July 1999 to June 2001 I was engaged in PhD fieldwork in Meghalaya, India. For most of this time I lived with my wife and field assistants in Sadolpara, a village of about sixteen hundred inhabitants. This allowed for casual, everyday (and night) engagement with the residents. The fieldwork was conducted with financial support of the Netherlands Organization for Scientific Research (NWO/WOTRO) and the Indian Council for Social Science Research (ICCR). It was conducted under the auspices of the North Eastern Hill University (Shillong and Tura) as well as the Research School CNWS (Leiden).

2. Metcalf and Huntington, *Celebrations of Death*.

3. Bloch and Parry, *Death and the Regeneration of Life*.

4. Hertz, *Death and the Right Hand*.

5. See Davies, "Robert Hertz," 97 Walter, "The Sociology of Death," 317.

6. See Randeria, "Mourning, Mortuary Exchange and Memorialization," 88–111.

7. Bloch and Parry, *Death and the Regeneration of Life*, 218.

8. Garos categorize funerary practices as "ritual" in the sense that they acknowledge that a funeral creates a time and space set apart from daily life. A Garo mortuary ritual (*mangona*) lasts up to two days. It is conducted from the house of the deceased person and confined to the village in which that person lived. Ritual activities do not exceed these temporal and spatial boundaries.

9. See Gregory, *Gifts and Commodities;* Laidlaw, "A Free Gift Makes No Friends," 617–34.

10. Mauss, *The Gift*.

11. Rio, "Denying the Gift," 449–70.

12. See, among others, Chattopadhyay and Sangma, *The Garo Customary Laws;* Costa. "The Garo Code of Law," 1041–66; J. L. R. Marak, *Garo Customary Laws and Practices;* K. R. Marak, *The Garos and Their Customary Laws and Usages.*

13. In South Asia the term "tribe" has acquired great political weight (Beteille, "The Idea of Indigenous People," 187–91). Being "tribal" brings important benefits, due to the Indian government's policy of preferential discrimination (Bayly, *Caste, Society and Politics in India*). Given the politicized use of "tribe" in South Asia, I am using quotation marks to indicate that it is not being used in a general academic sense.

14. Burling, *Rengsanggri.*

15. De Maaker, "From the Songsarek Faith to Christianity," 517–30.

16. See Lévi-Strauss, "Maison," 434–36; Carsten and Hugh-Jones, "Introduction," 1–46.

17. Garo kinship stresses descent along the female line. That is, relationships between mothers and daughters and mothers and sons are attributed far more importance than those between fathers and sons and fathers and daughters. People who claim a common female predecessor are said to originate from a single womb. They belong to a single *ba•saa* (localized matrilineage); these can vary in size from a few dozen to a few hundred people, and frequently most female members will be concentrated in a single village. Localized matrilineages that are believed to share a joint origin constitute a *ma•chong* (mother core). Related *ma•chong*s belong to a single *chatchi,* or "matriclan," the most comprehensive unit of descent.

18. This does not imply that a House cannot exist without a husband. If a House is without a husband, the most senior female spouse acts as the head of that House.

19. Perhaps equally important is the fact that the value of a monetary gift can easily be adjusted—a great advantage when it comes to bargaining over acceptance or refusal.

20. People stated that, until recently, gongs, heirloom jewelry, and weapons were made by Bengalis from the nearby plains. Nowadays this production has virtually come to a halt, largely because of the sharp increase in the number of Christian converts. Compared to Songsareks, Christians attach little value to heirlooms.

21. The only restriction is that an heirloom should never be offered as *ma•gual* to the House from which it has been received as *ma•gual.* Therefore someone explained the term *ma•gual* as "valuables that are forgotten" (*ma,* "valuables"; *guala,* "to forget").

22. Apart from the most recently deceased persons, all these dead are anonymous. That is, the dead that these heirlooms were previously associated with are not known by name. Yet the longer an heirloom object has been circulating, the larger the number of funerals where it has been transferred, and the greater the number of dead it has been related to. Because the names of these preceding dead are not remembered when an heirloom is transferred, the transfer of an heirloom results in the anonymization of the preceding deceased person that that particular heirloom was associated with.

23. The closeness or distance of kin ties depends on the extent to which the ties are regarded as biological relationships (involving blood ties or an extensive period of cohabitation), or are merely considered broad, classificatory categories. In the latter sense, all children of women who consider each other sisters, however distant, are siblings. However, experiencing kin ties as close or distant depends to a considerable degree on the way people approach them. If people behave as if a certain person is close kin, the relationship involved is likely to be perceived (and talked about) as such, and the other way around. Perceptions of closeness and distance of kin relationships thus depend on the level at which the people involved interact with each other.

24. A House is apical to the Houses that have emerged from it, that is, to Houses that have been founded by women who were born or raised in the apical House. Apicality thus indicates the relative seniority of Houses. The most apical House is the most senior House to which a House traces its origin.

Bibliography

Bayly, Susan. *Caste Society and Politics in India: From the Eighteenth Century to the Modern Age.* Cambridge: Cambridge University Press, 1999.

Beteille, Andre. "The Idea of Indigenous People." *Current Anthropology* 39, no. 2 (1998): 187–91.

Bloch, Maurice, and Jonathan Parry. *Death and the Regeneration of Life.* Cambridge: Cambridge University Press, 1982.

Burling, Robbins. *Rengsanggri: Family and Kinship in a Garo Village.* 1963. Tura: Tura Book Room, 1997.

Carsten, Janet, and Stephen Hugh-Jones. "Introduction." In *About the House: Lévi-Strauss and Beyond*, ed. Janet Carsten and Stephen Hugh-Jones, 1–46. Cambridge: Cambridge University Press, 1995.

Chattopadhyay, S. K., and Milton S. Sangma, eds. *The Garo Customary Laws.* Shillong: Directorate of Arts and Culture. 1989.

Costa, Giulio. "The Garo Code of Law." *Anthropos* 49, no. 28 (1954): 1041–66.

Davies, Douglas J. "Robert Hertz: The Social Triumph over Death." *Mortality* 5, no. 1 (2000): 97.

de Maaker, Erik. "From the Songsarek Faith to Christianity: Conversion, Religious Identity and Ritual Efficacy." *South Asia: Journal of South Asian Studies* 30, no. 3 (2007): 517–30.

Gregory, Christopher A. *Gifts and Commodities*. London: Academic Press, 1982.

Hertz, Robert. *Death and the Right Hand*. 1907. London: Cohen & West, 1960.

Laidlaw, James. "A Free Gift Makes No Friends." *Journal of the Royal Anthropological Institute* 6, no. 4 (2000): 617–34.

Lévi-Strauss, Claude. "Maison." In *Dictionaire de l'ethnologie et de l'anthropologie,* ed. Pierre Bonte and Michael Izard, 434–36. Paris: Presses Universitaires de France, 1991.

Marak, Julius L. R. *Garo Customary Laws and Practices: A Sociological Study*. New Delhi: Akansha, 2000.

Marak, Karnesh R. *The Garos and Their Customary Laws and Usages*. Tura: Brucellis Sangma, 1964.

Mauss, Marcel. *The Gift: The Form and Reason for Exchange in Archaic Societies.* London: Routledge, 1990.

Metcalf, Peter, and Richard Huntington. *Celebrations of Death: The Anthropology of Mortuary Ritual.* Cambridge: Cambridge University Press, 1991.

Randeria, Shalini. "Mourning, Mortuary Exchange and Memorialization: The Creation of Local Communities among Dalits in Gujarat." In *Ways of Dying: Death and Its Meaning in South Asia,* ed. Elisabeth Schömbucher and Claus Peter Zoller, 88–111. New Delhi: Manohar, 1999.

Rio, Knut. "Denying the Gift: Aspects of Ceremonial Exchange and Sacrifice on Ambrym Island, Vanuatu." *Anthropological Theory* 7, no. 4 (2007): 449–70.

Walter, Tony. "The Sociology of Death." *Sociology Compass* 2, no. 1 (2008): 317.

3

"The Clitoris Is Indeed Your Sweet"

NEGOTIATING GENDER ROLES IN THE RITUAL SETTING OF THE SWAHILI NEW YEAR'S FESTIVAL

Magnus Echtler

Wauzeni baba zenu, tembo njo utamu wenu—Ask your fathers, the clitoris is indeed your sweet

Wanawake si kama hatuwataki, tukiwatomba, wanalima kama komba—It's not that we don't like women, when we fuck them, they cry like bush babies

Kama hulinunulia kitenge, nyama yangu huitende—If you don't buy me clothes, you shall not work my flesh

Wanawake wananitia huruma, bora nitombe kima—The women frustrate me, better to fuck a monkey

In the midday heat, at the center of town and in front of thousands of spectators, groups of women and men insulted and entertained each other with obscene songs.[1] These songs formed part of the New Year's festival in Makunduchi, Zanzibar, whose rituals protected the borders of the town and established reciprocal relations between its citizens and local spirits, thereby reproducing local space and identities. But the rituals did not simply ensure the continuity of the local sociocultural order, as ritual innovations in the context of the festival formed part of the religious and political struggles over the definition of Zanzibari cultural identity.

The ambiguous role rituals play with regard to sociocultural reproduction and change can best be analyzed if rituals are understood as negotiations, as "processes of interaction during which differing positions are debated and/or acted out," as argued by Hüsken and Neubert in the introduction to this volume. In my interpretation of the obscene songs of the Swahili New Year's festival I will be concerned with negotiations on two levels: with the negotiation of ritual frames in the successful establishment of the songs as a new feature of the festival, and with the negotiation of gender roles through the songs, made possible by but not limited to the ritual frame. Throughout its history the New Year's festival formed a locus of contestation, as various actors struggled to participate and take leading roles, or refused to participate and challenged the whole festival or its parts as illegitimate. Young women and men began to sing obscene songs only after the colonial state had prohibited the festival's traditional transgressions, the fighting of the young men, and both local religious experts and advocates of reformist Islam criticized these songs. But as enough people participated in the singing, the ritualized subversion of religious authority was established in practice, and I argue that this innovation was successful because it referred to similar ritualized transgressions, both within the history of the festival itself and in the wider religious context.

Just as the New Year's rituals oscillated between social reproduction and change, the songs themselves played an ambiguous role in the negotiation of gender roles and regional identities. Though the obscenities did not lead to a sexual revolution in Zanzibar, they were not restricted to the inside of the ritual frame. As examples for the interpenetration of ritual and context (Hüsken and Neubert), the obscene songs played with and subverted the wider sociopolitical structures as they cut across the established oppositions between urban and rural, modern and traditional positions. The obscenities turned out to be effective transgressions because they challenged increasing strictures in gender segregation and women's roles, introduced into Swahili society since the late nineteenth century by reformist movements of Islam. When the women of Makunduchi sang "Ask your fathers, the clitoris is indeed your sweet" and the men answered "The women frustrate me, better to fuck a monkey," they certainly challenged the gender roles propagated by the modern religious movements, as well as the traditional authority of the male elders, who led the New Year's rituals and controlled legitimate access to women.

THE SOCIOCULTURAL CONTEXT

In the second half of the twentieth century obscene songs became the most popular form of transgressions in the context of the Swahili New Year's festival in Makunduchi, a town of ten thousand inhabitants located in the rather marginal southeast of Zanzibar Island (Unguja).[2] In 2001–2, the time of my research, New Year's Day was celebrated on July 22, a date calculated according to the traditional solar calendar, which had been used alongside the Muslim lunar calendar but which had lost most of its practical significance. These New Year's rituals were central to maintaining reciprocal relations between the citizens and local spirits. Two weeks before New Year's Day local religious experts invoked the power of Allah when circling the town and sacrificed a cow to local spirits. One week before New Year's Day the experts burned incense and recited from the Qur'an at the spirits' shrines (*mizimu*); the spirits received further sacrifices and in turn were thought to protect the town and its people. Although these religious practices made use of the Qur'an and were in part directed toward Allah, they were considered religious custom (*mila*) as opposed to orthodox Islam (*dini*). Specifically the New Year's rituals (*uganga wa mwaka*) were classified as religious practices of healing (*uganga*), but they also included religious practices of harming (*uchawi*), such as planting damaging substances at strategic locations as a measure to protect the town from malevolent outsiders. Although there was little disagreement over such classification, the moral consequences of the classification were highly contested: representatives of reformist Islam condemned the New Year's rituals as superstitious practices that should be avoided by all Muslims, while the citizens of Makunduchi not only rejected this judgment, but they also participated without regarding the rituals as interfering with their being good Muslims. Thus participation and nonparticipation were the principal options for negotiating Muslim identity in ritual practice, as argued by Hüsken and Neubert, and the New Year's festival in Makunduchi constituted the primary site for acting out difference to reformists' notions of orthodox Islam because it constituted the largest and best known religious practice of the *mila* kind for the whole of Zanzibar. And it was participation in ritual practice that defined the religious experience of most people, rather than participation in the discourses about ritual practices, discourses that were dominated by male religious experts especially of the reformist kind, and that in turn tended to dominate academic discourse about Swahili Islam.[3]

The fighting and singing of obscene songs formed part of the public performances on New Year's Day. The fighting took place between groups of young men from the northern and southern moieties of the town, and the obscene songs were exchanged between northern and southern groups of either men or women or between groups of women and men, irrespective of northern or southern affiliation. Both the singing and the fighting were restricted in space and time within the liminal phase of the New Year's festival and considered illegitimate activities outside this ritualized frame. While these transgressive acts were not classified as religious practices (*uganga* or *uchawi*), they did constitute part of the local tradition (*mila*), and the spilling of blood in the traditional fighting was linked to the animal sacrifices.[4] These negotiations of ritual frames and the struggles over what kind of transgressions should or should not be part of the festival will be discussed in the next section.

But the obscene songs as a new type of transgression was not the only innovation at the New Year's festival in Makunduchi. Since colonial times a commercial fair has developed and grown into an important part of the festival. In the 1980s political rituals were invented, and since then a representative of the political establishment has been invited as guest of honor every year. By 2001–2 New Year in Makunduchi had turned into one of the biggest religious festivals in Zanzibar, second only to the celebrations of the Muslim holidays in Zanzibar Town, and close to twenty-five thousand people visited during the five-day celebration. Despite this growing regional impact, the New Year's rituals remained the most important religious practices on the local level, integrating relations with local spirits into a coherent system. These relations served as a marker of citizenship, as every citizen was linked with at least one of the local spirit shrines.[5] The rituals were, in effect, spatial practices that used and produced the representational spaces of the town's descent groups—the spirit shrines—and contributed to the construction of representations of space by reinforcing the border between the "civilized" space of the town and the "wild" space of the surrounding bush lands.[6] In addition the rituals produced the local system of authority. Within the communal rituals the position of the religious experts—positions based on their knowledge and skill, as well as their standing within their descent groups—was publicly acknowledged; that is, their cultural and social capital was transformed into symbolic capital.[7] In precolonial times the political leadership and control over the economic resources of the town had been based on the authority produced through communal religious practices. During colonial times the religious leaders lost control over the economic resources in the wake of the rise of a capitalist economy. These leaders were able to retain some of their political power within the British system of indirect rule, but they lost all political significance within the one-party system of the postcolonial state after the Zanzibar revolution of 1964.[8] Throughout this period the New Year's rituals provided an important site for the negotiations between state power and local authority, and with the invention of the political rituals created in cooperation between the religious experts and state representatives in the 1980s, local authority was acknowledged by the state, while the state gained legitimacy through the religious rituals. A strictly local festival had ostensibly become a national one, at least according to claims of the visiting politicians.[9] The New Year's festival in Makunduchi was thus not only the site for acting out differences in the religious field, but also the public event that negotiated the relationship between traditional authority and state power. In their joint participation in the political rituals the conflicting parties reached some sort of agreement in the production of symbolic capital, despite the fact that they continued to compete over the economic spoils of the festival.[10]

NEGOTIATING RITUAL FRAMES

According to the editors' introduction, applying the notion of negotiation to rituals serves to "deepen our understanding of how the poles of stability/change, structure/performance, and tradition/innovation are mediated in social encounters." With regard to the invention of rituals, Victor Turner argues that rituals are flexible and adaptable to change because their multiple elements and liminal creativity enable them "to portray, interpret, and master radical novelty."[11] Conversely Roy Rappaport emphasizes the invariance of rituals and argues for a limited invention where there is "room for the rearrangement of elements, and even for discarding some elements and introducing others," but where "the sanction of previous performance is maintained."[12] Both these aspects of ritual change are important for interpreting the New Year's festival, whose transformation into a regional festival can be linked with two inventions: the political rituals and the obscene songs. I argue that the innovations were successful because they were limited, linked to preexisting rituals, and thus framed as rituals.[13]

The political rituals, which were built around established religious rituals, made use of other more or less ritualized practices from the political field such as ribbon cutting and a banquet for and a speech by the guest of honor. But the recombination of customary elements that framed the innovations as rituals also created something new as the elements were orchestrated to stage a ritual passage for the visiting politician. In ritual practice the political rituals publicly produced mutual acknowledgment between the state and local religious authority. Likewise the creation of the obscene songs as a new form of transgression was based on limited inventions.

Since the 1930s the colonial state had been interfering with the traditional form of transgression—the fighting of the young men—and by the early 1950s the fighting had been prohibited completely.[14] In the following years the people of Makunduchi filled the resulting gap in public performances of New Year's Day with dance performances taken from other ritualized contexts.[15] Still these substitute performances lacked the transgressive power of the violent fighting of old. Even when fighting was permitted again after the revolution of 1964, it returned in a tamed version only; in place of real weapons fighters were allowed to use only the stems of banana leaves, which broke into fibers quickly, thus preventing serious injuries.

In this situation, likely in the late 1950s or early 1960s, somebody started to sing obscene songs.[16] It is unclear whether the women, divided into northern and southern groups when singing the traditional, nontransgressional songs, started to abuse each other, or the men, possibly bored with the lack of violence in the dancing and fighting, started to insult the women. Regardless of who began the practice, I argue that the first singing of an obscene song in this context did not strike the listeners as a "creation of unpredictable novelty."[17] As the invention was based on the habitus of the inventor, and the other citizens present partook in the historical and social situation that produced this habitus, everyone immediately understood the obscenity as breaking social rules licensed by the ritual context, and rather than rejecting the new practice, they joined in. If anything, participants developed a special taste for the insults between men and women and began creating new songs every year. Nevertheless the creation of this new form of transgression remained a limited invention for three reasons. First, the midday performance on New Year's Day had already been established as a slot for transgressive acts in the ritual proceedings by the men's violent fighting. Second, sexual transgressions were already part of the New Year's festival. In late colonial times, for instance, young women sang obscene songs (*shindwe*) when they collected money for the communal rituals in the weeks before New Year; some of the fighters dressed in women's clothes; and the festival's evening entertainment consisted of a variety of dances, some of which included sexual allusions sung back and forth between men and women.[18] Third, obscene songs with explicit sexual content formed the transgressions in other ritual contexts, especially in the initiation of girls and boys.[19] Given this common background, such singing on New Year's Day was not unprecedented, and even as a new liminal practice it carried the sanction of previous ritual practices. These links with other practices framed the singing as legitimate transgression and enabled spectators to identify it as a new element of the New Year's celebration rather than an unacceptable breach of customary behavior. But as the new songs resembled a variety of more or less ritualized practices it can be argued that the ritual framing was "*context-sensitive*, rather than context-dependant."[20] That the context did not determine the ritual frame is supported by the fact that the legitimacy of singing these newly created obscene songs was contested. Local religious leaders criticized the songs as inventions not sanctioned by the religious tradition, and in 2001–2, as in several years earlier, the New Year's committee tried to stop the singing.[21] The eventual success of the innovation depended on negotiation, a process that was decided through singing rather than discourse. The elders' critique proved unsuccessful because the women and young men continued to sing anyway; not only had they already established the legitimacy of the obscene songs in practice, but the songs had now become part of festival tradition.

While ritual precedents provided some sanction for the invention of the new form of transgression, the obscene songs did not simply copy other practices. With new songs being invented every year, the practice of singing provided a space for creative freedom, and the songs commented on a variety of current issues.[22] With regard to their transgressive quality, the main innovations of these festival songs were that they addressed gender relations in explicit sexual terms in public and that they were sung back and forth between women and men. While transgressions in the context of initiations were equally explicit, these were performed in a less public setting and attendance was restricted to either women or men. And at the public dances for entertainment the songs passed back and forth between men and women alluded to sexuality but did not employ explicit terms. Thus the obscene songs formed a new, singular type of transgression based on the combination of the confrontation between men and women with sexual explicitness.

As argued by Hüsken and Neubert in their introduction, ritual negotiations are often dependent on bodily participation. In the case of the New Year's festival, both the fighting and the singing produced embodied subjectivities, but these subjectivities differed. The transgressive quality of the men's fighting was based on the bodily thrill of physical violence. The aggressiveness of hitting one another with all one's strength and the ability to endure the bodily pain produced male "body-selves" by "perceptual experience and by mode of presence and engagement in the world," an incarnate male subjectivity bound to the sociocultural opposition between the town's northern and southern moieties.[23] Next to this direct intersubjectivity of the fighting's physical violence, the obscene songs referred to sexual acts as another form of relational bodily techniques. Like the fighting, the singing produced embodied subjectivities, but apart from the opposition between northerners and southerners, it produced a difference between female and male selves based on sexual interaction. With this opposition between men and women the New Year's songs transcended the frame of local identities, which in turn contributed to the songs' success on the regional level. But their popularity was mainly due to their transgressive quality: the songs violated the concealed "social" body by revealing the sexuality of the "natural" body. In breaching the cultural norms regarding the representation of the sexual body, the obscene songs voiced what could not be talked about, thereby taking a stand in the "body politics" of gender relations in Zanzibari society.[24]

As transgressive acts the obscene songs recall the themes of the "grotesque body" or the "bodily lower stratum," which, according to Bakhtin, formed part of the popular counterculture of early modern Europe. But the singers at New Year in Makunduchi were not "outside of and contrary to all existing forms of the coercive socioeconomic and political organization, which is suspended for the time of the festivity."[25] On the contrary the singing produced social structure. Some of the songs, like the fighting, were sung back and forth between groups from the north and south of Makunduchi, thus producing an overarching opposition into which conflicts from all levels of the social structure could be channeled. In this sense the obscene songs can be interpreted as rituals of rebellion that renew or reproduce the unity of the social system.[26] Even the songs that were passed back and forth between groups of women and men did not revolutionize gender relations. As transgressions the songs remained bound to the very rules they violated.

These necessary ties between prohibitions and transgressions impose specific limitations on the invention of transgressive acts. Bataille argues that a prohibition always entails the possibility of breaking it, and is thus completed by the transgression that surpasses it, while the transgression depends on the validity of the prohibition and cannot negate it, because once the prohibition ceases to be in effect, the once transgressional act ceases to be a transgression.[27] In addition transgressions do not entail freedom, for in breaking the prohibitions transgressions remain just as rule-bound as the prohibitions themselves.[28] For Bataille, transgression "is in no way the abandonment of that world which the prohibitions *humanize*: it is the festival, it is of course, for a moment, the cessation of work, the unrestrained consumption of its products and the deliberate violation of the most hallowed laws, but the excess consecrates and completes an order of things based on rules; it goes against that order only temporarily."[29] While the prohibitions deny man's dependence on blind animal needs, and thus form the basis of the profane world of social existence, the transgressions make use of the animal forces transformed and increased through social repression in order to contest temporarily the "*lucid* and *voluntary* servility" of the profane world, thereby establishing the divine and the sovereignty of man.[30] As universal targets for prohibitions, and therefore transgressions, Bataille identifies death (i.e., corpses and deadly violence) and sexuality.[31] The necessary link with prohibitions restricts the creative scope to fashion transgressional acts, and Schechner, who is concerned with the creativity of what he calls "performed dreams" in rituals and art, notes that "performed dreams appear always to have been erotic and violent."[32] Sex and violence certainly played major roles in the New Year's rituals in Makunduchi, where sexual transgressions were invented once the violent transgressions had been stopped by the colonial state.

So far I have emphasized the limitations on the invention of rituals and transgressive acts and the contribution of both to the reproduction of social structure. But it would be wrong to reduce the singing of obscene songs in the ritual context of the New Year's festival to mere acts of ritual rebellion that served only to ensure the continuity of social order. As ritual actors the women and men of Makunduchi were empowered to voice their challenges of the customary gender roles precisely by the restricting ritual frame with its deferral of the agents' "intentional sovereignty" because they were just following time-honored tradition when they transgressed social strictures on New Year's Day.[33] Within the ritual frame they were empowered to sing what they could not voice on any other day. And the obscenities they sang were effective transgressions because they surpassed the strictures of gender relations without negating them, and therefore shocked and delighted Zanzibaris from other parts of the island who visited the festival in growing numbers. But let me add a word of caution. These interpretations are of course my own. The people of Makunduchi sang obscene songs, and these songs were important for the outside perception of the festival.[34] However, for the people of Makunduchi, the singers were "just having fun."[35] I offer an explanation of why the obscene songs were fun. In the next section I analyze how these extraordinary songs related to ordinary gender relations and how ritualized transgressions negotiated social structure.

NEGOTIATING GENDER ROLES

While the ritual frame empowered the singers to transgress strictures of ordinary life precisely because it differentiated this practice from other more mundane practices—in and through the actual singing, and not through any metalevel declaration about the singing—the framing did not cut all links with the everyday experiences of the singers. Quite to the contrary, it is the tension with the strictures embedded in the micropolitics of gender relations that makes the obscene songs effective transgressions. Following Hüsken and Neubert, ritual negotiation calls for contextualization of rituals; thus I will analyze the interpenetration of ritual and sociopolitical context, of inside and outside.

In Swahili society there are a number of more or less public practices that comment on, play with, reproduce, and alter gender relations. I interpret these practices as strategic, as negotiations of gender relations, in which the body acts "as the meeting ground of both hegemony and counterhegemonic practices, power and defiance, authority and subversion."[36] These practices ranged from marital relations and other everyday activities (such as working, moving through gendered space, dressing up for various occasions, the communicative use of sayings imprinted on women's dresses [*kanga*], and gendered recreational activities) to more ritualized practices like *taarab* and other musical performances, marriages, funerals, and initiations.[37] However, most of these practices lacked the transgressive quality of the New Year's songs. What made the obscene songs singular—what constituted their radical novelty—was that men and women used blatant sexual terminology in public, a terminology that was totally unacceptable in everyday contexts. To understand why this form of transgression was so much fun, as well as such a successful innovation, it is necessary to locate the transgression within the wider processes of sociocultural change.

Throughout the twentieth century Swahili society had been characterized by rather strict rules of gender segregation, although there were also marked regional differences in gender relations. This division has been interpreted as constituting female and male subcultures, an opposition linked with other dichotomies such as African versus Arab, slave versus freeborn, *mila* versus *dini*, oral versus literate, and rural versus urban.[38] Other authors regarded these relations as complementary rather than opposing.[39] Askew holds that the strict gender segregation dates back only to the nineteenth century and that it forms part of wider processes of social change resulting in a loss of female autonomy in the political, economic, and social spheres.[40] From this perspective, gender relations in Swahili society are the result of social struggles or cultural negotiations, in which variously configured local traditions face the overarching challenges of "Arabization" in the wake of the political dominance of the Omani sultanate and Islamic reformism.[41] With their emphasis on equal access to cultural capital acquired through Islamic education, the reformists challenged traditional hierarchies based on descent and offered new ways to gain symbolic capital; however, the positions of religious leadership they offered were restricted largely to men. With regard to women, the reformists emphasized the purity of women's bodies, demanding their concealment as "part of a whole domain of morality which urges people not only to cover their bodies and dress modestly but also to behave reservedly,"[42] thus restricting women to the domestic realm and curtailing their relative autonomy.

While attacks on traditional religious practices formed part of the reformists' moral struggle, they also reinforced the social strictures of the traditional system of gender relations, wherein the elders controlled the access to women. Legitimate sexual relations were based on marriage, which included economic transactions between descent groups, as the groom had to pay bride-price to male representatives of the bride's descent group. Within this structure of gender relations the disadvantaged groups were the young and, especially after the reformists' impact, the women. Parkin describes the ethic of gender relations as a social game of concealment and disclosure, and notes with regard to the urban youth in Zanzibar Town in the early 1990s: "In the young men's case, it concerns how they can retain dignity and a sense of the aesthetic in the face of joblessness and late marriage, while for the young women the concern is more directly with how their bodies are presented."[43] The obscene songs of the New Year's festival became popular precisely because they offered young men and (young) women the opportunity to violate the prohibitions and rules of the social structure of gender relations at a time when this structure imposed increasing strictures on both sexes.[44]

But gender relations were altered not only through the sociocultural effects of reformist Islam. Another decisive factor was the modern state. In Zanzibar the colonial state did not interfere with the traditional or reformist marital system, and the opportunities it offered in its administration were largely restricted to men. But the increased incorporation into the capitalist economy offered opportunities to women as well. In the late 1960s and early 1970s the postrevolutionary state enforced a cultural revolution that restricted hair and clothing styles as well as leisure activities of young women and men in an attempt to implement its own version of "African tradition" as a guard against the "western degeneration" of the Zanzibari youth, and in 1970 some "Asian" girls were forced to marry "African" high-ranking state officials, a notorious policy aimed at breaking the "racist" divisions of the old system.[45] In keeping with its socialist ideology, the postrevolutionary state decreased the economic opportunities for all, but it also increased women's opportunities within state institutions. The Revolutionary Council of 1995 included two women; in 2001–2 the majority of the state school teachers in Makunduchi were women, and the local police force consisted of women and men. With the economic liberation of the 1980s, and especially with the promotion of tourism since the 1990s, economic opportunities increased once again for both men and women, although the economic situation remained harsh for most Zanzibaris in general. But the political, economic, and cultural liberalization also led to Westernization. Urban youth especially strained against the strictures of the traditional structure of gender relations; significantly this modernized youth formed a significant portion of the visitors to the New Year's festival in Makunduchi.[46]

This scenario forms the sociocultural backdrop to these enormously successful obscene songs. The women and young men of Makunduchi invented the songs around the time of the revolution, when the reformists' impact on the town had reached a high point and strictures on gender relations had increased, only to be called into question by the revolution, whose violent transgressions were not confined to a ritual frame but affected the whole existing social and political structure. In the following years the postcolonial state took control over the festival and started to advertise it. Especially since the 1980s, with the invention of the political rituals, the festival was featured in state-owned radio and television programs, and the obscene songs were included in these features. Media exposure meant the obscene songs dominated outside perception of the festival and contributed significantly to its regional success.[47]

The common feature of the songs was their use of explicit sexual terms. This obscenity constituted the transgression, as the singers sang the unspeakable, exposed the "animality" of the naked body, revealed its smell, its pubic hair, and its rank sexuality, thus violating the ostensibly preferred, culturally concealed body. Swartz links the concept of shame (*aibu*) with the fear of public exposure (*aziri*): "Aziri is what happens when clothes fall to reveal the naked body, and it is also the word used to refer to having one's private deeds revealed publicly. Aziri is something to be avoided. Community members speak of it with enough feeling so that to say it is dreaded is not to put the matter too strongly."[48] This excess constituted the main attraction of the obscene songs: to reveal the naked body was indeed shameless behavior, a transgressive act acceptable only within the ritual framework. And although thus restrained, the liminal transgressions effectively challenged the established state of gender relations. One striking example of these songs was directed by the women toward the men:

> Wauzeni baba zenu, tembo njo utamu wenu—Ask your fathers, the clitoris is indeed your sweet.

With this song, the women revealed their bodies as sexual, they claimed control over their sexuality, and they demanded their satisfaction from the men. Not only that, but the women legitimized their demand with reference to tradition by proclaiming that the sexual satisfaction of women belonged to the ways of their forefathers.[49] This message can be linked to the latest influx of reformist Islam, which took hold in Zanzibar in the 1980s and whose main proponents were young men. In the men's struggle against the "corrupting" influence of tourism in the 1990s, the female body and its concealment formed a central site. Reformists put up posters in the streets of Zanzibar Town, depicting a properly dressed Muslim woman next to a crossed-out, bikini-clad Western woman. Swahili inscriptions, clearly aimed at the locals rather than the tourists, identified the woman in hijab as a woman "of pious virtue, who covered her Muslim body . . . and whose clothes indicated her self-respect," while the Western woman was referred to "as the Devil's whore, an unbeliever who walks naked."[50] With the obscene songs the women of Makunduchi violated the reformists' image of womanhood: women revealed their Muslim bodies, proclaimed sexual autonomy, and based their right to sexual satisfaction on their own cultural tradition, in direct opposition to the reformists' position. Swahili women played the social game of bodily concealment and disclosure within a number of public practices, but none of these were as explicit as the obscene songs. Indeed as public performances the New Year's songs were singular in their transgressive force. Of course the reformist young men heeded the command of their leaders and did not attend the "superstitions" of the New Year's festival, but they and others could hear the songs on the radio as well as see the singing women on TV. The political guests of honor at the festival, whose speeches emphasized the importance of the local customs for society as a whole, contributed to the medial construction of social significance, and when the president of Zanzibar declared in 2002 that the culture of the New Year's festival belonged to all the people of Zanzibar,[51] that culture included the obscene songs.

The transgression of revealing the body was also employed in the songs passed between groups of women. Here other women were shamed by the public revelation of their bodies by pointing out that they did not shave their pubic hair, or by referring to the bodily smell during sexual intercourse:

> Wanawake wa kaskazi mavuzi hawana nyoa—*The women of the North do not shave their pubic hair.*
>
> Ukatomba uzibe pua, harufu mpaka urejua—*You better hold your nose when you have sex, it smells up to the East.*

But the insults between the women also introduced the economic aspect of gender relations:

> Wale hao hawana hongwa, wanatombwa bure—*Those over there did not get presents, they are fucked for free.*

This song referred to the customary rules of engagement and marriage. In Makunduchi, a rather small town, gender segregation was reinforced by tight social control. Unmarried women and men were not supposed to meet in public, and girls were supposed to leave the house only in groups. When a man fancied a woman, he was supposed to ask her parents' permission, after which he and she would become an engaged couple (*wachumba*, sing. *mchumba*). At this stage sex was still prohibited, but the couple could meet under parental control. They exchanged presents, but the main direction of the gift exchange was from the man to the woman. Sexual relations were legalized through marriage, when the groom, with the assistance of his descent group, paid the bride-price to the bride's descent group. Because of the financial strain, many men married late, and some not at all. Of course it was possible to break the customary rules and to have illegitimate sex, but to do so brought on the danger of becoming pregnant and the public humiliation of bearing an illegitimate child; such pregnancies resulted in forced marriage if the perpetrator could be identified. During the liminal time of the festival social control of gender segregation slackened. For five days, and especially nights, unmarried men and women could talk and dance together at the fairground. And there was ample opportunity to find some privacy in the adjacent groves of trees. Young people used this opportunity to flirt, especially since the young men had been busy earning money in the weeks before New Year to buy presents for the girls they fancied.[52] Given this context, women insulted other women by pointing out that they were not smart enough to benefit from the established structure of gender relations, that they were unable to manipulate the men into giving them presents, in short, that they were so stupid as to be "fucked for free."

The women voiced their economic demands also vis-à-vis the men:

> Kama hulinunulia kitenge, nyama yangu huitende—*If you don't buy me clothes, you shall not work my flesh.*

The men responded by emphasizing sexual reciprocity:

> Maungo kwa maungo tena ujira huwa nini—*Body on body, what is the payment?*

And they threatened to leave the established structure of gender relations altogether:

> Mwaka uno mwaka wangu, nchatomba mpaka wazungu—*This year is my year, I will fuck even the whites.*

Wanawake wananitia huruma, bora nitombe kima—*The women frustrate me, better I fuck a monkey.*

I interpret the singing of obscene songs as a strategic practice. The songs were transgressions because they revealed the naked animality of the sexual body hidden beneath the restrained and concealed social body, thus calling into question any form of socially structured gender relations, be they traditional or reformist. But through the songs the women and young men also voiced personal choices, choices that took advantage of or rejected existing social structures. By voicing particular interests the songs translated the discourse on gender roles into concrete struggles over social and economic capital. In their songs the women advocated the traditional system, a system controlled by old men. But in the regional context the women of Makunduchi did have a rather strong position and supported the local structure of gender relations because they stood to lose part of their autonomy if they were to be subjected to the gender roles proposed by the advocates of reformist Islam. In their songs the women confidently proclaimed their sexual and economic autonomy. In the regional context where women were disempowered and restricted to the domestic sphere, these songs had revolutionary potential. In short, within the field of gender relations the women played an ostensibly conservative game because it was in their interest to support the local tradition against reformist Islam.

The young men, on the other hand, opted for change. In the middle of the New Year's rituals that reproduced traditional authority they challenged the elders' control over women. In their songs the men threatened to leave the customary structure of gender relations altogether by turning to Western women or even animals, thus circumventing the economic problem of paying the bride-price in order to gain legitimate access to women. In rejecting the obligations of the traditional descent-based structure, the young men of Makunduchi shared a common target with the modernizing reformist movements, which provided young men with the dignity of moral rigor and access to symbolic capital at the cost of sexual constraint. But by participating in the New Year's rituals and by unveiling the naked animality of their sexual bodies in the obscene songs, the young men rejected the reformist option in practice. The way out they proposed was based on the tourist women, in other words, on the Westernization of Zanzibari society.

This negotiation of gender roles in and through the practice of singing obscene songs was not detached from wider sociocultural processes. Legitimized within the liminal frame of the religious rituals, the songs challenged religious authorities, both traditional and modern, and called into question rules of ordinary social conduct. In public performance the singers transgressed the everyday boundaries of the local discourses on gender roles. These discourses were closely related to the religious conflicts between orthodox Islam (*dini*) and popular religion (*mila*), as well as to the three-way cultural tensions between tradition, Western modernity, and Islamic modernity. As the best known part of a politicized festival, the obscene songs were also part of the ongoing negotiation of national identity, which had formed the ideological backdrop of the political struggles leading up to the revolution in 1964 and which was reactivated in the political conflicts within the multiparty system introduced in 1995.

CONCLUSION

Using the concept of negotiation rituals can be analyzed as processes of interaction between differing positions, and with this (re-)turn to social conflicts the question of how rituals contribute to social reproduction and change is reframed. In the introduction to this volume Hüsken and Neubert suggest that participation, subversion, and contextualization form the major themes of this new analytical angle. The New Year's festival has been celebrated for centuries in East African coastal towns, and the struggles over participation in its rituals negotiated membership in the volatile Swahili society. Since independence New Year in Makunduchi has developed into the biggest celebration of "traditional culture" on the Zanzibar islands. As such it was attacked by proponents of reformist Islam, who urged their followers not to participate in its "superstitious" rituals. Conversely the participation of some twenty-five thousand visitors acted out their difference to reformist ideas, and thus contributed to the ongoing negotiation of Muslim identity in the Swahili cultural context. The growing regional importance of the festival in Makunduchi was in turn based on innovations like the invention of political rituals, in which the joint participation of local elders and state officials renegotiated the relation between traditional authority and state power. But my analysis focused on the second ritual innovation, the singing of obscene songs that certainly subverted cultural conventions and that can be analyzed only by taking into account the wider context of the micropolitics of gender relations within Swahili society.

The invention of obscene songs contributed to the popularity of the festival because they introduced a new division into its liminal transgressions: the opposition between men and women. Rather than the traditional northern and southern division, this new division addressing gender relations related to all Zanzibaris and targeted one of the central lines of conflict in Swahili society. The choices the songs voiced, as well as the ways they were voiced, made the songs popular, especially with young people, who faced similar problems and who accounted for the majority of participants in the festival in 2001–2. The songs contributed to the negotiation of gender relations by opposing men and women in a way that violated cultural conventions like no other public performance in Swahili society. Especially the transgression of unveiling the sexual body surpassed and completed the prohibitions of both local tradition and reformist Islam. While the obscenities as transgressions remained linked to the social strictures, the singers made use of the creative freedom provided by the ritual frame to reflect on gender relations, and were thus able to play with the sociocultural dichotomies that structure Swahili society, such as those between women and men, rural and urban, *mila* and *dini*, and African and Arab. At least two divergent voices can be detected in these songs. The women proclaimed their autonomy against the increasing strictures of reformist Islam on the basis of the local tradition, which fits the usual line-up of sociocultural dichotomies. Likewise the young men rejected the moral restraint of reformism, but they also used the liminal license provided by local religious rituals to attack the traditional gerontocracy by referring to the possibilities of Western modernity. It was precisely this hybridity, this mix of old and new, that ensured the success of the obscene songs and that turned the traditional festival of the town into a regional festival of Zanzibari popular culture.

Regarding the interpenetration of ritual frame and social context, I argued that the transgressions were legitimized through the ritualization of the songs, through the acknowledgment of a ritual frame by the participants in and through the practice of singing, despite the contestation of the elders. As liminal transgressions the songs did not lead to a revolutionary change in gender relations, and necessarily so, because if the songs would lead to sexual liberation they would cease to be transgressions. But they did voice actors' choices and as such contributed to the ongoing negotiation of gender roles. Significantly these choices were not removed from social reality. Women were able to defend their relative autonomy within the local structure, some were sexually satisfied and reached a high social standing as successful businesswomen, and some men were successful in avoiding the traditional strictures; a few of them even married Western women. Thus although the songs' obscene transgressions remained bound within a ritual frame, the choices they voiced certainly did not.

Notes

1. This essay is based on research conducted in 2001 and 2002, made possible by a scholarship granted by the University of Bayreuth. I collected empirical data during two six-month periods of fieldwork, employing the classic methods of anthropological research: participant observation and interviews. Of special importance for this paper were the songs recorded during the New Year's rituals in 2001 and 2002, as well as my understanding of the songs' sociocultural context acquired through uncounted informal conversations while living with the people of Makunduchi. The empirical research was supplemented with historical sources at the Zanzibar National Archive. My thanks go to the people of Makunduchi, especially to my host, Dume; to Stefanie Kolbusa (Bayreuth) for our discussions of obscenity in Swahili songs; and to panel participants at the 2006 American Academy of Religion meeting. Thanks also to Ute Hüsken, Frank Neubert, and the anonymous reviewers for their critical comments on this essay.

2. This section provides a brief overview of the cultural and historical context of the New Year's festival with its obscene songs. For a detailed discussion see Echtler, "Changing Rituals." For data collection I participated in the New Year's rituals in 2001 and 2002 and conducted forty-seven formal interviews. For the history of the festival the most important sources are the "Annual and Monthly Reports on District Administration," ZNA BA 30/2–8, 12–14 (1928–53), Zanzibar National Archives, Zanzibar Town, Tanzania.

3. Regional discourses on the orthodoxy of various religious practices were dominated by reformist groups in Friday prayers disseminated via audio cassettes or the newspaper *An Nuur*, which urged the faithful to "avoid the superstitions of the New Year's festival" ("Epukeni ushirikina wa Mwaka Kogwa," *An Nuur*, July 20–26, 2001, 3), but these interpretations were

rejected by religious experts from Makunduchi (interviews with Amina, Baraka, Hassan). For an extensive overview of the interrelated religious and academic discourses see Echtler, "Changing Rituals," 80–92. During my fieldwork I participated in numerous religious practices of the spirit shrines (*mizimu*), the spirit possession groups (*viringe*), and other forms of healing (*uganga*). For a detailed account of the religious field in Makunduchi see 92–169.

4. Interview with Selemani.

5. Social identity in Makunduchi is based primarily on descent group membership, but as they use a cognitive system of descent, every individual is (potentially) a member of a large number of groups. I argue that individuals choose membership in practice by participating in the rituals of the spirit shrines (*mizimu*), which serve as markers of the descent groups. See Echtler, "Changing Rituals," 147–52. The most important political units in Swahili society are the towns. Citizenship in these towns is highly volatile, and I argue that the New Year's rituals produce *Wamakunduchi*, the citizens of Makunduchi (227–44). For a similar argument with regard to participation in communal rituals and citizenship in a Swahili town in the late nineteenth century see Glassman, *Feasts and Riot,* 174.

6. I argue that ritual practices produce (sacred) space, and that (sacred) space is used to frame activities as rituals. The communal New Year's rituals not only produce citizens of the town, but also the space of the town. See Echtler, "Changing Rituals," 137–47, 227–44. My discussion is based on the distinction between spatial practices, representational spaces, and representations of space. See Lefebvre, *The Production of Space,* 38–39.

7. For my interpretation of the New Year's rituals as strategic practice see Echtler, "Changing Rituals," 265–76. For social and symbolic capital see Bourdieu, "The Forms of Capital," 241–58; Bourdieu, *The Logic of Practice,* 122–34; Bourdieu, *Méditations pascaliennes,* 285.

8. Interviews with Ali, Ameir, Haji, Jecha, Mussa; Zanzibar National Archives BA 30/2:3; BA 30/4:11; BA 30/13:4. For the political history of Makunduchi see Echtler, "Changing Rituals," 60–66.

9. As the guest of honor in 2002 "the president [of Zanzibar] explained that the culture of the celebrations of *mwaka kogwa* . . . is the culture of all Zanzibaris" ("Rais alielezea kuwa utamaduni wa sherehe za Mwaka Kogwa . . . ni utamaduni wa Wazanzibari wote"). Mwantanga Ame, "Utamaduni wa Mwaka Kogwa kuendelezwa–Karume," *Zanzibar Leo*, July 22, 2002, 1, 3.

10. This open conflict informed my understanding of the relations between religious authorities and state officials. In the very first interview, when I was still completely unaware of the local discourses, I was told that this year's festival had been a bad one because state administrators stole the money that belonged by right to the religious experts, and that the religious experts would not tolerate this development (interview with Mussa). For the political rituals, in which the management of participation and the interrelation with both the religious and the political field provide another test case for the concept of ritual negotiation as proposed by Hüsken and Neubert, see Echtler, "They Bewitched the Generator," 51–68; Echtler, "Changing Rituals," 200–16.

11. Turner, "Variations on a Theme of Liminality," 40.

12. Rappaport, *Ritual and Religion in the Making of Humanity,* 32.

13. In this sense ritual framing is metacommunicative: "Any message, which either explicitly or implicitly defines a frame, *ipso facto* gives the receiver instructions or aids in his attempt to understand the messages included within the frame" (Bateson, *Steps to an Ecology of Mind,* 188). Don Handelman criticizes Bateson's frames as "lineally defined and hierarchical" and suggests more flexible Moebius frames instead (Handelman, "Re-Framing Ritual," 11) that are

in turn criticized by Jan Snoek as "a logical impossibility, which we did not need in the first place" ("Some Thoughts about Handelman's Moebius Framing Theory," 36).

14. Interviews with Baraka, Hanafii, Selemani, Vatima (August 16, 2001); Zanzibar National Archives BA 30/6, 3rd quarter 1935: August 8, 1937: 12; BA 30/7, August 1939: 8, August 1940: 2; BA 30/8, August 1945: 2, August 1949: 4; BA 30/12, August 1950: 2, August 1952: 3.

15. For example, the *nyange*, *shandwa/kiumbizi*, *sendemre*, or *bondogea* dance. See Gray, "Nairuzi or Siku ya Mwaka," 15–17; Horton and Middleton, *The Swahili*, 130; Ingrams, *Zanzibar*, 483–88; Velten, *Sitten und Gebräuche der Suaheli*, 145–47, 159–60; Bakari, *The Customs of the Swahili People*, 83, 90.

16. Interviews with Ali, Mussa, Mzee, Ramadhani, Vatima (August 25, 2002). Only Mussa held the view that men invented the obscene songs; only Vatima somewhat dated the invention: "Haya matusi yamekuja miaka ya hivi karibuni, lakini wakati wetu sisi hakukuwa na nyimbo za matusi, wakati wa ukoloni huo" (These obscene songs have begun in recent years, but in our times, the colonial times, there were no obscene songs).

17. Bourdieu, *The Logic of Practice*, 55.

18. Interview with Amina. See also Chum, "The Impact of Mwaka Kogwa Festivals on the Development of Zanzibar," 15; Campbell, "Nyimbo za Kiswahili," 39–46, 225–33; Decken, *Reisen in Ost-Afrika*, 6; Velten, *Sitten und Gebräuche der Suaheli*, 158–60, 164–65, 170–73; Bakari, *The Customs of the Swahili People*, 89–90, 92, 95–97; Stefanie Kolbusa, personal communication.

19. See Zache, "Sitten und Gebräuche der Suaheli," 72–76; Velten, *Sitten und Gebräuche der Suaheli*, 81–82, 95–99; Bakari, *The Customs of the Swahili People*, 48–49, 56–58, 269n17, 271nn10–11; Fair, "Identity, Difference, and Dance," 156–57.

20. Handelman, "Re-Framing Ritual," 19. The links with different contexts could also be interpreted as multiple double framing, which would provide a number of backgrounds against which the innovative act could be delineated (Bateson, *Steps to an Ecology of Mind*, 188–90).

21. Interviews with Ali, Makungu.

22. For example, in 2002 one song commented on the recent practice of handing out condoms as part of the HIV/AIDS prevention program: "Mbona kunletee kondom, utamu ngozi kwa ngozi" (Why do you bring me a condom, sweetness is skin on skin).

23. Csordas, "The Body's Career in Anthropology," 182; Van Wolputte, "Hang On to Your Self," 261.

24. See Csordas, "The Body's Career in Anthropology," 177.

25. Bakhtin, *Rabelais and His World*, 255.

26. Gluckman, *Rituals of Rebellion in South-East Africa*, 3. For the application of this concept to the New Year's rituals see Echtler, "Changing Rituals," 244–51.

27. "La transgression n'est pas la négation de l'interdit, mais elle le dépasse et le complète" (Bataille, "L'érotisme," 66).

28. "Souvent la transgression de l'interdit n'est pas elle-même moins sujette à des règles que l'interdit. Il ne s'agit pas de liberté: *à tel moment et jusque-là, ceci est possible* est le sens de la transgression" (Bataille, "L'érotisme," 68).

29. Bataille, "The History of Eroticism," 90. In this context Derrida insists that Bataille's conception of the dialectical relation between prohibition and transgression displaces the Hegelian notion of *Aufhebung* as "to surpass while maintaining" ("From Restricted to General Economy," 127–28). But when discussing feasts and orgies, Bataille emphasizes the limited or framed character of these transgressions, which negate the secular world without destroying the cultural prohibitions or the social order ("Théorie de la religion," 312–15; "L'érotisme," 113–17). For the limits of transgression see Klaus Köpping, "The Transgression of Limits and

the Limits of Transgression"; on transgression generally, see Taussig, "Transgression."; On the relevance of Bataille for the study of religion, see Olson, "Eroticism, Violence, and Sacrifice"; Urban, "The Power of the Impure."

30. Bataille, "The History of Eroticism," 93.

31. Bataille, "L'érotisme," 43–57; Bataille, "The History of Eroticism," 51–58, 79–86.

32. Schechner, *The Future of Ritual,* 263.

33. Humphrey and Laidlaw, *The Archetypal Actions of Ritual,* 99. For limited agency as a feature of rituals see also Kelly and Kaplan, "History, Structure, and Ritual," 140; Rappaport, *Ritual and Religion in the Making of Humanity,* 32–33.

34. When I told people from outside Makunduchi that I did research on the New Year's festival there, they invariably joked about the apparent sexual license of the celebrations. Virtually everybody knew about the festival and the songs, as the festival was covered by Zanzibari radio (STZ) and television (TVZ), and the obscene songs formed part of all the features I had access to.

35. When I asked people about the meaning of the singing (or the fighting), the standard answer was "Wanafurahi tu" (They are just having fun; e.g., interviews with Makame, Nafasi and Mwandini, Vatima [August 16, 2001]). Maryam explained that people sing to insult each other: "Kusini wengine na kaskazi wengine, tena mnaimba mnakwenda kukutana katikati, tena mnatukana kwa mida" (A group from the South, another from the North, you sing and meet in the middle, you insult each other with the songs; interview with Maryam 25.6.2002). Beyond that, local discourse on the obscene songs centered on their legitimacy, with representatives of the New Year's committee criticizing them as illegitimate inventions (interviews with Ali, Makungu).

36. Van Wolputte, "Hang On to Your Self," 260.

37. See Campbell, "Nyimbo za Kiswahili"; Fair, "Identity, Difference, and Dance"; Ntarangwi, *Gender, Identity, and Performance;* Parkin, "The Power of Incompleteness"; Swartz, *The Way the World Is.*

38. Caplan, "Gender, Ideology and Modes of Production on the Coast of East Africa"; Eastman, "Women, Slaves, and Foreigners."

39. Lambek, *Knowledge and Practice in Mayotte,* 334–35; Nisula, *Everyday Spirits and Medical Interventions,* 154–63.

40. Askew, "Female Circles and Male Lines."

41. For the impact of reformist Islam on Swahili society, see Loimeier, "Patterns and Peculiarities of Islamic Reform in Africa"; Loimeier and Seesemann, *The Global Worlds of the Swahili.*

42. Parkin, "Blank Banners and Islamic Consciousness in Zanzibar," 212.

43. Ibid., 208.

44. My understanding of gender relations is based on my long-term fieldwork in Makunduchi and the informal conversations that living with the people allowed for. To put a check on this necessarily subjective understanding, I make use of the work of colleagues in my reconstruction of Swahili gender relations. One example from my fieldwork for gendered body techniques that shows the difference between the rather "traditional" Makunduchi and the much more "reformist" regional center, Zanzibar Town, is the way women dress. In Makunduchi women wore *kanga*, two pieces of brightly colored cloth, one worn as a skirt and the other covering the upper body, shoulders, and head, leaving the face uncovered. But they were not meticulous about it even in public, and in private, which included the semipublic verandahs in front of the houses, women would have their heads and hair uncovered even in the presence of male

visitors, a practice completely unacceptable within reformist circles. Only when traveling to Zanzibar Town would the women of Makunduchi don the black *buibui*, leaving only the face visible. The strictest type of women's clothing was a black hijab that left only the eyes uncovered. This was called *ninja* locally, and I never saw a woman wear one in Makunduchi.

45. Burgess, "Cinema, Bell Bottoms, and Miniskirts"; Clayton, *The Zanzibar Revolution and Its Aftermath*, 123–24.

46. Again my description of the local situation is based on my fieldwork experience. Being classified as a young man myself, my contact with young people, and young men especially, was closest. For an account of Swahili female youth in Mombasa see Fuglesang, *Veils and Videos*.

47. See note 34.

48. Swartz, *The Way the World Is*, 183.

49. This is my interpretation of the meaning of the song. For the people of Makunduchi, singing the songs is "having fun" (see note 35). I analyze why some of the songs are fun to sing, why they function as effective transgressions, by relating them to increasing strictures in the relations between women, young men and old men. I interpret a cultural text within its sociocultural context, and I specify the relation between text and context as ritualized transgression based on the use of explicit sexual terminology. The women (and young men) use the liminal space provided by the New Year's rituals to make specific statements about gender relations, and I analyze these specific statements by linking them with specific social relations. With regard to the relation between the obscene songs and "real life" outside the ritual frame, I merely hold that social rules can be broken; that is, I know people from Makunduchi who had sexual relations outside marriage, and I know some men from Makunduchi who married Western women without paying any bride-price. But the point here is that it is not possible to talk about these and other sexual relations explicitly and in public in Swahili society; one can only sing about them on New Year's Day.

50. Parkin, "Blank Banners and Islamic Consciousness in Zanzibar," 208.

51. Mwantanga Ame, "Utamaduni wa Mwaka Kogwa kuendelezwa–Karume," *Zanzibar Leo*, July 22, 2002, 3.

52. As mentioned earlier, my primary peer group was the young men, and I witnessed endless discussions about young women, growing anticipation before New Year, efforts to earn money in order to buy presents, and the collection of condoms from NGOs. At the festival I participated in the talking, flirting, and dancing with the women but did not venture into the thickets where actual sex supposedly happened. But as one of the young men commented, "Bila mwanamke haina mwaka" (Without a woman there is no [New] Year; interview with Makame).

Bibliography

Published Sources

Askew, Kelly. "Female Circles and Male Lines: Gender Dynamics along the Swahili Coast." *Africa Today* 46 (1999): 66–102.

Bakari, Mtoro bin Mwinyi. *The Customs of the Swahili People*. Ed. and trans. J. W. T. Allen. Berkeley: University of California Press, 1981.

Bakhtin, Mikhail. *Rabelais and His World*. Bloomington: Indiana University Press, 1984.

Bataille, Georges. "L'érotisme." In *Œuvres Complètes*, 10:7–270. Paris: Gallimard, 1987.

———. "The History of Eroticism." In *The Accursed Share*, 2–3:11–191. New York: Zone Books, 1993.

———. "Théorie de la religion." In *Œuvres Complètes*, 7:281–361. Paris: Gallimard, 1976.

Bateson, Gregory. *Steps to an Ecology of Mind*. Chicago: University of Chicago Press, 2000.

Bourdieu, Pierre. "The Forms of Capital." In *Handbook of Theory and Research for the Sociology of Education*, ed. John G. Richardson, 241–58. New York: Greenwood Press, 1986.

———. *The Logic of Practice*. Stanford: Stanford University Press, 1990.

———. *Méditations pascaliennes*. Paris: Seuil, 1997.

Burgess, Thomas. "Cinema, Bell Bottoms, and Miniskirts: Struggles over Youth and Citizenship in Revolutionary Zanzibar." *International Journal of African Historical Studies* 35, nos. 2–3 (2002): 287–313.

Campbell, Carol A. A. "Nyimbo za Kiswahili: A Socio-Ethnomusicological Study of a Swahili Poetic Form." PhD diss., University of Washington, 1983.

Caplan, Pat. "Gender, Ideology and Modes of Production on the Coast of East Africa." *Paideuma* 28 (1982): 29–43.

Chum, Lahdad H. "The Impact of Mwaka Kogwa Festivals on the Development of Zanzibar." Unpublished research report, Kivukoni Academy of Social Sciences, Dar Es Salaam, 2000.

Clayton, Anthony. *The Zanzibar Revolution and Its Aftermath*. Hamden: Archon Books, 1981.

Csordas, Thomas J. "The Body's Career in Anthropology." In *Anthropological Theory Today*, ed. Henrietta L. Moore, 172–205. Cambridge, UK: Polity Press, 1999.

Decken, Carl Claus von der. *Reisen in Ost-Afrika*. Vol. 2. Ed. Otto Kersten. Graz: Akademische Druck- und Verlagsanstalt, 1978.

Derrida, Jacques. "From Restricted to General Economy: A Hegelianism without Reserve." In *Bataille: A Critical Reader*, ed. Fred Botting and Scott Wilson, 102–38. Oxford: Blackwell, 1998.

Eastman, Carol. "Women, Slaves, and Foreigners: African Cultural Influences and Group Processes in the Formation of the Northern Swahili Coastal Society." *International Journal of African Historical Studies* 21 no. 1 (1988): 1–20.

Echtler, Magnus. "Changing Rituals. The New Year's Festival in Makunduchi, Zanzibar, Since Colonial Times." Unpublished PhD thesis, University of Bayreuth, 2008.

———. "They Bewitched the Generator: State Power and Religious Authority at the New Year's Festival in Makunduchi, Zanzibar." In *Exercising Power: The Role of Religions in Concord and Conflict*, ed. Tore Ahlbäck, 51–68. Stockholm: Almquist & Wiksell, 2006.

Fair, Laura. "Identity, Difference, and Dance: Female Initiation in Zanzibar, 1890 to 1930." In *Mashindano! Competitive Music Performance in East Africa*, ed. Frank Gunderson and Gregory F. Barz, 143–74. Dar Es Salaam: Mkuki na Nyota, 2000.

Fuglesang, Minou. *Veils and Videos: Female Youth Culture on the Kenyan Coast*. Stockholm Studies in Social Anthropology 32. Stockholm: Gotab, 1994.

Glassman, Jonathan. *Feasts and Riot: Revelry, Rebellion, and Popular Consciousness on the Swahili Coast, 1856–1888*. London: James Currey, 1995.

Gluckman, Max. *Rituals of Rebellion in South-East Africa*. Manchester: Manchester University Press, 1954.

Gray, John M. "Nairuzi or Siku ya Mwaka." *Tanganyika Notes and Records* 38 (1955): 1–22.

Handelman, Don. "Re-Framing Ritual." In *The Dynamics of Changing Rituals: The Transformation of Religious Rituals within their Social and Cultural Context*, ed. Jens Kreinath, Constance Hardung, and Annette Deschner, 9–20. New York: Peter Lang, 2004.

Horton, Mark, and John Middleton. *The Swahili: The Social Landscape of a Mercantile Society*. Oxford: Blackwell, 2001.

Humphrey, Caroline, and James Laidlaw. *The Archetypal Actions of Ritual: A Theory of Ritual Illustrated by the Jain Rite of Worship*. Oxford: Clarendon Press, 2004.

Ingrams, William H. *Zanzibar: Its History and Its People*. London: Frank Cass, 1967.

Kelly, John D., and Martha Kaplan. "History, Structure, and Ritual." *Annual Review of Anthropology* 19 (1990): 119–50.

Köpping, Klaus-Peter. "The Transgression of Limits and the Limits of Transgression." In *Rituale erneuern: Ritualdynamik und Grenzerfahrung aus interdisziplinärer Perspektive*, ed. Henrik Jungaberle, Rolf Verres, and Fletcher DuBois, 267–92. Gießen: Psychosozial-Verlag, 2006.

Lambek, Michael. *Knowledge and Practice in Mayotte: Local Discourses of Islam, Sorcery, and Spirit Possession*. Toronto: University of Toronto Press, 1993.

Lefebvre, Henri. *The Production of Space*. Oxford: Blackwell, 1991.

Loimeier, Roman. "Patterns and Peculiarities of Islamic Reform in Africa." *Journal of Religion in Africa* 33, no. 3 (2003): 237–62.

Loimeier, Roman, and Rüdiger Seesemann, eds. *The Global Worlds of the Swahili: Interfaces of Islam, Identity and Space in 19th and 20th-Century East Africa*. Münster: Lit, 2006.

Nisula, Tapio. *Everyday Spirits and Medical Interventions: Ethnographic and Historical Notes on Therapeutic Conventions in Zanzibar Town*. Saarijärvi: Gummerus Kirjapaino Oy, 1999.

Ntarangwi, Mwenda. *Gender, Identity, and Performance: Understanding Swahili Cultural Realities through Songs*. Trenton, NJ: Africa World Press, 2003.

Olson, Carl. "Eroticism, Violence, and Sacrifice: A Postmodern Theory of Religion and Ritual." *Method and Theory in the Study of Religion* 6 (1994): 231–50.

Parkin, David. "Blank Banners and Islamic Consciousness in Zanzibar." In *Questions of Consciousness*, ed. Anthony P. Cohen and Nigel Rapport, 198–216. London: Routledge, 1995.

———. "The Power of Incompleteness: Innuendo in Swahili Woman's Dress." In *Pour une anthropologie de l'interlocution: Rhétoriques du quotidian*, ed. Bertrand Masquelier and Jean-Louis Siran, 155–82. Paris: Éditions L'Harmattan, 2000.

Rappaport, Roy. *Ritual and Religion in the Making of Humanity*. Cambridge: Cambridge University Press, 1999.

Schechner, Richard. *The Future of Ritual: Writings on Culture and Performance*. London: Routledge, 1993.

Snoek, Jan. "Some Thoughts about Handelman's Moebius Framing Theory." In *Rituale in Bewegung*, ed. Henrik Jungaberle and Jan Weinhold, 33–36. Berlin: Lit, 2006.

Swartz, Marc J. *The Way the World Is: Cultural Processes and Social Relations among the Mombasa Swahili*. Berkeley: University of California Press, 1991.

Taussig, Michael. "Transgression." In *Critical Terms for Religious Studies*, ed. Mark C. Taylor, 349–64. Chicago: University of Chicago Press, 1998.

Turner, Victor. "Variations on a Theme of Liminality." In *Secular Ritual*, ed. Sally Moore and Barbara Myerhoff, 36–52. Amsterdam: Van Gorcum, 1977.

Urban, Hugh B. "The Power of the Impure: Transgression, Violence and Secrecy in Bengali Sakta Tantra and Modern Western Magic." *Numen* 50 (2003): 269–308.

Van Wolputte, Steven. "Hang On to Your Self: Of Bodies, Embodiment, and Selves." *Annual Review of Anthropology* 33 (2004): 251–69.

Velten, Carl. *Sitten und Gebräuche der Suaheli*. Göttingen: Vandenhoek & Ruprecht, 1903.

Zache, Hans. "Sitten und Gebräuche der Suaheli." *Zeitschrift für Ethnologie* 31 (1899): 5–86.

Archival Sources

Zanzibar National Archives (ZNA), Zanzibar Town, Tanzania
ZNA BA 30/2–8, 12–14: Annual and monthly reports on District Administration, 1928–53.

Interviews

I have changed the names of all my informants, as some of them did not want to be identified by name.

Ali, June 13, 2002.
Ameir, June 18, 2002.
Amina, August 6, 2002.
Baraka, June 5, 2002.
Haji, June 19, 2002.
Hanafii, June 7, 2002.
Hassan, June 9, 2002.
Jecha, September 3, 2002.
Makame, August 30, 2002.
Makungu, June 17, 2002.
Mussa, August 1, 2001.
Mzee, August 30, 2002.
Nafasi and Mwandini, August 23, 2001.
Ramadhani, June 11, 2002.
Selemani, July 8, 2002.
Vatima, August 16, 2001; August 25, 2002.

4

Ritual Negotiations in Lutherland

Barry Stephenson

FESTIVITY IN WITTENBERG

AN HOUR'S TRAIN RIDE southwest of Berlin lies the city of Wittenberg, home to Martin Luther for thirty-six years and the seat of the German Reformation. For centuries the city has played host to public ritual; in the past 150 years Wittenberg has also become a venue for Protestant pilgrimage and cultural tourism. Luther festivity has a long and checkered history, dating back to the first Reformation Jubilee in 1617, celebrating the hundredth anniversary of Luther's posting of the ninety-five theses, the so-called *Thesenanschlag*. This chapter presents three scenes from the larger drama of contemporary Luther and Reformation festivity, framed by a discussion of Carnival and the carnivalesque and Victor Turner's theory of social drama. These scenes, offering glimpses of on-the-ground tensions in contemporary Luther festivals, demonstrate the role played by ritual and performance in negotiating matters of memory, identity, beliefs, and values attached to and emanating from the figure of Martin Luther. I am chiefly interested in developing a notion of ritual negotiation grounded in processual dynamics, and so my discussion of contemporary Luther festivity begins with its social-historical context.

The reunification of Germany in 1989 stimulated a Luther renaissance. Pushed off the cultural map at the end of the Second World War, since the fall of the Berlin wall Luther has reemerged as important to cultural and economic renewal in the former East Germany. For a region suffering high unemployment and struggling with cultural memory, identity, and reintegration into the new Germany, Luther has become a renewable cultural resource. Today Wittenberg is a UNESCO World Heritage site, a magnet for Lutheran and Protestant pilgrims and visitors, and the capital of the thriving tourist and heritage region known as Lutherland.[1]

At the heart of Wittenberg's cultural and economic renewal efforts are two annual festivals. Reformation Day, held each October, is a centuries-old celebration of Luther's posting of the ninety-five theses; in principle Reformation Day is a church festival, but its ecclesiastical dimensions are rivaled by the secular, the aesthetic, and the popular; the festival attracts as many as twenty thousand visitors. The other festival, Luther's Wedding, held each June, was inaugurated in 1994 around the theme of the wedding of Martin Luther and Katharina von Bora. Upwards of a million people pour into the old city for the three-day wedding festivities. Both festivals include medieval markets, traditional arts, handicrafts, and cuisine, parades and processions, theater and street performers, food and drink, concerts, and special worship services, including the opportunity to renew wedding vows in "Luther's Church."

SCENE 1: A BEER FOR MARTIN

On Saturday, October 30, as the bells of Wittenberg's *Stadtkirche* struck four, the 2004 version of Wittenberg's annual Reformation Day festival kicked off in the *Marktplatz*. The geographical center of the old town, the Marktplatz is also a focal point for the festivities, host to the "Historical Market Spectacle." The festival fool and his music-playing, juggling, comic, ironic, tongue-twisting, theatricalizing cohorts called the crowd to order, aided by a trumpeted "Da-Da-Da-DAA!" On this warm, sunny afternoon the crowd of 250 or so festival-goers gathered in the Marktplatz was in good spirits, and the spirits—beer and a little wine—were beginning to flow. After a few jokes satirizing clergy with sexual innuendo about monks and nuns, the fool procured a beer from a nearby vendor. Balancing the brew on his cocked head, he wove through the crowd, navigating cobblestones, chairs, tables, and bodies, to return to the stage, tucked away in a corner of the town square.

There the fool waited, beer on head, as his fellow *Spielleute* volunteered a heavy-set, grizzled member of the crowd for their merry band. Hands thrust deep inside the pockets of a worn leather bomber jacket, an apprehensive look on his face, the man edged into the middle of the U-shaped circle of onlookers formed in front of the stage. As fate (or good performance) would have it, the man's name was Martin. The fool, nodding and smiling in approval at the fortuitous name, looked up to Johann Gottfried Schadow's Luther (the heroic statue unveiled on Reformation Day in 1821) and back to Martin, at once equating the two figures with the movement of his hand. Martin the monument was now Martin the man. His task? To down the fool's large mug of beer without coming up for air. Hoisting the mug, Martin started chugging, and the beer was downed in a few seconds; the players had chosen well and received the crowd's praise by way of rousing applause, helped along with a few more blasts on the trumpet. The performance, though, was not over. One of the fool's men flipped his trumpet end for end and, holding it to his ear, listened attentively for stirrings in Martin's belly.

Satisfied that all was settling well, the fool then spun Martin around like a top. Dizzy from the spinning—not to mention the beer—the poor man was bent over and listened to again; this time the short end of the trumpet probed the air at his backside, the large end funneling fumes back to the player's nose. Martin produced the desired wind, the crowd cheered, and the fool pronounced the annual Reformationsfest underway.

The performance of a bawdy, beer-guzzling, farting Martin Luther that afternoon in Wittenberg's Marktplatz lasted all of ten minutes, but the scene opened a window onto the dynamics of contemporary Luther festivity. Marking the beginning of the festival, this improvised scenario set a tone of playful—albeit, for a few attendees, offensive—merrymaking. Significantly the scene was not listed on the program schedule. The impromptu opening of the festival was primarily satire of medieval Luther-era clergy and monastics; by implication the performers satirized the liturgical dimensions of contemporary Luther festivity. Coming on the eve of Reformation Day, the opening in the Marktplatz pushed the traditionally liturgical basis of the festival in the direction of the carnivalesque.

"A Beer for Martin," as I have dubbed the scene, was, as street theater is, primarily visual: people watched it. But gustatory, olfactory, auditory, and kinesthetic qualities were also present, literally and metaphorically. "A Beer for Martin" was expressive and entertaining, aimed at getting people into the mood for celebrating, but it also embodied meanings. Historically the herald's trumpet was used to signal orders during military combat and to announce the arrival of royalty. The horn's contemporary use by clowning festival performers suggests social inversion: turning the trumpet end for end to use not with the mouth (the origin of speech, words, texts, and logos, the tools of Lutheran tradition), but to expand the sensitivity of ear and nose to detect nefarious sounds and odors amplified by this inversion. Beer has the effect of altering sensory states. The spinning of Martin, coupled with the chugged beer, played havoc with the man's kinesthetic sense. Martin was off balance, a model of and for the carnival-like, topsy-turvy atmosphere of contemporary Luther festivity. The kinesthetic sense of the scene suggested derangement: the sensory focus was on the lower senses associated with the genitals, mouth, gut, and bowels. Martin the culture hero who posted the ninety-five theses became, for a moment at least, a beer-loving stumblebum. Reformation Day on the liturgical and civic calendars in Sachsen-Anhalt is an elevated, special, extraordinary occasion whose liturgical focus is on the text and the preaching of the Word. Still the meaning embodied in the postures and gestures that Saturday afternoon in the Marktplatz seemed to be "Let's not forget that Reformation Day, however elevated, is also guttural, an event of and for the folk, a time to praise, but also to poke fun—maybe something about Luther or the festival even stinks."[2]

Characterized by spontaneity, improvisation, and a weakening of the performer-audience boundary, "A Beer for Martin" was something between play and theater. *Spielleute* (players) are not *Schauspieler* (actors), nor was there a script, for this performance was an age-old scenario around which the players and spectators improvised: on the precise day set aside to honor an important figure, he drinks too much, gets horny (the herald trumpet was briefly transformed into a phallus and thrust at a "nun") and dizzy, farts, and makes a fool of himself in public. The scenario not only lowered Martin Luther from his pedestal in the Marktplatz, but invited the public to poke fun at the high and mighty.

The performance heightened its entertainment value by drawing spectators into the play. The crowd formed a performance space in the Marktplatz by gathering in a semicircle, thereby placing people on the border between on and off stage, between audience and Spielleute. The volunteer Martin served as the crowd's representative, while others contributed with shouting, clapping, comments, and catcalls. One of the characteristics of festivity is that festival-goers are part of the production; this active participation is quite unlike, say, proscenium theater or political ceremony, where an audience-performer boundary is demarcated and maintained throughout the performance. In festivity spectators and consumers are also performers and producers. If you can consume a large mug of beer in a single, long gulp, if you dress up and perform your character, if you spend beyond your means, you amplify the ethos of festive celebration.

The performance theorist Richard Schechner distinguishes performance in terms of an efficacy-entertainment dyad. To call a performance efficacious is to emphasize that its "purpose is to effect transformation" at a social, personal, or even physical level; a rite of passage, an ecstatic trance, and a healing rite are examples of such purposeful performance. Schechner's basic opposition is not between ritual and, say, theater, but the degree to which any type of performance slides one way or another on the efficacy-entertainment dyad.[3] Where does "A Beer for Martin" fall on Schechner's continuum? Is it doing any kind of ritual work? If, as I have suggested, festival culture in Wittenberg is implicated in processes of social change, must not this change also be processed in the particular scenes, rites, and performances that compose the larger abstraction called Reformation Day?

Consider that the former East Germany was a repressive state. People lived in a world where the Stasi would entice or coerce family members to spy on one another, and speaking out against authority or the state was an act that drew serious repercussions. Extend this historical context back to include the Holocaust, the Second World War, Nazism, the depression of the 1930s, the legacy and waging of the Great War, and the absolutism of Prussian-era Germany, and it is evident that the past century in eastern Germany was anything but playful. It was a time of quiet or forced acquiescence to the authority of the state, an authority incarnated in the public and near god-like stature and power of individual men, among them the heroic Luther. If, broadly speaking, "one's religion is . . . one's way of valuing most intensively and comprehensively," then in the context of such militaristic-authoritarian history, the ability to defy and laugh at authority is intensely valued.[4]

Laughing at authority figures or fooling with prominent cultural-religious symbols may seem trivial, but engaging in public performance of political satire and critique is a measure of the health of democratic processes. Historically in European culture Carnival provided the occasion for the public display of popular sentiments, ideas, and opinions, a tradition that continues in the *Fasnacht* and *Fasching* traditions in southern Germany and Switzerland. It is important to realize, however, that the carnivalesque character of "A Beer for Martin" is a relatively new experience in Wittenberg. It exemplifies the return to popular street culture of a kind of playful, irreverent performance rooted in mockery, parody, satire, and clowning. Spielleute—literally, "play-people"—once again walk the streets at festival time. Sylvia, a consultant and member of the performance group Scharlatan, explains her understanding of the connection between historical and contemporary Spielleute: "What we do is basically try to transport what the medieval *Spielleute* did—to transport this into modern times. Because what we do is make fun of the system sometimes . . . and of political things, and combine this with music and fun. And this is what they did in earlier times."[5] In sum, Luther, the raison d'être of the festivals, is also the target of the Spielleute slings and arrows.

SCENE 2: RENEWAL OF VOWS

The Renewal of Vows service that takes place Saturday evening during Luther's Wedding is the creation of the Wittenberg English Ministry, an on-the-ground ministry affiliated with the socially and theologically conservative American Lutheran Church Missouri Synod.[6] The service, which has been part of Luther's Wedding since 2002, takes place in the Stadtkirche. In 2005 there were approximately twenty-five congregants, predominantly American Lutherans, though the service was conducted in both English and German. In 2006 more than sixty people took part in an English-language service on the tenth anniversary of the ministry. Keith Loetsch, the ministry's founder, had led a tour group from his home parish in Virginia to Wittenberg in order to help mark the anniversary with a large, if largely foreign, congregation.

A key aim of the Wittenberg English Ministry is to provide an explicitly Lutheran confessional context to Luther-themed tourism, festivals, and heritage culture. The renewal of vows during Luther's wedding is an opportunity for Christians to attend worship and renew their vows in a place of historic and religious value on an occasion of festive celebration. The practice of renewing one's wedding vows, although not widespread in either Europe or North America, is increasing in popularity, especially in the context of travel and tourism.

The service follows a familiar liturgical form: a "service of the word" shaped with readings and a sermon emphasizing the importance of the institution of marriage, love between husband and wife, and the exemplary marriage of Martin Luther and Katharina von Bora.[7] Luther and "Katie" are held up as role models to the Lutheran community, and the service provides the opportunity for couples to renew their own marriage vows. During the greeting the congregation responsively reads Psalm 100: "Shout for joy to the Lord, all the earth / Worship the Lord with gladness / come before him with joyful songs." The occasion is framed as celebratory, but in both services

I attended there was a distinctly ideological undertone suggesting there was more at work in the service than praise and the reaffirmation of vows.

Reverend Loesch introduced the service renewing wedding vows in an effort to "uplift the festival" by "tak[ing] a large beer fest, a party, and inject[ing] it with some spirituality, with some connection to Lutheran theology." In fact the renewal service developed in part as a result of reactions of American Lutherans to the carnivalesque character of Luther's Wedding. For the Wedding festival, two small stages for pipe and drum music are set up just outside the walls of the Stadtkirche. During the service the drumming, piping, singing, and shouting outside is so loud that it pours through the walls of the church. If the service aims to "uplift" the festival, the festive sounds of street celebration threaten to drown out the attempt. One of the most popular New Testament readings at weddings, and part of the renewal service, is 1 Corinthians 13, Paul's meditative celebration of love. The first line reads, "If I speak in the tongues of men and of angels but have not love, I am a noisy gong or a clanging symbol." During the sermon, as the rising music and noise from outside compete with the action inside, the American pastor was moved to comment, "I was thinking while you were reading the Corinthians section about [the] gonging symbols that are outside of our church here. A little added emphasis for the Holy Scripture." A good-natured laugh rippled through the congregation, but the "gonging symbols" comment did not diffuse the palpable tension.

A few minutes later, during the middle of the sermon, the noise once again became a nuisance. The sermon's theme was that the good news of the gospel is the answer to dealing with whatever "crosses one's path." With the noise from outside crossing the path of the service, the pastor implicitly pitted the church and faith against the festive outdoor celebrations: "The church is a refuge, is a place where we can come and spend time with God and say to him, 'Help me deal with the rest of the world that crosses my path every single day.' [A world that] is loud and full of debauchery, and full of kinds of temptations out there that cross my path every single day." The Wedding festival does indeed become raucous, but characterizing it in terms of "debauchery"—synonyms for which include "wickedness," "corruption," "depravity," and "sin"—would be considered laughably puritanical by the vast majority attending the festival, including most German Lutherans. The pastor's comment had effectively turned the small group worshipping in the church into a bulwark against a sea of corruption outside, as the tone of the service became defensive. Meanwhile the outside noise continued to interfere with worship.[8]

A sure indicator that the Spielleute and other performers in the Marktplatz and Wittenberg's streets are not merely, or only, playing around is that not everyone is thrilled with the performers. Events in the Marktplatz streets and *Hofs* (courtyards) constitute the public face of both annual festivals, where cultural performances such as "A Beer for Martin" often bump into the attitudes and values embodied by liturgical and ceremonial rites, most of which generally take place indoors. In conversations with some local church members and Lutheran visitors to Wittenberg, I heard concerns expressed over the carnivalesque nature of both Reformation Day and Luther's

Wedding. One consultant, a trained pastor, associated the ethos of the "medieval Marktplatz" with a wider "medieval movement" afoot in German culture. She was referring to neopagan forms of spirituality that are present not only in Germany, but around the globe. An American visitor noted with contempt that in Wittenberg bars Halloween parties were taking place alongside Reformation Day celebrations. Another consultant, in response to a question about the role of the church in planning Luther's Wedding, made a distinction between a *Volksfest* and *Religion*: "Luthers Hochzeit," she said, "ist ein Volksfest. Es hat nichts mit religion zu tun" (Luther's Wedding is a folk's festival. It has nothing to do with religion). Lurking in the background of such critical comments is the old cultural tension in Protestant Europe: the relationship between the feast days of ecclesiastical religion and the ethos of Carnival, the "battle between Carnival and Lent." Contemporary Luther celebration is informed by a concern for "getting it straight." For some, Luther cannot simply be the occasion for celebration; rather a Luther festival ought to embody and project Lutheran values and a worldview.

SCENE 3: "CHANNELING WITH THE DEAD"

In May 2005, in the days leading up to the annual Luther's Wedding festival, many of the city's heritage sites were sprayed with graffiti, and the *Thesenportal* of the *Schlosskirche* commemorating the mythical-historical posting of the ninety-five theses, as well as Luther's monument in the Marktplatz, were hit with paint-bombs. Wittenberg residents woke the next morning to find a leaflet, supposedly from the Nationaldemokratische Partei Deutschlands (NPD), the right-wing, neo-Nazi party in Germany, announcing a rally in Wittenberg. The leaflet called for a "national procession" in Wittenberg's Marktplatz, in the context of Luther's importance to questions of national identity and the welfare of Germany's youth. According to a consultant who participated in politicized street theater a few days later in Wittenberg, the leaflet likely did not come from the NPD; more likely it was planted by those critical of the revitalization of the figure of Luther in order to stir up debate and controversy: "My hunch is that people who are critical of Luther put out the leaflet to call attention to the fact that the Nazis and Hitler himself found much in Luther to praise; they [National Socialists] saw themselves as fulfilling Luther's [anti-Semitic] ideas." Clearly there is more at work here than concern for historical memory.

In state elections in Saxony in September 2004 the neofascist NPD received 9.2 percent of the vote, just 0.5 percent less than the leading Social Democrats. New right parties also made gains in state elections in Thuringia and in elections for the European Parliament.[9] Through the 1990s the federal government made several unsuccessful attempts to ban *Neuerecht* (new right) parties such as the NPD. Far right ideologies, disseminated via websites, CDs, and rallies, are gaining a foothold in some schools and are being articulated by an increasing number of educated professionals and politicians who are slowly migrating from the fringe to the mainstream. In short the 2004 elections were something of a wake-up call for antifascist groups in Germany. One of the key principles and aims of the new right in Germany is the establishment of a *Volksgemeinschaft*, "a mythical society of the German people."[10] Historically Luther was instrumentalized for precisely such purposes.[11] In the context of rising neofascism leftist protesters are concerned about public and media events that uncritically elevate Luther to the status of a national culture hero.[12]

On the heels of the graffiti and the leaflet, members of a small theater group descended on Wittenberg for a street theater event. The performance, "Channeling the Dead: Today, Martin Luther" ("Channeling: Gespräch mit Toten. Heute: Dr. Martin Luther"), was held in the plaza in front of the *Thesenportal*. As often happens in Wittenberg, Luther was brought back to life through performance, only this performance did not portray the man as an ancestor or culture hero, but as an anti-Semite, a political conservative and reactionary, and a bigot. "Dr. Luther" was questioned through a loudspeaker, to which he responded with answers culled from his published works. A selective handling of the sources cast Luther in a less than favorable light. But the performance did get people talking. As my consultant commented, "Passersby got interested. They thought we had to something to do with the graffiti and paint-bombs . . . and wanted to talk with us. Many of them stood there and just shook their heads over the bullshit that Luther spewed out."[13]

Luther's Thesenportal is the most visited tourist destination in all of Lutherland. Used by the church as part of an annual confirmation event to encourage group identity among young Lutherans, the Thesenportal is an impressive setting for heritage tourism and theatrical performances. It has also been used as a site for the performative subversion of normative narratives. Several factors make the Theses Door a natural setting for protest and debate: the troubled nature of the figure of Luther in the wake of the World Wars and the Holocaust, the ubiquitous presence of cameras and media in Wittenberg during festival time, and the power of the portal to attract large numbers of visitors.

NEGOTIATION, THE CARNIVALESQUE, AND SOCIAL DRAMA

Applied to ritual, the term "negotiation" draws attention to the debates, reflexivity, and grievances—expressed in a shout, delivered with a glance, carried on a banner—that are generally present in diverse rites and cultural performances. In a narrower sense the term points to a ritual type, to a genre of rites grounded in processes of negotiation aimed at settling something: a Catholic papal election, a Northwest Coast potlatch, a *kaiko* pig festival in New Guinea, a nineteenth-century Yiddish wedding, a modern-day courtroom. The ritual frame of such negotiating rites must be flexible enough to allow for movement and shifting, yet solid enough to contain and ultimately to resolve differences: a pope must be elected; the parents must agree on a contract; the jury must deliver a verdict.

One ritual type that can be imagined as a flexible container is festivity, especially festivity characterized by the carnivalesque. Festivity sprawls across cultural domains in large-scale public gatherings that convene remarkable concentrations of diverse individuals and groups. Moreover festivals informed by the tradition of European Carnival include reflexivity, critique, experimentation, and play as integral features of the form. In a festival what is explicitly or implicitly acted out and/or debated one year may lead to changes the next, yet it will still be the same festival. If the frame is too tight, processual dynamics suffer, normativity rules, difference is elided, and schism may result; if too loose, there is nothing to carry or hold the social-cultural tension necessary to drive processes of negotiation. Festivity has been theorized as a "safety-valve" mechanism, a minor "rite of rebellion" that ultimately serves the needs of hierarchical power; is has also been described as a vehicle of critique, liberation, destruction, and renewal, a "second-life" of the people.[14] A more balanced view avoids the dualist either/or of these two theories, claiming that carnivalesque festivity is an arena or stage for the negotiation of identity, memory, beliefs, values, and political, economic, and sacred power.

Not only do certain ritual genres contribute to cultural and religious processes of negotiation, but the negotiating power of ritual and performance become especially important at certain social-historical moments, events Turner referred to as social drama. Turner describes social processes in terms of patterned, dramatic action. A social drama unfolds when there is a *breach* of normative modes of social life that, if not sealed off or addressed, can lead to a state of *crisis* capable of splitting the social fabric into two or more contending groups. In response to this situation *redressive* action arises. In general "redress" refers to any action evoked in response to social crisis, for instance, political debate, legal procedures, or military action. But Turner is particularly interested in the role of ritual and other genres of cultural performance as instruments of redress. Ritual and performance are potentially liminal and reflexive. They have the power to communicate about the communication system itself. Redressive ritual is potentially transformative because it allows "the contents of group experiences [to be] replicated, dismembered, remembered, refashioned, and mutely or vocally made meaningful."[15] If successful, redressive action leads to *reconciliation* and *reintegration*, but it may also serve to fuel a crisis and lead to recognition of an *irreparable breach*, with a radical restructuring of social relationships as the inevitable result. In either case redress involves a "clash between conserving and reforming parties."[16] Social drama is fraught with negotiating rites and performances; "redress" is Turner's term for negotiation.

A fine example of Turner's social drama is the Reformation. The drama of ritual and performance propelled the Reformation: there were protests in the streets, mock burnings of the pope, public debates, one of history's great trials (the Diet of Worms), the public burning of the papal bull calling for Martin Luther to recant, and the wedding of a defiant monk and an escaped nun (Luther and Katharina von Bora). Ultimately normative redressive efforts to contain the Reformation (through formal debates, threats, and trial) failed, while attempts at reconciliation and reintegration (ritual negotiations) ended in an irreparable breach (excommunication and schism).

During the Reformation the reflexive, critical, and transformative power of Carnival was put to good use. The historian Robert Scribner identified seventeen Carnival events during the pivotal years between 1520 and 1525, consisting of anti-Catholic processions, plays, street theater, and mock sermons. Pelting with dung a figure representing the pope, hunting the Carnival pope and bishops through the streets, performing Carnival plays ridiculing indulgences, a fiddler and lautist leading a relic procession consisting of the jawbone of a cow and two horse legs—these and other carnivalesque events were not merely reflections or symbols of anti-Catholic sentiment; they were the thing itself.[17] Carnival, in other words, was one of the means by which the Reformation turned the world upside down; in fact the Reformation was the world turned upside down.

DISCUSSION: THE EXILE AND RETURN OF THE CARNIVALESQUE

The contemporary fair and festival movement in Germany and other European countries, of which the Luther festivals are compelling examples, is influenced by the tradition of Carnival. Central to European social-cultural life in the late medieval and early modern eras, Carnival was performed prior to Lent, the period of fasting preceding the high liturgical Easter celebrations. The figure of Carnival, typically represented as a bawdy, beer-drinking, flesh-eating, rotund male surrounded by revelers, was pitted against Lent, a withered fish-eating hag surrounded by the pious aged. Carnival in the early modern era was characterized by three chief themes, "food, sex, and violence,"[18] which in turn stirred suspicion among clergy, nobility, and officials of the state. Carnival, the domain of the lower and middle classes, was the "world turned upside down," a time to invert gender roles and class structures, to impugn the haughtiness of religious and political elites, and to go ritually crazy—if only so as not to go actually crazy. Carnival emphasized masking, costuming, processions, the overconsumption of food and drink, and farcical plays and skits, music, revelry, and dance. The travesty, mockery, and indulgence of Carnival was regarded as a threat to the moral fiber by those holding the reins of temporal power, who knew that during Carnival the horses might run wild, that the ritualized violence that often accompanied Carnival could spill over the festival play frame.

In post-Reformation Europe, as the historian Peter Burke has shown, reformers of all stripes (Lutheran, Calvinist, and Catholic) took heavy aim at the practices of "simple folk":

> The reformers [mostly Protestant, but some Catholics] objected in particular to certain forms of popular religion, such as miracle and mystery plays, popular sermons, and, above all, religious festivals such as saint's days and pilgrimages. They also objected to a good many items of secular popular culture. . . . Actors,

> ballads, bear-baiting, bull-fights, cards, chap-books, charivaris, charlatans, dancing, dicing, divining, fairs, folktales, fortune-telling, magic, masks, minstrels, puppets, taverns and witchcraft. A remarkable number of these objectionable items could be found in combination at Carnival, so it is no surprise to find the reformers concentrating their attack at this point. . . . This cultural reformation was not confined to the popular, for the godly disapproved of all forms of play [including theater]. Yet one is left with [the] impression that it was popular recreations which bore the brunt of the attack. . . . What, according to the reformers, was wrong with popular culture? . . . In the first place, [as Erasmus explained] Carnival is "unchristian" because it contains "traces of ancient paganism." In the second place [again according to Erasmus] it is unchristian because on this occasion "the people over-indulges in licence."[19]

Carnival and other forms of popular culture and religion were sharply curtailed across much of Europe, especially Protestant Europe, by 1800. In Wittenberg at least what emerged in Carnival's place was ideologically driven political ceremony. Throughout the nineteenth century Prussian kings deliberately transformed the city into a symbolically significant place in the landscape of the modern German nation. Upon taking the throne Friedrich Wilhelm IV (1795–1861) announced his plans for the Schlosskirche, which had suffered extensive damage in 1760 during the Seven Years War and again during the Napoleonic Wars of 1813–14: "If it is no longer possible to restore the church to its original state, then I will focus on the Theses Door. This Door is a monument to Reformation history. Let us renew them in kind, poured in ore, and, just as Luther attached his 95 Theses, engrave the Theses on the Door in gold."[20]

In 1858 Friedrich's wishes were fulfilled, and the bronze Thesenportal was installed in a ceremony on Reformation Day, the year coinciding with Luther's 375th birthday. Kaiser Wilhelm I (1797–1888) and Kaiser Wilhelm II (1859–1941) would pursue Friedrich's vision for the city with large statues of Luther and Melanchthon in the Marktplatz, the conversion of Luther's former home into a museum (the Lutherhalle or Lutherhaus, opened in 1883), and further costly renovations to the Schlosskirche, which were finally completed in 1892. Under the kaisers Wittenberg became hallowed, ceremonial ground. Indeed Kaiser Wilhelm II spared no expense in making the 1892 *Reformationsfest* something to remember. The highest officials from the Evangelical Church attended, as did members of the German parliament. Wilhelm personally invited the queens of England and Holland and the kings of Denmark and Sweden. The kaiser made his way in a procession from Wittenberg's train station to the Schlosskirche, taking his throne on a large stage built for the occasion and positioned with a view to the Thesenportal. After listening to numerous speeches and sermons, he gave permission for the key ceremony to begin. The architect of the portal came forward carrying the golden key on a cushion. The kaiser stepped down and, in front of the doors given to the church by his ancestor, Frederick IV, with Germany's and Europe's political, economic, and religious elite looking on, passed the key on to the president of the Evangelical (Lutheran) Church, who received it with hyperbolic deference: "Your

Highness, greatest of Kaisers and Kings, most merciful gentleman! With deep reverence and thanks I take the key from your noble hands."[21] The Schlosskirche was the church that Luther built; at the 1892 celebration the church became the emperor's too. Two cultural domains and social institutions—religion and politics—were fused.

Such ceremonial rites make little room for processes of negotiation. Rather the mood is officious, the narrative sharply ideological, the aim to compel, not mediate and negotiate, group assent. "Ceremony symbolizes respect for the offices, histories, and causes that are condensed into its gestures, objects, and actions"; it "invites [I would say demands] the participant to surrender idiosyncrasies and independence to some larger cause, for which one is willing to fight, to die, or pay homage."[22]

In nineteenth-century Germany, Carnival—the mood of which is anything but ceremonious—persisted in small pockets in the primarily Catholic southwest while virtually disappearing in the Protestant northeast. France invaded southern Germany in 1794, and the Prussians invaded from the northeast in 1815, and, like the church before them, these state powers worked to suppress Carnival. Carnival became institutionalized and partly secularized in the southwest through the founding of Carnival societies (*Vereine*), but in the Nazi era Carnival all but disappeared or was employed strictly for ideological purposes, for cross-dressing, satire, parody, masking, and transgression were targets for the Nazis. Similarly in communist-controlled East Germany Carnival was banned.[23] In the second half of the twentieth century, however, the carnivalesque returned to European popular culture, and more recently to Wittenberg, the heartland of German Protestantism. Costuming, satire, mockery, fools, masks, inversion, theatrical skits in the streets, farces, folktales, dances, drum and pipe music, long hair, boots, buckles, and beer—this is standard fare at both Luther's Wedding and Reformation Day. Though the festivals have liturgical and ceremonial dimensions, it is the carnivalesque that dominates.

Frank Manning, writing in the early 1980s, claimed, "Throughout both the industrialized and developing nations, new celebrations are being created and older ones revived on a scale that is surely unmatched in human history."[24] Manning may have been overstating the case, but there is evidence that festive celebration in Europe and North America has experienced a renaissance.[25] Why is carnivalesque festivity reviving?

Typically this question receives two different answers. First, festival renewal is a response to modernity: feelings of placelessness and the loss of tradition; secularization and the inability of the church to serve as a center for collective identity; the shrinking of social life to the family and workplace; the loss of seasonal rites that accompany the shift from agriculture to industry; and the attempt of urban populations to get back, however metaphorically, to roots and the land. Second, festivals are understood as examples of the commoditization of culture: Lutherland functions as a kind of Disneyland or Reformation-era theme park, packaged and sold to the omnivorous gaze and stuffed wallets of the consumer-tourist. While each of these answers has merit, they are also limited. Festival culture is more than nostalgia or a cog in the economic flywheel. The *Wende* is a social drama that is still playing itself out, as the former East tries to find its footing in the new Germany. In Wittenberg Luther festivity is a vehicle for processes of redress, a way of "submitting culture to observability." Festivity is the embodiment of conviviality, a broadening and deepening of an engaged public sphere, and a time for ludic, subjunctive play—all necessities in the creation of new social forms and relationships.

Burke's list of what Reformers and others rejected in popular culture shared the common denominator of mimetic behavior: dressing up, masking, puppets, charlatans, mystery plays, magic, role-playing. People are doing these things once again—the return of the repressed—in the Wittenberg festivals' mimetic play. Schechner writes about "twice-behaved behavior" or "restored behavior." "Restored behavior is symbolic and reflexive" and comes down to a single principle: "the self can act in/as another. . . . Restored behavior offers to both individuals and groups the chance to rebecome what they once were—or even, and most often, to rebecome what they never were but wish to become."[26] Reformation-themed festivity in Wittenberg reenacts what the Reformation would ultimately do away with, what the people, who for centuries now have located their origins in Luther and the Reformation, never were but wish to become: actors in the "battle" between Carnival and Lent that defined Carnival in the early modern era. Wittenbergers "actually relive" a pivotal historical-mythical moment in and through mimetic performance—not photographic replication but streaming metaphors and metonyms; not magic by likeness but magic by contact and contagion. Spielleute mock priests and nuns, they turn the everyday man in the street into Martin Luther, and vice versa. Meanwhile the pious complain about drums and pipes, a "medieval movement" in the Marktplatz, the contamination of Reformation Day with Halloween celebrations, and try to uplift Luther's Wedding in a renewal of vows ceremony while the sounds outside disrupt the service. Processions elevate and dignify Luther, as street theater criticizes and mocks him. Luther has become the occasion for a kind of modern, secularized magic that drums and dances into being the spirit of a lost world.

Peter Burke sees the battles between Carnival and Lent performed in the streets at the height of Carnival season as "two rival ethics or ways of life in open conflict." Shored up on the side of Lent were the values of "decency, diligence, gravity, modesty, orderliness, prudence, reason, self-control, sobriety, and thrift, or to use a phrase made famous by Max Weber, 'this-worldly asceticism.' . . . [This] ethic of the reformers was in conflict with a traditional ethic which is harder to define because it was less articulate, but which involved more stress on the values of generosity and spontaneity and a greater tolerance of disorder."[27] In short Wittenberg's festivals are an occasion for ordered disorderliness. Ironically the city's fame as a site of Lutheran heritage, a tradition that once rejected popular culture, is now the site of festive celebration informed by the traditions of poplar culture that thrived at the time of Reformation.

Festivals are commonly understood as times of expressive joy, but they are also a periodic and temporary agonistic framing of social-cultural life. The streets and plazas become a giant game board as the game's principals and pawns simultaneously cooperate and compete for the public's eye and ear. The aim of the game is to project one's own values, worldview, concerns, and beliefs. As Roger Callios notes, the goal of agonistic play or games is for players to assert and to be recognized for their "superiority," while also recognizing the friendliness of the game frame.[28] During the game we respectfully compete, even beat each other up; after the game we shake hands and go for a beer. By competing we may even arrive at mutual respect and understanding; we may, to use the lingo of popular psychology, bond. A festival creates a bounded cultural space and time that allows for the articulation of both difference and unity, debate and solidarity, criticism and jubilation.

One of the defining characteristics of the genre of spectacle is the presence of a sharp distinction between audience and performers. John MacAloon writes, "Spectacles institutionalize the bicameral roles of actors and audience, performers and spectators. Both role sets are normative, organically linked, and necessary to the performance." A spectacle is also something primarily watched or observed. The actors perform the event, the spectators watch—at a distance. In festivity, in contrast, everyone is called to celebrate together. Watching is part of festival action, but only a part. Finally, to name an event a spectacle is to introduce a certain suspicion or criticism, as in "He is making a spectacle of himself." A festival is different. Rather than generating a sense of diffuse awe and wonder, emotions that captivate while distancing the spectator from the action (think of gladiatorial games), festivals are joyous occasions, or are meant to be so. The "genres of spectacle and festival are often differently valenced. While we happily anticipate festivals, we are suspicious of spectacles, associating them with potential tastelessness and moral cacophony."[29] The French sociologist Guy Debord argues that modernity is a "society of the spectacle," which is to say, "an epoch without festivals."[30] The distinction here is between the production of spectacle by elites for nationalist, consumptive-commercial purposes and a more organic, cyclical domain of festivity that emerges from a people's productive labor and full participation. In Wittenberg participation is a key feature and aim of public festivals.

CONCLUSION

Festivals are a form of mimetic play incorporating dress-up, masquerading, role-playing, and travesty. The effectiveness of such mimicry relies on both the abilities of the performer and the willingness of the spectator to suspend disbelief, thereby entering into the spirit of the *Spiel*.[31] Mimetic play is inherently ambiguous, and the creation of ambiguity is a necessary element in successful negotiation. What mimicry negotiates is identity. Mimetic play is a way of displaying one's being in the world, while exposing the perceived vices and follies of particular others. Mimicry provides for the possibility of recognition, identification, and sympathy, but also dissonance, derision, and even fear.[32]

By copying or imitating, writes Walter Benjamin, "a palpable, sensuous connection between the very body of the perceiver and the perceived" is made possible.[33] Becoming something other than what one is, is the heart of mimetic behavior. For this reason, as far back as Plato mimesis has provoked both fascination and enmity since it disrupts a stable ontology and an Aristotelian epistemology in which A is A precisely because it can never be B.

Festivals are magical. Magic is contact, producing an effect, making a connection to something or someone through mimetic behavior. Magic is a power that a copy extracts from an original, or the power a copy has to influence or infect the original; magic thus involves a relationship between self and other, which is why Michael Taussig, following Benjamin and Adorno, connects mimesis with alterity. Just how mimesis establishes a connection to others is, of course, a complex question; psychological, social, cultural, and biological factors are all involved. In Wittenberg at least, as part of the effort to deal with the problems and prospects of reunification, people are dressing up as their ancestors, enacting foundational myths of the city and region, and re-creating a medieval world on the verge of tipping into the modern. And they do so out of a sense that all this will somehow make a difference. Luther festivity in Wittenberg involves negotiations among participants, but it also negotiates a complex relationship with the past through mimetically re-presenting and reconstituting aspects of that past. We might call this transformation magical. It certainly is not, in the language of Clifford Geertz, "commonsensical"—it is not ordinary, everyday behavior—which is to say that the quotidian world leaves something to be desired, and magic, above all, is driven by desire.

Notes

1. This chapter is based on fieldwork conducted in and around Wittenberg on four separate occasions in 2004–6. The project focused on Protestant pilgrimage, religious and heritage tourism, and Luther-themed festivity. The research was funded through a postdoctoral fellowship granted by the Canadian Social Sciences and Humanities Research Council.

2. Moreover a subtle allusion is likely at play. It is common in Germany to ascribe to Luther the query, supposedly posed to his guests after a large meal, "Why don't you burp and fart? Did you not like the food?"

3. See Schechner, *Performance Theory*, 129–36. Since the pioneering work of Victor Turner ritual has been largely understood as a potential motor for transformative social processes, whereas games, theater, and music tend to be viewed primarily as forms of entertainment (though avant-garde and experimental theater attempt to push back in the other direction).

4. Ferre, "The Definition of Religion," 11. Citizens of the former East Germany are still developing the willingness to engage in public criticism. "A Beer for Martin" embodies critical values; it is playful, but also serious work.

5. Sylvia is a member of the performance group Scharlatan, based out of Leipzig. On the road for several months of the year, Spielleute around Germany animate public festivals with their antics, music, and street theater.

6. The two main wings of North American Lutheranism are the Evangelical Lutheran Church of America and the Lutheran Church Missouri Synod. The Missouri Synod is the smaller of the two and theologically, socially, and liturgically more conservative. There are tensions between the two groups in America—over issues such as ordination of women, same-sex marriage, and ecumenical communion practices—and these tensions are brought back to Wittenberg, the homeland of Lutheranism.

7. The historical Reformation was not only a theological and political revolution. The Reformers also revolutionized sexuality, arguing against clerical celibacy and advocating married life as a thoroughly godly institution. The Reformers' writings against celibacy and monasticism led many to leave their convents and monasteries. Katharina von Bora arrived in Wittenberg in 1523; she and several other nuns were smuggled out of the convent in wine and fish barrels. In 1525 she and Luther were married, an act that shocked many of Luther's friends and colleagues. In the nineteenth century Luther and Katie became the paradigm of married and family life in Prussian, patriarchal Germany.

8. In retrospect the extra-ecclesiastical celebrating could have been interpreted in terms of Psalm 100—people shouting for joy, praising with joyful songs—but it was not.

9. The federal states of Saxony and Thuringia are the heartland of Lutheran Germany.

10. Brinks "Germany's New Right," 125.

11. "Immediately after 1945 the Reformer Martin Luther, and with him often German Lutheranism in general, were seen in certain circles as one of the spiritual roots of national socialism. Luther had helped, so his critics argued, to prepare the mentality structures, especially the servility towards the state, which had resulted in the creation of the Third Reich" (Brinks, "Luther and the German State," 1).

12. In November 2003 the national broadcaster Zweites Deutsches Fernsehen asked Germans to vote for the greatest German of all time. The event was called "Our Best" ("Unser Besten"), and when the votes were tallied Martin Luther stood in second place. Around this same time a new motion picture, *Luther*, funded by Lutheran Thrivent, a financial company, played in Europe and North America. The film has been criticized for its uncritical depiction of Luther as a heroic figure.

13. My consultant, Jörg, is a member of Projekt Werkstatt (Project Workshop), a nationwide group of social activists of the political left. Direct action is one of the guiding principles of the group, whose members are actively engaged in taking their positions and protests to the street, using a variety of means, including what Richard Schechner refers to as "guerilla theatre."

14. Ritual as "safety valve" or "rite of rebellion" is associated with the thought of Max Gluckman, who argues that a controlled, ritualized, periodic public display of social-political tension and conflict serves the interests of social-political hierarchy and stability. Mikhail Bakhtin, in contrast, sees festivity, especially Carnival, as an instrument of social criticism and empowerment.

15. Turner associates ritual (in a strict sense) with liminality, reflexivity, and a subjunctive mood: "Liminality can perhaps be described as a fructile chaos, a fertile nothingness, a storehouse of possibilities, not by any means a random assemblage but a striving after new forms and structure, a gestation process, a fetation of modes appropriate to and anticipating postliminal existence" ("Are There Universals of Performance in Myth, Ritual, and Drama?," 12–13). Normative, traditional forms of ritualized action Turner refers to as *ceremony*, which serves to structure social relations that mirror the status quo. A broad definition of ritual would include both ritual as liminal and potentially transformative and ceremony as normative and conservative.

16. Turner, *From Ritual to Theatre*, 109.

17. Scribner, influenced by the work of Mikhail Bakhtin and Natalie Davis, sees the Reformation-era carnivalesque as flowing "out of the second life of the people . . . seek[ing] to expose and degrade the values and style of official culture, to submit it to observability" (*Popular Culture and Popular Movements in Reformation Germany*, 93).

18. Burke, *Popular Culture in Early Modern Europe*, 186.

19. Ibid., 208–9. The excerpt here is from Burke's chapter "The Triumph of Lent: The Reform of Popular Culture."

20. Quoted in Schröder, "Die Baugestalt und das Raumprogramm des Berliner Doms als Spiegel der Ansprüche und Funktionen des Bauherrn Kaiser Wilhelms II," 144.

21. Quoted in ibid., 142.

22. Grimes, *Beginnings in Ritual Studies*, 47–48.

23. See McMahon, "The Aesthetics of Play in Reunified Germany's Carnival."

24. Manning, *The Celebration of Society*, 4. Frank E. Manning was professor of anthropology at the University of Western Ontario. His work focused on the study of popular and public culture.

25. See Boissevain, *Revitalizing European Rituals*, a collection of case studies on the revitalization of traditional celebrations across Europe.

26. Schechner, *Between Theatre and Anthropology*, 36–38.

27. Burke, *Popular Culture in Early Modern Europe*, 213.

28. Callois, *Man, Play and Games*, 15.

29. MacAloon, *Rite, Drama, Festival, Spectacle*, 243–46.

30. Debord, *The Society of the Spectacle*, 113.

31. "Mimicry is incessant invention. The rule of the game is unique: it consists in the actor's fascinating the spectator, while avoiding an error that might lead the spectator to break the spell. The spectator must lend himself to the illusion without first challenging the decor, mask, or artifice which for a given time he is asked to believe in as more real than itself" (Callois, *Man, Play and Games*, 23).

32. The original Greek meaning of "mimesis," according to Walter Benjamin and Theodor Adorno, consists of "making *oneself* similar to an other." See Cahn, "Subversive Mimesis," 34.

33. Benjamin, "The Work of Art," cited in Taussig, *Mimesis and Alterity*, 20–21.

Bibliography

Boissevain, Jeremy, ed. *Revitalizing European Rituals*. New York: Routledge, 1992.

Brinks, Jan Herman. "Germany's New Right." In *Nationalist Myths and the Modern Media*, ed. Jan Herman Brinks et al., 125–38. London: I. B. Tauris, 2005.

———. "Luther and the German State." *Heythrop Journal* 39, no. 1 (1998): 1–17.

Burke, Peter. *Popular Culture in Early Modern Europe*. New York: Harper Torchbooks, 1978.

Cahn, Michael Cahn. "Subversive Mimesis: Theodore W. Adorno and the Modern Impasse of Critique." In *Mimesis in Contemporary Theory: An Interdisciplinary Approach*, ed. Mihai Spariosu, 27–64. Philadelphia: John Benjamin, 1984.

Callios, Roger. *Man, Play and Games*. Champaign: University of Illinois Press, 2001.

Debord, Guy. *The Society of the Spectacle*. New York: Zone Books, 1995.

Ferre, Frederick. "The Definition of Religion." *Journal of the American Academy of Religion* 38, no. 1 (1970): 3–16.

Grimes, Ronald L. *Beginnings in Ritual Studies*. Columbia: University of South Carolina Press, 1995.

MacAloon, John, ed. *Rite, Drama, Festival, Spectacle: Rehearsals toward a Theory of Cultural Performance*. Philadelphia: Institute for the Study of Human Issues, 1984.

Manning, Frank E. *The Celebration of Society: Perspectives on Contemporary Cultural Performance*. Bowling Green, OH: Bowling Green University Press, 1983.

McMahon, Felicia Faye. "The Aesthetics of Play in Reunified Germany's Carnival." *Journal of American Folklore* 113, no. 450 (2000): 378–90.

Schechner, Richard. *Between Theatre and Anthropology*. Philadelphia: University of Pennsylvania Press, 1985.

———. *Performance Theory*. New York: Routledge, 2003.

Schröder, Jochen. "Die Baugestalt und das Raumprogramm des Berliner Doms als Spiegel der Ansprüche und Funktionen des Bauherrn Kaiser Wilhelms II." PhD diss., University of Marburg, 2003.

Scribner, Robert. *Popular Culture and Popular Movements in Reformation Germany*. London: Hambledon Press, 1987.

Taussig, Michael. *Mimesis and Alterity*. New York: Routledge, 1993.

Turner, Victor. "Are There Universals of Performance in Myth, Ritual, and Drama?" In *By Means of Performance: Intercultural Studies of Theatre and Ritual*, ed. Richard Schechner and Willa Appel, 8–18. Cambridge: Cambridge University Press, 1991.

———. *From Ritual to Theatre: The Human Seriousness of Play*. New York: Performing Arts Journal Publications, 1982.

5

Negotiating Rites in Imperial China

THE CASE OF NORTHERN SONG COURT RITUAL DEBATES FROM 1034 TO 1093

Christian Meyer

INTRODUCTION: THE CONCEPT AND RELEVANCE OF CHINESE RITUAL (*LI*, 禮)

IN IMPERIAL CHINA (221 BCE–1911 CE) the concept of *li* (禮), translated here as "rite" or "ritual," played a major role in Chinese thinking. In encyclopedias such as the Tang Dynasty (618–907) work *Tongdian*, the chapters on *li* alone comprise one hundred of its two hundred chapters (*juan*, 卷).[1] Furthermore ritual (*li*) has been called one of the three major discourses in traditional China in addition to *xiao* (孝, filial piety) and *wen* (文, text, culture, literature).[2] An important preliminary question, then, is what the Chinese term *li* means. While the explanation of the graph is not fully clear (although it probably indicates a sacrificial vessel), the traditional concept of *li* has at least three basic meanings: (1) concrete, standardized symbolic actions such as sacrifices and offerings to spirits, gods, or ancestors, as well as more or less profane (in a Western sense) ritualized ceremonies such as visits or local meetings that feature bowing and a detailed standardized order or sacrifices (as part of banquets); (2) concrete, normative patterns of behavior, including ethical patterns that almost always imply complementary, hierarchical roles practiced in normal, obedient behavior but also in more ritualized ways, as described in (1),[3] and after parents' death in ancestral service to them; and (3) ritual as an abstract, comprehensive principle, general norm, or virtue, as, for example, the standard against which behavior is judged in the classic *Zuozhuan* (i.e., as "against *li*," *feili*, 非禮), or a concept ranked together with humanity (*ren*, 仁), wisdom (*zhi*, 智), and other virtues.[4] Note that the first two categories denote different types of concrete actions (symbolic and ethical), while the third represents an abstraction, principle, or virtue. Significantly the characteristics of *li* were not restricted to religious "rituals" as communication with gods or spirits; indeed following its later dominant ethical implication, *li* has also been translated as "decorum" or "propriety."[5] On the other hand, *li* has never lost its connection to concrete sacrifices and other major symbolic actions such as ancestral rites, sacrifices to heaven at the imperial level, or detailed local and family rites on the lower levels.[6]

In any case the term *li* was never strictly descriptive but implied normative rules, which were nevertheless debatable on the basis of more fundamental standards.[7] As early as the late pre-Qin time (until 221 BCE i.e., before the imperial era) Chinese thinkers had speculated about the psychological and natural base or necessity of the norms of *li*.[8] Because human relations played a major role in concrete rituals, ritual came to be seen as primarily a human matter; even sacrifices to gods or (ancestral) spirits were interpreted as primarily relevant to the moral formation of the human agent performing the sacrifice,[9] to the point that assuming the existence of superhuman beings did not appear to be necessary. However, although the pedagogical aspect always played a major role, other Confucians continued to maintain the idea of a real existence of superhuman beings as objects of veneration.[10]

It is one of the stereotypes of Chinese history that the foundations of China's intellectual, social, and political system were established in antiquity and remained largely unchanged thereafter. However, if that were the case, later negotiation of rituals would have made little sense. An examination of the Song Dynasty shows that Chinese ritual was a matter of permanent negotiation, never a set of rules fixed once and for all. This dynamic of negotiating remained true despite the fact that the Confucian canon, which provided the most important and detailed rules and data for rituals, had already been basically defined in the early imperial time and constituted the matrix of all later performance.[11] Why, then, were ritual matters often fiercely discussed in later ages? The following contextualizing analysis reveals how and why Chinese scholars, politicians, and even rulers debated about ritual and what was actually negotiated in these discussions.

NORTHERN SONG DEBATES BETWEEN 1034 AND 1093

In the time of the Song Dynasty we find not only clearly defined canonical scriptures as bases for discussions on ritual, but also rich records of ritual discussions. The period of the middle Northern Song especially provides much material along these lines, probably due to a stronger emphasis on Confucian values than was the case in both earlier and later periods.[12] Two cases from this period,[13] the case of "correcting ritual music" and "the debate of addressing the Prince of Pu," serve to illustrate this point.

The Case of "Correcting Ritual Music" (zheng yayue 正雅樂)

Ritual music (*yayue*), especially the question of the basic tone pitch, had been a matter of permanent negotiation from the early beginnings of the Song Dynasty (960–1279). In contrast to the banquet court music and ordinary, popular music, ritual music was the exclusive accompaniment to the imperial sacrifice to heaven or the ancestors. This music was highly charged symbolically, involving a full set of symbolic devices such as the correct pitch of the fundamental note with the associated bell (the "yellow bell," *huangzhong* 黄鍾); the music also had political implications by virtue of the fact that it legitimized the emperor as the exclusive performer of the sacrifice.

The early emperor Taizu decided in 966 to choose a lower basic pitch for the hymns of imperial ritual music, probably according to his personal predilection, but a practical matter in 1034—the disastrous state of the bells—brought up the question again. The bells had been painted over for ornamentation several times and some had even cracked. However, instead of simply repairing them or recasting new ones, one official, Li Zhao (李照), made the matter a more fundamental issue. Li Zhao, who probably had at least some musical expertise and saw his chance to distinguish himself in order to further his career in the Chinese imperial bureaucracy, based his argument for a lower basic pitch as well as different instrumentation on the ancient classics and earlier historical accounts of the Han Dynasty (202 BCE–220 CE). Still his project eventually failed and his alterations were again revised due to disagreements on the committee, distractions caused by rising border tensions with the Xixia kingdom, and the likely unsatisfactory performance of the new bells.

In the 1050s two other scholars, Hu Yuan (胡瑗, 993–1059) and Ruan Yi (阮逸), took another approach. After the emperor had officially called for musical experts, the scholars were recommended and summoned to court in 1035 to an ad hoc committee (a special administrative instrument of the earlier Northern Song Dynasty until 1082), where they were to examine and possibly revise the pitch pipes made by Li Zhao in the 1030s. Hu Yuan and Ruan Yi developed a new theory for reconstructing the shape and sound of ancient bells according to measures mentioned in the classics and historical accounts.[14] their approach, however, ultimately failed like Li Zhao's before them, partly because reconstructing the bells based only on descriptions in the classical records proved an apparently impossible task at that time.[15] Furthermore another scholar-official, Fan Zhen (范鎮, 1008–88), who was not a musical expert but held the position of censor, criticized the experts' approach, basing his own interpretation on another version of the same basic historical account.[16] Later, in the 1080s, he joined a group of more pragmatic scholar-officials on an ad hoc committee whose opinion was that music should primarily match the human voice (*rensheng*, 人聲). This view represented a very flexible approach to the problem, thereby differing from the earlier "orthodox" solutions based on classical precedent. Fan's chance for testing his own ideas came only in 1088, after a major political shift, when he was allowed to cast his bells, build his instruments, and have them presented to the reigning empress dowager. Even so, his type of music seems never to have been used in ritual afterward.[17]

The Debate of Addressing the Prince of Pu ("Puyi", 濮議)

A second revealing example is that of the "Puyi" debate (*yi,* 議), about how best to address the prince (*wang,* 王) of the fief of Pu (濮), the biological father of the new emperor, Yingzong (英宗, reigned 1063–67) and a cousin of the previous emperor.[18] This particular case shows to what extent the term *li* represents standards of Confucian ethical behavior, measured according to relational, hierarchical patterns.[19] The filial relationship to parents (*xiao*) was one of the major aspects of *li* that had to be embodied in suitable behavior. While it was basically clear how to behave toward and address one's biological parents (in contrast to addressing one's uncles, etc.), the case grew much more complicated if a son was adopted. This relationship involved not only a legal but also a ritual aspect in that all patterns of behavior in interpersonal relations, including terms of address, had to be reconsidered. In the special instance of the adopted son actually being emperor, the case constituted a critical matter for the entire state. Apart from the question of legal legitimization, this case became a question of the ritual-ethical credibility of the adopted successor; the emperor was generally regarded as a role model for the whole country, and through his behavior as a filial son, especially an adopted son, he had to prove his worthiness. Moreover the incorrect title and form of address might also have interfered with the order of the imperial ancestral shrine.[20]

The main questions in the Puyi case were as follows: Could the adopted son still maintain a special relationship with his biological father, even addressing him as "(deceased) father" (*kao,* 考), the same term the son would use to address his adoptive father? Alternatively should the son instead address his biological father as "uncle"? Or would that violate "natural human feeling" (*renqing*), as some argued? In the case of the adopted emperor Yingzong, the government sided with the emperor and supported addressing the biological father as "imperial deceased father" (*huangkao,* 皇考) or, in a later, toned-down version, at least as "parent" (*qin,* 親).[21] The other party in the debate—the clear majority of censors, but also supposedly a majority of officials—fiercely opposed this position as questioning the unique and exclusive honor of the father and the emperor; opponents argued that, just as there could be only one sun in the sky, there could be only one ruler over the empire and only one father.[22] The elevated, quasi-religious dignity of not only the family and its order but also of the state seemed to be at stake. Eventually the less emphatic option of addressing the biological father as "parent" (*qin*) was chosen. Even so, ritual announcements were never performed by the emperor in person (but rather by officials and descendants of the Prince of Pu),[23] and the Prince of Pu, Yingzong's biological father, was never inducted into the imperial ancestral shrine (*taimiao,* 太廟), as opponents had feared. Thus this case not only bore political consequences but also raised important ideological-hermeneutical questions regarding a more or less flexible approach to ritual.

PATTERNS: CONTEXTUALIZING THE RITUAL DEBATES

These two cases reveal markedly different aspects or motivations behind their respective negotiating positions. Clearly these matters were not just cases of different "beliefs." The concept of *li* cannot be clearly separated from political or sociological matters, just as the idea of religion as a sphere beyond or apart from the secular and political did not exist in traditional, especially Confucian China. But parallel to the dignity of the classics with their socioethical message, which served as a source of Confucian ethical and ritual ideas, rituals were also deemed of higher value in constructing interrelational meaning and in embodying that meaning concretely. Although they are interrelated, it is useful to distinguish three levels of negotiations: (1) of imperial power, (2) of bureaucratic power, and (3) of personal and intellectual convictions.

Negotiating Imperial Power: Ritual, Legitimacy, and the Role of the Emperor

Although both cases show the importance of imperial legitimization, the emperors' role could appear quite different depending on the matter in question, personal character, or interest. In the long period from the 1030s to the early 1060s we find Emperor Renzong (仁宗, reigned 1033–63) especially interested in the question of music. New standards for ritual music could not only have immortalized his name,[24] but also legitimized his power, both visibly and audibly, at a time when he had to justify having deposed his first wife as empress (née Guo, 郭). With respect to the question of ritual music, officials basically tried to cooperate with the emperor while competing with one other in offering the best solution. But in the Puyi case a majority of officials, except those in the government, opposed the ruler's wish because they allegedly feared that his ritual plans would endanger his moral legitimacy. In other words, moral norms of behavior that were defined by the Confucian classics effectively put the Confucian scholar-officials in a position of power that in turn enabled them to criticize and restrict the emperor.

Negotiating Bureaucratic Power: Ritual Debates and the So-Called Faction Struggles

Another aspect of ritual debates was competition among officials themselves. The notorious struggles of factions (*pengdang*, 朋黨) of the Northern Song Dynasty provide an important underlying pattern for both cases; in the period from 1034 to the end of the Northern Song Dynasty (960–1126) there were several constellation changes in these struggles. While they were connected to political and ideological positioning, these struggles may also be regarded as effects of the complex antithetical structure of

Chinese bureaucratic institutions in Song times, as well as by-products of intergenerational conflict. An additional factor also partly connected to faction struggles was interest in promoting or safeguarding one's career.

The most important institutional elements that allowed relatively open discussion lay in the rule that officials were generally encouraged to freely express suggestions, even criticize the government. In addition there were censors, whose particular responsibility it was to criticize officials at different levels, including the government and even the ruler. This arrangement often allowed for the formation of two groups comparable to a ruling party and an opposition based on the institutions of state council (government) and censorship. Another institutional characteristic conducive to lively court debate was the possibility of the emperor's summoning ad hoc committees (at least this was the case until a major administrative reform in 1080). Both instruments put the emperor in the comfortable position of standing above conflicts and deciding between opinions put forth by groups of officials once arguments and majorities had become substantially clear. Thus he could avoid getting caught up in the details—a situation that worked, provided the person in question was not the emperor himself.

The influence of faction struggles on ritual discussions becomes even more telling when these debates are related directly to one other. The first reform group under Fan Zhongyan (范仲淹, 989–1052) succeeded in seizing power in the 1040s and, after a backlash, regained key positions and influence in the 1050s; the first music debate in the 1030s took place while this faction was taking shape. Indeed some officials on the committee, such as Feng Yuan (馮元, 975–1037) and Song Xiang (宋祁, 998–1061) can be identified as partisans of Fan. In the 1050s the musical and classical expert Hu Yuan was, by virtue of his personal networks, clearly connected to the faction of Fan and Ouyang Xiu. Indeed the promotion of his bells' cast and musical project in the early 1050s matches the gradual re-ascendency of their group. In the 1060s the Puyi case took place when the group around Ouyang Xiu and Han Qi had become the establishment, serving as state councilors. While the Puyi struggle dealt with the role of the emperor in relation to his biological father, the target of direct attacks by both the censors and administrative officials was the state councilors who had allegedly influenced the emperor. These officials, including the famous politician and historian Sima Guang (司馬光, 1019–86), were mainly representatives of a younger generation; some in fact had originally been recommended by the very councilors the young officials now attacked. In fact a partial explanation for the struggle is that the councilors, who at that point had already held high governmental positions for a long time, were seen as blocking the careers of younger, ambitious officials. The latter's frustrations resulted in especially harsh attacks. In this case, then, a ritual question was not only connected to major factional struggles but also constituted a major reason for the formation of political front lines.

But Sima Guang was only one representative of the younger generation. After the withdrawal of the old government in the late 1060s a new group of reformers under Wang Anshi (王安石, 1021–86) dominated the government for more than a decade. Ritual music debates were again featured in factional struggles between the dominant "reform group" and their "conservative" opponents, led by Sima Guang (ca. 1080). After the death of Emperor Shenzong (神宗, reigned 1067–85) the constellation changed again. Only now could Fan Zhen, friend of the new chancellor Sima Guang, present his version of musical instruments in 1088.

From an individual, utilitarian perspective, ritual debates were relevant not only to group interests but also to personal careers. Ritual matters such as ritual music (*yayue*) were prestigious, offering the chance to make a name for oneself as an expert or as the successful leader of a project. Furthermore bold criticism as a censor, as well as networking and distinguishing oneself through ritual matters, could help promote one's career.

Negotiating Personal and Intellectual Convictions

Factional struggles and ritual positions were also related to intellectual positions and movements. This first reform group of the 1030s to 1060s was very much connected to the Guwen (古文) movement, which propagated a "return to antiquity" and its institutions (*fugu,* 復古) and therefore a reorientation toward the canonical scriptures and their ancient style (*guwen*). One of this group's leading intellectual figures was Ouyang Xiu, and Hu Yuan's attempt at reconstructing the ancient bells was in accordance with these ideals.

The next struggle, the Puyi, although partly a generational conflict, also revealed deeply differing positions. While all participants in the struggle shared the ideal of returning to antiquity, the government's position, and that of its leading figure, Ouyang Xiu, emphasized the principle of "natural human feelings" (*renqing*) as a basis for understanding ritual norms in the classics, thereby allowing the expression of the emperor's personal feelings toward his biological father. Sima Guang's ideological position was much stricter, contending that adoption meant a radical break with former kin relationships. According to him, the classical idea of rituals (*li*) expressing "natural human feelings" (*renqing*) should not be interpreted so as to allow changes of classical norms due merely to personal circumstances.

In the following generation positions diversified yet again. The argument dividing Wang Anshi, state councilor and chancellor since 1069, and his main opponent, Sima Guang, was not only about practical matters of reform but also the interpretation of the classics. However, ritual matters did not loom large in their exchanges. Decisions in the later ritual music debate around 1080 may have been much more influenced by general power constellations and networks than ideological arguments applied to ritual music. The change of government in 1085 was mirrored in the matter of ritual music, when Fan Zhen could now use his good relations with the new leaders to test and present his ideas about music. Still this case also demonstrates how positions in ritual questions could diverge within a given political faction, as Sima Guang held a different view on music than did his friend Fan Zhen.[25]

The diverging interpretive patterns of ritual found in the Puyi case continued within the conservative group after the early death of the leading figure, Sima Guang, in 1086.

Representatives on one side included Cheng Yi (程頤, 1033–1107), who had supported Sima Guang in the Puyi case, and on the other the Su brothers, Su Shi (蘇軾, 1037–1101, also known as Su Dongpo) and Su Che (1039–1112), both famous literary figures who were followers of Ouyang Xiu. Like Ouyang the latter group preferred a flexible, down-to-earth application of the models of the classics, which should be close to "natural human feelings" (*renqing*). This term could even imply people's "commonsense opinion," which could then serve as a reason for a more flexible application of classical rules. In contrast the group around Cheng Yi were strict classicists. They proposed acting as closely as possible in accordance with models and institutions thought to originate from the perfect Sages (*shengren*, 聖人) of that ancient golden time, claiming that these norms would fit "natural human feelings" (*renqing*) the best; only minor adaptations to the present should be allowed. Major members of this mostly "fundamentalist" group constituted the later so-called Neo-Confucianism.[26] This school established the orthodoxy after the Song Dynasty, when their interpretations were taken as normative for the state's bureaucratic entrance exams. In this group Cheng Yi, who called his teaching the "teaching of the [correct] Way" (*daoxue*, 道學), placed an especially strong emphasis on ritual. Cheng Yi had not only contributed to the Puyi case, but had also been consulted as ritual expert for imperial tombs and private grave arrangements.[27] Furthermore he was the author of a collection on family ritual that was later used as one of the main sources for the influential handbook compiled by the most important Neo-Confucian, Zhu Xi (朱熹, 1130–1200).[28] Cheng Yi's attitude was expressed in his scrupulous and rigorous insistence on ritual decorum in all social interactions.[29] In his theoretical writings he placed a strong emphasis on ritual (*li*) and the attitude of (ritual) attentiveness (*jing*, 敬). Taken together, his acknowledged expertise and attitude provide ample reason to speak of him most explicitly as a "ritualist."

CONCLUSION

China has always been regarded as having an elaborate "high culture of ritual."[30] It is thus not surprising to find never-ending debates on ritual from the very beginning, including in Song times. However, what remains an open question is *why* ritual matters had to be discussed again and again and what ritual debates were *actually* negotiating. My answer is as follows.

The Basic Concept of li *as a Reason for Permanent Renegotiation*

First of all it must be said that the Chinese concept of *li* does not wholly match the Western term "ritual." On the one hand, *li* involved behavior that is easily categorized as ritualistic, that is, associated with concrete sacrifices, bowing, and so on. But on the other hand, in contrast to the Western concept of ritual, *li* also included an ethical, hierarchical aspect, which not only was embodied in special forms of respect (e.g., bowing to the living and ancestral service to deceased parents) but could simply be correct moral behavior (i.e., being a pious, obedient son). Besides, from the very beginning *li* had a strong political connotation and clearly functioned with respect to legitimizing both social order and political power.

Li was also one of the main concepts in Chinese traditional culture. Imagined to originate from the normative past, the matter of ritual was highly charged symbolically and included not only representation but also ethical norms for the ruler that thereby restricted and legitimized the emperor's power. However, the classics did leave space for interpretation and even encouraged some adaptation. And as times changed and *li* had to be applied to new constellations, the very concept itself invited divergent interpretations and thereby manipulations of its symbolic potential.

(Chinese) Rituals Negotiated: Symbolic Value and Power Struggle

Although court rituals mainly represented imperial power, the matter of rituals was in the hands of the scholar-officials, who, by virtue of their knowledge of the classics, served as ritual experts despite the fact that they had no priestly function. Their power was not directly enacted or made apparent through public ritual performance,[31] but they were institutionally involved as state officials who were required to draw up ritual details in advance. Furthermore because they had been educated in the Confucian classics, these scholar-officials were well aware of the value of ritual in validating ethical norms that could be used to restrict imperial power. Ritual matters, especially the court rituals discussed here that could represent imperial power, were thus subject to the expertise of the Confucian-educated scholars. From a different perspective, however, the emperor, although dependent on the cooperation and compliancy of his officials, had the power of final decision. He could thereby strengthen one group or faction over another and reward single officials and promote their careers. Therefore ritual decisions were subject to permanent negotiation between the emperor, different groups of educated officials, scholars outside the court, and even the broader public. In sum ritual was a major medium of power struggles; significantly it was these struggles, more than the performance of ritual itself, that made the actual distribution of power visible and apparent.

Ritual as a Medium for Creating a Public Sphere

Not only was *li* (ritual) a comprehensive concept in political, social, and intellectual domains, but it bound together two aspects of power and conceptions of the public sphere: a *representative* mode, as provided by ritual in its public performance, and the mode of *reasoning* in ritual discourse. Ritual thus provided a forum for negotiating differing worldviews as well as for making them visible by representing them in concrete practices.

A major precondition of this particular constellation was the institutional base in the Northern Song Dynasty which made relatively free speech possible and allowed the debate of important matters by changing groups of scholar-officials as well as the ruling emperor. At the center were two opposing groups of officials who often rotated in the roles of government (chancellor and vice chancellors) and opposition. The latter was institutionalized particularly in the position of the censors, who were allowed to frankly criticize the government and, indirectly, even the ruler. This arrangement constituted a dynamic triangular constellation that often resulted in two opposing groups of officials, with the emperor in the dual role of primary ritual performer and arbiter of final decisions. Although this role was in some ways a powerful position, the emperor was still dependent on the compliancy of his officials and was interested in the smooth operations of his bureaucracy, or at least support by its majority.[32] Certainly free discussion at court could help to reveal the majority public opinion before the emperor gave his vote.

Around this three-sided center there were wider, court-centered circles of audiences who partly participated in the debates. These audiences were connected in three ways, which in turn widened participation in the negotiating process, thus making it more dynamic, perhaps even more democratic, and possibly of course even more unstable. First, major ritual questions—for example, nominating the heir, deposing the empress, or pronouncing on the (un)virtuous behavior of an adopted heir—could apparently affect wider public opinion; this public opinion (*gonglun,* 公論; *gongyi* 公議) could then be quoted and used in argumentation.[33] Second, the borders of participating groups fluctuated; new discussants could accrue from the examination system and be summoned to court as experts in ad hoc committees and so enter the bureaucracy as officials. Third, external ritual (and other intellectual) experts could influence, and were influenced by, discussions of ritual matters at court. This was certainly the case, for example, with those Neo-Confucians such as Cheng Yi whose main roles were as teachers in private academies.

Ritual Theory Negotiated: Interpretations, Neo-Confucian Ritualism, and Identity

As I stated earlier, ritual was a matter within Confucian circles that could attract more or less interest according to intellectual conviction and/or personal character; although scholars such as Ouyang Xiu and Su Shi were in fact interested in ritual too, they had a rather loose affinity to it compared to downright "ritualists" like the so-called Neo-Confucians Cheng Yi and Zhang Zai.[34] For the first group, a lively and lifelike expression of correct relationships performed in ritual was deemed the most appropriate; exemplary models could be found in the classics but did not have to be applied normatively in every detail. Hermeneutically key terms for this group were "natural human feelings" and the "commonsense opinion of the people" (*renqing*); rituals should follow, express, and thereby strengthen these "natural" feelings. Importantly, then, rituals could and should be redesigned with respect to different times and situations "according to the original intention of the Sages."[35]

For the more ritualistic Neo-Confucians ritual was an important matter that also played a role in embodying Confucian values, in contrast to Buddhist, Daoist, and popular religious (e.g., geomantic) practices that had become common even in families educated in the "Confucian" classics (so-called *shidafu,* 士大夫). Although minor adaptations to the times were not categorically rejected, the Neo-Confucians regarded ritual as created and designed by the Sages of the past and thus as the best form for expressing and exercising Confucian values and attitudes. For example, a strict adherence to the classics could help one to attain sagacity, which would be applied in each situation as attentiveness (*jing*); in the state of perfection (as a sage [*shengren*]), one would act according to the norms spontaneously.[36] For the Neo-Confucians not only were rituals the best exercise of Confucian values on a personal level, but ritual (and ritual debates) should be pursued also in the higher (and more "public") imperial arena, as their embodied visibility and visible embodiment enacted by the emperor as the father of and role model for the whole empire.[37]

Because it had to be performed regularly, ritual provided periodic occasions for discussion. It thereby functioned as a practical motive and catalyst for intellectual diversification. From the participants' perspective, ritual raised important questions of how to deal with the past if one wanted to adapt its rules to the present or to determine how much flexibility should be allowed in dealing with the canon. To the modern scholar, the ensuing debates reveal other connections with the ongoing power struggles at court. In other words, the Song sources yield detailed insight into ideological, political, and personal motivations for negotiating rituals;[38] indeed often extrinsic reasons such as career interests or political factions had more influence on ritual matters than ideological views and convictions, yet even these are intertwined in complex ways. Thus negotiating rites in Song China reveal a complex structure involving distinct and opposing groups of participants (including the emperor and different groups of officials). This structure was partly shaped by external factors, based on institutional conditions, and colored by political reasons such as factional front lines and jockeying for career advancement. Simultaneously ritual matters had also their own intrinsic weight, connected as they were to Confucian (*ru,* 儒) identity. And so debates inside as well as outside the court were deeply connected both to ideological diversification and to hermeneutical decisions in Confucian scholarship.

Notes

1. Or two of five volumes in the Zhonghua edition; see Du You, *Tongdian.*

2. Zito, *Of Body and Brush,* 58. Surely these discourses, as well as the key terms of the said discourse fields, are overlapping. It could be argued that it remains unclear why *xiao* (孝, "filial piety") is different from ritual in its *ethical* meaning, and why, for example, other terms like *de* (德, often translated as "virtue") or *ren* (仁, "humanity") as the highest estimated virtue (especially by Confucius in the Lunyu) could not replace *xiao.* As the most comprehensive key word, the term *dao* (道) summarizes all three discourses as modes of practicing and realizing the Way (*dao*).

3. These hierarchical roles are defined by the five basic relationships (*wulun,* 五倫): father-son, ruler-subject, husband-wife, older brother–younger brother, and among friends, the only nonhierarchical of the five.

4. *Feili* often occurs in the *Junzi yue* (君子曰) paragraphs, for *li* (禮) in the *Zuozhuan*; see Pu Weizhong, *Chunqiu sanzhuan zonghe yanjiu*, 78–86. Especially for *feili ye*(非禮也) see, for example, 80 (quoting Zuozhuan, chap. Wengong 4).

On the virtues see, for example, Mengzi (孟子) 2A.6 or 6A.6, also called "five virtues" (*wude*, 五德; or *wuchang*, 五常). For the three meanings, see also Meyer, *Ritendiskussionen am Hof der nördlichen Song-Dynastie*, 45–46. See also Pines, "Disputers of the *Li*," 3–4, who differentiates practical rituals and rules from "a more abstract mode of social and personal conduct that could serve thinkers analytically as a tool to address the concerns of social order and hierarchy." For another recent attempt at classifying four basic aspects of the term *li* (禮, "Ritualität") and two basic ways of arguing about ritual since the Zhanguo period, see Gentz, "Ritus als Physiognomie."

5. For example, Fehl, *Li;* Brooks and Brooks, *The Original Analects*, 110 to Lunyu 2, 5.

6. *Rites de passage* as described in the ritual classic *Yili*, and later in Zhu Xi's family rites handbook, *Zhuzi jiali*, translated by Ebrey as *Chu Hsi's Family Rituals*.

7. The basic understanding of rituals as primarily denoting *rules* seems to accord with Frits Staal's perception of Indian Vedic ritual: "The chief concern of the ritual is with rules" ("The Sound of Religion," 58–59). According to his interpretation, Indian ritual rules would work "without meaning"; they only had to be perfectly performed. See his monograph *Rules without Meaning;* Bell, *Ritual Theory, Ritual Practice*, 121. Although this characteristic of rules that had to be followed *as fixed tradition* (something that may be typical for "written cultures") could also partly be shown to be true of Chinese rituals in Confucian tradition (*li*), there is a major difference: in Confucian Chinese interpretation ritual is regarded as being close to human feelings and as rational; it appears therefore as fundamentally *meaningful*. Besides, according to its explicit hermeneutical tradition, ritual was always open to minor changes according to higher principles of propriety. As loci classici for this, see Lunyu (Analects) 9,3 (about the change of a minor detail—wearing a silk instead of a linen hat—but not of a more meaningful aspect) and Lunyu 2,23 und 3,14 (about changes of ritual rules during the course of the earlier three dynasties).

8. For elaborations on the psychological basis of rituals the most important and influential thinker was Xunzi (荀子, ca. 300–230 BCE), who connected *li* (禮) to *tian* (天, "heaven"); see Knoblock, *Hsün-tzu*, 3:58 ("Discourse on Ritual Principles"). But Knoblock also regarded *li* primarily as based on human feelings (see 3:69). For Xunzi rituals were necessary to channel human desires but were also expressions of and in accord with human feelings (3:55).

9. For example, Xunzi mostly regards heaven (*tian*, 天) as a natural force ("nature") rather than as a normative moral institution; see ibid., 3:3–22.

10. In (Northern) Song times, for example, it was said of the important Neo-Confucian philosopher and distant uncle of the famous Cheng brothers, Zhang Zai, that he "taught [moral behavior] by means of ritual" (*yi li wei jiao*, 以禮為教). See Chow, "Ritual, Cosmology, and Ontology," 202; similarly in *ECJ*, *Yishu* 2A.23: "子厚以禮教學者，最善，使學者先有所據守." See also Ebrey, "Education through Ritual."

In a memorial to the young Emperor Zhezong (哲宗, 1077–1100, reigned 1085–1100) it is mentioned that only if the emperor were to fast seriously would the spirits come down in the ancestral shrine and communicate (*jiao*, 交) with him (see *zouyi* 934). Another ritual debate about sacrifices to heaven and earth deities mentions that, as the highest triennial sacrifice to heaven and earth were separated at this period, the emperor had not yet "seen" (or "met"; *jian*, 見) the deities of earth, but only of heaven (see *XCB* 477.11359–71). Both ideas are based on two quotations already found in the *Liji* (chap. *Jiaotexing* 郊特牲: "君子三日齊．必見其所祭者"; similarly in chap. *Jiyi* 祭義; chap. *Yucao*: "玉藻：凡祭．容貌顏色．如見所祭者"). There is also a substantial chapter about "ghosts and spirits" (*guishen* 鬼神) in the selected sayings of the most important Neo-Confucian philosopher, Zhu Xi (1122–1200), *Zhuzi yulei* (朱子語類).

11. The basic "Confucian" classics date back for the most part to pre-imperial times (i.e., the Zhanguo period), although some parts were written or compiled later. An initial canon of five scriptures grew to nine in early Song, while in the course of the Song Dynasty the Neo-Confucians suggested including Lunyu (論語) and Mengzi (孟子), using them together with the treatises *Zhongyong* (中庸) and *Daxue* (大學) from the *Liji* (禮記) as the foundational canon of study and instruction. By Qing times there were full editions of the thirteen classics with commentaries. However, the major base of canonical scriptures for ritual matters was already laid in Han times (206 –BCE–220 CE).

12. The reigns of Zhenzong (真宗, 997–1022) and Huizong (徽宗, 1100–25) showed a strong Daoist influence. In the years after the death of Zhenzong and before 1034 the Empress Dowager Liu (劉, 968–1033) reigned on her son's behalf; the period 1086–93 (Yuanyou period) was the last one in the Northern Song (960–1126) in which major antireformers prevailed; for the political contexts of reform and antireform, see below.

13. For a more detailed discussion, including more debates in the same period, see Meyer, *Ritendiskussionen am Hof der nördlichen Song-Dynastie,* especially part 2 for a detailed account and part 3 for analysis.

14. Like Li Zhao they collected millet, trying to find the right sort and the correct way of arranging the grains to reconstruct ancient measures of length, weight, and volume for proper bell casting.

15. A few years later ancient bells were found that showed how far removed the sophisticated reconstruction had been from its ancient ideal.

16. A version of the *Hanshu* (the historical record of the former Han Dynasty) that contained eight characters (之起，積一千二百黍) not found in the textus receptus, the common version of that time as well as today (see *Hanshu* 21A.966). Due to a compromise the bells and music standards provided by Hu and Ruan were only partly used for the ritual music, namely for audiences and normal sacrifices, but not for the important triennial Nanjiao sacrifice to heaven.

17. See *SS* 128.2988–2991.

18. For a detailed account of the complicated case, see Meyer, *Ritendiskussionen am Hof der nördlichen Song-Dynastie,* 256–88; Fisher, *The Chosen One,* 25–45; or Ji, *Politics and Conservatism in Northern Song China,* who treats the matter from the perspective of Sima Guang.

19. The case was explicitly categorized under the heading of *liyue* (禮樂, "rituals and music") in the *zouyi*.

20. The order of the imperial ancestral shrine represented the legitimate order of succession of the dynasty. The other main source of legitimization was the mandate of heaven (*tianming,* 天命), which was represented by imperial sacrifice to heaven.

21. Although this term could also just mean (closer) "relative."

22. 天無二日王，地無二，家無二主，尊無二上. A quotation from *Liji*, chap. *Fangji* (1997: 718); similarly in *Liji*, chap. *Zengzi wen* (1997: 286), *Sangfu sizhi* (1997: 935), or Mengzi, chap. *Wanzhang shang* 5 A 4. It is quoted explicitly in the memorials of Wang Gui, Sima Guang, Fan Zhen, and Cheng Yi (*zouyi* 957, 958, 961, 979–80).

23. See *SS* 13.258–59, *XCB* 207.5030,12, and *SHY* 1371/3–4 Li 40–42.

24. Codifications of the music standards would have borne his reigning periods (*nianhao,* 年號) in their title. If he was successful the codification would have kept the memory of his achievements alive for a long time.

25. See *SS benmo* 28.219. Both had prior exchanges about their divergent views on music. In the Puyi case, however, both had shared positions.

26. The group of early Neo-Confucians included also the ritualist Zhang Zai (張載, 1020–77), the cosmologists Zhou Dunyi (周敦頤, 1017–73) and Shao Yong (邵雍, 1011–77), and Cheng Yi's brother Cheng Hao (程顥, 1032–85). All of them had died earlier so that Cheng Yi was left as representative of this direction after the change of government in 1085–86. The term "fundamentalist" is meant here to describe this group's strict adherence to the ancient ideals as described in the canon.

27. In the Puyi case Cheng Yi contributed a memorial to the throne written on behalf of Peng Siyong, the father-in-law of his older brother Cheng Hao (*ECJ*, *Wenji* 5.515–18; *zouyi* 979–80). His expertise is further documented for the private burial of the father of the befriended Neo-Confucian thinker Shao Yong, Shao Gu, as well as in memorials on behalf of Fu Bi (*ECJ*, *Wenji* 5.532–34) and his father (*ECJ*, *Wenji* 5.527–29). For a detailed argument on behalf of Cheng Yi as a recognized "ritualist," see Meyer, "Cheng Yi as a Ritualist."

28. For a translation and analysis of this manual for family rituals, see Ebrey, *Chu Hsi's Family Ritual*; see also Ebrey, "Conceptions of the Family in the Sung Dynasty," and *Confucianism and Family Rituals in Imperial China*. The other main source was a ritual manual composed by Sima Guang; on his ritual thinking, see Clart, "The Concept of Ritual in the Thought of Sima Guang (1019–1086)."

29. Once as a tutor of the young emperor he scolded the boy ruler for thoughtlessly plucking off a twig from a tree.

30. From early on China has called itself the "country of rites" (*liyi zhi bang/guo,* 禮儀之邦/國); see He Xiu (Commentary), *Chunqiu Gongyangzhuan juan* 3 (Yin 7).

31. Except on the local level as magistrates, within their family, or on behalf of the emperor.

32. The emperor relied on the support of his officials not only in ritual matters (to support the legitimacy of his rule) but also in political and administrative matters. The main reason for the major faction struggles in Northern Song time were in fact fiscal issues, including questions of taxation and social ascendancy that endangered the established, more "conservative" families from the North.

33. Whether these terms refer to the general public or the court and the status group of officials is ambiguous. The terms are in fact often used in the Puyi case (see, for example, in general *zouyi* 961, 969, 970 and 975). In *zouyi* 964 the term specifies the "public opinion of the whole empire" (*tianxia zhi gongyi,* 天下之公議), while the use in *zouyi* 972–73 is narrowed to speak of the "general or public opinion of the court (officials)" (*juchao gongyi,* 舉朝公議) only; in *zouyi* 977 the term is again widened by quoting the general opinion of scholars with or without position (*shidafu*) (*shidafu gongyi,* 士大夫公議). The people "of the streets and lanes," however, could also be quoted as representing so-called ordinary people's opinion. In general the local and national elite of *shidafu* were seen as the most representative of general opinion outside the court, as they made up the "interested and informed public," but pro- or antigovernment (or -ruler) sentiment could apparently also be gauged among the broader public in the capital.

34. For other genuine ritualists such as Li Gou (李覯, 1009–59) or Lü Dalin (呂大臨, 1046–92), see Meyer, *Ritendiskussionen am Hof der nördlichen Song-Dynastie;* Hsieh, *The Life and Thought of Li Kou.*

35. See XTS 11.307–8; Bol, *This Culture of Ours,* 195–96. Cheng Yi's writings offer similar quotations, as he may have been influenced by contemporary discourses; these were at least partly dominated by Ouyang, a major influence on opinion in his time.

36. This is described programmatically in Cheng Yi's early "Treatise on What Yen Tzu Loved to Learn" (*ECJ* 577–78), translated by Chan in *A Source Book in Chinese Philosophy,* 547–50.

37. "Public" here refers to representability rather than general or public access. For the role of the emperor as father and role model, see, for example, the struggle about deposing the Empress Guo.

38. The advantage of this period in contrast to the earliest or earlier dynasties is that the richness of material allows scholars to reconstruct detailed discussions on a single topic. Contributors to the accessibility of this discussion were the long tradition of writing and administrative practice, the invention of printing, and a high standard of literacy and social mobility in Song society.

Abbreviations

ECJ	Cheng Hao (程顥) and Cheng Yi (程頤), *Er Chengji* (二程集).
Hanshu	Ban Gu (班固), *Hanshu* (漢書).
Liji	*Xinyi Liji duben* (新譯禮記讀本).
SHY	Xu Song (徐松), ed., *Songhuiyao jigao* (宋會要輯稿).
SS	Tuo Tuo (脫脫) et al., *Songshi* (宋史).
SS benmo	Chen Bangzhan (陳邦瞻), *Songshi jishi benmo* (宋史紀事本末).
XCB	Li Tao (李燾), *Xu zizhitongjian changbian* (續資治通鑑長編).
XTS	Ouyang Xiu 歐陽修, *Xin Tangshu* 新唐書
zouyi	Zhao Ruyu (趙汝愚), *Songchao zhuchen zouyi* (宋朝諸臣奏議).

Bibliography

Primary Sources

Ban Gu (班固). *Hanshu* (漢書). Peking: Zhonghua shuju, 1962.

Chen Bangzhan (陳邦瞻). *Songshi jishi benmo* (宋史紀事本末). Taibei: Liren shuju, 1981.

Cheng Hao (程顥) and Cheng Yi (程頤). *Er Chengji* (二程集). Peking: Zhonghua shuju, 1981.

Du You (杜佑). *Tongdian* (通典). Peking: Zhonghua shuju, 1988.

He Xiu (何休) (Commentary) *Chunqiu Gongyangzhuan* (春秋公羊傳). 28 juan. Taibei: Xinxing shuju, 1964.

Li Tao (李燾). *Xu zizhitongjian changbian* (續資治通鑑長編). Peking: Zhonghua shuju, 1979–95.

Tuo Tuo (脫脫). *Songshi* (宋史). 2nd ed. Peking: Zhonghua shuju, 1990.

Xinyi Liji duben (新譯禮記讀本). Commentary by Jiang Yihua (姜義華). Taibei: Sanmin shuju, 1997.

Ouyang Xiu 歐陽修. *Xin Tangshu* 新唐書. Peking: Zhongua shuju, 1975.

Xu Song (徐松), ed. *Songhuiyao jigao* (宋會要輯稿). 3rd ed. Peking: Zhonghua shuju, 1997.

Zhao Ruyu (趙汝愚). *Songchao zhuchen zouyi* (宋朝諸臣奏議). 2 vols. Shanghai: Shanghai guji chubanshe, 1999.

Zhu Xi 朱熹. *Zhuzi yulei* 朱子語類. Peking: Zhonghua shuju, 1986.

Secondary Sources

Bell, Catherine. *Ritual Theory, Ritual Practice*. New York: Oxford University Press, 1992.

Bol, Peter K. "Examinations and Orthodoxies: 1070 and 1313 Compared." In *Culture and State in Chinese History*, ed. Theodore Huters, R. Bin Wong, and Pauline Yu, 29–57. Stanford: Stanford University Press, 1997.

———. *This Culture of Ours: Intellectual Transitions in T'ang and Sung China*. Stanford: Stanford University Press, 1992.

Brooks, E. Bruce, and A. Taeko Brooks. *The Original Analects: Sayings of Confucius and His Successors. A New Translation and Commentary*. New York: Columbia University Press, 1998.

Chan, Wing-tsit. *A Source Book in Chinese Philosophy*. Princeton: Princeton University, Press, 1963.

Chow, Kai-wing (周啟榮). "Ritual, Cosmology, and Ontology: Chang Tsai's (1020–1077) Moral Philosophy and Neo-Confucian Ethics." *Philosophy East and West* 43 (1993): 201–28.

Clart, Philip. "The Concept of Ritual in the Thought of Sima Guang (1019–1086)." In *Perceptions of Antiquity in Chinese Civilization*, ed. Dieter Kuhn and Helga Stahl, 237–52. Heidelberg: Edition Forum, 2008.

Ebrey, Patricia Buckley. *Chu Hsi's Family Rituals: A Twelfth-Century Chinese Manual for the Performance of Cappings, Weddings, Funerals, and Ancestral Rites*. Princeton: Princeton University Press, 1991.

———. "Conceptions of the Family in the Sung Dynasty." *Journal of Asian Studies* 43 (1984): 219–45.

———. *Confucianism and Family Rituals in Imperial China: A Social History of Writing about Rites*. Princeton: Princeton University Press, 1991.

———. "Education through Ritual: Efforts to Formulate Family Rituals during the Sung Period." In *Neo-Confucian Education: The Formative Stage*, ed. William Theodore de Bary and John W. Chaffee, 277–306. Berkeley: University of California Press, 1989. Reprint, Taibei: Nantian shuju, 1994.

Fehl, Noah E. *Li* 禮 *Rites and Propriety in Literature and Life: A Perspective for a Cultural History of Ancient China*. Hong Kong: Chinese University of Hong Kong, 1971.

Fisher, Carney T. *The Chosen One: Succession and Adoption in the Court of Ming Shizong*. Sydney: Allen & Unwin, 1990.

Gentz, Joachim. "Ritus als Physiognomie: Frühe chinesische Ritentheorien zwischen Kosmologie und Kunst." In *Ritualdynamik: Kulturübergreifende Studien zur Theorie und Geschichte rituellen Handelns*, ed. Dietrich Harth and Gerrit J. Schenk, 307–37. Heidelberg: Synchron, 2004.

Hsieh, Shan-yüan. *The Life and Thought of Li Kou 1009–1059*. Asian Libraries Series 14. San Francisco: Chinese Materials Center, 1979.

Ji, Xiao-bin. *Politics and Conservatism in Northern Song China: The Career and Thought of Sima Guang* (A.D. 1019–1086). Hong Kong: Chinese University Press, 2005.

Knoblock, John, trans. *Hsün-tzu: A Translation and Study of the Complete Works*. Vols. 1–3 (books 1–6, 7–16, 17–32). Stanford: Stanford University Press, 1988, 1990, 1994.

Meyer, Christian. "Cheng Yi as a Ritualist." *Oriens Extremus* 46 (2007): 211–30.

———. *Ritendiskussionen am Hof der nördlichen Song-Dynastie 1034–1093: Zwischen Ritengelehrsamkeit, Machtkampf und intellektuellen Bewegungen*. Nettetal: Steyler Verlag, Monumenta Serica, 2008.

Pines, Yuri. "Disputers of the Li: Breakthroughs in the Concept of Ritual in Preimperial China." *Asia Major* 13 (2000): 1–41.

Pu Weizhong (浦衛忠). *Chunqiu sanzhuan zonghe yanjiu* (春秋三賺綜合研究). Taibei: Wenjin chubanshe, 1995.

Rickett, Walter Allyn. *Kuan-tzu: A Repository of Early Chinese Thought. A Translation and Study of Twelve Chapters*. Vol. 1. Hong Kong: Hong Kong University Press, 1965.

Staal, Frits. *Rules without Meaning: Ritual, Mantras and the Human Sciences*. Toronto Studies in Religion 4. New York: Lang, 1989.

———. "The Sound of Religion." *Numen* 33 (1986): 33–64 (parts 1–3) and 185–224 (parts 4–5).

Zito, Angela. *Of Body and Brush: Grand Sacrifice as Text/Performance in Eighteenth-Century China*. Chicago: University of Chicago Press, 1997.

PART TWO

Getting It Straight

6

Performing the Ancient Ones

THE BODY-IN-PRACTICE AS THE GROUND OF RITUALIZED NEGOTIATION

Nikki Bado

> The locus of the sacred is the body, for the body is the existential ground of culture. (Thomas, Csordas, "Somatic Modes of Attention")
>
> The most immediate and concrete means of persuading people of the reality of divine power is to involve their bodies. (Thomas Csordas, "Somatic Modes of Attention")

In a wooded clearing at a small farm in northern Ohio, a group of Witches meets to initiate a new priest into their coven. Under a sable canopy studded with stars and a brilliant full moon, they begin the ritual movements that will create the magic Circle.[1] *Traced thrice with fire, then smoke, blessed by water and earth, and protected by the Guardians of the Watchtowers of the four directions, the Circle is consecrated and made ready for the magical act of transformation. The Witches raise their voices in chants to call the Gods, while one High Priestess assumes the deeply ingrained ritual postures that bring the Goddess into manifestation within her.*

This moment of ritual performance holds a key to understanding the role of the body as the ground or site of interaction and negotiation with what scholars often call the sacred, including those "other-than-human persons" who populate the ritual landscape. While negotiation frequently brings with it connotations of disagreement, conflict, and even violence, I use the term to highlight processes of interaction that facilitate the crossing or transgression of boundaries and expectations. In the context of ritual performance I use "negotiation" in two explicit senses: (1) ritual as a contextual frame and a medium for traversing or mediating between two distinct and sometimes conflicting ways of knowing and socially relating—integral and intimate; and (2) embodied ritual praxis as a complex process of interaction and mediation between humans and other-than-human persons such as Gods and Goddesses and what I term *Nature-as-Person*.

The opening description of ritual performance derives from several years of extensive empirical observation of and participation in initiation rites and other religious rituals performed by a group of Wiccans, or Witches, in Ohio. The initiation process employed by these Wiccans serves as a fruitful source of study because it emphasizes a lengthy period of somatic training that negotiates a perceptual reorientation in the practitioner, making possible interaction with the various beings who populate the Wiccan religious landscape. This somatic training begins with the introductory classes and continues throughout the life of the Witch.

My own training and initiation into this group occurred more than thirty years ago, identifying me as both scholar and practitioner—an often perilous identity that crosses the dichotomy of insider/outsider, and one that is therefore itself habitually hotly contested and carefully, even cautiously, negotiated within religious studies.[2] This dual identity frequently transgresses the expectations of methodological atheism that typically pass as scholarly objectivity. But it allows for a form of reflexivity that admits the inclusion of the scholar in the material studied and dismantles an insider/outsider dichotomy that hides perspectives beneath a cloak of presumed objective analysis.

Wicca—referred to interchangeably in this essay as Witchcraft, the Craft, or the Old Religion[3]—is one of a host of contemporary Pagan religions that describes its practices as a modern-day revival or re-creation of shamanic techniques and indigenous religious practices of pre-Christian Pagan Europe. Wicca is often described as a "nature" religion—although precisely what this means is debated by practitioners and scholars alike—because nature figures prominently in the ritual and mythological landscape of many Wiccan groups whose ritual spaces are blessed by the four elements (earth, air, fire, and water) and whose Gods and Goddesses are immanent presences arising from the natural world. Because covens are autonomous and vary widely in composition, size, and organizational structure, descriptions of ritual training and initiatory processes are characteristic of the coven in question and those that practice similar rites, and must not be assumed to apply to all Wiccan groups.

Scholars have traditionally approached initiation as an isolated ritual moment with a simple unilinear directional movement. My study of the rituals performed by this group reveals that initiation, far from being a discrete event, is embedded in a long and complex multidirectional process of increasingly somatic practice that involves a shift in perceptual orientation as well as the formation of an intimate community. This ritual process functions pedagogically to transform the natural body into what I term the *body-in-practice*, a particular mode of perception necessary for successful communication, identification, and negotiation with other-than-human persons that entails a shift from what philosopher Thomas P. Kasulis terms an "integral" to an "intimate" perceptual orientation.[4]

In this context "integral" and "intimate" refer to two substantially different ways of knowing, relating to others, and perceiving the world. Among their general attributes, Kasulis describes integrity as primarily conceptual, intellectual, or rational, ideally empty of affect or feeling and distinct from the somatic. Intimacy is affective and empathetic, somatic as well as psychological. The body is centrally involved as both knower and doer. Integrity is "bright" and open; knowledge is self-conscious, reflective, and aware of its own grounds. Intimacy is "dark" or esoteric, the ground of its knowing not generally self-conscious or self-illuminating.

An integrity understanding of relationship might be characterized schematically as two separate beings, A and B, related to one another by a third, completely separate outside agent, C, where C might stand for an item such as a contract or agreement. In contrast an intimacy understanding of relationship might be characterized as two overlapping circles in which A and B intersect, their boundaries made fluid and transparent as they share parts of themselves with the other. For the Witches, the intimacy mode of perception or way of knowing is negotiated *with* and *through* the body with the development of the body-in-practice and is made meaningful by performed ritual identification and negotiation with the spirits during invocations.

In other words, the Witches' initiation process and its attendant focus on ritual praxis act as a learning curve in which the initiate's body-in-practice develops and acquires those skills necessary for successful ritual work within this community.[5] The body of the student Witch is the site or ground of contestation and negotiation between these two different ways of knowing, thereby mediating a shift in consciousness from an integral to an intimate frame of reference. This ritual training produces a paradigm shift in the understanding of religion itself from a kind of disembodied belief that resides "in the head" (an integral framework) to an embodied practice that includes the body as active learner (an intimate framework). The body-in-practice is an achieved state that cultivates what anthropologist Thomas Csordas calls "somatic modes of attention," "culturally elaborated ways of attending to and with one's body in surroundings that include the embodied presence of others."[6]

Here "others" include not only other practitioners in the rite, but an entire range of other-than-human persons, including the four elements, spirits and Guardians of the Watchtowers, Gods and Goddesses, and Nature-as-Person. The Witches' body-in-practice illuminates the concrete reality of those who inhabit the intersubjective and liminal field of ritual space and enables the complex and intimate dance of ritualized interaction with these Ancient Ones. In the "calling down" portion of the ceremony, the ritual praxis of the trained body-in-practice also enables the High Priestess to attain the delicate balance of consciousness negotiated between Goddess and woman during the invocation of the Goddess into the Circle.

A few illustrations of the learning process suggest how the body becomes somatically tuned to and adept at interaction with the sacred.[7] While initial classes are basic and informative in nature—explaining what the Craft is and is not, the organizational structure of the group, particular deities worshipped, their mythologies, the cycle of seasonal holidays, and so forth—subsequent classes increasingly focus on more somatic activities, for example, designing a ritual tool for one of the four elements after an initial lecture or presentation about the element by the teaching Witch. Such activities provide hands-on familiarity with the element, presenting a satisfying creative, even tactile connection between theory and practice.

The design of a tool for the element of air is easily described. One major representation of the air element on the Witch's altar is incense, so the student might design a fan of some sort to help waft the incense around the Circle. Here the aspiring Witch draws on a storehouse of interrelated and interlocking meanings and correspondences for inspiration. In this community air *means* the direction of east, dawn, wakefulness, beginnings, and communication. Air *means* the delicate cloud of incense that rises from the charcoal burner to sweeten and cleanse. Air *means* the trilling cacophony of songbirds conjuring up the morning light. Air *means* the striking note of a bell rung, commanding our attention, then fading on the air toward eternity. A tool designed to capture or evoke such a cluster of meanings might make use of feathers, decorated wood for a handle, bells to evoke sound, and paint, cloth, or beads that use colors associated in this community with the air element and direction. The student might also add to the tool herbs and essential oils or incense resins that correspond to the air element.

To say simply that the student is learning the correspondences of air is a shallow description that conceals the degree of sensual engagement between the student's body and the multiple meanings of air. Through sound and hearing, color and sight, aroma and smell, touch and movement as the student fans the incense around the Circle, the student's *body*, as the active learner in this process, participates in the creation of a whole complex of meanings of air by becoming more attuned to and aware of the presence of air. In other words, the student both discovers and creates meaning through bodily engagement, through sensual and participatory conversation and growing awareness of his own intimate entanglement and interaction with the element of air itself.

This simple and creative somatic exercise is the first of many that engage the student's whole body in the learning process, breaking what anthropologist Johannes Fabian calls our cultural dependence on "visualism" in knowledge production. Describing the problem with visualism, Fabian writes, "Vision requires distance from its objects; the eye maintains its 'purity' as long as it is not in close contact with 'foreign objects.' Visualism, by instituting *distance* as that which enables us to know, and purity or immateriality as that which characterizes true knowledge, *aimed to remove all the other senses and thereby the body* from knowledge production."[8] Although vision is certainly one of the body's senses, relying solely on vision masks the degree to which the body as a whole participates in the production of knowledge, particularly spiritual knowledge. Thomas Csordas echoes the problem with visualism: "We less often conceptualize visual attention as a 'turning toward' than as a disembodied beam-like 'gaze.' We tend to think of it as a cognitive function rather than as a bodily engagement."[9]

The distancing phenomenon innate in vision assists in concealing bodily engagement and the role of the whole body as active learner and knower.

Air is a particularly useful element for somatic exercises that begin to break visualism's hold precisely because it is *invisible* to the eye and yet sensually pervasive. While we can see its effects in the world—the flutter of leaves in a brisk autumn wind, the lazy movement of clouds across a summer sky, the flapping motion of laundry hung out to dry—our most direct apprehension of the presence of air is through senses other than sight. Ecologist and philosopher David Abram poetically notes the all-encompassing presence of air in *The Spell of the Sensuous*:

> Enveloping, embracing, and caressing me both inside and out, moving in ripples along my skin, flowing between my fingers, swirling around my arms and thighs, rolling in eddies along the roof of my mouth, slipping ceaselessly through throat and trachea to fill the lungs, to feed my blood, my heart, my self. I cannot act, cannot speak, cannot think a single thought without the participation of this fluid element. I am immersed in its depths as surely as fish are immersed in the sea.[10]

Through somatic exercises that engage the body as knower and producer of spiritual knowledge and meaning, the student gradually connects what his body does with religious practices. This is a critical moment in the training process and the beginning of the construction of an *embodied* imagery that the student will later perform in the Circle during ritual. In fact the exercise with air significantly lays the groundwork for the kind of somatic awareness the student will cultivate with his body-in-practice. Like the air, some of the other-than-human beings who inhabit the ritual landscape are presences who are felt, but not necessarily seen.

This immediate exposure to the sensual, tactile dimension of Wiccan religious experience counteracts the notion that religion is only, or even primarily about belief systems, memorized sets of abstract concepts, or texts. Wiccan training introduces students to a theological world within which religion as *practice*—practice that centrally includes the physical body *as the doer of spiritual learning*—emerges as equally important to belief or intellectual knowledge.

The notion that the body is an active agent of spiritual learning and activity surprises and may even disturb those who think the body has little to do with the sacred. The idea that body and spirit are somehow antithetical or antagonistic to one another is reinforced by a number of factors. Some religions reject or devalue the body, which must be ignored as a source of spiritual distraction or overcome as temptation, even a source of evil. This idea has been prevalent in Christianity, for example, since at least Augustine, who devalued the body as the carrier of original sin. Even those religious movements for whom the body is a "temple" overlook the body's *active* role in spiritual achievement by framing the body as a passive vessel of spirit.

Although Western philosophy is far from monolithic, the body occupies a problematic place at least as far back as Plato, who sometimes refers to the body as a kind of "prison" for man's reason, making incessant demands and eventually succumbing to disease and decay. Plato understands body and reason as more cooperative, if occasionally fragmented, rather than strictly partitioned within the person.[11] By far the most significant examples of the apparent antagonism between body and mind are found in Western philosophy after Descartes, who cast mind and body as not merely occasionally distinguishable from one another, but as ontologically distinct entities. And, as in the old nursery rhyme about Humpty Dumpty, once the unity of mind and body is broken, it is extremely difficult to put together again.

After Descartes body and mind become locked in a dualistic and polarized hierarchy with mechanical, unthinking matter—including the human body as well as the natural world—on the one hand, and the rational mind—the province of God and man (I use the gendered word deliberately)— on the other. In fact it is possible to consider Descartes's mind/body split as a secularized version of the wrestling match between divine spirit and unruly and wayward flesh. For Descartes, one half of the dichotomy—mind or reason—is primary; the other half—the body—is of secondary importance. As Foucault notes in *Discipline and Punish*, the devaluing of the body as an object to be controlled and disciplined, "made docile and productive," yet "economically and politically valuable,"[12] is reflected and reinforced throughout secular culture, which treats the body as an inconvenience at best, its need for rest and play ignored or repressed for the sake of artificial deadlines and corporate profit, social control, and political power.

A host of familiar and deeply entrenched Western dichotomies springs from this fracturing of world—mind/body, spirit/matter, sacred/profane, subject/object, theory/practice, masculine/feminine, nature/culture, emotion/reason—and the valuation of one side of the dichotomy over the other continues throughout each of the pairs. These dichotomies inform our understanding of every aspect of what it means to be human. They inform how we interpret and process what it is we perceive. They are the lens through which we look at the world, so much so that we have difficulty imagining any other way to be. Somatic exercises help the student gradually to break through established and dualistic ways of thinking about mind and body, spirit and nature that will later enable him to develop the body-in-practice and realize the intimate relationship with nature that already exists. Here the somaticity of Wiccan ritual praxis negotiates the shift to an intimate consciousness that reaches across the split in the world.

Study of the effects of Cartesian dualism on Western philosophy, particularly on epistemology (theories of knowledge), is vast and multidisciplinary, and it is not my intention to provide a review of them here. However, I find two broad lines of philosophical thinking particularly valuable in dismantling the dichotomies that erase the body as an agent or doer of spiritual learning and in revealing the body-in-practice as the ground of ritualized negotiation. One is anchored in the Western philosophical tradition of phenomenology, particularly in the works of Merleau-Ponty. The other is an Eastern philosophical tradition that includes contemporary philosophers such as Yuasa Yasuo and Thomas K. Kasulis. This tradition has a pedigree stretching back at least as far as eighth-century Japan to the philosopher Kūkai, the eighth patriarch of Shingon Buddhism, particularly his principle of *sokushin jōbutsu,* "attaining enlightenment with this very body."[13]

I return now to the Witches' training process and continue the lessons of air, albeit in a slightly different way, in order to discover the ways these philosophical traditions shed light on the body-in-practice. At this point in the training process small hands-on projects are slowly mingled with somatic exercises that focus on mastery of the breath. The first step is simply to notice one's breathing, followed by control of the pattern of breathing—for example, having students breathe in for a particular count, hold the breath in for a count, breathe out for that count, and hold the breath out for the same count. As much as possible students time the breath to the feeling and sound of their own heartbeats rather than an external clock. Once the student has mastered the breathing pattern, he learns to simply *be* in his body, feeling where his body is tight or tense and releasing that tension until he has achieved a feeling of deep relaxation.

For this group of Witches, control of the breath is the foundational or premier *technique du corps*, as sociologist Marcel Mauss might say, the gateway to all other ritual practices. Mastery of the breath is not only the initial somatic practice through which the Witch develops her spiritual being, that total integration of mind, body, and spirit that is the goal of spiritual practice, but also the technique that enables her to attain the level of somatic awareness that makes possible successful ritual work, including the casting of the ritual Circle, invocation of the Gods and spirits, divination, and healing.

The introduction of breathing exercises at this stage in the learning process is important for a number of reasons. Breath control and relaxation is the first step in learning a host of other meditative techniques: concentration, review and release of thoughts, visualization, creation of thought forms, and more. Relaxation is something nearly everyone can do, although students may have to use more effort at first than they expect; beginning relaxation and mastery of breathing is actually more difficult than it sounds, and students typically report initial difficulty following the count, sometimes a feeling of hyperventilation, a tendency to fall asleep, and a surprising number of places that itch. The exercises are also boring. Because of this, daily breathing exercises are often a way to weed out students who are not really serious about practice. This part of the training process occasionally evokes impatience on the part of the student to get on to "real" magic. But simple somatic exercises, which are not really very simple at all, *are* the beginnings of magic—the transformation of person that is the Witch's ultimate goal. Mastery of the exercises also signals the initial stages of a significant transformation or paradigm shift from religion as disembodied belief to religion as embodied practice.

I want to linger for a moment on the phrase "embodied practice" because this concept is essential to understanding Wiccan ritual performance as the site of ritual negotiation. The term consists of two words of equal weight: "embodied" immediately foregrounds the body, while "practice" suggests training, repetition, disciplined and conscious doing. Westerners have little problem understanding the body as trainable, as in the context of developing athletic dexterity and prowess, yet it is unusual for us to think of spirit in quite the same way. And it is even more uncommon to think of training the spirit *by means of* the body, achieving an increasingly well-integrated mind-body-spirit complex in the process. Yet this is exactly what the Witches' disciplined and somatic meditative and ritual practices are designed to do.

This training cultivates what I term the body-in-practice to differentiate it from how we typically think of the body in a world still very much influenced by Cartesian dualism. The body-in-practice is not a passive receptacle for spirit, but the active agent through which spirit is transformed—body and mind working together to achieve the whole person. Such embodied practice is the process—the *magic*—through which the Witch transforms herself into her most perfect form and attains an ever-increasing integration of body-mind-spirit. As Kasulis observes, a spiritual practice that engages both body and mind engages a "process by which we can gradually change what we existentially are."[14]

This training seems on the one hand to contradict a sense that spirituality is somehow equally and democratically given rather than a talent that varies from person to person and a skill that might be developed through somatic practices—other than, say, ascetic practices of denial in order to avoid and overcome the temptations of the flesh. On the other hand, the training contradicts a Western philosophical assumption that the mind-body relation, whatever it might be, is fixed rather than one that varies and changes based on the degree of one's ability and practice.[15] But by assuming that mind and body are distinct entities with a fixed relationship and even conflicting attributes, we overlook the ways mind and body communicate and actually do become increasingly well integrated through training and practice.

Yuasa Yasuo provides a schema of consciousness that may help to explain why somatic practices such as control of the breathing are connected to the integration of the mind-body-spirit complex. He suggests that consciousness itself is "double-layered," composed of a self-consciously aware surface ("bright" consciousness) over a deeper layer ("dark" consciousness) that is not itself capable of reflection. While there are no exact correlates, this deeper layer resembles the unconscious and parallels the autonomic nervous system. In phenomenological terms, dark consciousness is similar to Merleau-Ponty's lived body and Bergson's sensorimotor circuits.[16] Dark consciousness also resembles no-mind in Buddhist terms, that moment of prereflective experience when reality engages us before we chase it away by thinking. More accurately, however, dark consciousness is none of these things. "It is rather their common ground, a single aspect of consciousness viewed from various perspectives."[17]

In the introduction to Yuasa's *The Body: Toward an Eastern Mind-Body Theory*, Kasulis illustrates how bright and dark consciousness work together by considering the case of a woman driving her car who goes into an "unanticipated but controlled swerve to avoid hitting a dog." He unpacks the complicated maneuver of what went into her reaction: "In a sense, the act was an *impulse*, the triggering of a conditioned response. That is, the specific rationale of what had to be done and how to do it was dark; it was not something of which the driver was self-conscious." But while the temptation may be to explain away her response as simply an unconscious impulse, Kasulis points out that the "motorist's impulse is a *learned* response, the result of months of disciplined training and years of practical experience."[18]

The same sort of communication between bright and dark consciousness can be seen in a host of other activities: martial arts, professional sports, dance, even typing, as well as Buddhist meditation practices. Kasulis observes, "The initial step in all these disciplines is that the mind (the bright consciousness) deliberately places the body into a special form or posture." Like the experience of the student Witch learning to control the pattern of his breathing or learning to ritually create the magic Circle, the initial stages are awkward and the body uncooperative. Eventually the "knowledge in the bright consciousness"—the posture, the pattern of breathing, the movement—is "internalized through praxis" into the dark consciousness and becomes second nature, freeing the person to respond creatively and spontaneously without deliberation.[19]

While we can readily see how somatic practices develop learned responses that become mundane habits, Yuasa suggests that spiritual development occurs in a similar fashion. Here he is consistent with a tradition of Japanese philosophy that goes back at least as far as Kūkai and the concept of *sokushin jōbutsu,* "attaining enlightenment with this very body." Kūkai uses somatic ritual practices of word (*mantra*), thought (*mandala*), and deed (*mudra*) as a kind of pedagogy, a tool for teaching us to become enlightened "*with/through/by* and *in* this very body."[20] For Kūkai, disciplined ritual praxis not only trains the spirit by means of the body, but also reveals the nature of reality itself as it engages us in lived experience. Ritualized actions of thought, word, and deed immerse us in the actions of the Buddha and establish a resonance in which practitioner and Dharma flow into one another in mutual empowerment[21]—something that becomes an important point in the Witches' ritual invocation of their Gods and Goddesses.

Using Yuasa's map of consciousness, we find ritual praxis begins with the creation of a "psychophysical pathway" that allows free and direct communication between the bright and dark consciousness. Yuasa observes that most contemplative traditions begin with control of breathing, which he calls a "direct route by which the bright consciousness can contact the dark." For Yuasa, once the initial path has been opened by mindfulness or control of breathing, further possibilities for interaction between bright and dark consciousness may develop.[22]

The student of Wicca who has successfully forged this psychophysical pathway now works on an increasing variety and intensity of ritual practices in preparation for initiation. The student and teaching Witch address the *practice* of the religion itself, at first in limited and controlled exercises with the body in meditation postures or in simple rituals within the Circle. Eventually the student engages in more challenging and creative expressions of religious practice, incorporating ever more complex forms of visualization, concentration, ritual gesture, and other forms of somatic practice that develop the body-in-practice as the student proceeds through the learning process to initiation.

In terms of the initiation rite itself, I want to highlight two interactive moments of the ceremony in particular: the emergence of Nature-as-Person in the location of the ritual and the moment of invocation of the Goddess by the priestess. These interactive moments emphasize the engagement of the body-in-practice with other-than-human beings in ritual performance.

Because these Witches understand their practice as a nature religion, they hold as many of their ceremonies as possible outdoors. While there are practical and logistical reasons for doing so, the primary reasons are theological, or perhaps more accurately, praxological. Not only does the natural environment set the stage for the performance of the rite, but it also foregrounds Nature as a living *presence*, a member of the spiritual community whose attendance at the rite is made apparent and engaged by the worshippers through outdoor ritual praxis. Nature becomes an active participant—a *person*, or another *myself*, as Csordas would say—with whom the Witches interact somatically, thereby establishing a relationship of intimacy.

In this sense initiation will not bring the candidate into community with Nature so much as it will awaken him through the experiences of his body-in-practice to the community *that is already there*. This intimacy with Nature-as-Person is one of the critical lessons of the entire learning process of becoming a Witch. And it is vital that the initiate learn this lesson—not just intellectually or emotionally, but somatically, *with and through his body*.

Nature-as-Person gently caresses our skin with the breezes of the night air, murmurs secrets in our ears with the sighing wind in leaves, mischievously plays hide-and-seek with the full moon and twinkling stars through clouds and branches, and powerfully punctuates the ritual with the clap of thunder behind a now solid curtain of clouds. For the Witches, Nature-as-Person is not a metaphor, but a *being* as alive and present and interactive as are the human participants in the ritual Circle.

A typical reduction of all the above might be "Nature is personified," but I feel this passive-voice construction inadequately captures, even discounts, the level of intimate and somatic interaction between Witch and Nature and suggests a false distance—an estrangement—between them. Not only does this tepid description overlook the role of the human body in sensory conversation and mutual entanglement and engagement with the natural world; it also overlooks and dismisses the very presencing of that world in human experience—the deeply "mysterious powers and entities" of the natural world "reduced to so much scenery." Abram attributes much of this oversight to the "modern, civilized assumption that the natural world is largely determinate and mechanical, and that that which is regarded as mysterious, powerful, and beyond human ken must therefore be of some other, nonphysical realm *above* nature, 'supernatural.'"[23]

Spatiality and movement through the landscape also cultivate awareness of Nature-as-Person. The first spatial action in the rite is the placement of the candidate for initiation near a small pond that lies between the farmhouse and the area in the woods that will become the site of the ritual Circle. While this serves the practical purpose of getting the candidate out of the way during final ritual preparations, it also gives him an opportunity simply to *be* with the presence of Nature, intertwining bodies waiting together for the rite.

Initiation is the means by which the "ordinary" body is ritually remade into the body-in-practice and marks the student's successful learning of somatic practices that will begin to open him to an awareness of the lived reality of the world, awareness of Nature-as-Person and the beings who inhabit the Wiccan religious landscape. This is accomplished in large part through the initiate's symbolic death, his journey around the perimeter of the Circle, and his encounters with the Guardians of the elemental forces of Nature: earth, air, fire, and water, and also spirit—the five points of the Witch's sacred pentagram.

The ritual begins with the construction of the magic Circle, space transformed and made sacred through invocation of fire and air, earth and water. To be sure, sacrality of place is not an ontological given; a place is made sacred through interaction, by deliberate and practiced ritual negotiation and transformation using skills developed by the bodies-in-practice of the Witches performing the rite.[24] In fact transformation of both space and the person about to be initiated are mutually interdependent and dynamically related. As I observe in *Coming to the Edge of the Circle*, the transformation of the person "depends upon the presence of the Circle's elemental Guardians who perform the actions necessary to change the Dedicant into a new Witch and Priest. Just as the Witches invoke each element and direction to purify and consecrate the Circle, so, too, do the Guardians of the four directions employ their elemental powers to purify and consecrate the Dedicant,"[25] to accept or deny initiation.

While there are points in the rite at which initiation may fail either because the candidate withdraws or is denied, in practice this seldom (if ever) occurs. Mostly this is a result of extensive learning and careful screening processes that work in both directions: not only can the Coven reject the student as an inappropriate candidate for initiation, but the student can also reject the Coven. It might be argued that the success of the initiation ritual itself, as well as the likelihood of the initiated Witch continuing as a successful member of the Circle, depends on how well he develops a body-in-practice that is capable of negotiating the transition from an integrity to an intimacy consciousness. Without such a transition the candidate neither encounters Nature-as-Person, nor does he genuinely engage the many other-than-human persons necessary for ritual work.

Somatic awareness of and ritual negotiation with other-than-human persons such as the elementals and Guardians are essential to creating the ritual space. Witches consider the Circle a place "between the worlds" in which both Gods and humans meet and interact through ritual praxis. The Circle is thus an intersubjective field in which the Gods and those persons who have developed the body-in-practice *engage one another* in *shared* consciousness. In other words, as intersubjective field, the Circle is constituted by multiple sensing subjects, *both human and other-than-human persons,* negotiating a collective reality. The ground of this negotiated reality is the disciplined ritual praxis of the body-in-practice.

Through the body-in-practice the Witches cultivate what Csordas calls somatic modes of attention, those "culturally elaborated ways of attending to and with one's body in surroundings that include the embodied presence of others." In this case the "embodied presence of others" includes not only the Witches, but entities invoked into the Circle, such as the Gods, who are made manifest in and through the bodies-in-practice of the Priests and Priestesses invoking them. In other words, when the High Priestess invokes the Goddess in the portion of the ritual termed " the calling down ceremony," she *becomes present with and through* the Priestess's body-in-practice.

It is here tempting to borrow Daniel Valentine's term "consubjectivity,"[26] in the sense of "acting with/as one," in attempting to describe the complex negotiation—that degree of intimacy, identification, and mutual engagement—that occurs during the performance of deity invocations. Witches do not consider invocations to be spirit possessions; the consciousness of the Priestess does not leave and another consciousness take its place. The ritual invocation is instead a cautious negotiation between woman and Goddess, a delicate balance of power, a complex dance of control and surrender, a mutual embrace, a flowing into one another in mutual empowerment, a sharing of consciousness. Perhaps following in the spirit of Merleau-Ponty, we should speak of the carnal entanglement of the visible woman/priestess and the invisible Goddess as an embodied relationship of mutually interpenetrating and interdynamic transformation, a non-reductive intertwining and interweaving of different spheres negotiated through the body-in-practice. It is at once both Priestess *and* Goddess who perform the rite—as Kūkai would say, "different, but yet the same; not different but yet different."[27]

In the end we are perhaps left with a choice between paradox and poetry to suggest what cannot really be known except through the body-in-practice:

> An alder leaf, loosened by wind, is drifting out with the tide. As it drifts, it bumps into the slender leg of a great blue heron staring intently through the rippled surface, then drifts on. The heron raises one leg out of the water and replaces it, a single step. As I watch I, too, am drawn into the spread of silence. Slowly, a bank of cloud approaches, slipping its bulged and billowing texture over the earth, folding the heron and the alder trees and my gazing body into the depths of a vast breathing being, enfolding us all within a common flesh, a common story now bursting with rain.[28]

Notes

1. Witches use the term "circle" in a variety of ways: for consecrated ritual space, for a rite or ceremony in that space, or for the coven itself. The term is capitalized in this paper whenever so used.

2. For extensive analysis of the insider/outsider problem in religious studies and its root in dichotomous thinking, see chapter 1 of Bado-Fralick, *Coming to the Edge of the Circle*, 3–21.

3. For the purposes of this essay, I make no distinctions between the terms Wicca, Witchcraft, the Craft, or the Old Religion, and use the terms Wiccan and Witch interchangeably. Because they refer to religions, these terms, including the word Pagan, are all capitalized.

4. Kasulis, *Intimacy or Integrity*, see especially chapters 2 and 3.

5. I use the term "praxis" to mean a system of related practices forming a self-disciplinary process that involves the whole person—body, mind, and spirit—emphasizing that body is as much involved in the process as is mind or spirit. This disciplinary process is performed as a way of integrating the self and transforming the way one thinks and acts in the world.

6. Csordas, "Somatic Modes of Attention," 138.

7. Readers who desire a more complete description of the community and the learning process used in this essay should refer to Bado-Fralick, *Coming to the Edge of the Circle*.

8. Fabian, "Ethnographic Objectivity Revisited," 98–99.

9. Csordas, "Somatic Modes of Attention," 138–39.

10. Abram, *The Spell of the Sensuous*, 225.

11. Personal communication with Professor Travis Butler, specialist in Plato at Iowa State University.

12. Foucault, *Discipline and Punish*, 25.

13. Kūkai's concept of *sokushin jōbutsu* is particularly useful for understanding ritual praxis as pedagogy that not only trains the spirit through the body, but reveals our intimate connection with reality itself. I explore parallels between the esoteric ritual praxis of both Shingon Buddhism and Wicca in Bado-Fralick, "With This Very Body."

14. Kasulis, introduction to Yuasa, *The Body*, 3.

15. Kasulis, "The Body—Japanese Style," 303.

16. Kasulis, introduction to Yuasa, *The Body*, 5.

17. Ibid.

18. Ibid.

19. Ibid., 5, 6.

20. While for Kūkai somatic ritual praxis is the key to resonating with the Dharmakāya and attaining enlightenment, for these Witches it is the key for resonating with Nature-as-Person and successful invocation of deity. See Bado-Fralick, "With This Very Body" for an exploration of pedagogical parallels between the somatic ritual praxis of Shingon Buddhism and Wicca.

21. Dharma is frequently used to mean three things: right actions, true teachings, and phenomena as they really are. Here Dharma might be usefully translated as simply "reality."

22. Kasulis, introduction to Yuasa, *The Body*, 6, 6–7.

23. Abram, *The Spell of the Sensuous*, 9.

24. Bado-Fralick, "Mapping the Wiccan Ritual Landscape," 45–65.

25. Bado-Fralick, *Coming to the Edge of the Circle*, 129.

26. A neologism from "The Pulse as an Icon in Siddha Medicine," Daniel Valentine's study of diagnostic pulse-taking by practitioners of Siddha in South Asia, "consubjectivity" refers to the ability of doctors who are able to make their own pulses mirror those of their patients, thus experiencing, at least in part, their patients' suffering.

27. This rather paradoxical statement from Kūkai is translated in *The Body* (156) thus: "This body is my body, the Buddha body, and the bodies of all sentient beings. They are all named the 'body.' All of these bodies are interrelated horizontally and vertically without end, like images in mirrors, or like the rays of lamps. *This* body is, no doubt, *that* body. *That* body is, no doubt, *this* body. The Buddha body is no doubt the bodies of all sentient beings, and the bodies of all

sentient beings are no doubt the Buddha body. They are different, but yet identical. They are not different but yet different."

The third line (omitted in Yuasa) is adapted here from Hakeda, *Kūkai*, 92–93, replacing the word "existence" in his version with "body," in keeping with Yuasa's style. The original is taken from Kūkai's *Shokushinjōbutsugi* (Meaning of becoming a Buddha in this very body), published in *Kōbō daishi chosaku zenshū* (The complete works of Kōbō Daishi), ed. Katsumata Shunkyō (Tokyo: Sankibō, 1968). *Shokushinjōbutsugi* appears in vol. 1, 41–58.

28. Abram, *The Spell of the Sensuous*, 274.

Bibliography

Abram, David. *The Spell of the Sensuous*. New York: Vintage Books, 1996.

Bado-Fralick, Nikki. *Coming to the Edge of the Circle: A Wiccan Initiation Ritual*. London: Oxford University Press, 2005.

———. "Mapping the Wiccan Ritual Landscape: Circles of Transformation." *Folklore Forum* 33, nos. 1–2 (2002): 45–65.

———. "With This Very Body: Or What Kūkai Has to Teach Us about Ritual Pedagogy." In *Educations and Their Purposes: A Conversation among Cultures*, ed. Roger T. Ames and Peter D. Hershock, 177–89. Honolulu: University of Hawai'i Press, 2008.

Csordas, Thomas. "Somatic Modes of Attention." *Cultural Anthropology* 8 (1993): 135–56.

Fabian, Johannes. "Ethnographic Objectivity Revisited: From Rigor to Vigor." In *Rethinking Objectivity*, ed. Allan Megill, 81–108. Durham, N.C.: Duke University Press, 1994.

Foucault, Michel. *Discipline and Punish: The Birth of the Prison*. London: Penguin Books, 1979.

Hakeda, Yoshito S., trans. *Kūkai: Major Works*. New York: Columbia University Press, 1972.

Kasulis, Thomas P. "The Body—Japanese Style." In *Self as Body in Asian Theory and Practice*, ed. Thomas P. Kasulis, Roger Ames, and Wimal Dissanayake, 299–319. Albany: State University of New York Press, 1993.

———. *Intimacy or Integrity: Philosophy and Cultural Difference*. The 1998 Gilbert Ryle Lectures. Honolulu: University of Hawai'i Press, 2002.

———. Introduction to *Self as Body in Asian Theory and Practice*, ed. Thomas P. Kasulis, Roger Ames, and Wimal Dissanayake, xi–xxii. Albany: State University of New York Press, 1993.

Mauss, Marcel. "Les Techniques du Corps." *Journal de Psychologie* 32(1934): 1–23.

Valentine, Daniel E. "The Pulse as an Icon in Siddha Medicine." *Asian Studies* 18 (1984): 115–26.

Yuasa Yasuo. *The Body: Toward an Eastern Mind-Body Theory*, ed. Thomas P. Kasulis, trans. Nagatomo Shigenori and Thomas P. Kasulis. Albany: State University of New York Press, 1987.

7

Negotiating Tantra and Veda in the *Paraśurāma-Kalpa* Tradition

Annette Wilke

In 1832 the Maharashtrian Brahman and Veda-Mīmāṃsā scholar Rāmeśvara presented the public with a voluminous commentary on the *Paraśurāma-Kalpasūtra* (*PKS*).[1] The book started with a long defense of Tantra against common reproaches, such as that Tantrists have left the Vedic path, that they are greedy and self-indulgent, and that they were following rites that were acceptable for women and Śūdras, but certainly not for Brahmans. This was not what Rāmeśvara thought. He defended left-hand Kaula Tantra, a Tantric ritual tradition that made use of "forbidden" substances, in particular alcohol, meat, sexual fluids, and sexual intercourse, the last preferably practiced with women of untouchable castes. These rites (which were not shared by other Tantric traditions) have remained a highly contested issue ever since they emerged, because they challenge the codes of purity and caste hierarchy of normative Brahmanism. Rāmeśvara presents us with the interesting case that a Kaula-Tantric insider speaks as a Vedist pro Tantra, and he disagrees with a widespread opinion in emic as well as etic discourses that Vedic traditionalism and (Kaula-)Tantra exclude each other. Indeed both Hindus and scholars of Hinduism have tended to consider Veda and Tantra, that is, the Vedic and the Tantric (*vaidika* and *tāntrika*), as opposite ends of the spectrum of Hinduism. The relationship is actually far more complex, fluid, and variegated,[2] but certainly it was a field of negotiation, dispute, and contest. Such negotiations are also reflected in Rāmeśvara's source, the *PKS*, a ritual script probably composed in the sixteenth century or earlier that both partakes of and subverts a general trend of domestication within Tantric history.[3]

MAPPING THE CONTEXTS AND ENSUING QUESTIONS

Hindu-Tantra is a complex pluralist phenomenon that refers to a vast number of South Asian ritual systems derived neither from Vedic rites nor the Smārta tradition, that is, *dharma* literature, epics, and Purāṇas that are considered Veda-based.[4] Tantric rites were a predominant religious paradigm from the fifth century to the thirteenth, giving a prime place to the body, the senses, the iconic power of language, and visualizing practices. Some of these practices have since been wholeheartedly added to the traditional Smārta mainstream, and they deeply informed the temple culture. Others have been judged heterodox and polluting by normative Brahmanism. The Kaula Tantra tradition grew out of early radical Śaiva cults that considered as emancipatory wisdom and divine empowerment what was commonly regarded as deviant. Most of their revolting "left-hand" practices (such as necrophilia, embodied imitation of the liminal god Bhairava-Śiva and wild female folk deities, sexual intercourse, use of liquor, menstrual blood, and feces) did not survive or gained gnostic revalorization when moving from lonely places and cremation grounds to palaces and private homes. Between the ninth century and the thirteenth nondual Kashmir Śaivism played an essential role in making these practices acceptable to elite circles by finding deep interior sense in subaltern body practices and recoding radical and popular cults through a sophisticated discourse of spiritual self-cultivation.[5] The Kaula Tantra was part of this process of increasing sublimation.[6] The Śrīvidyā, in particular, the latest Kaula branch and nowadays the most widespread Tantric tradition, witnessed a high degree of interiorization in which ritual became in effect gnostic contemplation—a shift resulting in what the Tantra scholar David Gordon White calls the "end of ritual."[7] In Tamil Nadu the Śrīvidyā merged with Smārta Brahmanism to such an extent that some scholars speak of a "deviant and bowdlerized" Tantra, or even refuse to call the tradition Tantra anymore.[8] This indicates the extent to which the negotiations about Tantric rituals and "proper performance" have always been a matter of constant dispute not only among participants and Tantric specialists, but also among outsiders. I do not agree with either the "end of ritual" or the "bowdlerization" thesis. Rather I would like to draw attention to the fact that even in the ("right-hand") south Indian Śrīvidyā, wherein Kaula was "purged" of all "impurities,"[9] internalized sensuality was retained in the form of *kuṇḍalinī-yoga*, which centered on visualization practices, breath control, and the yogic body scheme. The validation of the inner senses as realities and important ritual instruments provided a basic form of agreement within a field of dissent.

The source text for the following considerations, the *PKS*, also belongs to late Kaula Śrīvidyā and also emerged in south India, but in contrast to the better known "right-hand" Śrīvidyā just mentioned, the little-studied *PKS* is pronouncedly "left-hand" Kaula and betrays common expectations that would consider the term "left-hand Śrīvidyā" almost a contradiction in itself. I see the *PKS* as an interesting "betwixt and between" regarding the processes summarized above. It confirms Alexis Sanderson's characterization of the Tantrists as "super-ritualist."[10] The *PKS* is definitely "gnostic" with respect to contemplating one's own Śivahood (thereby combining Kashmir Śaiva, south Indian Śaiva-Śākta, and Vedāntic concepts of nonduality)[11] and making rich use of interior yoga practice, but it makes also use of the most powerful exterior ritual media to attain emancipation and cosmic awareness: the sensual life of the body. This emphasis on sensuality centers on the secret Kaula *pañcamakāra* ("five m's"), considered the most important (*mukhya*) ritual elements and consisting of items that start with the letter "m": (1) alcohol (*madya*); (2) meat (*māṃsa*); (3) fish (*matsya*); (4) roasted and spiced chickpeas, beans, grains, or wheat (*mudrā*); and (5) sexual intercourse (*maithuna*).[12] At the same time the *PKS* makes extensive use of the Veda, integrating, subordinating, reinventing, and transforming it. Quite in contrast to the right-hand Śrīvidyā that heavily "vedicizes" the Tantra by excluding the revolting parts of Kaula practice, the *PKS* heavily "tantricizes" the Veda by making it completely its own and claiming its conformity with the Kaula tradition. The *PKS* apparently negotiates orthodoxy and orthopraxy within both the Vedic and the Tantric fold by means of symbolic manipulations, ritual transfers, and textual reinterpretations. Its deliberate attachment to the Vedic lore differs greatly from the nondual (left-hand) Kashmiris (by whom it is otherwise heavily influenced), and so does its chief deity, the mild and beautiful great goddess Lalitā, worshipped in her *śrīcakra* diagram.[13] While these features coincide with the right-hand Śrīvidyā that was adopted even by staunch representatives of orthodox Brahmanism such as the monastic Śaṅkarācāryas, the mingling of Tantra and Veda in the *PKS* is of a different brand and comes from different social elites: an avant garde of Brahman intellectuals, elegant urban householders, and royal customers who seek to break the narrow grid of caste society and transcend the normal, everyday *dharma* values. This typical Kaula feature is, however, much more evident in earlier Kaula sources, such as the *Kulārṇava-Tantra* (*KT*), one of the most authoritative Kaula sources, composed between the eleventh and sixteenth century, wherein caste-free intercourse and ecstatic transgressiveness are explicitly spoken about.[14] The *PKS* selectively borrows a great number of core ideas from the *KT* but is far more secretive and conventionally decent.[15] In the *PKS* there is no reference to sexual liberty or wild drinking parties, as found in the ecstatic Kaula of the *KT*. Rather excess control and governance by strict ritual rules dominate in the confrontation with ecstatic Kaula.

Within the field of combating Tantra receptions, interpretations and recodings that mirror underlying conflicts of social identity formation and a constant contestation of cultural values, social hierarchies, competitive ways of world making, tensions and clefts between tradition and creativity, normative behavior and subjective sense, the *PKS* exerted considerable influence. It provided a ritual setting that was both an inherently dynamic frame and a virtual space of the extraordinary that related the exterior to the interior and vice versa. Ritual scripts based on the *PKS*, elaborations, and commentaries extend to the present day. In fact the manual seems to be enjoying a renaissance in present-day Vārāṇasī and has a strong living tradition in Kerala.[16] Here I focus on the textual tradition, which has a life of its own.

The later *PKS* tradition continued the multifaceted negotiating process outlined above, for example, by refuting a Veda-Tantra opposition or by debating whether substitutes of alcohol and sexual rites should be allowed. While Umānanda had already elaborated and restructured the *PKS* according to the mystical grades of the *KT*, Rāmeśvara adopted the method of Veda hermeneutics to stress strict rule governance. They vary in details of *mantra* performance, but not in their acceptance of Kaula body practice. It is only in the twentieth century that we witness (almost complete) evaporation of the physical body within the *PKS* tradition, which is largely equivalent with the conversion of the *PKS* ritual into right-hand Tantra. One may interpret these processes as the final triumph of Brahman orthodoxy. The enduring success of the Tantric domestication process was further reinforced by the changing power structures in colonial and postcolonial India and by the nineteenth-century trend to universalize, spiritualize, and ethicisize Hinduism (by means of Śaṅkara's nondual Vedānta) to fit it into the choir of "world religions." In addition to these factors, my argument will be that the modern transformation followed an inner logic rather than deviating from the ritual path outlined by the legendary great Kaula master Paraśurāma, to whom the *PKS* is ascribed in the colophon (*PKS* 10.85). The original text already calls itself proudly "great Upaniṣad" (10.83), thus merging the peak of Vedāntic knowledge and Tantric esoteric wisdom (1.5–12). Within this wisdom *mantra* practices, visualizations, and interior body processes, including various techniques of mentally shaping and expanding interiority and subjective sense, are ultimately given much more credit than corresponding physical acts. In fact the borders between the real and the virtual become extremely fluid. The mental activation of the yogic body centers, the repetition of erotic goddess names and diverse imagined forms of intercourse are so prominent that they gain a hyperreality which is perceived as "more real than the real." I suggest that such imaginative strategies and interiorized sensuality paved the way to a ritual enactment in which physical intercourse was no longer necessary. Already in the *PKS* the real and the virtual merge to such an extent that it is often unclear where active imagination starts and physical body-practice ends. I reckon this de-differentiation to be deliberate due to a soteriological ritual program typical of the Kaula, namely to merge flesh and spirit by placing the mind in the body and the body in the mind. The aim was to expand the human frame into a cosmic one, experience Brahman bliss in a body-mind continuum, and become one with the bodiless Śiva and his powers in "all one's bodily limbs" (which naturally involved ritual scrutiny as well as a high degree of active imagination and focus on interiority and gnostic insight). The *PKS* is particularly interesting in regard to opposing trends raised by scholars of high Hindu Tantra, such as gnostification and embodiment, super-ritualism and the "end of ritual," Veda and Tantra. In the *PKS* these dichotomies are being dissolved. It is a rare case of left-hand Śrīvidyā promoted by Vedic Brahmans who reinvented the Vedic tradition to fit it with genuine Kaula Tantra, and at the same time adjusted the "impure" rites to the Vedic-Upaniṣadic worldview and the blissful experience of nondual reality, making the "bliss of Brahman" a corporal experience.

In accordance with the overall perspective of this volume, I understand negotiation as referring to "any process of interaction in which differing positions and concepts are explicitly or implicitly acted out and/or debated."[17] Negotiations, then, are the normal state of affairs in religious history, if one understands history as a series of discourses.

Rituals are no exception, despite emic and etic claims about ritual's stable, unchanging nature. A common characteristic of ritual negotiations is the reinterpretation and reworking of traditions, which may involve reworking hierarchies, power structures, definitions of orthodoxy, and so on. Rituals tend to be useful instruments to do so, since there is no need for real-world face-to-face interactions; virtual encounters are good enough, as the exploration of the *PKS* will show. The *factual* negotiating interactions with other Tantric traditions and the Veda are virtual rather than real, spiritual rather than profane, as well as unilateral; that is, they self-position toward, as well as selectively integrate and transform, other traditions.[18] The *PKS*'s interest in the Veda is extraordinary within the Tantric traditions, but interactional processes and hybrid forms are not.

What is negotiated in the *PKS* are not "worldly matters," but spiritual perfection, a new body-mind awareness, the very existence in the world as a holy cosmos. The ritual efficacy does not aim at solving social problems, maybe with the exception of the Vārāhī worship, which promises the conquering of enemies and uninhibited commanding power (*PKS* 7.28, 7.37–38), a topos known from other Tantric sources and far from clear, whether spiritual or worldly "commanding power" (*ājñā-śakti*) and autonomy are hinted at. Typically the *PKS* does not specify the enemies; they may be inner psychic ones such as doubt and fear, demonic numina, political foes, or hostile fellow men who are critical of the Kaula conduct. Even if social conflicts or power contests should be the unseen background, their "solution" lies precisely in the fact that the ritual agent performatively resolves them, whereas the invisible others cannot react within the self-sufficient ritual frame.

My major focus is the *PKS* construction of a Veda-Tantra continuum in which the Tantra becomes the "real Veda." Besides negotiations of the body-mind relationship, I want to stress the negotiation of socioreligious hierarchies that are ritually acted out by discursively negotiating the relationship with the transcendent. This focus accords with a practice-theory approach to rituals emphasized, for instance, by Catherine Bell. Bell is concerned with the way rituals "construct and inscribe power relationships" by means of totalizing strategies, that is, by expressing and drawing from an "authority of forces deemed to derive from beyond the immediate situation."[19] While I would not go so far as to postulate that the major characteristic of ritual action lies in manipulating power relationships, I do agree with Bell's more general statement that rituals have multiple dimensions, and that they *do*, rather than just mean, something. The performance aspect of ritual is crucial, because the style of doing as well as the aesthetic setting create a framework that communicates the message "This has extra significance," thereby evoking strong situative presences. I consider this self-referential meaning and effectiveness a major reason why rituals inherently possess "the power to define what is real and to shape how people behave."[20] Owing to my sources I am concerned not only with the performance of ritual but also with the performance of the ritual script that *does* something by virtue of the fact that religious ideas and actions are selected, expressed, and orchestrated.

RITUAL PERFORMANCE IN THE *PKS*

It is noteworthy that the *PKS* belongs to later Kaula, Trika, and Śrīvidyā, in which, according to David Gordon White, "practice" was reduced to "knowing" in what he terms "the end of ritual." In the strain of postcolonial criticism and subaltern studies White heavily criticizes Arthur Avalon's "essentialist" Tantra representation as well as the native "elitist" high Hindu Tantra. White assumes an original Kaula "hard-core Tantra" among subaltern circles of Śaiva worshippers, which involved violent practices of sexual fluid exchange that would have been "too shocking and perverse" for medieval and modern urban consumers.[21] To the nondualist Kashmiris in the eleventh century are attributed a gnostified "internalization," "aesthetication," and "semanticization" of Kaula ritual that produced an elitist high Hindu "soft core Tantra," designed for "conformist" urban consumers who secretly enjoyed forbidden things, promoted a "cult of ecstatic bliss," and could turn to substitutes if they were too afraid of pollution.[22] This trend culminated in the Śrīvidyā, wherein, according to White, semen and female discharge were replaced with asexual terminology and verbal "seeds" (*bījas*), ritual by the meditative practice of *mantras*, and doing by knowing. [23]

I agree that high Hindu Tantra augmented the verbal media, but I am reluctant to concede that there is an opposition of doing and knowing or a total move to abstraction. Rather sensory attention shifted to sound, to internal body practices, and to the power of metonymic imagination. Even the most gnostified Śrividyā did not forsake ritual, that is, formalist, rule-governed activities that deliberately differed from daily routine. Certainly the *PKS,* in which body practices play a substantial role, is a highly ritualistic text. Indeed the term *kalpa* signifies anything but the "end of ritual"; the term means "ritual," "ceremonial," "practice," "procedure," "method." Remarkably the term *kalpa* as well as *Kalpa-Sūtra* deliberately alludes to the Vedic tradition; *PKS* 1.1 even copies the style of the initial *Sūtras* in the Vedic counterpart.[24] The ritual also fulfills all formal criteria suggested in etic ritual theories,[25] such as membership condition, formality, performance, sacral symbolism or extraordinariness, and transformation.

The daily rites stipulated by the *PKS* consist of well-ordered ritual sequences (*krama*) dedicated to the elephant-headed god, Gaṇapati (chapter 2); the chief, highly erotic goddess Lalitā (chapters 3–5); her closest attendant, Śyāmā, the goddess of song, dance, and music (chapter 6); the sinister boar-faced Vārāhī, who is Lalita's fierce commander in chief (chapter 7); and a fourth, "Supreme" goddess form, Parā, called Lalita's "heart," consisting of the seed-sound of liberating wisdom (SAUḤ) (chapter 8). The cycles involve recursive ritual figures who appear slightly changed in each sequence. Each of the deities has his or her own ritual universe in which the manifold powers associated with them are invoked and made present by *mantra* repetition, meditation verses and litanies, diagrams, active imagination, and *kuṇḍalinī-yoga*. Besides verbal and mental acts, the deities' worship includes a high degree of sensory pageantry (flowers, colors, perfumes, etc.), to which one or more items of the "five m's" or their combination belong. Fire sacrifice (chapter 9) and a chapter devoted to "all *mantras*" as well as an integral perspective (chapter 10) conclude the *PKS*. The rites effect emancipation (*jīvanmukta*) (*PKS* 10.82) and transformation of the mortal body into a cosmic body; the practitioner becomes an embodiment of Śiva "in all the limbs" (10.50) and obtains omniscience (10.21) as well as the goddesses' supermundane powers.[26]

Merging Body and Mind as Soteriological Program and Ritualized Excess Control

The *PKS* illustrates that embodiment and gnostification may well go hand in hand. Although verbal material predominates, bodily awareness is inherent in all deity cycles, even the *Parā-krama,* wherein the gnostic tendency is strongest (chapter 8). Consider how Parā is visualized according to her two meditation verses (*dhyāna*): according to *PKS* 8.16 she holds a piece of *meat* and the "water of immortality" (i.e., wine) in her two hands, whereas in *PKS* 8.20 she carries a *book* and shows the "gesture" (of consciousness). This image of Parā seems to symbolize a major aim of Kaula, namely to unite flesh and spirit. The ritual agenda to relate inner and outer worlds involved a number of ritual strategies to place the body in the mind and the mind in the body.[27] The description of the chief goddess Lalitā in the *PKS*, for instance, is notably erotic: she is "ever wet" (*PKS* 3.28–30),[28] and each of her fifteen emanations is characterized by highly sexual terms, such as vulva and sperm (4.9), but the framing of ritual is to create the erotic goddess via one's mind and withdraw her after worship (4.1, 5.23). During the meditation of her "parts of love" (*kāmakalā*) (White's example of "the end of the ritual"), the practitioner must mentally expand the central dot (*bindu*) in Lalitā's ritual diagram and visualize the "parts of love" of the goddess: her face, breasts, and vulva (5.16). Remarkably this mental exercise precedes the "sacrifice" of physical ritual intercourse. After "satisfying" the human Śakti, "the rest of sacrifice" is to be offered "into the fire of consciousness" (*cidagnau havis*, 5.22).[29] The fruit of sacrifice is said to be the inner vision of one's objectless awareness (*nirviṣaya-cid-vimṛṣṭiḥ phalam*, 1.27).

In the *PKS* the real and the virtual or visionary merge to such an extent that it is difficult to decide which practices are real and which actively imagined, and whether they are literary topoi or real-world phenomena. This is also the case in earlier Kaula Tantric literature, but compared with them the *PKS* is notably sober. Although it borrows heavily from the *KT*, the *PKS* does not include the passages of *KT* 8, wherein the "post-mature" Kaula Tantrics' divine possession (*praudhānta-ullāsa*) that transgresses any normative behavior is so described: "Exhilarated Yogīs fall on ladies, and intoxicated Yoginīs fall upon men" (*KT* 8.74). While the *KT* explains such behavior by the exalted state of mind of ritual agents who have reached the stage of superior Yogīs (8.4, 8.75ff.) beyond normal consciousness (8.66) and engrossed in ecstatic god-consciousness (*devatā-bhāva*), rapture, and divine madness (*unmanā*), the *PKS* simply speaks of consuming the rest of sacrifice—which may mean nothing more than sipping from the ritual alcohol vessel and partaking of a fine communal meal.[30] In any case the *PKS* seems to mirror negotiations within the Kaula fold and to promote excess control by ritual rule governance, gnostified cognitive attractors, and cultivated behavior.

Cultured Cosmopolitans: The Ritual Agents

Although there is constant vacillation between the real and the virtual in the *PKS*, the "real thing" is definitely condoned. The acceptance of alcohol and sexual rites has both an emancipatory and a worldly connotation, and there is appeal to common sense and cultured behavior. *PKS* 10.56 states that one should consider the social customs, the (conditions of different) countries, and one's health before one decides to consume the fifth (sexual intercourse) and the other m's.[31] *PKS* 10.62 suggests that the liquor should be produced according to the custom of the country, but if harmful, drinking should not be indulged in (10.61). *PKS* 10.69 stipulates that a woman who is sexually aroused should not be left untouched, whereas if not sexually inclined, she should by no means be approached. Apparently it is left to the woman whether or not she wants intercourse (*maithuna*).

Whereas the goddess's epithets and visualizations are sexually explicit, the hints at physicalized sexual rites are indirect, even cryptic. We know only that a *Śakti- pūjā* belongs to each deity cycle (except for the one of Parā), but for the want of further information the commentators disagree to what extent this also involves sexual intercourse. The commentator Rāmeśvara (1832) considers it a daily duty only in the Lalitā-Krama (*PKS* 5.21–22), but seems to restrict it to the practitioner's own wife (or wives).[32] The *PKS* and Umānanda (1745) do not know such a restriction. In the *Śakti-pūjā* of *PKS* 7.36 (ending the Vārāhī cycle) three female partners are required who are in the "blossom of their youth" and "extremely beautiful" and "infatuating." They should be bathed, decorated, perfumed with fragrances and the like, and here the passage ends, except for a short note that thereafter they should be "gratified with all substances," which may or may not include sexual intercourse. Notably the merger of erotics and aesthetics, both strikingly vivid in this passage, combines with the verbal invocation of a gruesome goddess who is asked to strike and kill, then drink the blood and sperm (*PKS* 7.28).[33]

Accordingly I am hesitant to call such practitioners "conformist." Rather I see them as cosmopolitan freethinkers who seek to cross religious and social boundaries. It is part of the *PKS*'s ethical norms that an initiate must gradually emancipate himself from caste and creed (*PKS* 10.70), and even Rāmeśvara (a self-conscious Vedic Brahman) makes a special point that no caste restrictions pertain to the Tantric peer group. (This idea, however, is much more pronounced in the *KT*.) The *PKS* apparently addresses the kind of clientele White describes: liberation-seeking householders, luxurious urban consumers, including members of royal courts.[34] In short, the *PKS*, like most of the Tantras, is designed for a cultural elite.[35] Style and content both suggest that the ritual agents must know a good deal of Sanskrit, be well-educated in Vedic literature, poetry, and sciences, and be well-traveled. It is reasonable to infer that practitioners must be quite well-off (considering the many decorations, spices, perfumes, and gifts the ritual requires) and have ample leisure time (considering that the ritual process consumes more or less the whole day). Notably all commentators were Brahmans, and at least two had close affiliations with the court of Tanjore.[36] The *PKS*, in other words, presupposes a clientele of cultivated and refined connoisseurs of beauty. The ritual agent enjoys a perfumed body, good drink, fine food, erotic pleasure, and philosophy. But the drink, the food, and the erotic pleasures have changed by virtue of the ritual act from profane substances into sacred substances of immortality and blissful trance. The practice, however, is not a "cult of ecstasy" (see White's argument above), but rather a rule-governed ritual of self-transcendence and the construction of a Tantric identity, which in this case means a specific Śaiva-Śākta (versus Vedic) identity.

NEGOTIATING THE VEDIC TRADITION

The Kaula family of initiates was a spiritual elite and presumably also a cultural, political, and economic elite who enjoyed forbidden things and esoteric knowledge and who regarded their own ritual and worldview as superior to the Vedic. This secret society of freethinkers or cosmopolitan avant-garde tried to cross borders, and, at least within the realm of the Kaula "family," transcend purity rules and caste society. In their negotiation of power relationships and redefinition of orthodoxy, the initiates gave the Veda an essential role and drew heavily from the Vedic tradition. The *PKS* is not in opposition to the Veda but includes a number of Vedic *mantras*, particularly from the *Ṛgveda* and the *Upaniṣads* (*PKS* 2.2, 2.6, 3.26, 3.31, 10.10–11, 10.20). Besides involving fire sacrifice (*PKS* 9), as do other Tantric traditions, the *PKS* invents a new Gāyatrī for its major goddess (3.5); presents another variant of the Vedic Gāyatrī for Gaṇapati (2.2); and incorporates the real Vedic Gāyatrī (10.10), that is, the most important Vedic *mantra*.[37] The *PKS* presents itself as belonging to Vedic heritage by self-referential terms such as *Kalpa-Sūtra*, by its *Sūtra*-style (particularly 1.1), and not least by calling itself "great *Upaniṣad*" and Tantric performers "the sacrificers of all sacrifices" (10.83). But this kind of integrative and transformative "borrowing" from and absorbing of the Veda is not a smooth Veda-Tantra continuum, as it is in the south Indian Śrīvidyā.[38] Remarkably the subordination and inversion of the Veda become clear straightaway from the first *Sūtras* on:[39]

1.1 Hence we unfold initiation (*dīkṣā*).
1.2 The great lord, the supreme Śiva, issued the Veda and the rest of the eighteen sciences and other systems of knowledge, by playfully assuming different states . . . and from his five mouths came forth the five Tantric lineages which are given reverence for granting the supreme human aim [i.e., emancipation].
1.3 This is the final doctrine (*siddhānta*).
1.4 Thirty-six principles make up the world.
1.5 Śiva armored with a body is the human individual, without armor he is the supreme Śiva.
1.6 Self-reflection is the aim of men.
1.7 Phonemes (*varṇa*) [constitute] the eternal words [mantras].
1.8 The inherent power of mantras is unimaginable.

1.9 The school tradition and confidence lead to success [of the mantras].
1.10 The best [thing for] confidence is evidence (*pramāṇya*).
1.11 Because the fruit of unification of guru, mantra, deity, one's self (*ātman*), mind and breath is the cognition of the inner self (*antarātman*).
1.12 Bliss (*ānanda*) is the form of Brahman and resides in the body. The five m (*pañcamakāra*) make it manifest. The worship by means of these [five m] [should be performed] secretly, for public display [leads to] hell.
. . .
1.28 There is nothing higher than reaching the Ātman.
1.30 The public sciences (*vidyā*), such as the Veda, are like prostitutes (*veśyā*). Among all worldviews (*darśana*), our [*mantra*] science is the esoteric ("hidden," "secret") one (*gupteyaṃvidyā*).

This agenda is the school's "final doctrine," their *Siddhānta*, which is actually taught during the threefold initiation rites.[40] In terms of negotiation, the Siddhānta is noteworthy for three reasons: (1) the initial statement proclaims the Veda's subordinate position versus the priority of the Tantric revelation as liberation-granting oral teaching from the mouth of the supreme godhead; (2) the Tantra's most efficient ritual instruments, namely the *mantras*, grant success in everything due to their inherent extraordinary power, and the secret *pañcamakāra* (alcohol, etc.) make the bliss of Brahman in the body manifest; and (3) a public-secret opposition is constructed. All three are part of a continuum of one and the same discourse for reordering socioreligious hierarchy. Calling the Veda a "prostitute" (as does also *KT* 11.85) sounds like a severe criticism, but given that the *PKS* stipulates reverence for prostitutes (10.66) and given the inclusion of Vedic *mantras*, it is fair to conclude that it is not so much anti-Vedic opposition that is expressed, but rather an explicit and implicit dialectical negotiation.

Symbolic Subordination of the Veda

The negotiation starts with the proud claim that the Supreme Śiva is the divine originator of the Veda,[41] in explicit contrast to the Veda-orthodox Mīmāṃsākas, who consider the Veda "authorless" and "eternal." The Pūrva-Mīmāṃsākas "prove" this doctrine—which also entails proof of the Veda as a verbal means of knowledge or direct "word evidence" (*pramāṇa*)—by a sophisticated linguistic theory of the permanence of words and phonemes, which in turn the *PKS* implicitly makes use of by transferring it to Tantric *mantras*. While the *PKS* claims Śiva is the source of both the Vedic and the Tantric revelation, only the Tantric lineages issue directly from the godhead's mouth. The supreme god Śiva is the primordial Tantric preceptor, and only the Tantric lineages are associated with liberation. The "eternal words" are the (Tantric) *mantras*, consisting of "eternal phonemes," the letters of the alphabet, which are called "mother(s)" (*mātṛkā*) because they constitute the primary material or energy forms of the universe.[42] The alphabet rites during initiation and daily ritual therefore effect omniscience (*PKS* 10.21). To the *mantras* are attributed inconceivable "power" because they grant success in everything and embody the goddesses (i.e., are immediate self-communicating "hierophanies" of the divine, thereby making their power present). Initiation is primarily *mantra* initiation. Its performance transforms the unredeemed body into a cosmic one, the body of Śiva. This is the first and primary step of emancipation. Emancipation does not necessitate renouncing the world, but is achieved while enjoying sensual delight; the consumption of the (ritualized) forbidden substances is explicitly equated to Brahman bliss.

The Most Efficient Ritual Instruments

The most efficient ritual instruments for emancipation are the *mantras* and the five m's (*pañcamakāra*).

Mantra Power: Negotiating Soteriology

While ideas of holy sound and *mantra* power affecting reality are deeply rooted in the Vedic tradition, probably the Tantra's most important contribution to Indian religious history was a new form of *mantra*. Tantric *mantras* often consist only of (strings of) monosyllabic sound codes, so-called seeds, or *bījas*. But invariably Tantric *mantras*, unlike the Vedic ones, verbally embody the divinities and all their powers.

The *PKS* belongs to a stage when Tantra is largely "*mantra* science" (*mantra-śāstra*). During the initiation rites the novice is led into a ritual diagram, called "mother-*yantra*," the eight lotus leaves (the eight directions of the compass) inscribed with the letters of the alphabet, and in whose center stands the syllable HSAUḤ (*PKS* 1.38). Apparently HSAUḤ denotes the *maithuna* (sexual intercourse) of the supreme male (HA) and female (SAUḤ), which is the energetic center in whom all plurality merges and from whom creation emanates. Parā encompasses the alphabet "mothers" in one single goddess form, in whom all thirty-six principles of the universe are present and absorbed (*PKS* 8.17–18, 8.22). She is not only the cosmos and all knowledge; she also transcends the world by her single seed-syllable SAUḤ, the *bīja* of liberation, of pure light and self-reflexivity (8.1, 8.21). In her own ritual worship the thirty-six principles ("all what can be known") and the "alphabet mothers" are mentally sacrificed—immersed, burned, and absorbed—in the goddess, the "fire of consciousness," whose presence has been ritually established in the lower yogic body centers (8.10, 8.17, 8.21–22). In her dimension as great light of consciousness, Parā is undifferentiated from the Supreme Śiva (the *bīja* HA), the supreme "I" and pure knowledge (10.26) activated in ritual.[43] Whereas the first chapter states that Śiva, "when armored with a body," is the human individual (*jīva*), while "without armor" he is the "Supreme Śiva" (1.5), the last chapter asserts that by the mantra rites the ritual agent attains a body of pure knowledge and becomes the Supreme Śiva in all his limbs (10.50).

If there is a practice common to all Tantric traditions, it can be said to be *mantra* utterance and ritualization as an instrument of power, control, and self-transformation.

By contrast not all Tantric traditions include sexual rites. The identification of Tantra with sexuality is rather the fanciful projection of popular Western Tantra images on the World Wide Web, a move that may itself be seen as the reversal of colonial and missionary fantasies. Since earliest times, however, the Tantrics' "body laboratory" included *mantra* rites and experiments with sound. Due to its immaterial and yet physical nature, sound was a real, potent symbol of cosmic unity, which in turn made the *mantras* excellent ritual instruments for merging interior with exterior space and for bringing about the sphere of the "bodiless" in the body. The later "seed *mantras*" are particularly designed for sound meditation. Most of these end in the nasal sound "ṃ," which has the effect of a bell or a gong: the sound is still heard after the bell has been struck. The Tantrics were very interested in this subtle vibrating sphere of "unstruck sound" or sound waves and devoted their practice to sound contemplation, following the "unstruck" sound in the ether and in the body, the *cakras*, the *mūlādhāra* near the genitals and particularly in the "ether of the heart," between the eyebrows, and ever new steps above the crown of the head.[44] Not least the *mantras*' capacity to effect physical nonduality, absorption, and experiential bliss was of particular interest. Moreover the cryptic sound codes were open to symbolic interpretation and made it possible to express complex cognitive concepts in a single syllable. The *bīja* HSAUḤ, for instance, communicates in a very compact way a holistic worldview.

Bliss in the Body: Negotiating the Body-Mind Relationship

While the *mantras* lead to omniscience, interiority, and bodylessness, the internal "bliss of Brahman" can be *corporally* experienced by the five ritual substances, starting with alcohol and ending with sexual intercourse. Bliss is the divine absolute, the *Brahman* (*PKS* 1.12), and it is the *Ātman*, one's own self, that should be sought (1.28). Here the *PKS* directly correlates with the (late Vedic) Upaniṣadic tradition. In contrast to the world-denying, totally interiorized, and unsensuous bliss of the usual Upaniṣad hermeneutics found in the Veda-orthodox Uttara-Mīmāṃsā or Advaita-Vedānta, the *PKS* asserts that bliss is not only an interior condition, but it has a corporal base. This assertion is taken from the Tantric source *KT* and differs completely from the bliss conception of the *Lalitātriśati-Bhāṣya* (a heavily vedānticized Śrīvidyā source composed in a Śaṅkara monastery of south India),[45] which gives interior bliss an emotional color by evoking the aesthetic *rasa* ("flavor") of the beautiful goddess Lalitā.

Ritual Exteriorization of Mental Concepts and Physical Embodiment of Bliss

The *mantra* initiation is the most elaborate (*PKS* 1.37–41) but is not purely verbal.[46] At the most crucial point meat and alcohol become part of the performance; after the *guru* projects the "mother(s)" (the alphabet) onto the disciple's body, the veil, which up until now has covered the disciple's face, is removed, and he is given flower petals and three pieces of meat soaked in liquor to eat, while the *mantras* of the principles that constitute the world are uttered (1.39). Here is the junction of the performative transubstantiation that transforms his body into a nonordinary, cosmic body, and where he leaves his old self and corporal existence to join the family of the holy, who are able to experience their self-own bliss. Characteristically the adept is given a new name, which ends in "lord of bliss" (1.40).

The *pañcamakāra* ("five m's"), said to make bliss in the body manifest, are considered the "most important" thing (*mukhya*) in the later *PKS* tradition as well. Umānanda (1745) and Rāmeśvara (1832) accept substitutes only if the real substances are not available.[47] They extract the rule from *PKS* 1.23–24, which enjoins that the daily ritual must be performed without exception, even if the "five m's" should not be present or available.

Singling out sexual rites from the integrated whole of the *pañcamakāra* may be a Western bias. In any case it is not by chance that alcohol is presumably called "the first." It is actually the most important ritual substance in the *PKS* as well as in the *KT*.[48] *KT* 5.77 equates liquor with the god Bhairava and the goddess, that is, their self-revelation. Excessive drinking was apparently a form of possession trance. *KT* 7.101 explains, "Only by ecstatic delight the goddess is satisfied. By his [alcoholic] swoon he [becomes] (Śiva-)Bhairava, and by his vomiting he [becomes] all gods."[49] Although there is nothing similar in the *PKS*, alcohol seems to play a similar role. It is a "must" in the special *arghya* offering that should be "sacrificed" into the practitioner's own *kuṇḍalinī* and consumed after sacrifice (*PKS* 3.22–31, 5.22).[50] In this passage the wine is transubstantiated by means of speech acts (including a fair amount of Vedic *mantras*) into the ever-wet goddess and her divine, intoxicating fluid. Alcohol is a physical manifestation of bliss, of the "water of immortality," and of the goddess herself. In singling out sexual rites, then, too much stress has been laid upon them. Indeed a stronger focus on alcohol than on intercourse is acknowledged in the commentary tradition too.[51]

Ritual Interiorization of the Body and Gnostification

Remarkably the cycle of Parā includes only alcohol (*PKS* 8.12) and no other m-substance. Instead there is an even greater degree of visualization than in the previous goddess cycles; one should imagine one's body flooded with the fluids of the "water of immortality" (8.4), exercise breath control and repetition of Parā's *mantra* SAUḤ, while mentally sealing the thirty-six principles of the physical universe in the navel region and burning them "with the fire of consciousness" in the *mūlādhāra-cakra* near the genitals. Then the melted world elements are transposed like a "fluid of heated metal" into the heart lotus (8.10, 8.17) to contemplate their unity in the mind as divine Parā (8.17, 8.19) who is to be worshipped as supreme light, that is, pure awareness and reflection merged (8.20–22). Parā worship is the least tangible and the most connected with internal yoga (*kuṇḍalinī-yoga*) and metaphoric sexuality, but the interiorization of the body by means of the yogic body schemes appears throughout the text, and the last chapter promotes integrative worship: in the morning Lalitā is worshipped in the *mūlādhāra*, in the afternoon Śyāmā in the heart, at night Vārāhī between the eyebrows, and before sunrise Parā is worshipped in the whole body and its yogic centers, starting with the "vessel of Brahman" (*brahmarandhra*), the fontanel or the yogic *cakra* of the thousand-petaled lotus above the crown of the head.[52]

The interiorizing tendency in the *PKS* reaches its peak in the combination of Vedāntic *Mahāvākyas* ("Great Sayings" of nondual existence) and Tantric imagery and ritual. The goddesses' sequences of worship contain ritual enactions of nonduality and *Mahāvākya*-like mystic formulas and prescriptions: enjoining the constant absorption (*samāveśa*) in the Śiva state (*śivatā*) (1.18) and interior sacrifice (1.26), whose fruit is objectless awareness (1.27); combining highly erotic goddess images with the formula "The *Brahman* am I" (3.31); stipulating to connect oneself with Śiva by means of the formula "I am He" (*Haṃsaḥ*) while concentrating on the lowest body *cakra* near the genitals and mentally dissolving ("burning," "cutting," "flooding") the physical elements of one's ordinary body (7.6); enjoining to meditate on the oneness of the cosmic principles (the "burned" and "melted" elements of the physical universe) in the pure light of consciousness (8.17–22); obliging one to visualize the union of the Lord and Mistress of Speech (9.8); prescribing the reflection on one's unity (10.49); describing the ritual agent's Śivahood and attributing the "highest priority" to the clear vision of pure light (10.73).

According to the *KT*, mental focusing, *kuṇḍalinī-yoga*, and the taste of internal blissfulness are necessary to create a sacramental attitude and to distinguish alcohol consumption and intercourse from normal sense indulgence.[53] This seems to be precisely the rationale in the *PKS* too, which augments the mental and verbal acts. Just as important as the physical acts, however, is the shaping of the interior body and senses. Indeed this emphasis on internalized spirituality made it possible to keep the ritual intact even when "purged" of all "impurities" and helped to spread the Śrīvidyā even in the most orthodox Brahmanic circles of the south Indian Śaṅkarācāryas, where sexuality retained a powerful metonymic-metaphoric character, while body practice was completely excised.[54] Instead interior body schemes of *kuṇḍalinī-yoga* and Vedic-Vedāntic influences were stressed, culminating in the assertion that Tantric *mantra* practice and contemplation were the third, secret contemplation part of the Veda, its so-called *upāsanā-kāṇḍa*. This claim of the Tantra to be the *upāsanā-kāṇḍa* of the Veda can also be found in the *PKS* commentary of Lakṣmaṇa Rānaḍe (1889), who while still speaking of "the real things," nevertheless claims to offer a more profound interpretation than previous commentators.[55]

Negotiating Social Space and Spiritual Power

The *PKS* stipulates strict secrecy concerning the "five m's" and eulogizes the "secret" Tantra rather than the "public" Veda. The public-secret opposition certainly reflects pragmatic reasons that are not hard to understand, given the background of the Vedic-Brahmanic value system based on caste society, purity and pollution, and gender difference. But this opposition also reflects theological and ideological reasons—once more, part of negotiating socioreligious hierarchies as well as relationships with the transcendent. Consider how Sanderson contrasts the Śaiva mainstream, whose scriptural revelations are the Tantras (or Āgamas), to the Veda:

> This corpus of *śruti* [the Veda] and *smṛti* [the Veda-based revelations] prescribes the rites, duties and beliefs that constitute the basic or orthodox order and soteriology of Hindu society. The Tantrics however saw their own texts as an additional and more specialized revelation (*viśeṣaśāstra*) which offers a more powerful soteriology to those who are born into this exoteric order. The Tantric rituals of initiation (*dīkṣā*) were held to destroy the rebirth-generating power of the individual's past actions (*karma*) in the sphere of Veda-determined values, and to consubstantiate him with the deity in a transforming infusion of divine power.[56]

This is a fitting description of the *PKS* theology. According to Sanderson (and the *PKS*), the public-secret opposition is a direct socioreligious expression of this more powerful soteriology and a display of reordering religious authority:

> All these Tantrics were similarly related to the traditional forms of religions . . . the Vaiṣṇavas and Śaivas to Vedic orthopraxy. They were excluded by the traditionalists because they went beyond the boundaries of these systems of practice. But the Tantrics themselves, while excluding these exclusivists, included their systems as the outer level of a concentric hierarchy of ritual and discipline. In those communities in which it was possible or desirable to add to the exoteric tradition this second, more esoteric level, there might be forms of the Tantric cult in which this transcendence entailed the infringement of the rules of conduct (*ācāra*) which bound the performer of the ritual at a lower, more public, level of his practice. Thus some rites involved the consumption of meat, alcohol and other impurities.[57]

Sanderson acknowledges a general trend of purging the elements of impurity, and the *PKS* is part of this trend of "domestication"; nevertheless it still keeps such elements intact at a relatively late date; that is, the *PKS* seems to belong to those "limited circles" wherein such trends survived almost unrevised.[58] To offer and consume the "five m's" and follow the Kaula ethical codes of behavior is the right and orthodox conduct (*samaya*) and a "higher" form of social practice, according to the *PKS* worldview and value system.

With respect to ritual and knowledge, the public represents the lower forms, whereas the esoteric represents the higher. This differentiation explains the phrase "like a prostitute" (*veśyā iva*), which is attributed to the Veda and other systems of knowledge by the *PKS* while it represents its own knowledge system as "most hidden" (i.e., superior, precious). While the text itself *performs* secrecy by virtue of its written encodings of the *mantras*, it also *enjoins* secrecy in the case of the "five m's." This stipulated secrecy is easily explained by the antinomian character of the "five m's," but it also has a social dimension. Secrecy is a particularly strong device for establishing group identity, and the *PKS* makes effective use of the different functions of secrecy. The secret of one's own tradition versus the public knowledge of the other, for instance, is a powerful strategy of demarcation and of superiority claims.[59] In this sense the encoded *mantras* are performances of preciousness. The secret performance of the "five m's," on the other hand, and the stipulation not to disclose the practices to noninitiates are both means of hiding heterodox behavior—in effect, to protect insiders from misunderstanding, social branding, and "unworthy" ones who would not understand the true sense of the rites—and cautioning initiates not to offend public norms.

So negotiation with the Vedic tradition by means of this public-secret opposition takes place on more than one level. There is on the one hand a new positioning of public and secret and of the Veda and Tantra, and on the other hand a concise parallelism: Vedic initiation happens undercover; Tantric initiation begins with a veiled face (*PKS* 1.34); Veda recitation may not even be heard by Śūdras; and Tantric *mantras* are given only in encoded form and communicated to morally qualified disciples. Indeed the *PKS* prides itself on being the most secret (i.e., most valuable) ritual system, and by contrasting itself to the Veda at the same time the *PKS* incorporates the Veda's sanctity. The Veda is integrated and thereby simulated, even inverted, since the *PKS* is ostensibly the Veda's equal and even its superior. By calling itself *Upaniṣad* the *PKS* claims to belong to the Veda's "knowledge part." And in fact the *PKS* replaces the entire Veda, both the "ritual part" and the "knowledge part." The ritual actor is the supreme sacrificer who can attain everything he likes (10.83); in his internal sacrifice (1.26) he realizes nonduality, and in his heterodox rituals, embodied *Brahman* bliss (1.12). The *PKS* ritual assures emancipation while the initiate is alive, and no rebirth after death, regardless of whether the performer dies in holy Vārāṇasī or "in the house of a dog-eater" (10.82).

The text thus reflects negotiation processes in the very definition of orthodoxy—including within the Śrīvidyā itself, whose south Indian members would usually shun the houses of the Cāṇḍālas, known as "dog-eaters." The later *PKS* tradition illustrates that even by the nineteenth century Śrīvidyā had retained traits that did not conform to mainstream culture. This is not to say there was an "unbroken tradition," for each of the commentators criticizes his predecessors, but it is noteworthy that all three—Umānanda (1745), Rāmeśvara, (1832) and Lakṣmaṇa Rānaḍe (1889)—were Maharashtrian Brahmans who accepted sexual rites and who disagreed on the use of substitutes. Further this earlier tradition projects an ideology free of caste, whereas Swami Karpatri, who composed the latest *PKS* elaboration, *Śrīvidyā-Ratnākara,* in the 1950s (1987), was not only a spiritual authority but also a national activist and defender of caste society. Karpatri augments the verbal material, while being silent about the "five m's." Here we witness a new vein of negotiation and the final merger of two originally opposed Śrīvidyā and late Kaula schools: the cosmopolitan Kaula of elegant freethinking householders and the heavily vedicized Śrīvidyā of the renunciate monks of the Śaṅkara tradition with whom Karpatri had close connections.

NEGOTIATING TANTRA AND VEDA: CONCLUSION

In introducing a little studied, late ritual manual that obliges the performance of so-called left-hand rites, I am presenting an example that on the one hand justifies Sanderson's proposal that Tantrics are "super-ritualist," while on the other hand illustrates how ritual and nondual gnostic contemplation and knowledge necessarily merge. Significantly it is precisely this necessity that also paved the way for more conformist forms of Kaula Tantra. My other objective in this essay has been to illustrate how rites express, create, and transmute religious ideas and power relationships. An essential part of the performative acts of the *PKS* appears to be the illocutionary negotiation with other traditions. While the negotiation with the Kaula-Tantra (e.g., the *KT*) appears in unmarked quotations and there is a tendency to reduce orgiastic ecstasy in favor of the apathic ecstasy of controlled ritual action, the negotiation with the Veda is more visible and in a certain way more daring, precisely because the *PKS* incorporates the former to such an extent that one can speak of an "invention of tradition," that is, a "(re-)invention of the Veda."

As a written script the *PKS* constructs an idealized vision of Tantric identity and Kaula ritual, and one may ask whether the agents of its negotiation have anything to do with real-world interactions. But the virtual and the real interface in many ways. Consider Bhāskararāya (late seventeenth to mid-eighteenth century), to whom is attributed the first (and now lost) commentary of the *PKS* and who, according to an apocryphal anecdote, was accused by the orthodox sixteenth-century Veda-Pandit Nārāyaṇa Bhaṭṭa of Varanasi of having "left the right path" because of following left-hand Tantra (*vāma-marga*).[60] In the early nineteenth century Rāmeśvara, the grand-disciple of Bhāskararāya, is still repeating these same reproaches, which he attributes to the famous seventh-century Mīmāṃsā theorist Kumārila Bhaṭṭa: Tantrics have left the Vedic path, they are greedy and self-indulgent, and Tantra is only for women and Śūdras.[61] But remarkably Rāmeśvara uses the very same Vedic authority, Kumārila Bhaṭṭa (besides Purāṇic sources), to defend the Kaula-Tantra and its propriety for Brahmans—possibly a secret protest in colonial times when the necessity of defense was greater then ever?

Note that Rāmeśvara and Lakṣmaṇa Rānaḍe, who defend the Tantra and its consonance with the Veda, flourished at a time when the British had firmly established rule in India, when the first translation of the *Bhagavad-Gītā* (1785) and first edition of the *Ṛg-Veda* (1849–73) were published and when other expressions of Hindu culture were regarded as "debased" and Tantra most despised. Rāmeśvara not only defends Kaula ritual by using Mīmāṃsā methods (Veda hermeneutics and Pāṇini's grammar), but he also strongly emphasizes *bhakti* (loving devotion) and faith, arguing that otherwise it would be hard to keep sense control and a controlled mind while consuming meat and alcohol, getting drunk, and seeing beautifully decorated young women.[62] Furthermore he apparently restricts the obligatory sexual intercourse to the practitioner's spouse. Here we glimpse the Tantra described with great empathy by Arthur Avalon (pen name of Sir John Woodroffe) some eighty years later.[63] Avalon had the courage to counter the negative missionary and colonial cliché of a degenerate and obscene religion by highlighting the great philosophical sophistication, high morality, and subtle metaphoric imagination of the Tantras, including their ingenious *mantra* practices, *cakra*- and *kuṇḍalinī-yoga* to attain internal bliss. Even so, be it Victorian prudery, Anglican morals, his Bengali Brahman informants, or simply because this was the Tantra of his time, Avalon restricted the sexual element either to matrimonial intercourse or to purely metaphoric and symbolic use.[64]

Avalon has since been subjected to heavy orientalist criticism, and it cannot be denied that he presented a highly unified and essentialized Tantrism. But even by the sixteenth century the *PKS* had produced a left-hand Tantra not so far removed from Avalon's unified Tantrism. I suspect that by compiling Tantra material of almost "global" pan-Indian spread the *PKS* attempted both a sort of *summa* of high Hindu Kaula orthodoxy and an *aggiornamento*,[65] thereby presenting a Tantra-Veda continuum that did not forsake Kaula and that met the needs of literary elites, elegant householders, and liberal cosmopolitans. Courtly milieus may also be suspected here. Umānanda, who wrote the first *PKS* elaboration and lived at the Tanjore court, says of Bhāskararāya, "There was no part of the earth unvisited by him, not any king known uninitiated by him."[66]

The (Kaula-)Tantra in general, and the *PKS* in particular, provided educated social groups and ruling classes, regardless of caste and gender, with a means to acquire sacred power. This power was deemed similarly potent and even better than the exclusivist orthodox sacred power of the Vedic Brahmans and their purity-ridden ritual and *dharma* codes. Recent publications have pointed out the special appeal of Tantric ritual and Tantric professionals to rulers who were in need of divine empowerment to establish social authority and protect their kingdoms. But there is no doubt that the Tantric ritual loaded with esoteric meaning was attractive also to the Brahmans and became an important social and religious as well as political factor due to its popularity among powerful social groups and royal sponsoring. An important factor was the agreement that the Tantrists accepted the "public" authority of the Veda, even when promising a higher "secret" esoteric knowledge, which itself was publically not to be offensive to normative Brahmanism and the Vedic *Leitkultur*. Nor were the Tantric *mantra* rites offensive; in fact they could easily be combined with Vedic recitation in coronation rites, temple services, festival culture, and private worship. Much of the Tantric ritual became completely uncontroversial and merged with the Vedic-purāṇic Smārta stream. To a certain extent even Kaula body practice became acceptable as a possible (albeit not commonly cherished) ritual form, provided it was secretly performed. Indeed there are Brahmans in Nepal and south India who first perform their Vedic daily rites, and thereafter their left-hand or right-hand Tantric ritual—the Nepalis usually being left-handers using alcohol, the south Indians right-handers using water. Such regional varieties must not be forgotten. Nor should it be forgotten that Rāmeśvara's solution to perform Śakti worship with one's own wife was likely not only a conformist turn, but simply pragmatism (considering that only in royal courts would a harem of beautiful young women have been daily available).

I have suggested that the cosmopolitan Kaula-Tantra of the *PKS* implicitly and explicitly mirrors a number of processes of negotiation. By being liberal the *PKS* challenges both ecstatic Kaula and conformist Śrīvidyā as well as traditional Vedic orthodoxy and Smārta mainstream culture. So-called left-hand rites are definitely present and certainly accepted, but there is also a high degree of gnostic overcoding and deliberate secrecy—and most prominently a strict ritual form. While the *KT* already discloses features of domestication, the ritual program of the *PKS* to locate the mind in the body and the body in the mind illustrates more clearly which kinds of practices and conceptual schemes exactly helped to pave the way for a Kaula completely "purged" of so-called left-hand features. The *PKS* is an impressive example of the fact that, even favoring embodiment, a pronounced emphasis on the *mantras*, the imaginary, and the virtual can become so prominent that finally only metonymy and metaphor are left—remarkably without substantially endangering the ritual.

Of course the replacement of the real by the virtual not only was a reaction to the fact that the virtual was seen as equally real as the real, but also was due to social constraints, sheer prudence, anxiety to be seen as a respectable part of the society, conformism, and monastic vows. Yet the virtuality argument is less idealistic than it may sound to a Western mind under the impact of the Cartesian body-mind split (including Platonic idealism, Aristotelian rationalism, Christian discourses of body and soul, and Protestant antiritualism). Remarkably the most prominent Kaula opponent, Lakṣmīdhara, a Brahman Śrīvidyā adept who lived in a royal court in Orissa around the same time the *PKS* was composed (fifteenth or sixteenth century), centered his critique precisely on the virtual, particularly on virtual sexuality, rather than corporeal intercourse. He heavily censored the imaginative practice to visualize the goddess's face, breasts, and vulva (*kāmakalā*) and the Kaula's emphasis on the lowest body *cakra*, the *mūladhāra*. That means he censured imaginative practices promoted by the *PKS* and found them disgusting and unworthy of Brahmans and twice-born (i.e., the three upper castes initiated into the Veda). According to him, Śrīvidyā is restricted to the twice-born, and the union of god and goddess must be contemplated in the topmost *cakra,* above the head. Any other practice would be unspiritual and must be shunned. Only spiritual worship is *samaya-ācāra*, correct and orthodox behavior. Lakṣmīdhara's innovation was to create a split between Kaula and Samaya that had not been known before. In this sense the *PKS* is more traditional, understanding the Kaula rules themselves as Samaya. Since Lakṣmīdhara's time, Samaya became a counterterm to Kaula and a synonym for "right-hand" ritual among Śrīvidyā worshippers, and the points he raised remained controversial issues. However, most "right-hand" ritual manuals of the Śrīvidyā contain the sexually connoted *kāmakalā* meditation. No one really wanted to dismiss its philosophic content. It was only the ritual act of imagination that incited controversy. We do not know whether the author of the *PKS* reacted to Lakṣmīdhara by showing how spiritual the Kaula really was or whether it was the other way around. They may not even have known each other at all. In any case the two protagonists provide us with a nice example of the role of the virtual in the field of ritual combat and its relations to real life and social reality. At the same time this example shows that the replacement of the real by the virtual that I claimed did not happen that smoothly and easily, and surely it opened new fields for negotiations. The virtual body, the inner senses, and the techniques of imagination themselves became a contested field. Different kinds of bodily awareness are created when contemplation is centered "above" the head or "in" different body places, including the lower body parts, or when imagining the body flooded with the "nectarine water of immortality" oozing from the topmost *cakra*, instead of keeping concentration there.

I should add a further differentiation. My contention was that the Kaulas belonged to an intellectual avant garde of freethinkers. In the cases of the Kashmir Śaiva Tantrist Abhivanagupta, the *PKS* author (anonymous), Bhāskararāya, and Umānanda, I maintain this claim. Rāmeśvara, however, seems to be a different character: a Kaula Tantrist more by family tradition than by personal charisma and enthusiasm. His commentary almost gives the impression that he is a Kaula Tantrist unwillingly and drinks his cups of wine because it is his ritual obligation, rather than enjoying them as "bliss of Brahman." This does not mean that he rejects ecstatic Kaula. In fact he quotes many extreme passages without being critical of them; he even does so with certain empathy because it belongs to the Kaula *dharma* to increase the cups of wine in the "mature" and "post-mature" states of the Tantric "hero." Rāmeśvara approaches the Tantric ritual and the ritual script of the *PKS* in precisely the same way that a classical Pūrva-Mīmāṃsā Vedist perceives the Vedic ritual and the Veda, namely as consisting of strict rules, ritual duties, and a number of do's and don'ts to be scrupulously followed in the minutest detail in order to get the unseen desired fruit (heaven in the case of the Veda, Śiva-hood in the case of the *PKS*). Rāmeśvara's outstandingly furious and pungent critique regarding Umānanda's *PKS* elaboration mostly concerns details in the *mantra* practice rather than big themes like the "five m's," sexual intercourse, or interior yoga, and one wonders why Rāmeśvara should be so much enraged about his co-disciple in the same Bhāskararāya lineage, treating him like the worst heretic. Be it due to Umānanda's success in the royal court, his lasting greater popularity among the Kaulas, his greater liberty in adding extra wine when consuming the rest of sacrifice—we can only speculate. Only one thing is certain: even within the same Tantric lineage do negotiations take place.

A final word should be added about the limited representation of Tantṛa in this paper. Owing to my textual sources I have spoken only about high-class issues, that is, problematic areas in the perception of cultural elites, where the debate of Veda and Tantra ranged foremost. There has always been a popular and "folk" Tantra that was little concerned about such issues and was much more pragmatically oriented and interested in coping with the difficulties of daily life, the Tantra of healers, astrologers, village shamans, wandering yogis, and wonderworking babas. All of them have their own little and large contests among each other and have to meet with the common reproaches against Tantra as brought forth by emic outsiders, such as "foul mumble-jumble" and "black magic." A further kind of Tantra is the mainstream Tantra of the common people which is not even perceived as Tantra anymore because it became the cultural knowledge of all sectors of society and fused completely with the epic-purāṇic performance culture, *bhakti* devotionalism, and popular Hinduism. I am speaking of "lighter forms" of Tantra that did not (necessarily) require initiation or special training and centered on *mantra* power and the utterance and repetition of simple holy formulas containing the name of god (e.g., "Prostrations to Śiva" and "Rām, Rām"). Like the complex Tantric ritual, the mere repetition of a sacred formula containing the name of god provided religious autonomy, a most direct contact with the divine, a feeling of being protected and invested with the god's transmundane power, a knowledge enabling one to absorb the god or goddess by uttering his or her name and to participate in the very substance of the divinity. Tantric and devotional *mantra* performance made the experience of the extraordinary a part of everyone's life, without the need of Vedic sacraments or the mediating priest in the temple, and even without a *pūjā* place at home. I suspect such subjective factors, such as the religious empowerment of laypersons, the easiness of performance, and the personal satisfaction it provided, were equally important as or even more important than royal sponsoring in the process of making Tantra a mainstream culture in middle-age and early modern India. Thus I would like to stress Tantra's quality not only as an important social, religious, and political factor, but also as an important cultural factor that directly and indirectly shaped the beliefs and practices of a great number of Indian religious traditions. *Mantra* practice became part of popular religion and mass culture, and the sacred power of the holy formula became an unquestioned reality. The semantically transparent prayer formulas needed no initiation, no training, no higher education, no wealth, no esoteric knowledge, no knowledge about the right time, place, or rules of performance, and provoked few conflicts, even being acceptable to staunch Veda Brahmans. The prayer formulas in which merged Tantric *mantra* conception and *bhakti* devotionalism of loving participation established an individualistic counterculture that enabled one to transcend the rigid grids of social life beyond Vedic or Tantric knowledge and ritual.

Notes

1. Although acknowledged as one of the most important Tantric ritual manuals (Brooks, *Auspicious Wisdom*, 52, 110, 239nn112–18; Bühnemann, *The Worship of Mahāgaṇapati According to the Nityotsava*, xv; Goudriaan and Gupta, *Hindu Tantric and Śākta Literature*, 150–51; Khanna, "The Concept and Liturgy of the Śrīcakra Based on Śivānanda's Trilogy," 77–79; Padoux, *Le Coeur de la Yoginī*, 7), neither the *PKS* nor its commentaries received translations or detailed studies. This essay is the preliminary result of research with Dr. Claudia Weber, "Vertextete Riten: Das Paraśurāma-Kalpasūtra (annotated edition, Erstübersetzung, Ritualanalyse) und seine 'Weiterschreibungen' in der Rezeptionsgeschichte." I want to express my gratitude to the German Research Council for granting support for this endeavor. Claudia Weber supplied me with translations of the commentary tradition, Rāmeśvara (1832), referred to as *PKS*(Ba); Lakṣmaṇa Rānaḍe (1889), whose commentary exists only in manuscript form and is referred to as "STV(Ms)"; and the ritual elaborations *Nityotsava* (*N*) of Umānandanātha (1745) and *Śrīvidyā-Ratnākara* (*ŚRĀ*) of Svāmi Karpātrī (ca. 1950).

2. Although most Tantric schools were not interested in the Veda, they have been informed since their first literary emergence by the Vedic deities Rudra-Śiva and Viṣṇu, as well as by features of the Vedic sacrifice and the Upaniṣadic worldview, and neither were various attempts of deliberate integration lacking. See also Goudriaan, "Tantrism in History," 15–17; Lorenzen, "Early Evidence of Tantric Religion"; Coburn, "The Structural Interplay of Tantra, Vedānta, and Bhakti"; Brooks, "Auspicious Fragments and Uncertain Wisdom."

3. The first mention of the *PKS* is found in Kṛṣṇānanda's *Tantrasāra* (ca. 1580); the oldest preserved manuscript dates from 1675. On the manuscript tradition, see Weber, "Manuskripte des Paraśurāma-Kalpasūtra und seiner Kommentartradition."

4. On the problematic term "Tantrism," see also Padoux, "A Survey of Tantrism for the Historians of Religion; Padoux, "What Do We Mean by Tantrism?"; Urban, *Tantra*, 1–43.

5. Sanderson, "Purity and Power among the Brahmans of Kashmir," 191. See also Sanderson, "Meaning in Tantric Ritual"; White, *Kiss of the Yoginī;* Hatley, "The Brahmayāmalatantra and Early Śaiva Cult of Yoginīs."

6. White, *Kiss of the Yoginī.*

7. White, "Transformations in the Art of Love," 174.

8. Padoux, *Le Coeur de la Yoginī*, 7–8; Khanna, "The Concept and Liturgy of the Śrīcakra Based on Śivānanda's Trilogy"; Padoux, "What Do We Mean by Tantrism?," 22; White, *Kiss of the Yoginī.*

9. This "purge" is attributed to the impact of the eighth-century philosopher Śaṅkara, but in fact it is the result of the adoption of *Śrīvidyā* by Smārta Śaivas and the Śaṅkarācāryas, the abbots of the south Indian Śaṅkara monasteries.

10. Sanderson, "Śaivism and the Tantric Traditions," 662.

11. See *PKS* 1.5–6, 1.11, 1.18–19, 1.21, 1.26–28, 3.14, 3.31, 7.6, 8.19–22, 9.9, 9.26–27, 10.23–28, 10.49–50, 10.63, 10.82. For the combination of Kashmir Śaiva and Vedic-Vedāntic terminology and conceptions in particular, see *PKS* 1.18–1.22, 1.26–27.

12. The third and fourth "m" word belong to a later, already codified phase of Kaula. Compare White, *Kiss of the Yoginī*, 83.

13. Characteristically the horrific Vārāhī is given a subordinate ritual role as Lalitā's commander in chief.

14. On the question of date see Goudriaan and Gupta, *Hindu Tantric and Śākta Literature*, 10, 14, 17, 18, 47, 93–96; Carlstedt, *Studier i Kulārṇava-Tantra*, 15, 65–66. White (*Kiss of the Yoginī*, 152) traces the KT to the thirteenth or fourteenth century.

15. See *KT* 3.6–7 (*PKS* 1.2); 5.51 (*PKS* 10.63); 5.80 (*PKS* 1.12); 6.41–48 (*PKS* 3.26); 6.50–52 (*PKS* 3.27–28); 6.53–55 (*PKS* 3.29); 6.56–58 (*PKS* 3.30); 6.61 (*PKS* 6.19); 6.69 (*PKS* 4.3); 8.4 (*PKS* 10.68); 9.42 (*PKS* 1.5); 11.57–58 (*PKS* 10.66); 11.66–68 (*PKS* 10.65); 11.85 (*PKS* 1.30); 16.129–30 (*PKS* 8.10, 8.21–22).

16. Lately there have been extensive editions and compilations: see the *Śrīvidyā-Ratnākara* (1991/92); the *Śrīvidyā-Vārivasyā* (1970); the *PKS*, ed. Misra (2000) and ed. Tripathi (2008), both containing a new Hindi commentary, the *Nityotsava*, ed. Misra (2005), with Hindi commentary, and the prefaces that accompany these texts.

17. This definition was suggested as a tentative starting point by the editors of the volume.

18. Certainly I concede social contests behind the scene. For instance, behind the *PKS* different elite groups compete about sacred and profane authority and power and alternative worldviews at a particular historical juncture. However, in this paper I will concentrate on the "virtual negotiations" as mirrored in the *PKS*.

19. Bell, *Ritual*, 81–83, 168–169.

20. Bell, *Ritual*, 83, 160–61, 165, 166, 168–69.

21. This is the major thesis of White, *Kiss of the Yoginī*. See, for instance, xi–xiii, 2–26, 70–85, and 188–218. A substantial critique on this was raised by Hatley, "The Brahmayāmalatantra and Early Śaiva Cult of Yoginīs," 11, *n*. 33.

22. White, *Kiss of the Yoginī*, xii–xiii, 3, 99, 241–45.

23. See ibid., 218–57, particularly 219–20, 242–43, 245–46; White, "Transformations in the Art of Love," 174–75.

24. *Athāto dīkṣāṃ vyākhyāsyāmaḥ* ||1|| (*PKS* 1.1).

25. Bell, *Ritual*, 138–72 suggests that common aspects of ritualization include formalism, traditionalism, invariance, rule governance, sacral symbolism, and performance. Michaels, "Rituelle Klangräume," 34–35 regards embodiment, formality, framing, transformation/effectiveness, and extraordinariness ("Überhöhung") as major criteria. Lawson and McCauley, *Rethinking Religion*, 84–136 and McCauley and Lawson, *Bringing Ritual to Mind*, 13–14, 17–19, 143–45 suggest that each religious rite necessarily implies membership, change in the religious world, and the foundational action of a superhuman agent in which the ritual is embedded. For the latter criteria, see also 6–37, particularly 20–23, 25, 33, 86.

26. *Sarva-gātraḥ śuddha-vidyā-maya-tanuḥ sa eva parama-śivaḥ* (*PKS* 10.50).

27. See the cognitive theory of Johnson, *The Body in the Mind*.

28. *PKS* 3.28–30 combines the erotic image with alcoholic liquor, which itself embodies the goddess and the nectar immortality.

29. The *PKS* invariably uses the term "Śakti" for the female partner whose worship may involve intercourse if she agrees. Other terms in Kaula sources are "Yoginī," "Dūti," and "Suvāsinī." See also Bühnemann, *The Worship of Mahāgaṇapati According to the Nityotsava*, xxvi, xxix; and STV(Ms), vol. 2, chap. 7, p. 71.

"The rest of sacrifice" possibly refers to the Tantric practice of collecting the sexual fluids produced by the ritual intercourse in the special *arghya* vessel into which the other four "m's" are also added; this is then offered to the deity and finally consumed by the ritual agent(s), the *guru* and disciples. Bühnemann (*The Worship of Mahāgaṇapati According to the Nityotsava*, xxvi) mentions a number of sources for this practice, but not the *PKS*. Lakṣmaṇa's STV(Ms), vol. 1, chap. 1, pp. 167–92 (particularly p. 190) and chap. 2, pp. 79, 117, indicate that the practice is known, and cryptically hinted at in *PKS* 2.6 by the word *ca* ("and").

30. The commentaries discussing *PKS* 5.22 do not disclose much more: see *PKS*(Ba), pp. 176–86; STV(Ms), vol. 1, chap. 2, p. 170; vol. 2, chap. 3, p. 168; chap. 4, pp. 37–38; chap. 5, pp. 51–52. STV(Ms), vol. 1, chap. 1, pp. 167–92 (particularly pp. 167, line 2ff., 170–71, 177, 182–86) emphasizes the symbolic and spiritual aspects and rule governance.

31. Rāmeśvara explains, for instance, that it would be very unwise to consume liquor if one has to meet worldly obligations to non-Tantrics after the ritual.

32. Regarding the restriction to matrimonial intercourse, Rāmeśvara quotes the *Svatantra-Tantra*. See *PKS*(Ba), p. 175, lines 4–10 and p. 278, lines 25–27; see also STV(Ms), vol. 1, pp. 847–49. Lakṣmaṇa agrees with Rāmeśvara concerning the obligation of "the fifth" in the Lalitā cycle and cites him quite frequently. See his opinion in more detail in STV(Ms), vol. 1, chap. 1, p. 170, lines 5ff.; p. 179, line 2; pp. 183–85; vol. 2, chap. 3, p. 168; chap. 4, pp. 37–38; chap. 5, pp. 51–52; chap. 7, p. 71.

33. This image (of the goddess Vārāhī) is closest to White's wild Yoginīs and subaltern Tantric practices.

34. The royal images associated with the goddess trinity (see, for instance, *PKS* 6.1–2) and a few other Sūtras may be taken as hints of a royal audience. But these hints are so metaphoric and general—in addition to which they also apply to other Tantric sources on gaining commanding

power (*ājñā-śakti*) and conquering one's enemies—that it seems too speculative to draw a definite conclusion. There can be no doubt, however, that highly cultured upper-class males are addressed, and that the *PKS* was known in the Tanjore court at the time of Umānanda (eighteenth century).

35. I doubt subaltern roots, as suggested by White, but I agree with the notion of growing inspiration from subaltern goddess traditions. Some early Tantras are definitely "folksy," that is, written in a highly hybridized Sanskrit that is not (yet) Kaula in outlook. But in general the authors of the Tantras (who wrote almost exclusively in Sanskrit) belong to literate, upper-caste, urban social groups. See also Lorenzen, "Early Evidence of Tantric Religion."

36. This is ascertained for Umānandanātha as well as his *guru* Bhāskararāya, the most eminent Śrīvidyā theoretician whose *PKS* commentary *Ratnāloka* is now lost.

37. It is not conclusive whether this is an invention of the *PKS*, since it is not uncommon in later Tantra that Gāyatrī variants are attributed to the deities. See also Brooks, *Auspicious Wisdom*, 92–97, 103–4. On the Vedic Gāyatrī see *Taittirīya Āranyaka* 10.1.

38. See Wilke, "A New Theology of Bliss."

39. *Athâto dīkṣāṃ vyākhyāsyāmaḥ* | |1| | *bhagavān parama-śiva-bhaṭṭārakaḥ śruty-ādy-aṣṭādaśa-vidyāḥ sarvāṇi darśanāni līlayā tad-tad-avasthā-"pannaḥ praṇīya, saṃvinmayyā bhagavatyā bhairavyā svâtmâbhinnayā pṛṣṭaḥ pañcabhiḥ mukhaiḥ pañcâmnāyān paramârtha-sāra-bhūtān praṇināya* | |2| | *tatrâyaṃ siddhāntaḥ* | |3| | *ṣaṭtriṃśat-tattvāni viśvam* | |4| | *śarīra-kañcukitaḥ śivo jīvo niṣkañcukaḥ para-śivaḥ* | |5| | *sva-vimarśaḥ puruṣârthaḥ* | |6| | *varṇâtmakā nityāḥ śabdāḥ* | |7| | *mantrāṇām acintya-śaktitā* | |8| | *saṃpradāya-viśvāsābhyāṃ sarva-siddhiḥ* | |9| | *viśvāsa-bhūyiṣṭhaṃ prāmāṇyam* | |10| | *guru-mantra-devatā-"tma-manaḥ-pavanānām aikya-niṣphālanād antarātma-vittiḥ* | |11| | *ānandaṃ brahmaṇo rūpaṃ, tac ca dehe vyavasthitaṃ, tasyâbhivyañjakāḥ pañca ma-kārāḥ, tair arcanaṃ guptyā, prākaṭyān nirayaḥ* | |12| | *[. . .] ātma-lābhān na paraṃ vidyate* | |28| | *[. . .] veśyā iva prakaṭā vedâdi-vidyāḥ* | *sarveṣu darśaneṣu gupt-eyaṃ vidyā* | |30| | The following translation is my own.

40. The initiation ritual proper starts with *PKS* 1.32, and the teaching of the doctrine of the previous verses is actually part of the ritual. Compare *PKS* 1.34 and 1.42, and *Nityotsava* p. 7, line 4 to p. 8, line 7. That the *PKS* begins with doctrinal issues shows its scriptural and idealistic-ideological character. This is also reflected in a few more inconsistencies concerning the ritual order (see *PKS* 1.32–33, in contrast to 1.35–36; 1.39 and 1.41; 1.13–25 and 10.57–81), which the *Nityotsava* seeks to eliminate, partly in disagreement with Rāmeśvara.

41. Historically this claim is much older than the *PKS* and was already known, for instance, to the Nāyaṉmārs.

42. See also Muller-Ortega, *The Triadic Heart of Śiva*, 59, 99. On the equation of the *tattvas* (the thirty-six principles of the cosmos) with the *mātṛkā* (the Sanskrit alphabet to which a nasal sound is added) and their ritual application, see *PKS* 1.38–39, 6.11, 8.17–18, particularly 10.21.

43. Whereas the Parā image of *PKS* 8.21 seems close to the nondual Kashmir Śaiva idea of the merger of light and self-reflection in the supreme godhead, *PKS* 10.26–27 is closer to the androgynous and ultimately genderless Ardhanarīśvara theology, which is typical for the south (and is also expressed by the *KT*, particularly *KT* 4.107–15).

44. See Bhāskararāya, *Vārivasyā-Rahasya*, auto-commentary to chap. 1, in *Varivasyā-Rahasya and Its Commentary Prakāśa*.

45. See Wilke, "A New Theology of Bliss."

46. The other two consist of visualizations of the *guru* who mentally projects the red and white feet of goddess and god onto the disciple's head (*śāmbhavī-dīkṣā*) and who burns away the disciple's sins by imagining a wave of light extending through the yogic centers of the disciple's body (*śāktī-dīkṣā*).

47. *Nityotsava,* p. 62, line 24 to p. 63, line 9 and *PKS*(Ba), p. 39.10–11 on *PKS* 1.24; p. 175, lines 4–10 on *PKS* 5.21; pp. 275–79 on *PKS* 10.62–63.

48. On the preference of alcohol, see *KT* 5.11–43, 5.77–85, 7.81–102.

49. *ānandāt tṛpyate devī mūrcchayā bhairavaḥ svayam* | *vamanāt sarva-devāś ca tasmāt trividham ācaret* | | This verse is also quoted in *PKS*(Ba), p. 184, lines 17–18, by Rāmeśvara.

50. While the ordinary *arghya* consists of water to which a drop of wine must be added (*PKS* 3.22), the "special *arghya*" involves plain wine.

51. Umānanda allows extra portions of wine at the end of the ritual (*Nityotsava,* p. 62.7ff.). Even Rāmeśvara, who disapproves of this custom, devotes long passages to all kinds of alcohol and defends alcohol consumption if not done out of passion and lust, but as part of the ritual. *PKS*(Ba) pp. 121–33 on *PKS* 3.31; pp. 176–86 on 5.22; pp. 274–75 on 10.62.

52. *PKS* 10.22–55, particularly 10.28, 10.33–47, 10.55. On worshipping Parā in different parts of the body, see her own cycle: *PKS* 8.4, 8.9–10, 8.16–17, 8.23. Her sunrise worship equals the one of Gaṇapati (*PKS* 2.2) in which the same imagery of mentally showering the body from the *brahmarandhra* occurs. The topmost *cakra* also plays a central role while worshipping the *mantra* of the *guru*'s "sandals" within each of the goddesses' cycles. The *PKS* uses different terms for the highest *cakra* (for instance, *brahmabila, brahmakoṭara* or *dvādaśānta*). The first two mentioned sometimes refer to the fontanel as a separate body place (maybe not a *cakra* in the proper sense), and sometimes they are identified with the thousand-petaled lotus.

53. See *KT* 5.68–72, 5.102–8, 5.111–12.

54. See Wilke, "A New Theology of Bliss."

55. STV(Ms), vol. 1, chap. 1, pp. 2–7. See also Sastri's preface to the *PKS*(Ba), xi–xiii.

56. Sanderson, "Śaivism and the Tantric Traditions," 660.

57. Ibid., 661.

58. Compare ibid.

59. It is a common topos in the Indian tradition to present a new text as "secret," a "great secret," or an "even greater secret" in order to designate a text as more important and more precious than its predecessor(s).

60. *Varivasyā-Rahasya and Its Commentary Prakāśa,* 18–19.

61. *PKS*(Ba), p. 3, lines 7ff; *PKS*(Ba), p. 7, lines 15ff.

62. *PKS* (Ba), p. 15, lines 24–27, on *PKS* 1.1.

63. See, for instance, Avalon, *Principles of Tantra,* which enjoyed a number of reprints.

64. See Avalon, *Śakti und Śākta*, 376–412, particularly 379–80, 385–87, 393–95.

65. The *KT* is not the only source. There seems to be a common stock of (Kaula-)Tantric ideas from which the *PKS* draws selectively. Textual parallels can be traced in Tantra literatures from virtually all regions of India, such as the *Subhagodaya* (Kerala?), *Śāradatilaka* (Kashmir?), *Śrītattvacintāmaṇi* (Bengal), *Śyāmarahasya* (Bengal), *Mantramahoddhati* (Varanasi), and other earlier and later Tantra works.

66. Quoted in Sastry, *Lalitā-Sahasranāma with Bhāskararāya's Commentary*, x.

Bibliography

Primary Sources

Kulārṇava-Tantra. Ed. and trans. Ram Kumar Rai. Varanasi: Chowkhamba Sanskrit Series Office, 1983.

Nityotsava, by Umānandanātha. Ed. A. Mahadeva Sastri. 1923. Revised by Trivikrama Tirtha. Vadodara 52000. Baroda: Central Library, 1930.

Nityotsava, by Umānandanātha. Ed. and Hindi commentary by Paramahamsa Misra. Varanasi: Chaukambha, 2005.

Paraśurāmakalpasutra. Ed. Claudia Weber. Göttingen: GRETIL, 2007. www.sub.uni-goettingen.de/ebene_1/fiindolo/gretil.htm#Paraks.

Paraśurāmakalpasutra, with Rāmeśvara-vṛtti [abbr. Saubhāghyodaya] and [Hindi commentary] Nīraksīraviveka, by Paramahamsa Misra. Ed. Vidyanivasa Misra. Varanasi: Sampūrnānanda Saṃskrita Viśvavidyālaya, 2000.

Paraśurāmakalpasutra, with Rāmeśvara-vṛtti and Hindi commentary, by Mrtyunjaya Tripathi. Varanasi: Caukhamba Sanskrit Series, 2008.

Paraśurāmakalpasutra (Ba), with Rāmeśvara's Commentary. Ed. A. Mahadeva Sastri. 1923. Revised and enlarged by Sakarlal Yajneswar Sastri Dave. Baroda: Oriental Institute, 1999.

Śrīvidyā-Ratnākara. Compiled by Karapātrasvāmi (ca. 1950). Enlarged ed. Ed. Sītārāma Kavirājaḥ. Varanasi: Śrīvidyā Sādhanapītham, 1991–92.

Śrividyā-Vārivasyā. Ed. Sītārāma Kavirājaḥ. Varanasi: Chaukambha, 1970.

Sūtratattvavimarśinī, by Lakṣmaṇa Rānaḍe [Paraśurāmakalpasutra commentary]. Manuscript nos. TR 587.1 and TR 587.2 (old book no. 38 C 20 de 802 [saṃ 1, 2]). Adyar Library, Chennai, Adyar.

Varivasyā-Rahasya and Its Commentary Prakāśa. Ed. Subrahmanya Sastri. Madras: Adyar Library, 1934.

Studies and Translations

Avalon, Arthur. *Principles of Tantra: The Tantratattva of Śrīyukta Śiva Candra Vidyārṇava Bhattacārya Mahodaya*. 1913. 2 vols. Madras: Ganesh, 1991.

———. *Śakti und Śākta: Essays and Addresses*. 1927. Madras: Ganesh, 1987.

Bell, Catherine. *Ritual: Perspectives and Dimensions*. New York: Oxford University Press, 1997.

Brooks, Douglas Renfrew. "Auspicious Fragments and Uncertain Wisdom: The Roots of Śrīvidyā Śākta Tantrism in South India." In *The Roots of Tantra*, ed. Katherine Ann Harper and Robert L. Brown, 57–75. Albany: State University of New York Press, 2002.

———. *Auspicious Wisdom: The Texts and Traditions of Śrīvidyā Śākta Tantrism in South India*. Albany: State University of New York Press, 1992.

Bühnemann, Gudrun. *The Worship of Mahāgaṇapati According to the Nityotsava*. Revised ed. Delhi: Kant Publications, 2003.

Carlstedt, Gunnar. *Studier i Kulārṇava-Tantra*. Uppsala: Almqvist & Wiksell, 1974.

Coburn, Thomas B. "The Structural Interplay of Tantra, Vedānta, and Bhakti: Nondualist Commentary on the Goddess." In *The Roots of Tantra*, ed. K. A. Harper and R. L. Brown, 77–89. Albany: State University of New York Press, 2002.

Goudriaan, Teun. "Tantrism in History." In *Hindu Tantrism*, ed. S. Gupta, D. J. Hoens, and T. Goudriaan, 13–46. Leiden: Brill, 1979.

Goudriaan, Teun, and Sanjukta Gupta. *Hindu Tantric and Śākta Literature*. Wiesbaden: Harrassowitz, 1981.

Hatley, Shaman. "The Brahmayāmalatantra and Early Śaiva Cult of Yoginīs." PhD diss., University of Pennsylvania, 2007.

Johnson, Mark. *The Body in the Mind: The Bodily Basis of Meaning, Imagination, and Reason*. Chicago: University of Chicago Press, 1987.

Khanna, Madhu. "The Concept and Liturgy of the Śrīcakra Based on Śivānanda's Trilogy." PhD diss., Oxford University, 1986.

Lawson, E. Thomas, and Robert N. McCauley. *Rethinking Religion: Connecting Cognition and Culture*. Cambridge: Cambridge University Press, 1996.

Lorenzen, David N. "Early Evidence of Tantric Religion." In *The Roots of Tantra*, ed. Katherine Anne Harper and Robert L. Brown, 25–36. Albany: State University of New York Press, 2002.

McCauley, Robert N., and E. Thomas Lawson. *Bringing Ritual to Mind: Psychological Foundations of Cultural Forms*. Cambridge: Cambridge University Press, 2002.

Michaels, Axel. "Rituelle Klangräume." In *Musik und Raum*, ed. Annette Laundau and Claudia Emmenegger, 33–44. Zürich: Chronos, 2005.

Muller-Ortega, Paul Eduardo. *The Triadic Heart of Śiva: Kaula Tantricism of Abhinavagupta in the Non-Dual Shaivism of Kashmir*. Delhi: Satguru, 1997.

Padoux, André. *Le Coeur de la Yoginī: Yoginīhṛdaya avec le commentaire Dīpikā d'Amṛtānanda*. Paris: Diffusion de Boccard, 1994.

———. "A Survey of Tantrism for the Historians of Religion: Review of *Hindu Tantrism*, by Sanjukta Gupta, Teun Goudriaan, and Dirk Jan Hoens." *History of Religions* 20, no. 4 (1981): 345–60.

———. "What Do We Mean by Tantrism?" In *The Roots of Tantra*, ed. Katherine Anne Harper and Robert L. Brown, 17–24. Albany: State University of New York Press, 2002.

Sanderson, Alexis. "Meaning in Tantric Ritual." In *Essais sur le Rituel III: Colloque de Centenaire de l Section des Sciences Religieuses de l'École des Haute Études*, ed. A. M. Blondeau and K. Schipper, 15–95. Louvain-Paris: Peeters, 1995.

———. "Purity and Power among the Brahmans of Kashmir." In *The Category of the Person: Anthropology, Philosophy, History*, ed. Michael Carrithers, Steven Collins, and Steven Lukes, 190–215. Cambridge: Cambridge University Press, 1985.

———. "Śaivism and the Tantric Traditions." In *The World's Religions*, ed. Stewart Sutherland et al., 660–704. London: Routledge, 1988.

Sastry, Ananthakrishna, trans. *Lalitā-Sahasranāma with Bhāskararāya's Commentary*. 1925. Madras: Adyar Library, 1988.

Urban, Hugh B. *Tantra: Sex, Secrecy, Politics and Power in the Study of Religion*. Berkeley: University of California Press, 2003.

Weber, Claudia. "Manuskripte des Paraśurāma-Kalpasūtra und seiner Kommentartradition." *Münchener Indologische Zeitschrift* 1 (2008–9): 186–207.

White, David Gordon. *Kiss of the Yoginī: "Tantric Sex" in Its South Asian Contexts*. Chicago: University of Chicago Press, 2003.

———. "Transformations in the Art of Love: Kāmakalā Practices in Hindu Tantric and Kaula Traditions." *History of Religions* 38, no. 1 (1998): 172–98.

Wilke, Annette. "A New Theology of Bliss: 'Vedantization' of Tantra and 'Tantrization' of Advaita-Vedānta in the Lalitātriśatibhāṣya." In *Sāmarasya: Studies in Indian Arts, Philosophy and Interreligious Dialogue. In Honour of Bettina Bäumer*, ed. Sadananda Das and Ernst Fürlinger, 149–75. New Delhi: D. K. Printworld, 2005.

8

Jewish Same-Sex Weddings in Canada

RITES OF RESISTANCE OR RITUALS OF CONFORMITY?

Shari Rochelle Lash

Sometimes the rose will lean towards the rose,
the jonquil to the jonquil.

In May 2006 two gay constables of the Royal Canadian Mounted Police (RCMP), representing the national police of Canada, were married in Nova Scotia to widespread media coverage.[1] Much to the consternation of the Conservative federal government at the time, the wedding of David Connors and Jason Tree took place close to one year after the previous Liberal government had extended the legal definition of marriage to include same-sex couples. Early in 2007 Ontario's health minister, George Smitherman, announced his intention to marry his partner, Christopher Peloso, in a wedding inspired by First Nations' ceremonies at a wilderness resort in the north of the province.[2] Smitherman downplayed the historical significance of his union in a statement to the *Toronto Star*, suggesting that his marriage to Peloso was "not that big a deal now," since same-sex marriage has been legal in Ontario since 2003, and federally since 2005.[3]

Across the border in the United States, however, marriage to a member of the same sex remains a politically charged issue fraught with controversy. During the 2006 Academy Awards broadcast the singer-songwriter Melissa Etheridge accepted her Oscar for Best Original Song by first thanking her "wife," Tammy Lynn, and their four children. The speech, seen by millions of viewers worldwide, lasted only a few seconds but created a firestorm of media reaction the following day. Many viewers were outraged, others absolutely delighted. By using language normally reserved for heterosexuals, Etheridge's remark struck a chord, in effect asserting the moral and cultural equivalency of family, whether or not the state recognized her same-sex "marriage" as legal.[4]

The fact that gay and lesbian couples are coming forward in greater numbers to declare the legitimacy of their relationships without fear of recrimination signals a turning point in the history and progress of the struggle for equality. Even though many disagree with and even vehemently oppose same-sex marriage, the publicly recognized commitments between lesbian and gay partners is becoming increasingly common in the twenty-first century, not only in North America but also in many other parts of the world.[5] In Canada in particular many now consider legalized same-sex marriage simply another facet of the country's growing diversity.[6] As such this essay focuses not on *whether* same-sex couples should marry but rather *why* and *how* they marry in a climate where contested secular rights may embolden a chosen religious rite of marriage.

By examining liberal Jewish wedding rituals, I highlight a previously underrepresented segment of same-sex marriage, most of whose coverage has centered on American data within a dominantly Christian or secular framework.[7] One advantage of focusing specifically on Jewish weddings is that they have consistent elements that are historically traceable and that have been adapted over time to changing circumstances. Because of its relatively coherent ritual structure, the Jewish ceremony adheres to, departs from, and innovates with respect to traditional liturgical and symbolic elements when the gender-complementarity paradigm of the wedding is altered. All Jewish weddings take place under a canopy, or *chuppah*, and feature the drinking of wine, a special betrothal blessing, the exchange of rings, the sharing of a marriage contract, the recitation of seven blessings, and the conclusion of the ceremony with the breaking of a glass.[8]

My fieldwork with lesbian couples in the Toronto area and with clergy members who officiate at same-sex Jewish weddings demonstrates the ways ceremonies are adapted to meet the challenges that new ritual actors pose to an existing ritual structure. It also examines how weddings are perceived to be religious, creative, political, and transformational. A central issue, I argue, is that the presence of legal entitlements in Canada diminishes the need for ritual innovation that might otherwise draw attention to sexual orientation or to larger issues of political injustice, as is often the case with commitment ceremonies in the United States. In other words, *because* they are legal, Jewish same-sex weddings in Canada are more likely to resemble liberal, egalitarian ceremonies for opposite-sex couples. Government sanctioning of these unions in effect encourages rituals of conformity rather than rites of resistance. In regard to its transformative potential, I suggest that the Jewish same-sex wedding, rather than altering the institution of marriage itself, promotes social and cultural receptivity to a marriage that departs from traditional understandings. By simply occurring in a climate of legal tolerance after a lengthy process of negotiation with both religious and civil authorities, the ceremony reinforces the status quo at the same time as it fosters greater acceptance of diversity.

RITUAL AS A SITE OF NEGOTIATION

Issues surrounding same-sex marriage cross a variety of disciplinary boundaries. Focusing on ritual performance, I approach the subject from a perspective that highlights the wedding itself. Because marriage facilitates a change in status of two single people into a publicly recognized couple, weddings are considered classic rites of passage. Ronald Grimes suggests that wedding rituals function to "carry us from here to there in such a way that we are unable to return to square one."He contends that the transformative impact of a rite of passage can affect both the individuals taking part as well as the communities that create and perpetuate them. This assertion is particularly salient with respect to the same-sex wedding, because the latter operates on two levels. First, long-held social assumptions about what constitutes committed, loving relationships are dismantled when the central ritual actors are changed. Second, a wedding establishes and confirms a particular couple's change in status. While theorists such as Victor Turner make a distinction between ceremony as a gesture of conformity and ritual as its creative counterpart, I argue that distinguishing between the two terms is almost impossible within the context of a same-sex Jewish wedding, which both conserves and transforms the status quo.[9] Catherine Bell calls this dance between conformity and resistance a fundamental dimension of ritual. Negotiating with time-honored elements is seen as a process of *traditionalization* and is especially necessary when a rite must be adapted to a new social context. Bell, insisting that the absence of familiar ritual components compromises authenticity, suggests, "A ritual that evokes no connection with any tradition is apt to be found anomalous, inauthentic, or unsatisfying by most people."[10] Traditionalization, she asserts, assists in converting familiar practices into a new setting by evoking a link with the past. Same-sex Jewish weddings in particular are evidence that a negotiation process is underway between what is traditional and what is innovative. Even though Jewish lesbians are in many ways positioned outside the parameters of religious tradition, the women I interviewed sought out familiar wedding practices as a way to assert their legitimacy and to feel linked to their Jewish ancestors and the continuing story of the Jewish people. They were, knowingly or not, engaged in a necessary process of reinvention.

Because these Canadian marriages were legal, my participants' stories contrast with their American counterparts, who did not have the privilege of government sanctioning.[11] My fieldwork took place in Toronto between August and December 2006, one year after the federal marriage laws were changed to include same-sex couples. One of the most multicultural cities in the world, Toronto has close to three million people in the metropolitan area alone and, significantly, the largest Jewish population in Canada.[12] During the course of my research I interviewed six couples and attended three weddings.

Unlike many who have written on this subject, I am a heterosexual woman with no direct experience of being marginalized because of sexual orientation. Being a liberal Jewish Canadian and a feminist has already situated me both within and outside of the boundaries faced by my consultants. When same-sex marriage was legalized I sought to observe the conversation between politics and religion when the central players in this familiar ritual performance were radically altered. As a starting point it was necessary to explore how wrestling with time-honored texts and theological understandings within liberal Judaism have made room for same-sex marriage within a ritual structure that was previously reserved exclusively for heterosexual relationships.[13]

NEGOTIATION IN PROCESS: MAKING ROOM FOR JEWISH SAME-SEX MARRIAGE

Jewish history is characterized by negotiation with surrounding cultures in order to ensure the survival of the tradition and its subsequent relevance for each generation. In the last third of the twentieth century in particular Jewish feminism had a tremendous impact on liberal Judaism by challenging the religion's patriarchal and androcentric biases and by interpreting texts and developing liturgy and symbols that reflect alternative metaphors and representations of the divine. Feminist critiques and innovations also highlighted the experiences of women and other excluded groups, including gay and lesbian Jews as well as unpartnered, childless, divorced, widowed, and elderly members of the community.[14] With same-sex marriage becoming more widely accepted in mainstream society, the movements within liberal Judaism have worked to revitalize traditional practices to accommodate an increasingly diverse population.[15] In 1984 the Reconstructionist Rabbinical College in Philadelphia established a policy of nondiscrimination on the basis of sexual orientation and in 2004 passed a resolution supporting civil marriage and rabbinic officiating at religious wedding ceremonies for same-sex couples despite the lack of government sanctioning.[16] The Reform movement passed a similar resolution in 2003, affirming rabbinic autonomy regarding the decision to officiate at same-sex weddings.[17]

Resolutions to perform same-sex marriages arose after years of discussion and debate around sacred texts that deny or reject homosexual behavior and the perceived holiness of Jewish marriage.[18] The two most contentious elements have been the prohibitions regarding sexual behavior found in the Book of Leviticus in the Hebrew Bible and the Talmudic concept of *kiddushin*, the theological designation for heterosexual Jewish marriage.

Leviticus 18:22, "Do not lie with a male as one lies with a woman; it is a *to-evah*" (often translated as "an abomination"), has proved to be the main obstacle for conventional or traditional Judaism in accepting same-sex couples as equal members of the community, particularly for the purposes of sanctifying marriage.[19] For observant gays and lesbians especially, coming to terms with this passage is most likely the greatest barrier to finding an equal place and a home within the Jewish community.[20]

In response to a literal reading of these verses, rabbis such as Rebecca Alpert and Joan Friedman insist on recognizing the cultural environment informing these texts in order to understand the meaning intended by these prohibitions. In the ancient world neither homosexuality nor heterosexuality was understood as an "orientation," as it is today. In the Ancient Near East as well as the Greco-Roman world sexuality comprised a wide spectrum of activity, which anyone might choose to engage in as a source of gratification. The kind of sexual behavior one participated in was directly related to one's social status and not to her or his sexual "nature" or proclivity for a specific gender. Gratification was most widely available to free adult males and significantly limited for women, children, and slaves.[21] (Hetero)sexual intercourse was symbolic of dominant and submissive relations that males and females were expected to engage in as part of the social order. If the power differential of this relationship was complicated by homosexual sex, then the dominant role of the male was exposed and left vulnerable to conquest.[22] Thus what was most likely of concern to the patriarchal biblical authors was not the sexual act itself, but the violation of these strict social categories of power and status.[23] Because the egalitarian movements of liberal Judaism contest hierarchical structures of social organization based on gender, many rabbis argue that the reasoning behind the Leviticus text is no longer relevant. Furthermore reproductive technology means couples can now have sex without having children and children without having sex. A vast array of sexual options places few constraints on the conduct of consenting adults. The feminist theologian Judith Plaskow further argues that confining sexuality to an ancient ideal is now a futile exercise, emphasizing that "there are many reasons to question and even undermine the centrality of sexuality as a topic of religious concern."[24] These contextualizing critiques of the Leviticus passages have helped liberal Jewish leaders move away from a literal reading of the text to make room for same-sex love and imbue it with a sense of holiness.

The second issue of contention that keeps same-sex couples from accessing a Jewish marriage is the concept of *kiddushin*. Rooted in Talmudic property law, the term literally means "holiness," and is currently understood as the consecrated designation of a husband and wife as a sanctified entity.[25] *Kiddushin* is the rooting of the human couple in the realm of the sacred. Theologically, as partners in creation the couple are meant to mirror the relationship between God and Israel and the continuation of the Jewish people.[26] The metaphor of husband and wife in relationship to God through the couple's sexuality is a powerful gendered image. However, even though the significance of *kiddushin* is intimately bound to heterosexual marriage, many liberal rabbis have argued that the union of two Jewish women or men is equally deserving of this holy designation. *Kiddushin* is only limited to heterosexual couples, rabbis contend, as long as one refuses to allow for the possibility of committed and monogamous same-sex couples—a reality that was not a functioning aspect of ancient and rabbinic culture.[27]

NEGOTIATED RITES

Once the textual obstacles are interpreted in such a way that same-sex marriage appears less onerous in liberal circles, the process of reframing a traditional Jewish wedding outside of a heterosexual model can begin. At this stage it appears that decisions about whether or not same-sex weddings should resemble heterosexual ones is decidedly influenced by the existence—or lack—of civil recognition.

In the United States the emphasis on maintaining the integrity of a Jewish marriage is balanced with a need to recognize the uniqueness of lesbian and gay relationships, which are not legally recognized in most parts of the country. The Reform rabbi and liturgical scholar Yoel Kahn argues that commitment ceremonies for same-sex couples must be analogous to those of heterosexuals in one sense, but also entirely innovative in another. He cites two main principles at work in the wedding ceremonies he performs for Jewish same-sex couples in the United States. The first is the recognition that lesbian and gay relationships are equally valid and as worthy of Jewish recognition as their heterosexual counterparts. The second is the acknowledgment that same-sex relationships are not exactly the same and as such need not do everything the same way.[28] In outlining this equal-but-different scenario, Kahn suggests the addition of ritual elements that highlight both the same-sex nature of the marriage partners and their contested status within American culture and its legal system. Specific innovations to traditional liturgy include the addition of gay and lesbian poetry, readings that call attention to issues of social justice, and texts that highlight the love between the biblical characters David and Jonathan (Samuel 18:3) and Ruth and Naomi (Ruth 1:16). Familiar ritual actions such as the breaking of the glass at the end of the ceremony can be newly explained as the breaking of the social order that rejects same-sex couples, the grief for the loss of friends and community members to AIDS, or the sadness at the absence of certain family who refused to attend the ceremony.[29]

In Canada rabbis who perform same-sex weddings now have the advantage of proclaiming them valid. Rabbi Michael Dolgin, a Toronto Reform rabbi, initiated a lengthy negotiation process with his fifty-year-old congregation on the issue of officiating at gay and lesbian weddings. In a discussion paper published in 2005 Dolgin asserted that the desire of lesbian and gay Jews to marry was not motivated by a need for extra recognition, especially within a country where legal sanctioning is equally available to all couples.[30] Marriage, he writes, is a model covenant, or *brit,* that can be compared to the relationship between God and the people of Israel. This *brit*, in Dolgin's view, defines the basis for Jewish responsibility and, in a modern context, is based on the commitment to being monogamous, the establishment of a Jewish home, and the affirmation of the values and practices of the community. If two Jewish women or men wish to marry each other according to these precepts, he argues, there is no rational reason to deny them the access and the blessing to do so.[31]

As a marriage that conforms to community expectations and standards, the wedding ceremony that Dolgin devised for same-sex couples is virtually identical to the egalitarian weddings he performs for opposite-sex couples; the exception is minor language changes, most notably the insertion of "loving friends" in place of bride and groom. Rabbi Daniel Gottlieb, another Toronto Reform rabbi, echoes Dolgin's insistence on performing a parallel ritual for same-sex couples. The service he delivers is "almost identical" to the ones he does for opposite-sex couples.[32] Both rabbis call these unions *kiddushin*, insisting that the term denotes legitimacy and spiritual equivalency to other Jewish marriages. "What I do is *kiddushin*," Rabbi Dolgin confirmed. "To say that same-sex weddings are not, and that egalitarian, opposite-sex weddings are, is not intellectually honest, in my opinion." Although both Dolgin and Gottlieb may incorporate personalized elements in consultation with couples, neither rabbi has been asked to provide any additional rituals or readings that highlight the difference of same-sex marriage partners or their status in the community—something that was noticeably encouraged in the United States.

Conforming to tradition, however, has not always been the case for lesbian and gay couples in Toronto wishing to make a public commitment to each other. Before provincial legalization in 2003, congregational rabbis in the city did not officiate at same-sex marriages; at that time ceremonies had a more intentional, creative tone that celebrated the unique nature of same-sex relationships. Aviva Goldberg, a ritual facilitator and university professor who has been conducting life-cycle events for Jewish lesbians since the early 1990s, was approached to officiate at her first same-sex commitment ceremony in 1994. She observed that at that time highlighting the lesbian aspect of the union had been extremely important to the couple. Goldberg worked with the two women for close to six months preparing for the ceremony, which included traditional elements and additional special readings that emphasized their identity as lesbian Jews. "It was important for them to do this within the context of Judaism and to be publicly recognized for their commitment as lesbians," said Goldberg. "It didn't seem to matter that it wasn't legally sanctioned. I would say that their decision was a radical one for that time because it was so new. The ceremony was more about pride and Jewish continuity and expressing individuality." Another lesbian couple Goldberg worked with had a *chuppah* created by the mother and grandmother of one of the women; the canopy featured an appliquéd rainbow fashioned out of material donated by family and friends as a way to symbolize wholeness and unity. A description of the *chuppah*'s significance was written into the ceremony: "These vivid colors represent all of us, including the symbols of the gay and lesbian movement. They are reminders of the unbelievable efforts, sacrifices, and strength of those who enabled us today to share and celebrate the diversity of love, and stand here openly proud and strong."[33]

Other lesbian weddings Goldberg conducted involved similar elements that celebrated the same-sex nature of the marriage partners, while acknowledging their inclusion within Jewish tradition. In this way prelegal Canadian weddings resembled more closely the American "same but different" model, though the former clearly lacked explicitly political references to the couple's marginal legal status. Nevertheless, Goldberg asserts, because they were commitment ceremonies that were not civilly recognized, the rituals themselves demanded more intentionality and allowed for greater creativity.

For most of the couples I spoke with, access to legal marriage was the primary motivation for enacting their Jewish ceremonies, and their emphasis for doing so was based on the idea of "being just like everyone else."[34] The American sociologist Kathleen Hull contends that the symbolism of law wields tremendous power in rendering the relationships of same-sex couples socially and morally equivalent to those of heterosexuals.[35] Hull's assertion certainly plays out in Canada, where lesbian and gay marriage really *is* legally equivalent to opposite-sex marriage. Supported by federal law, Jewish same-sex couples may now proclaim with confidence that their relationships are also equally worthy of inclusion in their respective religious communities. Michael Dolgin, the senior rabbi at Temple Sinai Congregation of Toronto, the second largest Reform temple in Canada, affirms this view. He admits that his congregants were divided over the same-sex marriage issue, but he feels they were more receptive to discussing it once the laws were changed: "It's amazing how much of an impact it had to be able to say to people, 'It's the law.' . . . It's easier to focus on the religious issues when the society has done the political work."

After a series of debates, discussions, and educational programs about the religious aspects of Jewish marriage, Temple Sinai voted in favor of same-sex officiating for synagogue members. This "growth opportunity" was precipitated once the civil marriage laws were passed and two men, long-time members of the temple, approached Dolgin to officiate at their wedding in the synagogue's main sanctuary.

When two of my consultants, Alisa and Michelle, were also married at Temple Sinai, I attended their ceremony. The wedding, which took place in the chapel of the large synagogue, was officiated by a congregational rabbi and a cantor and witnessed by approximately seventy guests.[36] The ceremony featured all the traditional elements of an opposite-sex egalitarian Jewish wedding, with only minor changes in language. The event was tasteful, elegant, and thoughtful and lacked any components that drew attention to the same-sex nature of the couple. In our discussions both women had admitted that their decision to marry was tied to politics; their ceremony, however, clearly was not. When the Conservative Party leader Stephen Harper was sworn in as Canada's new prime minister in February 2006 he vowed to keep his promise to revisit the issue of legalizing same-sex marriage to satisfy his right-wing supporters.[37] Many gay and lesbian couples, including Alisa and Michelle, feared their freedom to choose would be taken away and hastily took advantage of their fledgling civil rights. A legal marriage represented Alisa and Michelle's equality with other couples. Had it not been available, the two adamantly avowed, they would not have pursued a "mere commitment ceremony." Having a Jewish wedding featuring a *chuppah*, the seven marriage blessings, and the breaking of a glass was essential to linking these two women both to their community and to the long history of the Jewish people. It was important to them not to depart from what they understood to be the standard ritual practice for heterosexual couples. "The wedding had the same essence, the same feeling," Michelle told me in our interview. "That's why people felt so comfortable because it wasn't something big, bad, and scary, it was something that they've seen before over and over."

The legal designation of marriage was also important for another couple who traveled to Toronto from Washington, D.C. to have a Jewish ceremony even though their union was not civilly recognized in their home state. "Naomi" and "Chris" told me that their decision to marry in Canada was clearly political, but the cultural recognizability of their ceremony was a necessity. Having a traditional ceremony without calling attention to politics or sexual difference was a way for the couple to bridge any discomfort felt by conservative family members. "We have as much as possible laid things out in what I would consider a very traditional ceremony," Naomi told me. "It was intentional on my part to show my family that even though you see us as different, we're the same."

It was clear in my fieldwork that couples wanted their legal, "traditional" Jewish weddings to facilitate acceptance and to stress the equivalency of same-sex love to heterosexual love.[38] Yet to assume that weddings were always received in the way they were intended and that legalization automatically makes these weddings acceptable would be naïve at this fragile juncture in history. It is also important to recognize that the process of negotiation continues. While rabbis and couples may wish to assert sameness by adopting a recognizable ritual structure, not all agree that this is indeed effective in stemming the tide of discrimination and prejudice. Adopting a more cynical approach, "Rachel," an intentionally unmarried lesbian consultant I worked with during my research, suggested that the discourse of acceptance and equality surrounding same-sex marriage is suspect. A Jewish wedding for two lesbians may look the same in many respects, but the appropriation of ritual symbols and the heterosexist structure of marriage produces, in her view, a spectacle that will never be fully embraced: "Perhaps it is my bias, perhaps it is my internalized homophobia, but my sense is that you have to be careful whom you choose to come to your commitment ceremony or wedding. I don't think it's as acceptable [as one might expect]. I think there are still people who say, 'Isn't this strange?' And one becomes a monkey in a zoo."

While Rachel's comments contrast sharply with those of the other women I interviewed, I include her observations because it complicates the perception that a lesbian wedding, however legal or recognizable, is understood by all to be fully equivalent to a heterosexual one. Many participants pointed to some level of unease in their behind-the-scenes wedding preparations.

These confessions show how rocky the process of negotiating an equal space still is. Whether it was the refusal or reluctance of some family members to attend the ceremony, a delay in parents announcing their daughter's engagement to their friends, or couples simply feeling ostracized by members of the synagogue congregation, many of the stories I heard suggested that discrimination still runs deep despite the perception (and rhetoric) of institutional and cultural acceptance. However, regardless of whatever conflict or discomfort may surround the performance and reception of Jewish same-sex weddings, participants are still consciously or unconsciously active in a process of affirming social change that has been initiated both by the Canadian government and liberal Judaism.

CONCLUSION

In most of the United States same-sex marriage is still a political goal rather than a social reality. Even though many liberal rabbis routinely perform Jewish marriages for gay and lesbian couples, they do so in part as acts of civil disobedience.[39] Because of this extralegal status, it is reasonable to expect that same-sex ceremonies will likely continue to be more creative and self-conscious by including elements of resistance and attention to difference. In Canada, however, the scenario has shifted, at least among Jewish couples who wish to wed. Now that same-sex couples have access to equal marriage it appears that the need to call attention to the uniqueness of their relationship diminishes, if not dissolves completely. Unlike their predecessors who proudly walked before them, Jewish lesbian couples in Toronto no longer have to carefully think through the meaning behind their traditional Jewish weddings; rather they may simply step into the egalitarian model that has already been modified for them by the liberal movements of Judaism. These weddings can therefore more readily be considered rituals of conformity than rites of resistance.

Ritual performance may be only a small part of the complex and continuing controversial issue of same-sex marriage, but it may also be an important barometer that measures the impact of recent or potential changes to the legal definition of marriage. In light of the fact that some consider the institution threatened by including same-sex couples in this last bastion of heterosexual exclusivity, this essay gives some indication of what actually happens when both religious and political authorities negotiate with each other to make room for a "new" kind of marriage. My research suggests that legal entitlements actually encourage interest in conformity—at least conformity with respect to institutional expectations regarding the ritual performance. Rather than asserting difference, attention to sexual orientation, or political injustice, same-sex marriage rites are more likely to resemble traditional weddings.[40] In short, allowing same-sex couples to marry legally disrupts neither the social order nor the religious status quo.

Participants and rabbis I interviewed both stressed that same-sex weddings were intended to look equivalent to any other, and that the presence of legal recognition enabled the accepted performance of a parallel ritual. Although the roads that lead to weddings were not always smooth or obstacle-free, couples agreed that having the law behind them made it easier for both their families and their communities to accept their relationships as authentic. Grimes observes that rites, even as they adhere to tradition, are never static. They borrow from the past, mix with the present, and reach out toward the future in a process of reinvention: "Rites are not givens; they are hand-me-downs, quilts we continue to patch. Whether we call this activity ritual creativity, ritual invention, ritualizing, ritual making, or ritual revision does not matter as much as recognizing that rites change, that they are also flowing processes, not just rigid structures or momentary events."[41]

I would add that Jewish same-sex weddings in Canada, because they are both religious and legal, are participating in a process of reinvention simply by appearing familiar. In being virtually identical to other Jewish weddings, these same-sex ceremonies are, in Catherine Bell's words, "a powerful tool of legitimation"; their performance with a new set of actors assists in evoking a link with the past while simultaneously aiding in shaping the future.

A same-sex couple in Canada that has gained full access into the institution of marriage represents the culmination of several layers of negotiation. At the level of government the struggle for equal rights has been long fought for, and continues to be a source of political debate south of the border in the United States. Establishing equal *rites* in the religious sphere has also been a site of contest and negotiation for Jews who wish to adhere to the tradition of their ancestors while coaxing that tradition to make room for the existence of same-sex love and lifelong commitment. Finally, negotiation remains a theme for the individuals themselves who wish to proclaim the legitimacy of their same-sex relationship to their families and communities even as they are met with resistance and discomfort. The wedding itself is the result of these many layers of negotiation. It is not necessary for the same-sex wedding to look radically different from an opposite-sex ceremony. By simply featuring different actors, the rites themselves are fundamentally altered and, potentially at least, transformational.

Notes

The verse at the beginning of this essay is from Mathers, "The First Captain's Tale," 351.

1. The RCMP is a uniquely national, federal, provincial, and municipal policing body. Also known as the Mounties, the force has played a leading role in Canada's history and remains one of the country's most recognizable national symbols.

2. The term "First Nations" refers to an organized aboriginal group or community, especially those bands officially recognized by the Canadian government.

3. Rob Ferguson and Robert Benzie, "Smitherman Set to Say 'I Do,'" *Toronto Star,* February 12, 2007, www.thestar.com/pringArticle/180711 (retrieved March 27, 2007).

4. Melissa Etheridge and Tammy Lynn Michaels held a public commitment ceremony in Los Angeles in 2003. Their union was recognized as a domestic partnership under California state law. In June 2008 the state overturned the ban on same-same marriage and began issuing marriage licenses to lesbian and gay couples. Proposition 8, an initiative designed to overturn this new law, if passed in the November 2008 general election, would amend the California Constitution to prohibit same-sex couples from marrying in the state. Close to one thousand automatic federal and state protections, benefits, and responsibilities granted to married people are not available to gays and lesbians in most parts of the United States (*New York Times,* editorial, April 24, 2007).

5. Same-sex marriages are recognized in the Netherlands, Belgium, Spain, Canada, South Africa, Norway, and the U.S. states of Massachusetts, New Hampshire, Iowa, Vermont, and Connecticut. Civil unions, domestic partnerships, registered partnerships, and other legal recognitions of same-sex couples that offer varying degrees of benefits common to marriage are available in Andorra, Argentina, Brazil, Croatia, Czech Republic, Denmark, Finland, France, Germany, Iceland, Israel, Luxembourg, New Zealand, Portugal, Slovenia, Sweden, Switzerland, the United Kingdom, the Australian state of Tasmania, the U.S. states of Hawaii, Maine, New Jersey, and Vermont, and the U.S. District of Columbia http://en.wikipedia.org/wiki/Same-sex_marriage (retrieved February 2010). Couples must live in the state to qualify for a marriage license.

6. Civil marriages are processed in Canada for lesbians and gays from around the world, although these marriages may not be recognized in the couples' home countries.

7. See Ellen Lewin, Recognizing Ourselves: Ceremonies of Lesbian and Gay Commitment (New York: Columbia University Press, 1998); Hull, Same-Sex Marriage; Gretchen Stiers, From This Day Forward: Commitment, Marriage, and Family in Lesbian and Gay Relationships (New York: St. Martin's Press, 1999); Becky Butler, Ceremonies of the Heart: Celebrating Lesbian Unions (Seattle: Seal Press, 1990, 1997); Ladelle McWhorter, "Rites of Passing: Foucault, Power, and Same-Sex Marriage," in Thinking through Rituals: Philosophical Perspectives, ed. Kevin Schilbrack (New York: Routledge, 2004), 71–96; Suzanne Sherman, ed., Lesbian and Gay Marriage: Private Commitments, Public Ceremonies (Philadelphia: Temple University Press, 1992).

8. For more detailed and historical description of the ritual elements of a Jewish wedding, see Hoffman, "The Jewish Wedding Ceremony," 129–53; Lash "Fitting under the Marriage Canopy," 29–38.

9. Grimes, *Deeply into the Bone,* 6–7. Discussing Turner's contributions to ritual theory, Grimes writes, "In Turner's vision, ritual is a hotbed of cultural creativity; and its work is to evoke creativity and change, not to buttress the status quo" (121).

10. Bell, *Ritual Perspectives and Dimensions,* 145.

11. See the following for examples of Jewish lesbian weddings in the United States: Inbal Kashtan, "Breaking Ground: A Traditional Jewish Lesbian Wedding," in *Queer Jews*, ed. David Schneer and Caryn Aviv (New York: Routledge, 2002), 148–55; Paul Horowitz and Scott Klein, "A Ceremony of Commitment," in *Twice Blessed: On Being Lesbian, Gay, and Jewish*, ed. Christie Balka and Andy Rose (Boston: Beacon Press, 1989), 126–32; Lewin, *Recognizing Ourselves,* 79–81.

12. Almost half of the city's Jews are unaffiliated, while the majority of synagogues are either Orthodox or Conservative. Overall Toronto Jews are perceived as more conservative than those in the rest of Canada and the United States. Rabbi Michael Dolgin told me that the city is by far the most traditional Jewish environment in North America, even within the Reform movement, the most liberal of the three major streams—Orthodox, Conservative, and Reform (personal interview, March 6, 2007).

13. It is important to emphasize that same-sex marriage is not acceptable within all streams of contemporary Judaism. The more liberal branches—Reform, Reconstructionist, Secular Humanist, and Renewal—all share the principles of respecting individual autonomy in interpreting sacred texts as well as deciding on which observances are most appropriate to follow. Therefore these streams can more easily deal with challenges raised by the emergence of same-sex marriage, compared to their more Orthodox counterparts.

14. For examples, see Judith Plaskow, *Standing Again at Sinai: Judaism from a Feminist Perspective* (San Francisco: Harper, 1990); Tikva Frymer-Kensky, *Reading the Women of the Bible: A New Interpretation of Their Stories* (New York: Schocken Books, 2002); Marcia Falk, *The Book of Blessings: New Jewish Prayers for Daily Life, the Sabbath, and the New Moon Festival* (San Francisco: Harper, 1996); Alpert, *Like Bread on a Seder Plate;* Debra Orenstein, ed., Lifecycles: Jewish Women on Life Passages and Personal Milestones (Woodstock, Vt.: Jewish Lights, 1994); Balka and Rose, Twice Blessed; Elyse Goldstein, ReVisions: Seeing Torah through a Feminist Lens (Toronto: Key Porter, 1998); Lynn Gottlieb, She Who Dwells Within: A Feminist Vision of a Renewed Judaism (San Francisco: Harper, 1995).

15. This diversity includes single Jews, intermarried and interracial families, converts to Judaism, those with mixed ethnic backgrounds, and individuals returning to Judaism as

adults with little or no Jewish education or knowledge. Efforts made by liberal Jewish leaders address ways the synagogue can be more welcoming through educational and social programs, as well as prayer services that are more accessible to anyone unfamiliar with Hebrew. See Rahel Musleah, "Reinventing the Synagogue," *Reform Judaism* 28 (2000): 44–48; Lawrence A. Hoffman, "Why Congregations Need to Change," *Reform Judaism* 28 (2000): 78.

16. Alpert, "Religious Liberty, Same-Sex Marriage, and the Case of Reconstructionist Judaism," 36; Phill Goldberg, director of communications at the Reconstructionist Rabbinical College in Philadelphia, phone conversation with the author, December, 2005, and unpublished press release to the Associated Press dated November 24, 2005.

17. Rabbi Sharon Sobel, executive director, Canadian Council for Reform Judaism in Toronto, phone conversation with the author, December, 2005. CCRJ is the Canadian arm of the Union for Reform Judaism in New York. It is interesting to highlight that in the absence of civil law, institutional sanctioning necessitates that many Reform and Reconstructionist rabbis in the United States conduct same-sex weddings in violation of the Jewish principle *dina d'malchuta dina*, translated as "the law of the land is law," a rule established hundreds of years ago to prevent a Diaspora people, like the Jews, from conflicting with the regulations of their benevolent host culture. Rabbi Daniel Gottlieb explained the origins of this principle in Medieval Europe. When the law of civil society is more stringent than Jewish law, the secular law applies (personal interview January 18, 2007).

18. Even though scriptures are not always the ultimate authority in making religious decisions in liberal Judaisms, they must be carefully considered before the religion can bend to meet the needs of a minority group.

19. Later on in Leviticus (20:13), the restriction is restated to include the penalty of death. The precise historical meaning of *to-evah* is obscure. Although the word is related to negative consequences, the English word "abomination" is considered by some to be an extreme interpretation (Alpert, *Like Bread*, 27). In the Hebrew Bible the term *to-evah* can also refer to idolatry, manner of dress, the imitation of outside customs, and dishonest business practices. See Dolgin, "Officiating at Same-Sex Marriages," 179. By conventional or traditional Judaism, I mean mostly Orthodox and Conservative streams, both of which assert the enduring authority of *Halacha*, or Jewish law.

20. Two documentaries provide moving portraits depicting the struggles of being Orthodox and lesbian or gay: *Keep Not Silent*, DVD, directed by Ilil Alexander (Israel: Women Make Movies, 2004); *Trembling before God*, DVD, directed by Sandi Simcha DuBowski (New York: New Yorker Video, 2003).

21. Friedman, "Position Paper in Favor of Rabbinic Officiation of Same-Sex Ceremonies," 1.

22. Adler, *Engendering Judaism,* 131. For a detailed exploration of ancient sexuality, see Judith P. Hallett and Marilyn B. Skinner, *Roman Sexualities* (Princeton: Princeton University Press, 1997), in particular Holt N. Parker, "The Teratogenic Grid," 47–65. Parker argues that the ancient Greeks and Romans based their sexual classification on whether one assumed a passive or active role in a sexual interchange, and that contemporary categories of homosexual and heterosexual based on gender would have been far too limiting. The statement "(hetero) sexual intercourse" presumes not only the forms of sex but also the position in which they are enacted.

23. Adler, 131.

24. Plaskow, "Decentering Sex," 1.

25. Friedman, "Position Paper," 10; Adler, 169, Dolgin, "Officiating," 185.

26. The marital relationship between God (the husband) and Israel (God's wife) is a metaphor that is used frequently by the prophets Hosea, Jeremiah, and others (Friedman, "Position Paper," 10).

27. Friedman, "Position Paper," 11; Levi Elwell, "Honor the Holiness of Lesbian and Gay Marriages," 11; Levinson, "A Covenant of Same-Sex Nisu'in and Kidushin," 15; Dolgin and Gottlieb, personal interviews.

28. Kahn is citing Rabbi Janet Marder in "Why Union Ceremonies for Lesbian and Gay Jews?" from his manual, *Kiddushin: Union Ceremonies for Lesbian and Gay Jews,* Jeff Herman Virtual Resource Center, Institute for Judaism and Sexual Orientation (Hebrew Union College–Jewish Institute of Religion, 1989), www.huc.edu/ijso/jhvrc (retrieved March 2007), 3.

29. Levinson, "A Covenant," 18; Kahn and Hoffman, "Contemporary Challenges to Jewish Life-Cycle Events," 278.

30. Dolgin, "Officiating," 188.

31. Performing a wedding ceremony for two Jews of the same sex is seen as an entirely different issue from condoning religious intermarriage. In Toronto virtually no affiliated rabbi would agree to conduct a Jewish ceremony between a Jew and a non-Jew, of the same sex or the opposite sex. In the United States liberal rabbis routinely officiate at intermarriage ceremonies.

32. Rabbi Daniel Gottlieb, personal interview, January 18, 2007.

33. Aviva Goldberg. Used by permission.

34. My six months of fieldwork included interviews with six Jewish lesbian couples of diverse backgrounds and three rabbis in the Toronto area who officiate at same-sex weddings. I personally attended three wedding ceremonies.

35. Hull, *Same-Sex Marriage*, 24.

36. A cantor is a member of the Jewish clergy whose training centers on liturgical music. He or she often co-officiates at Jewish weddings.

37. A year later Parliament defeated Harper's motion to debate whether the traditional definition of marriage between one man and one woman should be upheld. The next day his minority government conceded not to revisit the issue (Lash, "Fitting under the Marriage Canopy," 19).

38. For a more detailed explanation of why marriage and public weddings are important markers of prestige, especially for marginalized groups, see Shari Lash, "Struggling with Tradition: Making Room for Same-Sex Marriage in a Liberal Jewish Context," *Ethnologies* 28, no. 2 (2006): 136–39.

39. See Lash, "Fitting under the Marriage Canopy," 107–13.

40. Further study is needed to determine whether similar results would be found if the focus were on other religious traditions across Canada.

41. Grimes, *Deeply into the Bone,* 12.

Bibliography

Adler, Rachel. *Engendering Judaism: An Inclusive Theology and Ethics.* Philadelphia: Jewish Publication Society, 1998.

———. *Like Bread on the Seder Plate: Jewish Lesbians and the Transformation of Tradition.* New York: Columbia University Press, 1997.

———."Religious Liberty, Same-Sex Marriage, and the Case of Reconstructionist Judaism." *Reconstructionist* 68, no. 1 (2003): 33–42.

Bell, Catherine. *Ritual Perspectives and Dimensions*. New York: Oxford University Press, 1997.

Dolgin, Michael. "Officiating at Same-Sex Marriages: A Discussion." In *This is Sinai: Values, Voices, and Vision,* 177–205. Toronto: Temple Sinai Congregation, 2005.

Friedman, Paula. "Position Paper in Favor of Rabbinic Officiation of Same-Sex Ceremonies." 1998. www.davka.org/what/text/publishing/samesexceremonies.html (retrieved November 2005).

Grimes, Ronald L. *Deeply into the Bone: Re-inventing Rites of Passage*. Berkeley: University of California Press, 2000.

Hoffman, Lawrence A. "The Jewish Wedding Ceremony." In *Life Cycles in Jewish and Christian Worship,* ed. Paul F Bradshaw and Lawrence A. Hoffman, 129–53. Notre Dame, Ind.: University of Notre Dame Press, 1996.

Hull, Kathleen E. *Same-Sex Marriage: The Cultural Politics of Love and Law*. New York: Cambridge University Press, 2006.

Kahn, Yoel, and Lawrence A. Hoffman. "Contemporary Challenges to Jewish Life-Cycle Events." In *Life Cycles in Jewish and Christian Worship,* ed. Paul F. Bradshaw and Lawrence A. Hoffman, 262–85. Notre Dame, Ind.: Notre Dame University Press, 1996.

Lash, Shari. "Fitting under the Marriage Canopy: Same-Sex Weddings as Rites of Conformity in a Canadian Liberal Jewish Context." Master's thesis, Wilfrid Laurier University, 2007.

Levi Elwell, Sue. "Honor the Holiness of Lesbian and Gay Marriages." *New Menorah* 59 (2000): 11–12.

Levinson, Eyal. "A Covenant of Same-sex Nisu'in and Kidushin." *New Menorah* 59 (2000): 15–18.

Mathers, Powys, trans. "The First Captain's Tale." In *The Thousand Nights and One Night,* Vol. 4, 341–51. London: Routledge, 1953.

Plaskow, Judith. "Decentering Sex: Rethinking Jewish Sexual Ethics." In *God Forbid: Religion and Sex in American Public Life,* ed. Kathleen M. Sands, 1–41. New York: Oxford University Press, 2000.

9

The Social Element of Visionary Revelation

PUBLIC RITES AS A MEANS OF NEGOTIATING AUTHENTICITY IN TIBETAN BUDDHIST VISIONARY LINEAGES

Amy Holmes-Tagchungdarpa

TREASURE CYCLES (*Gter ma*) are series of teachings, meditation practices, prophecies, and ritual texts that form both important and controversial parts of the Tibetan Buddhist canon.[1] They appear in all traditions of Tibetan Buddhism in varying degrees, though they are more closely associated with the Nyingma (*Rnying ma*) and Kagyu (*Bka' brgyud*) traditions. These sets of texts, or cycles as they are more commonly known, are "discovered" at prophesied times by a preordained individual, who may find them as physical objects in the earth or another location (*sa gter*), or who may reveal them from their mind-stream (*dgongs gter*) as part of a meditative experience. The Treasures are considered to have been originally hidden in the eighth century by the early propagator of Buddhism in Tibet, Guru Rinpoche (pronounced *Gu-ru rin-po-che*), or Padmasambhava, who left prophecies so they would be discovered later, in times of need, by specific people.[2]

The history of Treasures is filled with polemics, as by the nature of their discovery Treasures cannot coalesce easily with orthodox Buddhist canons. While other forms of Buddhist literature are traced back to the historical Buddha or a celestial realm, Treasures are discovered by individuals, who then become responsible for translating them into human language. Treasure authorship is thus ambiguous. While the revealer often goes through a process of "decodifying" a cycle into different sections, the authorship is ultimately considered to be by Guru Rinpoche, a celestial Buddha, or a ḍākinīs (*mkha' 'gro*), a female celestial being who in turn will help or hinder the revealer to guide him or her through the process of revelation. Due to this ambiguity and the difficulties verifying the true origins of Treasure, Treasure revealers (*Gter ston*) are often regarded as charlatans, tricksters who exploit religious institutions and the public for worldly fame and wealth by claiming to have revealed a text that they may have actually authored. The process of verifying the authenticity of Treasures has spawned an entire subgenre of polemical writings regarding Treasures, and the same debates continue today in the Western academy.[3] This essay is not concerned with the validity of the texts, however, but focuses rather on the process by which the veracity of these texts is negotiated and authenticated.

Treasure revelation, I argue, is not merely a personal, mystical experience. In order for a Treasure and a Treasure discoverer to be legitimated, community recognition of the veracity of that lineage must be acknowledged as part of a fluid, interactive process. In this essay I expand on the work of the Tibetologist Janet Gyatso, who, in laying out the steps that occur when a Treasure is revealed, develops the idea of an extra, crucial step: the importance of socially endowed legitimacy that takes place through community participation in initiation rituals. While the Tibetologist Alexander Gardner studies the importance of the actual ritual of discovering Treasures,[4] here I explore the importance of rituals for promulgating Treasure and creating lineage. These rituals, which are derived from the original Treasure texts, are performed publicly and are open to many different social groups, including Buddhist practitioners and laypeople. The public performance of secret Tantric ritual allows for groups that would not otherwise have the opportunity to take part in Tantric practice to derive some of the benefits or blessings of the practice. Rituals make Treasure revelation accessible, and public participation in rituals endow the practices in the ritual, as well as the revealer of the original Treasure, with veracity, while at the same time allowing different social groups to become insiders in the revelation process through a process of ritual negotiation. In keeping with the definition of ritual provided in the introduction to this volume, this essay explores how broader community and authority in Buddhism is negotiated in the field of rituals. The act of rites in assisting in the creation of a new, receptive environment is crucial in the authentication of Treasure. Rites expand Treasure revelation from an individual visionary experience that can be experienced only vicariously by the community into an environment where that experience is re-created and experienced by participants who are also crucial parties in its negotiation, which is taken here to mean the process of interaction between the differing positions of the Treasure revealer and the audience to create a new, powerful series of practices.[5]

In this essay I explore the stages by which a Treasure is authenticated by expanding on Gyatso's formula—adding an extra stage in which the community takes part in the construction of legitimacy through negotiation and participation in rites. The illustrations used include examples and excerpts from the biography and *Collected Works* of Togden Shakya Shri (*Rtogs ldan Śākya Shrī*, 1853–1919), a renowned teacher, meditater, and Treasure revealer based in the peripheries of Tibet between the late nineteenth and early twentieth centuries.[6] Although Shakya Shri had none of the other traditional mantles of authority available to religious practitioners of his time, such as incarnation status or aristocratic family lineage, he managed to become respected among the religious and politically powerful of the wider Himalayas and gain recognition in the lay community. He achieved this by using different localized forms and mechanisms available for power in his society. One of the most potent forms of power Shakya Shri exercised was his ability to reveal Treasure and Pure Visions (*dag snang*).[7] I translated Shakya Shri's biography and *Collected Works* and carried out fieldwork, interviewing surviving members of his lineage, in order to understand more about the space where Treasure texts meet human imagination in a Treasure revealer's community. My work has also been influenced by excellent secondary studies of Treasures, including those of Janet Gyatso, Alexander Gardner, and Sarah Jacoby.[8]

STAGES OF TREASURE REVELATION

The Tibetologist Janet Gyatso explains how Treasure is revealed in several stages. First, a prophetic injunction must be received from one of the original promulgators of the Treasure cult, preferably Guru Rinpoche. Following this injunction a vision will appear in which the actual Treasure is bestowed on the discoverer, or the discoverer will be led to the site of a physical Treasure. Then, in line with the prophecy, the practice contained within the Treasure must be both accomplished and kept hidden for a set time. Gyatso suggests that this period of secrecy is necessary because the discoverer needs to have mastered the practices within a Treasure cycle before promulgating a cycle's teachings. She also regards this secrecy as part of a wider effort to "regulate" the formation of Treasures in a prescribed manner, which will lend the Treasure authenticity, thereby avoiding some of the polemical fallout endemic to the tradition.[9] Different practices and rites may be involved in divulging the full contents of the revelation in a process of codification. These may or may not include practice with a sexual partner (a "consort") or a period of retreat. After intensive practice the Treasure can then be freely promulgated. Initially prophetically specified recipients known as Treasure regents (*chos bdag*) receive the transmission of the Treasure from the discoverer. The regents also transmit the Treasures to other students, and in this way the Treasure practice spreads. However, success in promulgation depends upon the accurate completion of the other prior prophetic steps. Taken together these steps lead to a unique lineage that perpetuates the practice of a Treasure cycle.[10] If one step is not correct, or, as Sarah Jacoby puts it, the auspicious connections (*rten 'brel*) that assist the revealer are botched, then promulgation will also be ruined. If the sequence of discovery and promulgation of a Treasure is not completed accurately, the entire lineage of a Treasure can disappear.[11]

These stages of revelation appear in many accounts of Treasure revelations. I argue, however, that the formula is oversimplified; an important part has been left out, namely the community. A Treasure revealer is a religious practitioner who, by perfecting lineage-transmitted practice passed down over generations, has attained yogic virtuosity. Through yogic practice signs appear that indicate to the discoverer that a revelation of a

Treasure is imminent. Practice in an already established lineage leads to mastery of techniques which then qualify the discoverer to become receptive to discovery processes. However, this process is not merely private and mystical; lineage transmission is also inherently social. The continuation of lineage depends not only on mystical processes and karmic connections but also on human interaction. A lineage is a human community, bound together by otherworldly substances such as vows of loyalty (*dam tshig*; Skt. *Samaya*) and the blessing power of previous masters (*byin rlabs*), as well as by human chemistry and social networks. Lineages of practice are transferred socially through teaching networks and also through rituals, or rites.[12] These rites are enacted performances of transmission of knowledge. Rites are performed in a prescribed manner from an original text in a Treasure corpus. The initial transmission of a Treasure is known as an empowerment (*dbang*), a rite that systematizes initiation into a Treasure cycle for a community of students who gather to receive teachings from that cycle.

NEGOTIATING RITES: COMMUNITY AND LINEAGE IN TREASURE PROMULGATION

It is in public rituals that a lineage community actively negotiates the full revelation of a Treasure and thereby takes part in consolidating its authenticity. The performance, structure, and content of a ritual are a source of ongoing negotiation between the participants in initiation rituals and the revealer, and thus they illustrate the ways differing positions and experiences are acted out as both the revealer and the participants experience the benefits of the Treasure through ritual. The public that participates in initiation rituals plays an important part in negotiating the revealer's legitimacy, as well as affirming the legitimacy of the original Treasure. Negotiation in this instance is composed of the actual decision to participate in rituals, participants' social as well as implied spiritual interaction with the revealer or ritual master, and the actions that constitute participation, which in turn endow the revealer with legitimacy. Treasures are not automatically legitimated through the discovery of prophetic injunctions or visions appearing to the discoverer. A Treasure is endowed with legitimacy through ritual performance, which is open to practitioners, lineage members, and laypeople who, significantly, provide economic viability by sponsoring the Treasure revealer and his or her community. This sponsorship is crucial for that community to pursue the transcendent Buddhist aim of Enlightenment through the perfection of the practices of the Treasure cycle. Thus these groups all have a stake in taking part in the negotiation of the Treasure's authenticity.

REVISED STAGES OF REVELATION

How does the communalization of Treasure practice fit into the wider scheme of the Treasure revelation process? The process of communalization takes place in several stages.[13] The first step is that of the discovery, where the practice is revealed, given to, or discovered by the practitioner. Then follows decodification, where the practice from the Treasure is undertaken by the practitioner and written as a text in a "decodifying process." At this point different practices and commentaries are written that have been inspired by the original Treasure. The third step is early propagation to students, in which select students are given initiation to study, or "empowerment," in the text that grant them permission to perform the practices. The fourth step is the spread of propagation through students, where students take that text and teach it in their own geographical regions to their own students. The fifth stage is public ritual consumption, where the text is adapted, added to, and censored in accordance with the needs of the audience, the lineage, and the laypeople who take part in its consumption. This process can be done by the original discoverer as well as his or her students and their students; in this way the original, personal experience in the visionary world of the discovery becomes accessible to community participation. These communities include both practitioners who, by mimicking the visionary episode through practice, hope to actualize the power obtained within, and laity, although they do not undertake the actual mimicking of experience through Tantric practice, but take part vicariously, on a ritualized level, where they may not understand the actual allegorical meaning of what is taking place but still partake in a form of the power produced by such realization. The participating lay community also validates the power of the authenticity within the Treasure, as their receptivity to the Treasure is a form of negotiation that enhances the veracity of the Treasure's practices. Before considering this further, however, I expand on each stage of revelation.

STAGE 1: DISCOVERY

The discovery of a Treasure is initially preceded by signs and prophecies and unusual experiences on the part of the revealer. These may include vivid visions of otherworldly beings, such as mentioned by Gyatso as a type of proof. The episode may itself be short, but it will be memorable. Shakya Shri's biography, *The Garland of Flowers*, gives many examples of visions that led to his discovery of Treasures. He mostly revealed either Mind Treasures or Pure Visions, both of which came out of meditative experience.

One colorful example precedes his discovery of the *Wrathful Guru* (*Gu ru drag po*) *Cycle*.[14] *The Garland of Flowers* recalls that the vision regarding the revelation of this cycle took place while Shakya Shri was at Drugu Monastery (*Gru gu dgon pa*) as a young man, a time in which he undertook many intensive retreats. This presumably would have been one of his earliest visions that led to the revelation of Treasure. According to the colophon of the texts born of this particular vision, the vision itself took place while Shakya Shri was at Samten Choling (*Bsam gtan chos gling*), a retreat center in Drugu.

The Garland of Flowers gives the following brief description of the discovery: "One day while in retreat while asleep [Shakya Shri] saw a vision of the Wrathful Guru

(*Gu ru Drag po*) and the assemblage of the sugatas stretching out into space in front of him.[15] Finally they dissolved in succession, departing into a state of naturalness. [Later he] completely codified the principal mind sādhana from the deep experience of the pure vision heart practice."[16]

The colophon of the "The Wrathful Guru and the Sugatas Practice Manual" elaborates on Shakya Shri's perception of events: "As for this text, [I] awoke once during the night session at the retreat centre of Samten Choling in Drugu to find the entire space in front of me taken up by the Wrathful Guru and the Assemblage of the Sugatas, with their customary ornaments, body color and symbolic implements. [They] remained for quite some time, and then finally, in stages dissolved into a natural state of voidness."[17]

In the following example regarding Shakya Shri's discovery of his *Bliss Lama* (*Guru Mahāsukha*) text, another form of veracity is suggested, that of a prophecy. Prophecies were often attached to or part of Treasure cycles and prescribed who should discover the Treasure and in what manner and place. This example is a prophecy regarding Shakya Shri's text and includes the attributed creator of many Treasures, Guru Rinpoche. As the prescribed source of the Treasure tradition, Guru Rinpoche is the ultimate legitimater for many cycles. This prophecy describes Shakya Shri as the revealer and gives detailed instructions about the means by which the practice should be first perfected and then promulgated. The prophecy appears in *The Garland of Flowers* before Shakya Shri's discovery of a Treasure.

This is from a prophecy of Orgyan Rinpoche [i.e., Guru Rinpoche]:

In the future, [at a time of] residual impurities
The heart essence of the conqueror of Māra (*Bdud 'joms*) will emanate:
A great hero that comprehends the practice of yogic discipline:
A compassionate one that has realized The Great Perfection (*Rdzogs chen*):
From a profound mind, the hero will be imbued with signs of success:
Without bestowing, [success] will spontaneously arise:
An auspicious connection will arise in due time and be resolved:
For three years, keep it secret having established a seal:
Through prayers of aspiration, the spiritual teacher will master it:
Gradually disseminate it through ripening and freeing teachings:
Bring great benefit to all sentient beings by realizing this.[18]

STAGE 2: DECODIFICATION

Physical Treasures are often found written on yellow scrolls in a unique script considered to be the language of the ḍākinīs; the revealer is then required to translate this language into human script. This translation takes place as the revealer practices the Treasure and familiarizes himself or herself with the teachings within—a period that can include intensive retreats and yoga practices. These yoga practices can also at times be done with a partner in the practice of sexual yoga; a consort is vital in the translation process, as he or she unblocks obstacles in physical channels of the Tantric body that are thought to obstruct the Treasure revealer's translation and reception of the Treasure.[19]

One example of this process featured in *The Garland of Flowers* follows the prophecy quoted above by narrating how Shakya Shri carried out the instructions: "Referring to this prophecy of the Guru, for three years [Shakya Shri] kept [the Treasure] secret."[20] The three years of secrecy refers to the period of retreat Shakya Shri undertook, during which time he decodified the original Treasure and perfected it. This excerpt also illustrates the other stages in the sequence of Treasure revelation: promulgation to students and then to the public throughout Kham and Tibet.

The colophon to the *Wrathful Guru* (*Gu ru drag po*) *Cycle* mentioned above also depicted the process by which Shakya Shri decodified the Treasure he had received. This took place at Samten Choling while Shakya Shri was in retreat, where the Wrathful Guru and the Sugatas had appeared before him: "The following morning [after the vision], I kept in mind a mind sādhana from that pure vision, and in relaxation but at attention remembered the event with longing while arranging a basic sādhana, a gaṇapūja and also a destruction of enemy ritual."[21]

The *Wrathful Guru Cycle* provides a striking example of the myriad potentials for decodification and the forms it can take. Also important is the fact that scribes were often used in the decodification process, several of whom are mentioned below. The decodification here resulted in a set of texts in the *Collected Works*:

> Ma. *A Supplication to the Lineage of the Wrathful Guru,*[22] which was recorded by the scribe known as "the one named son" (*Sras ming*). Shakya Shri had six male offspring, but the second youngest son, Phagchog Dorje (*'Phags mchog rdo rje*), often referred to himself as "the son" so it seems he was the scribe.
>
> Ma. *The Iron Hook That Draws Back Life Forces Empowerment from the Wrathful Guru and the Sugatas* was not written by Shakya Shri but by the third generation of his "bone lineage" (*gdung rabs*), his son's son, Pema Dechen (*Pad ma bde chen*).[23]
>
> Ca. The Wrathful Guru and the Sugatas Essential Heart Essence of the Lotus Sādhana.[24]
>
> Cha. A Secret Inner Life Accomplishment Practice.[25]
>
> Ja. Gaṇapūja Offiering.[26]
>
> Wa. The Razor Practice That Destroys Enemies of the Teachings through Wrathful Applications of Destruction.[27]
>
> Du. Exorcist Rites Arranged for Liturgical Recitation were written by another lineage member.[28]

The three texts mentioned earlier in the colophon—the sādhana, gaṇapūja, and destruction of enemies practice—are all featured here. However, the colophons of these texts show clearly that the decodification of Treasure texts is an ongoing process.[29]

For example, Shakya Shri wrote "The Razor Practice" at Akar Tenpal Monastery (*A mkhar bstan "phel dgon*) rather than at Samten Choling, where the vision occurred. Another telling point is that practices derived from the decodified Treasure do not have to be composed by the original revealer. Lineage descendants also compose texts inspired by the original Treasure, thereby amplifying the process of ongoing revelation. Indeed in other parts of the *Collected Works* the current incarnation of Shakya Shri's son Phagchog Dorje, who is still active in eastern Tibet, wrote new works related to the Treasure cycles of Shakya Shri as recently as the 1990s.[30]

STAGE 3: PROMULGATION TO STUDENTS

After the decodification process the Treasure revealer initiates his or her students into the Treasure cycle. This initiation is seen in several instances in *The Garland of Flowers*, such as when, following a three-year retreat, Shakya Shri initially gives empowerments for his *Bliss Lama* text, as seen earlier: "Thus, [Shakya Shri] initially bestowed ripening and freeing [instruction] on some few fortunate people. Gradually, [the Treasure] spread to all of Kham (*Khams*), and then Tibet like this."[31]

STAGE 4: LINEAGE CONTINUITY—PROMULGATION THROUGH STUDENTS

After students were given permission to perform practices from the Treasure, they would in turn initiate others into the Treasure and thereby carry on the lineage. While some students would have remained in the same area as their teacher, others traveled. Shakya Shri's students were from places as diverse as Ladakh, in the far western Himalayas, Bhutan in the east, and throughout Tibet. This movement meant that word of mouth and travel were important tools for social promulgation, particularly since a great many students not only traveled but also taught and set up practice centers. Thus the visionary products of Shakya Shri's internal worlds were initially spread.

STAGE 5: PUBLIC RITUAL CONSUMPTION

Although yogic virtuosity in practices is the most highly regarded method for continuing a lineage, and although Shakya Shri's students certainly covered enough territory to account for widespread propagation of these particular Treasure cycles, a crucial step in understanding the entire process is the often overlooked but vital aspect of public support for a cycle and a teacher. Personal family ties and other local, social relationships would have been critical to facilitating the positive reception of Shakya Shri's lineage practices in different areas of Tibet and beyond.

These practices would have become accessible through their availability and the method in which they were disseminated. The crucial method for being given permission to undertake any kind of Tantric practice in Tibetan Buddhism is the trilogy of taking empowerment (*dbang*), reading transmission (*lung*), and receiving personal instruction (*khrid*). The empowerment aspect of the process is often open to the public as well as full-time practitioners. There are different types of empowerment, depending on the interest of the receivers and the circumstances. For instance, *tsewang* (*tshe dbang*) are related to health and physical longevity; *tsok* (*tshogs*) are part of empowerments and are offerings of food and other substances to the presiding deities; more esoteric empowerments can be related to sādhana and other ritual practices. The point, however, is that all types of people, elite yogis as well as laity, could attend these different empowerments.

However, the transference of power in the ritual setting was not just one-sided. The public and the clergy also created power through their participation in the rites, representing their role in the negotiation of this rite. Their participation in the ritual dimension of the Treasure was a form of negotiating the authenticity of the Treasure, as their public recognition of the revealer's legitimacy increased his or her credibility. This is an important point because obscure Treasure revealers who may not otherwise be famous gained public recognition from the community's willingness to participate in the ritual.

Still, why would different sections of society want to participate in Tantric ritual? Their willingness could be attributed to the significance of the practices. For example, when Shakya Shri decodified the *Wrathful Guru Cycle*, he initially wrote a trilogy of practices: a sādhana, a gaṇapūja (*tshogs*), and a ritual for killing enemies. Reflected in these three practices are some of the most important concerns of regular members of society as well as practitioners. The sādhana relates to meditation and would be conceived as being the more secret practice; however, empowerment in a deity practice also gives the recipient permission to recite the mantra of the deity. This recitation is a popular pastime in Tibetan Buddhist cultures that is believed to accrue merit, and accruing merit is itself a widely felt concern throughout social hierarchies in Buddhist cultures. The gaṇapūja is related to making offerings to deities for success, prosperity, and long life. The ritual for killing enemies is an aspect of Tantric practice that appears contrary to depictions of Buddhists as nonviolent, but is the practice believed to clear all kinds of obstacles.[32] Prosperity, wealth, relationships, enemies, and relationships with higher forces are all major concerns of any society, besides which the enactment of these rituals also facilitated social relations.

Empowerments for long life and other such concerns can be attended by different social groups. The rituals described above can all be bestowed in such empowerments. There are, however, levels to understanding these empowerments, which are normally in heavily coded, allegorical language. A lay community with no education in Tantric symbolism would still be able to take part in the ritual on a vicarious level. Attending is itself considered to leave "traces" and also blessings (*byin rlabs*), which are often described as carriers of merit beyond time and space. This does not mean that people who attend empowerments become enlightened automatically. However, it does suggest that by creating public empowerments that are open to the laity, practices from

Treasure cycles and Pure Visions become communalized. In turn this communalization facilitates the public accessibility of Treasure practices. Even if the recipient does not become a practitioner who dedicates years of retreat to perfecting practices, he or she can, by virtue of taking part in the ritual, also experience the end-product of the practice. This may be vicarious accessibility, but it is through the accessibility that Shakya Shri and other Treasure revealers find their successes. A community of elite yogins who spend their lives in retreat is not enough for the ultimate conferral of power to take place. Instead socially construed and recognized power is also extraordinarily important.

The participants of the empowerment are not just receiving the initiation, then; they are also taking part in the negotiation of the effectiveness of the Treasure. Their participation lends the Treasure authenticity and credibility, as it removes the revealer from a potentially fraudulent status, endowing him or her with the status of an authentic emissary of Guru Rinpoche. Community members therefore become insiders in the process of revealing the Treasure, for though they did not participate in the original experience, they are providing essential veracity to the Treasure by virtue of negotiating its promulgation and reception. The rituals that make these powers accessible also give laypeople access points to higher powers, and their belief in the efficacy of such rituals leads to efficacies in the practice. This leads ultimately to a belief in the efficacy of the power of the revealer and the Treasure. This social power ushers mystical experience and realization out of a purely personalized realm of vision and into the public realm of ritual. Being in the public realm recognizes the power of the Treasure revealer in both the ultimate worldly and spiritual senses.

CONCLUSION: THE COMMUNITY AS EQUAL PARTNERS IN REVELATION

In the realm of Treasure literature, the original Treasure vision does not just end in the head of the visionary. Ultimately the real power involved in visionary activity and their respective lineages is their ability to be accessed by the wider world as well as the simultaneous correspondence of power endowed by that world onto the visionary. Examining the life of Shakya Shri, a Treasure revealer who was not conventionally recognized as a powerful being in his society, shows that the previous formula for the production of Treasure and its recognition is less than comprehensive. Overlooked is the fact that the community plays a crucial role in negotiating the authenticity and legitimacy of Treasures; it is through the gaze (and economic support) of laypeople, as well as the recognition of the religious elite, that a Treasure and its revealer became credible sources of power. Treasures therefore have social applications apart from their visionary context, something that is often overlooked in scholarship regarding such visionary products. Shakya Shri's case shows that uses of the genres were crucial to the promulgation of his lineage; by using public rituals he made his visions more accessible. In this way visionary and social worlds came together to create new veracity for different forms of Tantric practice. This case study gives us insight into the process by which visionary texts are legitimated through their social negotiation and the way that the lay community provides elite religious groups with crucial recognition through participation in rituals. The very act of participation in an enactment of mutual engagement between the ritual master and participant endows these rituals with efficacy and therefore legitimacy. Recognition of the importance of this process reveals a new insight into the importance of the lay community for Buddhist elite practitioners. Not only do these communities provide economic support, but they also provide social recognition that gives a Treasure text the opportunity to develop into a lineage. Social negotiation is a crucial part of this process.

Notes

1. At their first appearance Tibetan words are given phonetically, followed by their full spelling, in accordance with the Wylie transliteration system.

2 For an overview of categories of Buddhist Treasures and their revelation, see Thondup, *Hidden Teachings of Tibet;* Gyatso, "Drawn from the Tibetan Treasury"; Gyatso, *Apparitions of the Self.* There are also Bonpo Treasures, though these are beyond the scope of this essay; however, some of the processes suggested here may also be relevant in Bon. For more on Bonpo Treasures, see Martin, *Unearthing Bon Treasures.*

3. See Aris, *Hidden Treasures and Secret Lives,* for a particularly critical depiction of the life of the Bhutanese Treasure revealer Padma Lingpa (*Pad ma gling pa*, 1450–1521).

4. See Gardner, "The Twenty-Five Great Sites of Khams."

5. This definition is taken from the introduction to this volume.

6. Kaḥ thog si tu chos kyi rgya mtsho, *rJe stun bla ma rdo rje 'chang chen po Śākya Shrī dznya na rnam thar me tog phreng ba* (henceforth *The Garland of Flowers*); Grub dbang Śākya Shrī, *Grub dbang Śākya Shrī dznya' na'i gsung 'bum* (henceforth *The Collected Works of Shakya Shri*).

7. For more on Shakya Shri's life and his negotiations with different forms of power, see Holmes, "Mapping Constellations of Power in Himalayan Buddhism." "Pure Visions" refer to a different form of revelatory text that is believed to have been *inspired* by the visionary experience of a practitioner, as opposed to being *bestowed* by a deity upon a practitioner in its entirety. The differentiation is in the attribution of authorship from the practitioner to the deity.

8. Gyatso, "Signs, Memory and History"; Gyatso, "The Logic of Legitimation in the Tibetan Treasure Tradition"; Gyatso, "Drawn from the Tibetan Treasury"; Gyatso, *Apparitions of the Self;* Gardner, "The Twenty-Five Great Sites of Khams"; Jacoby, "Consorts and Revelation in Eastern Tibet."

9. Gyatso, *Apparitions of the Self,* 169.

10. Gyatso, "The Logic of Legitimation in the Tibetan Treasure Tradition," 97–134, sets out a particularly compelling structure for these events, and also suggests their interesting "doubling" effect on the practitioner and the original celestial bestowers, such as Guru Rinpoche, which again adds to veracity (132). The necessary components of a Treasure discovery are known as the right time, place, connections, consorts, and auspicious connections (*phun tshogs sogs lnga*), which all appear in a "Treasure registry" in the possession of the discoverer (Jacoby, "Consorts and Revelation in Eastern Tibet," 99).

11. Jacoby, "Consorts and Revelation in Eastern Tibet," 100.

12. These rites often take the form of empowerment ceremonies (*dbang*) in which a qualified practitioner who has undertaken the practices from within a Treasure corpus bestows instructions on how to carry out these practices on aspiring students in a ritualized setting.

13. Some of these stages are derived from Gyatso's, but here community participation is added.

14. The Wrathful Guru, Guru Dragpo, is one of the eight manifestations of Guru Rinpoche. Guru Rinpoche is said to have appeared in different manifestations to assist Guru Dragpo in teaching different types of beings, all of whom had individual needs and capacities.

15. *Sugata*, a Sanskrit term for "One Who Has Gone to Bliss," is a synonym for Buddha. Here the term refers to an assemblage of beings who have passed beyond saṃsāra.

16. *The Garland of Flowers,* 82. All translations in this essay are my own, unless otherwise noted.

17. *The Collected Works of Shakya Shri,* 362. The text in its entirety is found on 347–62.

18. Ibid., 88–89.

19. Jacoby, "Consorts and Revelation in Eastern Tibet," 101–8 and chapter 4 (especially 210–38) outline these processes and consort practice in detail.

20. *SSSB*, 88–89.

21. *The Collected Works of Shakya Shri,* 362. *Sādhana* is a Sanskrit term for Tibetan *Grubthab (sgrub thabs)*, which translates as a meditation- or visualization-related text. A literal translation would be "a means or method of accomplishment," referring to the practice's ability to assist the practitioner in attaining higher stages of realization. *Gaṇapūja* is *tsok* (*tshogs*) in Tibetan, an offering feast.

22. Ibid., 347–48.

23. Ibid., 349–50. This is given in the colophon. Pema Dechen was the son of Shakya Shri's second eldest child, Rigzin Tsewang Jigme (Rig 'dzin tshe dbang 'jigs med).

24. Ibid., 351–62.

25. Ibid., Cha 363–64.

26. Ibid., Ja 364–69.

27. Ibid., 371–78.

28. Ibid., 961–90.

29. Alexander Patten Gardner elaborates on ideas about stages of Treasure revelation in "The Twenty-Five Great Sites of Khams," 59–78.

30. Several of them appear in *The Collected Works of Shakya Shri.*

31. Ibid., 88–89.

32. For more on one of these rituals, see Sihlé, "Lhacho [Lha mchod] and Hrinan [Sri gnon]."

Bibliography

Tibetan-Language Sources

Grub dbang Śākya Shrī. *Grub dbang Śākya Shrī dznya' na'i gsung 'bum (Shakya Shri's Collected Works)*. Kathmandu: Ven. Khenpo Shedup Tenzin and Lama Thinley Namgyal, 1998.

Kaḥ thog si tu chos kyi rgya mtsho, *rJe stun bla ma rdo rje 'chang chen po Śākya Shrī dznya na rnam thar me tog phreng ba*. Ed. Sherab Gyalsten, Palace Monastery, Gangtok, Sikkim, 1980.

Additional Sources

Aris, Michael. *Hidden Treasures and Secret Lives*. London: Kegan Paul International, 1989.

Gardner, Alexander Patten. "The Twenty-Five Great Sites of Khams: Religious Geography, Revelation and Nonsectarianism in Nineteenth Century Eastern Tibet." PhD diss., University of Michigan, 2006.

Gyatso, Janet. *Apparitions of the Self: The Secret Autobiographies of a Tibetan Visionary*. Princeton: Princeton University Press, 1998.

———. "Drawn from the Tibetan Treasury: The *gTer ma* Literature." In *Tibetan Literature Studies in Genre*, ed. Joze Cabezon and Roger Jackson, 147–69. Ithaca, N.Y.: Snow Lion Publications, 1996.

———. "The Logic of Legitimation in the Tibetan Treasure Tradition." *History of Religions* 33, no. 1 (1993): 97–134.

———. "Signs, Memory and History: A Tantric Buddhist Theory of Scriptural Transmission." *Journal of the International Association of Buddhist Studies* 9, no. 2 (1986): 7–35.

Holmes, Amy. "Mapping Constellations of Power in Himalayan Buddhism: The Life and Lineage of Rtogs ldan Śākya Shrī (1853–1919)." PhD diss., Australian National University, 2008.

Jacoby, Sarah. "Consorts and Revelation in Eastern Tibet: The Auto/Biographical Writings of Sera Khandro (1892–1940)." PhD diss., University of Virginia, 2007.

Kapstein, Matthew. *The Tibetan Assimilation of Buddhism: Conversion, Contestation and Memory*. Oxford: Oxford University Press, 2000.

Martin, Dan. *Unearthing Bon Treasures: Life and Contested Legacy of a Tibetan Scripture Revealer, with a General Bibliography of Bon*. Leiden: Brill, 2001.

Sihlé, Nicolas. "Lhacho [Lha mchod] and Hrinan [Sri gnon]: The Structure and Diachrony of a Pair of Rituals (Baragaon, North Nepal)." In *Culture in Tibet. Tibetan Studies: Proceedings of the Ninth Seminar of the International Association for Tibetan Studies, Leiden 2000*, ed. Henk Blezer, 185–206. Leiden: Brill, 2002.

Tulku, Thondup. *Hidden Teachings of Tibet: An Explanation of the Terma Tradition of the Nyingma School of Tibetan Buddhism*. London: Wisdom Publications, 1986.

10

Negotiating Ritual Repair

THE *PRĀYAŚCITTA* MATERIAL IN THE BAUDHĀYANA ŚRAUTA SŪTRA

Kathryn McClymond

"You will have to answer to God on Judgment Day," he said, "if you make mistakes in the ritual."—Clifford Geertz, *The Interpretation of Cultures*.

In Frits Staal's well-known study of an *agnicayana* ritual in Kerala, India, he makes brief mention of how one woman's menses altered the performance of the elaborate Vedic sacrifice:

> In 1975, the menses of the wife of the Yajamāna [the ritual sponsor and beneficiary] began on April 13, scheduled on the second day of the ritual. The rites of the third and fourth ritual day, planned for April 14–15, could not be executed because of the ensuing pollution; expiatory rites were performed instead. Some of the ceremonies of the third and fourth ritual days were combined and performed on April 16. As a result, ceremonies that, in the Agniṣṭoma, are performed consecutively, but that are not consecutive in the Agnicayana, were also performed consecutively on April 16, 1975, but this time as a consequence of the menses of the wife of the Yajamāna.[1]

The wife's menses prompted an adjustment in the ritual performance, one that "corrected" problems caused by ritual pollution. In Vedic sacrifice even seemingly small mistakes in ritual execution can have serious consequences. Note, for example, the warning in the Baudhāyana Śrauta Sūtra, "If the oblation is pulled up or wavers or spills out or breaks or rolls down, what should be the expiation? It is said, if pulled up, it would injure the family; if [it] wavers, the progeny will be ruined; if it breaks into pieces or rolls down, the sacrificer will die."[2]

Experience suggests that ritual mistakes are not unusual; rather they occur frequently. Ethnographers have documented countless examples of specific ritual events that include ritual errors. In addition priestly manuals, which are commonly characterized as presenting "idealized" versions of ritual, frequently include passages that address ritual mistakes. Much of the richest, most extensive ritual literature available includes detailed discussions about how to negotiate the discrepancy between the ideal of how a ritual ought to be performed and the unsettling actuality of ritual mistakes. Within the Vedic tradition, for example, entire bodies of expiatory material developed over the centuries that identify and categorize ritual mistakes, warn of potential consequences, and prescribe redress. In fact the Vedic ritual specialists clearly thought long and hard about ritual "accidents," as evidenced by the fact that they list literally hundreds of specific ways that ritual mistakes can occur, how these accidents can be resolved, and how to anticipate potential mistakes in future performances, thereby establishing general rules to guide ritual performers.

Yet while ethnographers and indigenous ritual experts have repeatedly noted that rituals frequently do not play out the way they are described in ritual manuals, these observations have had little impact on general theorizing about overall ritual systems or the nature of ritual itself. Until recently ritual theorists have tended to bracket the issue of mistakes from general theories about ritual.[3] There is a sharp divide between the close study of specific ritual events, which notes and comments upon mistakes as they occur, and general theorizing about ritual, which tends to imagine—and then discount—ritual mistakes as anomalies. Mistakes—and the corrections for those mistakes—are treated as isolated elements that have little to contribute to our understanding of ritual systems overall. We frequently note that ritual performances can involve mistakes, but we tend not to think of ritual errors (and their remedies) as instructive elements of ritual systems. Instead we need to linger over discussions of errors in order to determine what they can tell us about specific ritual traditions and ritual in general.

This essay begins with the assumption that Vedic ritual events involve a constant negotiation between preferred practice, unintentional errors, and ritual correction, and that this fact is an assumed and integral element within the Vedic system. I examine one small sample of expiatory material from the Baudhāyana Śrauta Sūtra as an initial foray into one ritual tradition's thinking about ritual mistakes before offering general thoughts about how the study of ritual error and expiatory material as part and parcel of specific ritual systems can lead us to rethink the nature of ritual itself.

VEDIC SACRIFICE

The Vedic sacrificial system is one of the oldest and most complex sacrificial systems in the world. Scholars traditionally locate the Vedic period between 1500 and 500 BCE, with some texts dated as early as 900 BCE. The Vedic period is often referred to as the "brahmanical" period because a sacrificial system seems to have dominated religious life in this period, and this system is identified most closely with an ancient priestly class, the *brahmans*. Over the following centuries various Hindu and non-Hindu traditions developed in reaction to the complex hierarchical sacrificial system outlined in the Vedas, but Vedic practice continues within India to this day, and it offers some of the richest material for the academic study of sacrifice.

Vedic sacrifice has been examined in detail by numerous scholars, most notably Jan Gonda, Jan C. Heesterman, Stephanie Jamison, Nancy Jay, Charles Malamoud, Laurie Patton, Brian K. Smith, and Frits Staal, and I direct the reader to these scholars' writings for in-depth descriptions and analyses of Vedic practice.[4] Generally Vedic sacrifice is divided into two broad categories, public and domestic; this essay focuses on the public, or *śrauta,* sacrificial system. *Śrauta* sacrificial practice is remarkably complex, involving the construction of an outdoor temporary sacrificial space, the establishment of three ritual fires, the participation of numerous priests, and the presentation of multiple offerings, including milk products, grain cakes, animal substances, and *soma* (a plant). The selection, preparation, and manipulation of offerings made from these substances are prescribed carefully by the Vedas, the *apauruṣeya,* or eternal texts that are traditionally said to undergird creation itself. Correct performance of the sacrifice can lead to worldly benefits—progeny, wealth, military success, and so forth—as well as the attainment of heaven. Śatapatha Brāhmaṇa (ŚB) 14.3.2.1 states, for example, "This—that is, the sacrifice—is the self of all beings, of all deities; after its successful completion, the sacrificer prospers with wealth and cattle."[5] In addition the elements of the sacrifice are also correlated with elements on the macrocosmic level, and so ritual activity is said to sustain the entire cosmos through its regular performance as well as to generate specific benefits for an individual sacrificer. For all these reasons ritual theorists have frequently turned to Vedic material as they have developed their own theoretical approaches to ritual. Most notably Henri Hubert and Marcel Mauss developed their classic work on sacrifice, *Essai sur la Nature et la Fonction du Sacrifice* (1898), drawing on data from the Vedic and Jewish sacrificial systems.[6] More recently Frits Staal has offered his controversial discussion of the "meaninglessness" of ritual based on years of studying Vedic ritual.[7]

Ritual manuals known as *śrauta sūtra*s provide the most extensive textual descriptions of Vedic ritual available to us. Gonda summarizes, "The *śrautasūtras* are manuals compiled for a practical purpose, viz. giving directions to those who officiated at the several solemn sacrificial rites that were performed or recommended in Vedic times. Their authors provide us with many detailed and meticulously accurate descriptions of these ceremonies."[8] M. Winternitz concludes, "They [the manuals] are our most important source for the understanding of the Indian sacrifice-cult, and their significance as sources for the history of religion cannot be estimated highly enough."[9]

The various *śrauta sūtra*s developed out of distinct priestly schools, reflecting various priestly philosophical and practical approaches to the performance of Vedic *śrauta* rituals. The *śrauta sūtras*, often thought of as idealized ritual "manuals," build on teachings provided in the Vedas, and their content was originally transmitted orally from priest to priest. Winternitz provides an example to illustrate how the oral nature of the transmission affects the *śrauta sūtras*: "The Śrauta and Gṛhyasūtras of the Black Yajurveda . . . give only the first words of the verses or Yajus-formulas, which are taken literally from the Saṃhitā to which they belong, that is, taking for granted that they are known, while they give other mantras for instance those out of the Ṛgveda or Atharvaveda, in entirety."[10] In other words, the *śrauta sūtras*, though essential to an understanding of Vedic sacrifice, are incomplete; they assume a baseline of knowledge on the part of the reader. One cannot hope to replicate Vedic ritual practice from the material provided in the *śrauta sūtras* alone, but they are a necessary starting point.

The Vedic *śrauta sūtras* are also appropriate for this particular discussion because they offer numerous discussions of ritual errors and correction. As Samiran Chandra Chakrabarti summarizes, "The Vedic texts accordingly warn us that any flaw in the performance of a sacrifice may lead to disastrous results. For example, Tvaṣṭṛ's son (Vṛtra) was killed by Indra, Pūṣan lost his teeth, and Bhaga his eyesight, Bhāllaveya fell victim of a chariot-accident, and Āṣāḍhi Sauśromateya lost his life—all for committing errors in the sacrificial procedure."[11] Clearly in Vedic practice the consequences of ritual error are serious. As a result the Vedic tradition goes to great lengths to delineate what one has to do to correct a ritual mistake. Within the sacrificial arena the *brahman* priest is specifically charged with identifying errors as they occur and then performing (or directing others to perform) the appropriate corrective activity. Ritual reparations, or *prāyaścittas*, make it possible for rituals to continue and to accomplish their stated goals despite mistakes in their performance. Āpastamba Śrauta Sūtra 9.1.4 explains, "A *prāyaścitta* is a rite performed in order to get rid of errors," or, more accurately, the consequences of errors.[12]

It would be impossible to review all of the *prāyaścitta* material within the Vedic corpus. For the purposes of this essay, a small sample will suffice: a self-contained section of expiatory material within the Baudhāyana Śrauta Sūtra. The Baudhāyana Śrauta Sūtra was probably compiled between 800 and 400 BCE.[13] Although followers of the Baudhāyana school currently (at least since the fourteenth century) live in Kerala and Karnataka in south India, the Sūtra itself was probably composed in northwest India. C. G. Kashikar's recently published critical edition and translation makes this text more accessible to modern scholars.[14] Kashikar concludes from his research that Baudhāyana "orally transmitted the discourses to his disciples. Probably he was the first ācārya who set the ritual of the Taittirīya recension in order for the facility in performance, and orally explained it to his pupils."[15]

The Baudhāyana Śrauta Sūtra is a helpful resource for an initial study of ritual error because a large portion of its *prāyaścitta* material falls within a discrete *praśna*, or chapter.[16] Kashikar concludes that this organization reflects how the text was compiled:

> Baudhāyana intended to lay down the expiation-rites side by side with the Ādhvaryava; he did not intend to collect the expiation-rites separately in any Praśna. Some follower of the Baudhāyana school felt it necessary to devote special space to the expiation-rites in the Sutra-text following the practice of the

> other Śrautasutras. While doing so, he took care not to touch the expiation-rites already dealt with in the Sutra-text following the Taittiriya texts. He recorded such expiation-rites as had become established in his time.[17]

In other words, expiatory information is included both in the main discussions of the rituals and in its own distinct section; the distinct section probably includes later expiatory rites added by a disciple of Baudhāyana, not Baudhāyana himself.

The presence of this expiatory material suggests several assumptions. First, this expiatory material assumes that rituals can and should be performed according to certain guidelines; there are correct (and therefore incorrect) ways to conduct rituals. Second, the material assumes that if these guidelines are not met, a ritual will not fulfill its intended purpose. Even worse, the error may bring about unintended—and unwanted—results. Third, expiatory activity assumes that ritual mistakes can generate negative results no matter what the ritual participants intended. In other words, ritual action, rather than intention, is key here. For the most part it doesn't matter whether or not one intends to perform an action correctly; what matters is what actually occurs.[18] In fact several passages indicate that participants may not recognize that an error has occurred, so expiatory actions are performed just in case. For example, BŚS 27.2 notes, "He offers the Samiṣṭayajus offerings for the total offerings of the sacrifice. By means of them one compensates for whatever might have been ferocious in the sacrifice, whatever disjoined, whatever might have transgressed the normal procedure, whatever might not have sufficed for the needs of the procedure, whatever might have been overdone and whatever might not have been properly done."[19]

Finally, ritual reparation assumes that mistakes in ritual can be corrected—they are not irreversible. This point deserves further attention because this may be one way ritual differs from mundane reality. Ritual expiation allows ritual participants a do-over opportunity that minimizes or even eradicates the negative consequences of ritual errors. I return to this point in my conclusion, because the fact that ritual practitioners can negotiate their way forward in ritual activity even after committing mistakes deserves appreciation.

RITUAL MISTAKES

The expiatory material found in *praśna* 27 of the Baudhāyana Śrauta Sūtra addresses several key issues. First, it suggests general categories of errors that can occur during a sacrifice, followed by specific examples and descriptions of these errors. Mistakes can occur with virtually every concrete element of the ritual, including the *mantra*s, the sacrificial setting, the participants, the ritual activity, and the offering substances. As Axel Michaels points out, "The number of possible mishaps is almost infinite. . . . *Āśvalāna-Prāyaścittāni* 1b, for example, lists what could eventually be subject to errors: the sacrificial material, place and time of the ritual, the sacrificial fees, the priest and his wife."[20] Second, the *prāyaścitta* material prescribes specific remedies for specific ritual errors. I review these in more detail below, but in general ritual remedies in the Vedic context always involve action, specifically pronouncing a particular *mantra* coupled with ritual gestures or movements.

Mistakes can occur in many arenas. BŚS 27 begins by discussing errors associated with the *mantras*, a concern that reflects the Vedic sacrificial system's dependence upon sacred speech as a performative activity. Ritual speech makes things happen within the ritual arena, quite apart from any ritual actor's intentions, so errors in speech have to be corrected. Specific examples include skipping a required mantra, invoking the wrong deity, and mispronouncing a word, accent, or syllable (BŚS 27.2).

Errors can also arise in the natural setting of the sacrifice. The Vedic ritual system assumes the existence of unseen connections (*bandhus*) between the natural, ritual, and cosmological realms. As a result many ritual activities are correlated with specific geographical locations, cardinal directions, seasons of the year, and specific times of day. Problems with any of these natural elements can generate problems in the sacrifice. For example, BŚS 27.1 notes that if "the sun does not become visible while a sacrificial rite is going on," expiation is necessary. It is not unusual for rituals to begin or end at sunrise, so if the sun is not visible for some reason, logistical problems arise. To offset these problems, *ghee* offerings are made in conjunction with appropriate verses to make it possible for the ritual to continue relatively uninterrupted.

In addition any number of things can go wrong with the constructed sacrificial arena. In Vedic practice a temporary sacrificial space is laid out and constructed for individual *śrauta* sacrifices; no permanent ritual space exists. Priests are hired, land is cleared, utensils are fashioned, and offerings are obtained with a particular sacrificial goal (and beneficiary) in mind. Mistakes in any element of the ritual space—mismeasurements, inappropriate materials, and so forth—pollute the sacrifice and nullify its effect.

The texts are particularly concerned with the sacrificial fires, which are at the heart of Vedic sacrifice. Participants prepare offerings on certain fires and present offerings to others with the understanding that the consuming fires transport the offerings to the appropriate deities. When the gods receive offerings they are ritually compelled to respond—offerings are not mere gifts; they set cosmological forces in motion that prompt the gods to react. Ultimately, therefore, the fires make it possible for a sacrificer to manipulate the cosmos so that he can obtain his desires.

Unfortunately the fires are susceptible to numerous problems, such as ritual pollution: "The kindling woods become defiled on account of eight contingencies. The defilement of kindling woods occurs as a result of the contact with an impure object, a dog, a *cāṇḍāla*, a *śūdra*, a crow, a sinner, a donkey, or a woman in her menses" (BŚS 27.8). An earlier passage warns that "if a man, chariot, horse, ox, buffalo, boar, serpent, deer, dog or any quadruped passes between the fires," the fires are considered violated. Fortunately one can take specific expiatory measures to repair the damage. BŚS 27.2 generalizes, "In any case of damage to the sacred fires he should put a fire-stick on the fire with the verse, 'O wealth-bringing Agni, may the Vasus, Rudras and Ādityas reinstall you; may the priests reinstall you with offerings. Nourish your bodies with clarified butter; may the desires of the sacrificer be fulfilled.' He should also offer a spoonful [while pronouncing] this verse." Fires also are extinguished occasionally, so there are elaborate instructions on how to reestablish each fire.[21] Frederick M. Smith notes that references to "extinguished fires" may not refer primarily to fires that have actually "gone out"; they may refer more broadly to ritually useless fires: "Most of the contingencies are the result of not taking proper care of the fires, of allowing the fires or the sacrificer or his wife to become polluted, or of committing mistakes. In most cases the fire(s) are not actually extinguished but are rendered ritually useless, i.e., they are '(considered) lost' (*naṣṭa*)."[22] Michaels notes that fire "mishaps" could lead to death, the absence of heirs, and even "unpleasant things in this and the next world."[23]

Over time a retrospective interpretive move developed associated with the sacrificial fires. If major problems developed in a man's life, it became common to assume that there was a problem with his sacrificial fires. P. V. Kane explains, "When within a year after a man sets up the Vedic fires he suffers from severe illness (such as dropsy) or suffers loss of wealth or his son dies or his near relatives are harassed or made captive by his enemies or he becomes crippled in a limb, or if he is desirous of prosperity or fame he again sets up the fires."[24] In other words, if certain life difficulties arise, a householder may suspect that his sacrificial fires have become ritually useless, thus rendering his sacrifices ineffective. In response he can reestablish the ritual fires, starting afresh to correct the problem. Brian K. Smith has suggested that the householder may suspect or accuse a priest of "ritual sabotage," therefore shifting responsibility for his own life's failures onto a ritual specialist.[25] As Ute Hüsken has noted, "We have in each and every case of a report of ritual failure to try to disclose the motivation(s) behind the report: rituals are always represented by somebody to somebody. . . . It is common practice to accuse other members of the same tradition of making mistakes or even of messing up the entire ritual—one party's failure can be the other party's success."[26]

Problems can also arise with sacrificial utensils: they occasionally fall apart, break, become ritually polluted, are lost during the course of the ritual, or are manipulated improperly. BŚS 27.1 elaborates:

> In any case where a ladle or a bundle of grass or Prastara or an enclosing stick or sacrificial grass or a separating blade or a strainer or the Veda or a fire-stirring stick or a faggot or any other offering material is broken or burnt or damaged or lost or destroyed, he should prepare it correctly, put it down suitably and offer two spoonfuls with the verses," You are quick, O Agni. Being quick, you are placed in the mind. Being quick, you carry the oblation [as a messenger to the gods]. Being quick, grant us medicine. O Prajāpati, no one other than you has encompassed all beings. May that for which we make offering to you belong to us. May we be lords of wealth."

Problems also arise when the materials necessary to construct a ritual item are unavailable. For example, "It may so happen that the available piece of *khadira* wood is too small for binding the sacrificial animal. If the sacrificer uses it, though prescribed for making a *yūpa* [sacrificial stake], the purpose will not be served. The paribhāṣā [ritual guidelines] decides that it has to be rejected and a substitute (e.g., *kadara*) sufficient for binding the sacrificial animal should be adopted."[27]

Chakrabarti comments, "If a material of an archetype [that is, the preferred offering substance] is replaced, by virtue of an instruction, by another material in an ectype [the broad category of suitable offerings, of which the' archetype' is the primary, preferred offering], the new material imitates the features and embellishments of the normal material. For example, *śara* grass imitates the features of *barhis*, *śyāmāka* grains those of *vrīhi*, a vessel (*sthālī*), those of a potsherd, and a *caru* those of a *puroḍāśa*. The normal Mantras are suitably modified in such cases."[28]

Similar problems can develop with the offering substances themselves. An offering may be prepared incorrectly. For example, an offering may be "burnt," that is, prepared without clarified butter: "Indeed, he who without first pouring clarified butter offers the portions and does not pour clarified butter afterwards, burns them [the offerings]. Neither the gods nor the sacrificer become gratified by the burnt portions. [However], he who beforehand pours clarified butter, then offers the portions and then pours clarified butter over them, satiates them" (BŚS 27.12). Improperly prepared offerings do not generate the results a sacrificer wants.

The most common problem sacrificers face is the unavailability of an offering substance, and the Vedic system anticipates this problem by offering an elaborate, but limited, system of substitution. Chakrabarti explains:

> If a material originally prescribed for a sacrifice is not available or is spoilt in the course of the sacrifice, a similar material should be adopted as the substitute. A substitute can normally be adopted in an obligatory sacrifice. An optional sacrifice should not be commenced in want of the prescribed materials; but if a material becomes spoilt after the commencement of such a sacrifice, a substitute has to be adopted for completing the performance. If the available quantity of a prescribed material is sufficient for its main purpose, one should perform as much as can be done with the available quantity. A substitute, even if sufficient for all the purposes, primary and secondary, should not be adopted in such cases, because it is not considered reasonable to reject the prescribed material for the sake of its secondary purposes.[29]

The possibility of substitution opens up many options for ritual participants to continue a sacrifice when seemingly essential materials are unavailable. However, substitutes are clearly stand-ins for the preferred offerings. Instructions concerning their manipulation reinforce their replacement status and prevent "forgetting" that the substitute is indeed a substitute:

> A substitute is considered identical with the original material and the features of the original material are made applicable to its substitute. . . . Hence the name of the original material in Mantras is not replaced by that of its substitute in

a sacrifice. . . . If a substitute too becomes spoilt, another material similar to the originally prescribed material (and not similar to the substitute that has been spoilt) should be adopted for the purpose; there can be no substitute for a substitute.[30]

Clearly the mechanisms designed to incorporate substitutes are also designed to remind the participants that they *are* substitutes: verbal references to and manipulation of the substitute always point back to the preferred offering. A replacement substance is viewed as a last resort and should be used only when the preferred offering is not available.[31] A later text states this clearly:

That twice-born who performs his sacred duties (*dharma*) according to the regulations for an emergency (*āpat*), when there is no emergency, does not obtain the fruit of that (action) in the next world; thus discern (the sages). The substitution (*pratinidhi*) was created to serve the injunction (*vidhi*) by the Viśvedevas, by the Sādhyas, and by the great Brāhmaṇa ṛṣis who were afraid of perishing in times of emergency. He who is capable (of carrying out) the primary rule (*kalpa*) (but) lives by the secondary rule (*anukalpena*) is evil minded (and) does not obtain the fruit of that (action) after death.[32]

One way the primacy of the preferred offering is preserved is by retaining the name of the preferred offering in the ritual even when a substitute is being used. Perhaps the best example of this is the *soma* rite. Vedic *śrauta* sacrifices center on three primary offerings: grain, animal, and a plant known as *soma*. The *soma* rites, which are at the top of the ritual sacrifice hierarchy, require the pounding of the *soma* plant, whose juice is then consumed by ritual participants. The problem is that no such plant exists. Since recorded time a substitute has been used for the *soma* plant, often *pūtīkā*.[33] Yet despite centuries of substitution the priests still chant mantras that refer to the substitute as *soma* in the ritual as a constant reminder that the preferred offering is the *soma* plant, and whatever is being used is only a backup. Substitution makes the continued execution of a ritual possible, but by continuing to use the name of the preferred substance in the mantras, the tradition also establishes some boundaries against further change. Speaking the name of the preferred substance is like holding up a verbal picture of the preferred offering alongside the substitute: it invites comparison. While asserting similarity between two substances, it also circumscribes the range of acceptable substitutes by consistently pointing back to the prescribed offering and the qualities that make it the archetype.

Even when preferred sacrificial offerings are available, they can cause ritual dangers when they become defiled. The Baudhāyana Śrauta Sūtra goes on at great length to explain:

An oblation becomes defiled if it is vitiated by the touch of insects such as blue bee, *Āśātikā*, a bug, a louse occurring in a garment or in the head, or an insect

> causing a boil except a tiny insect or a fly or an ant, or it if is vitiated by the excrement of a dog or a cat or an ichneumon or a cock or a monkey or a crow or a rat, or vitiated by mud-sprinklings from the feet or by hair, or by pared out nails or by deceased nails or by pus or by sweat or by blood or by fat or by tears or by mucus from cough or by an oozing wound, or vitiated by the touch of any other thing; or if it is touched by a woman in menses or if is looked at by an impure person or by an embryo-killer, or if it is placed in an improper vessel or if it is placed on a spot which is unworthy of sacrifice.[34]

A defiled offering is dangerous because it brings pollution into the ritual arena and thus makes the sacrifice ineffective.

Finally, mistakes can occur related to the various ritual participants. For example, occasionally priests are unavailable for specific rituals. BŚS 27.6 explains, "There are four priests required for the Full- and New-moon sacrifices. If one is absent, three should function, or two. If there is only one [priest], before the Prayāja offerings he should offer the Edādhvaryava Prāyaścitta offerings by dipping the spoon into the vessel of clarified butter [ājya] with the accompanying verses, 'May I be agreeable to speech and agreeable to the Lord of Speech. O Divine Speech, move me to what is sweet of speech, to Sarasvatī, svāhā.'"

Occasionally the ritual participants become ritually defiled, therefore polluting the ritual as a whole. For example, rituals are considered polluted if the sacrificer or priests emit semen while sleeping, just as a sacrifice becomes polluted if the *patnī* (sacrificer's wife) begins her menses.[35] As in many sacrificial traditions, bodily fluids are considered contaminating. Perhaps less expected, expiation is also required "for the sacrificer who has vomited Soma, who has purged Soma, whose partaking of Soma is passed over, or who is deprived of partaking" (BŚS 27.5). Ultimately the concern is that ritually impure participants will pollute the sacrifice itself. Inappropriate or absent personnel contaminate the ritual as a whole, so the ritual as a whole must be purified. The relative insignificance of specific ritual actors is most clear in extreme situations. Certain texts indicate that occasionally ritual sponsors have died after making the initial commitment to perform a ritual but before the ritual's conclusion (KŚS 1.6.11). Clearly any ritual component is a potential opportunity for ritual error.

In general mistakes in Vedic ritual generate at least two types of problems. First, they create impurity that must be removed. More precisely, errors pollute the ritual arena itself, and the ritual space must be purged before the sacrifice can have its intended effect. Frederick M. Smith summarizes, "*Prāyaścitta* may either prepare a secondary object for ritual use, or it may rectify error or re-establish the purity of the sacrifice after it has been broken."[36] In addition ritual mistakes may generate a negative result that must be averted somehow. This is generally done by asking the appropriate deity to avert any impending danger. Note that the gods are never asked to ignore a mistake, but rather to avert the ill fortune that will naturally result: "In all instances of pronunciation of the divinity if one pronounces the name of the divinity other than the correct one, should offer a spoonful with the verse, 'O Maruts, the excess involving the offence towards gods which I have perpetrated with regard to you through speech, which seeks to harm us who are poor, do you place it away from us.'"[37] Thus the gods are not asked to ignore or override the rules governing the sacrifice; instead they are asked simply to avert the consequences of the ritual error. I read this as an acknowledgment that the gods themselves are subject to the metarules that frame sacrificial ritual.

Fortunately almost every ritual error has a remedy in the Vedic system. This auspicious balance is crucial to the survival of Vedic practices over thousands of years, but just as importantly to the authoritative weight Vedic sacrifice continues to have as a religious metaphor within the broader Hindu traditions. The following section notes the common elements of expiatory activity and examines some specific examples. For the time being it is important to note that any potential anxiety generated by the demands of the Vedic ritual system is somewhat offset by the broad array of remedies available when mistakes occur.

RITUAL REPAIR

Given the complexity of Vedic ritual and the countless opportunities for errors, it becomes increasingly apparent that the only way Vedic ritual could survive as a viable religious activity is through the possibility of ritual repair. There are no blanket remedies for ritual mistakes; as indicated previously, each specific error has its own specific correction. Some general principles can be discerned from this brief overview of the Baudhāyana Śrauta Sūtra *prāyaścitta* material.

First, the key figure responsible for identifying and correcting ritual errors is the *brahman* priest:

> For every sacred act, therefore, every sacrifice too is, according to the Indian view, exposed to a certain amount of danger; if an act is not performed exactly in accordance with the ritualistic prescription, if a spell or a prayer formula is not spoken correctly, or if a melody is sung incorrectly, then the sacred act may bring destruction upon the originator of the sacrifice. Therefore the Brahman sits in the south of the place of sacrifice, in order to protect the sacrifice: the south being the haunt of the god of death, and the haunt from which the demons hostile to the sacrifice, threaten people. He follows the course of the whole sacrifice mentally, as soon as he notices the least mistake in a sacrificial act, in a recitation or in a chant, he must, by pronouncing sacred words, make good the harm Therefore the Brahman is called in an old text "the best physician among the sacrificial priests."[38]

The *brahman* priest heals the living sacrifice so that it may continue its dynamic activity on behalf of the sacrificer and function in harmony with the cosmos. The ability to repair ritual—negotiating the ritual journey from "what should have been" through "what was" to "what can be"—gives the *brahman* great power within Vedic society, not only because he can correct ritual errors, but because he can identify them in the first place. In fulfilling these functions he mediates the actions of the ritual participants and the underlying framework of the cosmos, manipulating unseen forces so that the ritual can proceed effectively.

The BŚS material indicates that the foundational remedial activity is the offering of a *mantra*. BŚS 27.4 generalizes, "Whatever is deficient or superfluous in a *mantra* or what is wrongly offered—they (the Vyāhṛtis) [the syllables *bhuh, bhuvah, svaha*] drive away the blemish. Therefore they are known as the Vyāhṛtis."[39] *Praśna* 27 begins with a general rule: "In all cases, if an object placed to the accompaniment of a formula falls down, one should restore it to its proper place with the verse, 'The divine knowledge is the stability of mind, of speech, of sacrifice, of the oblations, of clarified butter. Compensating the rites which may be in excess or may be wanting, the sacrificer goes on furnishing the parts of sacrifice. May the Svāhā-utterance reach the gods.'"[40] The words themselves repair the sacrifice.

Expiatory *mantras* are usually coupled with ritual activity. The most basic expiatory activity is the recitation of a *mantra* accompanied by an offering of a spoonful, or multiple spoonfuls, of clarified butter. For example, "In all cases of invocations of divinities, if he invokes a divinity other than the correct one, he should offer a spoonful along with this very verse" (BŚS 27.1). Slight variations in the ritual activity are made depending upon the exact nature of the error.

Certain mistakes, however, require more complex correction. BŚS 27.3 describes problems that may arise with a grain-cake offering:

> If the potshards are not fully covered [by the grain-cake], he should offer spoonfuls on the *āhavanīya* with the *vyāhṛtis bhūḥ bhuvaḥ and suvaḥ*. The same expiation [should be undertaken] if the grain-cake is irregularly spread or overspread. Now regarding the expiation for the under-baking, flowing, burning, overflowing or flowing out of the oblations: if under-baked, he should offer a spoonful on the *āhavanīya* with "to Rudra *svāhā*." If it becomes flowing [he should offer a spoonful on the *āhavanīya* with] "to Vāyu." If it becomes burnt [he should offer a spoonful on the *āhavanīya* with] "to Nirṛti." If it becomes partly burnt, he should offer only that portion which is baked. If it becomes totally burnt, he should dispose of it in water and offer two *mindāhutis*. He should pour out paddy for another oblation or offer clarified butter. This is the expiation. He should make an offering to each of the divinities governing the respective direction towards which the oblation would have overflowed. If towards the east, "to Agni." If towards the south, "to Yama." If towards the west, "to Varuṇa." If towards the north, "to Soma." If it overflows in all directions, he should make offerings to all these divinities.

Note that for the most part the ritual participant's intention has nothing to do with the ritual mistake; a mistake is a mistake, which must be addressed whether or not it was intentional. In a few rare cases, however, intention becomes a factor. The BŚS itself discusses one such case:

> If one *deliberately* offers the Agnihotra on secular fire or if it is offered by an ignorant one or by a boy onto the fire spread out by the sacrificer's wife, one should consign the fires into the kindling woods. He should move out, churn out fire, and spread out fires. Pūrṇāhuti should be offered and then a cake on eight potsherds [should be offered] to Tantumant Agni. If one *non-deliberately* offers the Agnihotra on secular fire or if it is offered by an ignorant one or by a boy onto the fire spread out by the sacrificer's wife, one should spread out the fires with the Vyāhṛtis. Pūrṇāhuti should then be offered and then a cake on eight potsherds [should be offered] to Tantumant Agni. (BŚS 21.11)

However, changes in ritual expiation procedures according to the ritual performer's intent are the exception rather than the rule.

CONCLUSION: NEGOTIATING RITUAL REPAIR

A brief foray into Vedic *prāyaścitta* literature leads to several insights into the nature of ritual in general. Let's take them one at a time.

1. The fact that ritual can "go wrong" indicates that external standards determine when it "goes right."

This may seem an obvious point, but there are important implications to the notion that a ritual can "go wrong." The ability to identify ritual errors assumes that general standards for correct and incorrect ritual action exist, grounded in some authority beyond the realm of the ritual arena itself. Rituals are governed by rules that transcend individual ritual performances. These rules, grounded in a broader framework, determine what can go right and what can go wrong in any ritual performance. Rituals themselves don't do this; they are dependent on some logically prior system to establish right and wrong.

Here we may have a possible response to Staal's controversial notion of "meaninglessness." In his well-known work, *Rules without Meaning,* Staal argues that ritual is "meaningless"; that is, ritual activity has no meaning in the mundane world outside of ritual itself. Instead, he argues, ritual is self-contained, governed by internal rules that have no referent outside of the ritual arena. However, in making this argument Staal assumes that meaning must be found either through reference to the mundane world or within the boundaries of the ritual arena. I would argue instead that *prāyaścitta* literature points to a third realm of metarules that encompasses the ritual realm.[41] This realm of metarules, which is integrally connected with the metaphysics of the cosmos, is revealed by the *paribhāsṣās* as well as the *prāyaścittas* and is distinct from the realm of the mundane and the ritual arena itself. Therefore a ritual may have meaning with reference to metarules that transcend the ritual arena without necessarily having clear referents to elements of everyday life.

The *paribhāṣā* and *prāyaścitta* material, the fraternal twins of ritual error, coexist within and reveal this transcendent realm. As mirror images of one another they cooperate in navigating ritual participants between what should occur in ritual and what actually does. In the Vedic literature explicit *paribhāṣā* material probably developed relatively late in the composition of the various *śrauta sūtras*, but it builds on ideas that are assumed or implied throughout the *śrauta sūtras*.[42] Francis X. Clooney argues that the *paribhāsṣās*, "meta-rules[,] Sūtras about Sūtras," point to an awareness of an overarching logic that governs the sacrifice, grounded in a realm beyond the closed circle of the ritual arena.[43] I would argue that the *prāyaścitta* material functions in the same way, linking each particular ritual performance to a more foundational framework. Together ritual guidelines for correct action and expiatory activity that addresses incorrect action draw attention to the metarules that underlie ritual activity in general.

2. Prāyaścitta material points to the inherent "elasticity" of ritual.

While there are resonances between the *paribhāṣā* and the *prāyaścitta* material, there are also some important differences. While the *paribhāṣās* or metarules draw attention to the fixed nature of ritual, the *prāyaścittas* hint at elasticity. Ritual expiation suggests that rules are negotiable, that the boundaries between correct and incorrect performances of sacrifice are somewhat fluid, permeable. As a result rituals can accommodate themselves to a wide spectrum of circumstances, both foreseen and unforeseen. The mere fact of alternative possibilities, the constant deferral of an "ought" to a "can be," suggests a dynamism and fluidity in Vedic ritual that has often been overlooked. *Prāyaścittas* assume a level of organization beyond themselves, a system once-removed from each specific performance of a ritual. However, this system is elastic. It allows for the correction of errors—and thus alternative procedures—by drawing on homologous relationships between various elements of ritual activity. *Bandhus*, invisible connections between ritual elements, twist and stretch to accommodate ritual error, allowing individual ritual events to bend without breaking.

Frederick M. Smith makes a similar observation about substitution within the Vedic context: "Indeed, the system of substitution, embracing what Seidenberg calls 'a tradition of "tricks of the trade"' . . . has imbued a practicable degree of flexibility into an otherwise rigid sacrificial cult. Substitution has, therefore, in no small measure contributed to the survival of the sacrifice itself."[44] I would simply extend Smith's conclusion to all forms of expiatory activity.

3. Prāyaścitta material implies ritual made manifest.

Ritual error assumes action, either physical or mental. *Prāyaścitta* material grows out of the assumption that ritual is intended to be actualized, manifest in either directed thought or physical gesture. If discussions of ritual remain in the realm of the abstract, then there is no need to be concerned with mistakes. As Clooney notes in his discussion of later *mīmāṃsā* material, "The truth of Vedic language is not *satya* [being, existence], but *kriyā* [making, doing]; language is purposeful when it expresses *kriyā*."[45] This is made particularly clear in expiatory material. Discussions of ritual mistakes assume the actualization of sacrifice. The presence of expiatory material underscores the fact that rituals are intended to be performed; they are not fully realized except in execution, and even misexecution.

This point becomes particularly interesting when examining ritual correction in other sacrificial traditions, specifically traditions that are no longer performed. For example, the Jewish sacrificial tradition includes extensive discussions of correct ritual performance. The Mishnah (ca. 220 CE), Judaism's first systematic collection of rabbinic teaching, records literally thousands of corrections for potential ritual errors in the domestic and Temple rituals. What is remarkable about this is that the Temple, the original center of Israelite public ritual life, had been razed in 70 CE, well over a hundred years *before* the Mishnah was compiled. Unlike Vedic sacrifice, which continues to this day, Jewish Temple ritual ended for all intents and purposes in 70 CE. Yet for centuries afterward the rabbis continued to outline the proper procedures for dealing with ritual mistakes. Why? Most interpretations assert that rabbinic discussions of ritual activity were primarily a means of demonstrating mastery of Torah. The compilation of rabbinic teachings marked a shift in authority from priestly mastery of ritual to rabbinic mastery of Torah—yet this authority turned on knowledge about ritual activity. Rabbinic authority derived from the fact that the rabbis knew what *to do*, in both real and imagined situations. This observation leads to interesting questions about the power associated with *knowledge* of ritual repair and the religiosocial power dynamics displayed by a textual tradition controlled by one group describing the ritual power of another group that can never exercise that power.

4. Expiatory material works against the routinization of mistakes.

This point may seem counterintuitive. If *prāyaścitta* material provides for the continual correction of mistakes, doesn't that encourage sloppy behavior and lax enforcement of ritual guidelines? Surprisingly, no. By providing a release for the pressure that builds from ritual demands for perfection, expiatory material restrains ritual participants from allowing just any behavior to go unnoticed or unaddressed. Corrections draw attention to error; they don't condone it. In fact certain passages anticipate how tempting it may be to use an expiatory procedure when it is unnecessary: "Whatever lesser options have been prescribed for various incidences, one should not adopt them by way of preference. One should resort to them only in emergency" (BŚS 27.11, trans. Kashikar). Corrections actually reinforce the idea that there is a preferred action.

This point is worth lingering over for a moment because it suggests that one of the most common characterizations of ritual—as the "ought" to reality's "is"—may itself be incorrect. In a well-known discussion the religious studies scholar Jonathan Z. Smith explores the routinization of ritual accidents. He juxtaposes two texts, one from Kafka and the other from Plutarch:

> Leopards break into the temple and drink the sacrificial chalices dry; this occurs repeatedly, again and again: finally it can be reckoned on beforehand and becomes a part of the ceremony.
>
> At Athens, Lysimache, the priestess of Athene Polias, when asked for a drink by the mule drivers who had transported the sacred vessels, replied, "No, for I fear it will get into the ritual."[46]

Here Smith pairs two passages, implying that there are only two scenarios available involving mistakes: the strict prevention of errors or the gradual incorporation of errors that go unchecked. Expiation, however, offers a third possibility: acknowledging error, countering its negative effects, noting that error does not belong in ritual practice, and then returning to prescribed practice. One wonders, what if the Athenian mule drivers had had a drink without asking permission first? Presumably Lysimache could have addressed this problem with an expiatory act. The possibility of expiatory options defuses the potential danger of mistakes and simultaneously maintains the boundaries of ritual activity by demarcating where acceptable behavior begins and ends.

Expiatory texts act as a stop-gap measure, forestalling change by drawing attention to error. They say, "Look at this! This is unacceptable!" In so doing they actually preclude (or at least slow down) the routinization of errors by providing a mechanism for dealing with mistakes. If ritual is a way of "paying attention" to space, time, matter, and people, then expiatory actions are a way of "paying attention" to ritual itself. Expiatory actions force participants to pay attention to what should and should not occur in ritual precisely because there are mistakes to catch and opportunities to correct those mistakes.

Conversely as expiatory actions weaken or fall by the wayside, they indicate acceptance of deviation from standard practice. A contemporary example will illustrate this point. A recent BBC News South Asia story described what happened when a baby urinated inside an Indian temple in Kerala.[47] At first the father was asked by the temple priests to pay 1,001 rupees to cover the costs of the purificatory ritual required to resanctify the temple. (According to this community's tradition, priests maintain the general ritual traditions with their activity, but the costs are underwritten by the community as a whole. When a ritual is linked specifically to an individual, however, that person must subsidize the ritual activity.) Unfortunately the father could not afford this fee, and ultimately state officials in Kerala set the financial charges aside completely. K. C. Venugopal, the Kerala state minister responsible for temple activity, offered a comment: "I respect the views of the temple priests. *But this penalty business is very pre-historic*. . . . If they want to conduct a cleansing ceremony, let the money be taken from the temple funds. It should not be taken from worshippers" (my emphasis). It may be tempting to conclude from this example that the state minister's primary concern was not whether or not the purification should be performed, but the financial burden on the baby's father. I believe, however, that Venugopal's words indicate something far more troubling from a ritual perspective. His phrase "this penalty business" indicates that he thinks of the financial cost as some kind of fine ("penalty") for urinating in the temple, *not* the cost of an additional—and necessary—ceremony. He indicates that the priests can perform some "cleansing ceremony" if they want, but he draws a sharp dividing line between the priests and the worshippers. Venugopal's words suggest that *he* does not view the baby's father as responsible for providing a *ritual* solution to the contamination his baby caused. Venugopal's position—and the fact that it was unchallenged by the community at large—suggest that rules related to ritual repair are not widely viewed as significant.

My suspicion is that by tracing whether or not expiation guidelines are enforced, we can get a sense of the relative strength or weakness of a particular ritual rule. If support for a specific expiatory practice slips, this decline may reflect a lack of concern for the error expiation is meant to expunge. In the Kerala community public concern over the possible ritual consequences of urinating in a temple has diminished. This deterioration is reflected not in direct challenges to the rule, but in weakening enforcement of the expiatory activity designed to counter the resulting ritual pollution.

5. Expiatory material is fundamentally optimistic.

Mistakes are dangerous or threatening only when they cannot be corrected. Expiatory material neuters mistakes, making them innocuous and thus not to be feared. If ritual offers an "ought" to what "is," expiation offers a "can be" to what "should be." Expiation suggests that if participants don't get it right the first time, there is opportunity to try again. As a result ritual systems that incorporate expiatory material are self-preserving. This observation suggests a possible avenue for further study; it may in fact be helpful to examine which ritual systems do and do not accommodate errors effectively as an indicator of how healthy the ritual systems are. My suspicion is that those in decline tend not to apply their expiatory mechanisms as faithfully as vital systems do because fewer community members are invested in maintaining the ritual system overall. Similarly one sign that a ritual system may be failing is when it is unable to fix its own errors, when the indigenous *prāyaścitta* system is not adequate to address the mistakes that occur in ritual performances.

Virtually every religious tradition involves ritual practice of some kind, and one would be hard-pressed to find a ritual system that does not include expiation. This brief study shows some of the ways ritual errors and their companion strategies provide a unique lens for viewing the negotiation of actual ritual practice with ideal ritual paradigms. Expiatory material brings us into intimate contact with individual ritual systems and leads to broader insights into the nature of ritual in general. Expiatory activity reminds us that rituals are grounded in day-to-day reality, subject to the same conflicts, foibles, and limitations of all other expressions of religious life. The negotiation of ritual repair can be tremendously instructive for the understanding of specific ritual systems and for the broader understanding of ritual in general.

Notes

1. Staal, *Rules without Meaning*, 93. His discussion of this issue is just as brief in the 2-volume chronicle of the *agnicayana*. See Staal, *Agni*, 336.

2. Baudhāyana Śrauta Sūtra, trans. Kashikar. Hereafter BŚS.

3. See Ute Hüsken's edited volume *When Rituals Go Wrong*.

4. Jan Gonda, *Vedic Ritual: The Non-Solemn Rites* (Leiden: Brill, 1980); Jan C. Heesterman, *The Broken World of Sacrifice: An Essay in Ancient Indian Ritual* (Chicago: University of Chicago Press, 1993); Nancy Jay, *Throughout Your Generations Forever: Sacrifice, Religion, and Paternity* (Chicago: University of Chicago Press, 1992); Stephanie W. Jamison, *Sacrificed Wife/Sacrificer's Wife: Women, Ritual, and Hospitality in Ancient India* (New York: Oxford University Press, 1996); Charles Malamoud, *Cooking the World: Ritual and Thought in Ancient India* (Delhi: Oxford University Press, 1996); Laurie Patton, ed. *Authority, Anxiety, and Canon: Essays in Vedic Interpretation* (Albany: State University of New York Press, 1994); Brian K. Smith, *Reflections on Resemblance, Ritual, and Religion* (New York: Oxford University Press, 1989).

5. All translations are my own unless otherwise indicated, although I acknowledge a heavy debt to C. G. Kashikar for his recent translation of the Baudhāyana Śrauta Sūtra.

6. Hubert and Mauss, *Sacrifice*.

7. Staal argues, "Ritual is pure activity, without meaning or goal. . . . To say that ritual is for its own sake is to say that it is meaningless, without function, aim or goal, or also that it constitutes its own aim or goal" (*Rules without Meaning*, 12–13).

8. Gonda, *The Ritual Sūtras*, 489.

9. Winternitz, *A History of Indian Literature*, 272.

10. Ibid., 276.

11. Chakrabarti, *The Paribhasas in the Śrautasūtras*, 1.

12. Note that this essay restricts discussion of *prāyaścitta* to the Vedic context, in which the focus is on ritual sacrifice. See Michael Aktor's chapter in this volume for a discussion of *prāyaścitta* in the later Indian legal literature. While I would argue that Vedic *prāyaścitta* is largely about the nullification of the consequences of ritual activity, Aktor argues that, in the legal literature, *prāyaścitta* is about the penitence of the ritual actor.

13. There is considerable difference of opinion regarding the dating of the Baudhāyana Śrauta Sūtra. R. N. Sharma offers a date between 400 and 300 CE, and Louis Renou roughly agrees. C. G. Kashikar suggests an earlier dating, between 800 and 650 BCE. Chakrabarti points to Baudhāyana's use of the *pravacana* form—"a literary composition resembling the Brāhmanas . . . . [in which] the author shows little tendency towards succinctness which is evinced in the later sutra works"—as evidence of early dating (77, 78). Some scholars place the Vādhūla Śrauta Sūtra before or contemporaneous with the Baudhāyana Śrauta Sūtra. See Frederick M. Smith's discussion in *The Vedic Sacrifice in Transition*, 19n70. In general scholars agree that BŚS is the earliest of the *śrauta sūtras* in the Taittirīya school. See R. N. Sharma,

Culture and Civilization as Revealed in the Śrautasūtras (Delhi: Nag Publishers, 1977); *The Baudhāyana Śrautasūtra*, ed. Kashikar.

14. *The Baudhāyana Śrautasūtra*, ed. Kashikar.

15. Ibid., 1: xiii.

16. Kashikar comments, "The Śrautasūtra itself covers Praśnas I–XXIX. Its broad divisions are: the main Sūtra I–XIX, Dvaidha XX–XXIII, Karmānta XXIV–XXVI, and Prāyaścitta XXVII–XXIX" (ibid.).

17. Ibid., 1: xvii.

18. As always, there are exceptions to this, as later examples in this essay demonstrate.

19. Also, "Whatever might have been done unaware or in haste, is deemed to have been done correctly through the utterance of the Vyāhṛtis" (BŚS 27.4); "May Agni and goddess Śraddha release me from whatever evil the bewildered priests do knowingly or unknowingly, svāhā" (BŚS 27.6).

20. Axel Michaels, "Perfection and Mishaps in Vedic Rituals," in Hüsken, *When Rituals Go Wrong*, 122.

21. Note that each fire within the sacrificial arena must be reestablished slightly differently. See BŚS 27.10.

22. F. M. Smith, *The Vedic Sacrifice in Transition*, 79.

23. Michaels, "Perfection and Mishaps in Vedic Rituals," 122.

24. Kane, *History of Dharmaśātra*, 997–98.

25. B. K. Smith, "Ritual Perfection and Ritual Sabotage in the Veda," 285–306.

26. Ute Hüsken, "Ritual Dynamics and Ritual Failure," in *When Rituals Go Wrong*, 340.

27. Chakrabarti, *The Paribasas in the Śrautasūtras*, 176.

28. Ibid., 134.

29. Ibid., 175.

30. Ibid., 175–76.

31. One counterexample to this general rule is the increasingly prevalent custom of using grain-cakes as substitutes for animal offerings in contemporary India. In the 1975 *agnicayana* that Staal chronicled, he notes that "cakes made of a paste of rice flour" were substituted for the goats. This change, however, was offset by the fact that "the mantras were recited in the prescribed manner and it was felt that the essence of the ritual was thereby preserved" (*Agni*, 18).

32. Manu 11.28–30, trans. F. M. Smith, *The Vedic Sacrifice in Transition*, 77.

33. Several substitutes may replace *soma*. Most commonly *pūtīka* is used, but Staal lists several other potential replacements, including ephedra and sarcostemma. The *śrauta sūtras* even describe a procedure for transforming milk ritually into *soma* by adding the bark of the *parṇa* tree (ĀpŚS 1.6.8).

34. BŚS 27.9, trans. Kashikar, 1733. Note how gazing is considered comparable to physical contact. See, for example, Stephanie Jamison for further discussion of the importance of the sacrificer's wife gazing in Vedic sacrifice.

35. "[TKM] I. 84 states that an officiant must, as far as possible, substitute for the wife if she is in her menstrual period or has given birth. I.140c–143 declare that only the Agnihotra, the new and full moon sacrifices, and the Piṇḍapitṛyagña may be performed while the wife is in either of these two conditions of impurity. On the other hand, 'so passive is her role that the question of whether she need participate at all is raised.' II.8 and III.96 note that she may be replaced by a fistful of *kuśa* grass or, like Sītā in Rāma's Aśvamedha, by a golden image of her" (F. M. Smith, *The Vedic Sacrifice in Transition*, 89).

36. Ibid., 65n210.

37. BŚS 27.1, trans Kashikar, 1717.

38. Winternitz, *A History of Indian Literature,* 161.

39. "Les trois 'énoncés' par excellence (bhūr, bhuvaḥ, svar) . . . généralement murmurés par l'adhvaryu ou (expiatoirement) par le brahman" (Renou, *Vocabulaire du Ritual Védique,* 144).

40. BŚS 27.1, quoting TBr 3.7.11.1–4, trans. Kashikar, 1717.

41. Aktor makes a similar statement in his chapter: "Therefore 'negotiation' is not located *in* ritual but around it."

42. See Chakrabarti's discussion of this in *The Paribasas in the Śrautasūtras,* 47.

43. Clooney, *Thinking Ritually,* 81.

44. F. M. Smith, *The Vedic Sacrifice in Transition*, 64.

45. Clooney, *Thinking Ritually,* 115.

46. J. Z. Smith, *Imagining Religion,* 53.

47. "Peeing Baby Temple Fine Reversed."

Bibliography

Primary Source

Baudhāyana Śrauta Sūtra, vols. 1–4. Trans. and ed. C. G. Kashikar, Delhi: Motilal Banarsidass, 2003.

Secondary Sources

Chakrabarti, Samiran Chandra. *The Paribasas in the Śrautasūtras.* Calcutta: Shyamapada Bhattacharya, 1980.

Clooney, Francis X. *Thinking Ritually: Rediscovering the Pūrva Mīmāṃsā of Jaimini.* Publications of the De Nobili Research Library, ed. Gerhard Oberhammer, vol. 17. Vienna: Brill, 1990.

Geertz, Clifford. *The Interpretation of Cultures.* New York: Basic Books, 1973.

Gonda, Jan. *The Ritual Sūtras*. Vol. 1.2. *A History of Indian Literature*. Wiesbaden: 1977.

Hubert, Henri, and Marcel Mauss. *Sacrifice: Its Nature and Functions*. Trans. W. D. Halls. Chicago: University of Chicago Press, 1964.

Hüsken, Ute, ed. *When Rituals Go Wrong: Mistakes, Failure, and the Dynamics of Ritual.* Numen Book Series 115. Leiden: Brill, 2007.

Kane, P. V. *History of Dharmaśātra.* 2d ed. 5 vols. Poona: Bhandarkar Oriental Research Institute, 1968–75.

"Peeing Baby Temple Fine Reversed." BBC News South Asia. http://newsvote.bbc.co.uk/mppapps/pagetools/print/news.bbc.co.uk/2/hi/south_asia/4614719, accessed June 8, 2005.

Renou, Louis. *Vocabulaire du Ritual Védique.* Paris: Librairie C. Klincksieck, 1954.

Smith, Brian K. "Ritual Perfection and Ritual Sabotage in the Veda." *History of Religions* 35, no. 4 (1996).

Smith, Frederick M. *The Vedic Sacrifice in Transition: A Translation and Study of the Trikāndamandana of Bhāskara Miśra.* Poona: Bhandarkar Oriental Research Institute, 1987.

Smith, Jonathan Z. *Imagining Religion: From Babylon to Jonestown.* Chicago: University of Chicago Press, 1982.

Staal, Frits. *Agni: The Vedic Ritual of the Fire Altar*. Vol. 1. Berkeley: Asian Humanities Press, 1983.

———. *Rules without Meaning: Ritual, Mantras and the Human Sciences*. Toronto Studies in Religion 4. New York: Peter Lang, 1990.

Winternitz, M. *A History of Indian Literature*. Vol. 1, trans. S. Ketkar. 1927. New York: Russell & Russell, 1971.

PART THREE

Meanings and Values of Ritual

11

Hook-Swinging in South India

NEGOTIATING THE SUBALTERN SPACE WITHIN A COLONIAL SOCIETY

Ulrike Schröder

HOW DO RITUALS PROVIDE a dynamic resource for negotiating individual and collective identities within a society? The constitutive power of rituals for social and religious identity within a society has been a focus of ritual theory from the beginning, but few ritual theorists have gone so far as to inquire about the subversive potential of ritual action.[1] The question of how rituals serve as a focus for social and religious identity is significant—rituals not only preserve or strengthen an established socio-religious order,[2] they also undermine enhanced authorities and serve as spaces of subaltern action in predominant hegemonic structures. I am referring in particular to Comaroff's understanding of African syncretistic movements and their rituals as "purposive attempt[s] to defy the authority of the hegemonic order."[3] For a better understanding of the subversive power of rituals it is critical to focus on the discursive context of a ritual as much as on the ritual action itself. Ritual failure and ritual criticism, for example, often become important occasions for debates about ritual's deeper meaning and contents.[4] In this essay, I consider a specific ritual as a discursive formation in which aspects of ritual action and their discursive context merge, providing a dynamic resource for the negotiation of social and religious identity within a larger discourse.[5]

Grounded in the context of postcolonial studies, this essay focuses on rituals as a form of resistance within India's colonial discourse. As political and cultural practice, colonial rule led to a fundamental transformation of Indian society.[6] Because the nature of colonial discourse was principally hegemonic, characterized by dominance, representation, and suppression, it had a massive impact on Indian society as a whole, especially on subaltern and regional groups, who were widely marginalized by the dominant discourse. Moreover, established socio-religious identities were contested and newly negotiated between different groups as well as vis-à-vis the colonial establishment. Different claims for religious authority and the power of definition competed with each other.[7] But this process of identity formation was not completely in line with the colonial representation of the Other. Rather, the process contested the normative and coercive power of colonial rule in both direct and indirect ways, subverting the ruling norms of the colonial discourse by articulating and acting out alternative positions.[8]

The ritual of hook-swinging and its related controversy in nineteenth-century India merits consideration within this framework. During the colonial period, several rituals, such as *sati* (the self-immolation of widows) and hook-swinging, were subject to heated public debate and political interference by colonial authorities. Although there have been extensive historical analyses of contested rituals, these particular cases have received insufficient scholarly attention from the field of ritual studies. This essay addresses that gap by analyzing hook-swinging as a discursive formation in two ways.[9] First, I ask how colonial policy, which had a massive impact on the performance and meaning attributed to hook-swinging, as well as on its participants and socio-religious setting, determined the field of social and religious discourse about rituals. Second, I examine how, within this transformation, the ritual itself served as a space of subaltern agency and resistance to colonial and social suppression.[10]

Colonial attitudes to hook-swinging can be readily summarized from missionary sources. In 1858, the Reverend G.E. Morris, a missionary in South India, wrote to the local magistrate pressing for the abolition of hook-swinging:

> [Reverend Morris] disclaims all intention of wishing to interfere with the religious rites and ceremonies of the Hindoos, but he asks the permission of the Government in this instance on the grounds: 1) that this particular festival forms no part of their religious system, 2) that it involves unnecessary cruelty, 3) that it militates against public order and decency, 4) that it is an infringement of the common laws of humanity, and 5) that in this particular case it disturbed the residents in the quiet and orderly observance of the Lord's Day.[11]

It is remarkable that Morris could denote a ritual that was usually carried out in connection with temple festivals in South India as forming "no part of their religious system." This attitude already indicates the major reinterpretation of Indian religious folk practices that took place during the nineteenth century and early twentieth century. Hook-swinging, like *sati*, was a specific target of missionary polemic; hence, missionary criticism brought Hindu rituals to the center of colonial attention. As a result, the meaning and practice of the ritual became contested objects of colonial discourse.

Before an analysis of this debate, a short summary of what colonial and missionary sources say about the variety of hook-swinging practices is telling. This overview is not intended to provide a satisfactory explanation of the 'ritual itself.' In fact, it is questionable how much colonial sources can serve as reliable bases for a ritual theory of hook-swinging. As Andreas Nehring has observed, it is not fully clear from colonial sources what the meaning of the rituals really was, due to their stereotyped representation of Indian religious practices in general and hook-swinging in particular.[12] Therefore a careful consideration of colonial sources can only be a limited approach. Yet, what they reveal about the performance, the participants, and the context of hook-swinging deserves attention. The ritual was so diverse that the breadth of reports and sources reflects the varieties of hook-swinging practices quite precisely. The following is therefore little more than an attempt to carefully lift the curtain on colonial representation to see more clearly the varieties of ritual practice in colonial India.

THE RITUAL OF HOOK-SWINGING AND ITS PLURALISTIC PRACTICE

Unlike other ritual practices in Hinduism that are more or less attached to the ritual canon of brahmanical Hinduism, hook-swinging was not only linked to very different religious contexts, it was also a phenomenon of considerable regional and local variation in dispersion, meaning, and practice.[13] From a theoretical point of view one can even question the conceptualization of such diversity as a single (form of) ritual, or ask if certain common features allow for the consideration of hook-swinging as one and the same ritual. Nonetheless, the creation of a uniform perspective on hook-swinging regardless of its variations was precisely the most important effect of nineteenth-century colonial discourse. This holds true even if the reports and descriptions occasionally shed light on the religious variety of "folk Hinduism" that was otherwise fully neglected in the orientalist discourse and its preoccupation with text-based "higher religion."[14]

Reports and descriptions from around India show the ritual spreading along language lines in eastern and central regions of India (Bengal, Orissa, and hill regions) as much as in the west and south. The actual form of this practice differed substantially in Bengal compared to the south and west (i.e., Madras and Bombay presidency), but the usual method was to insert two iron hooks in a person's bare back, below the shoulder blades, and to tie the hooks together with a rope. The swinger was then suspended from a wooden apparatus mostly consisting of an upright pole and a horizontal cross beam. He or she was then pulled upwards off the ground and sometimes whirled.

In the Bengali form of hook-swinging the swinger was suspended from an immobile apparatus and then whirled around, sometimes while smoking, which was interpreted as a sign of ascetic endurance,[15] and sometimes while distributing flowers and fruits to the crowd below. The ritual that gave the festival its Bengali name is referred to as *charak puja* or *churuk poojah* in colonial and missionary sources. *Charak* or *churuk* was understood as a derivation of the Sanskrit word *cakra* (wheel), referring to circle rotation as the method of swinging the devotees.[16] In Bengal, the practice was linked to notions of ascetic self-torture and penance. Practices of self-torture played an important role in the cult of Shiva and his aspect as the god of the ascetics in the *samnyasa* traditions. The festival, which lasted several days, was carried out annually, before the beginning of the Hindu New Year, in April. On this occasion men mostly of low-caste origin, for example *Sudras*, adopted the temporary status of an ascetic (*sannyasi*) to perform a series of ascetic exercises, such as rolling one's body over rough and prickly plants, jumping from a scaffold into a bed of sloped knives, and piercing parts of the body with sharp nails, rods, and cords. The swinging ritual was the last and final exercise and the one that attracted the most attention from local people. The missionary accounts often note critically the carnivalesque character of the whole festival, with its fairs and gambling on the side.[17] The swinging ceremonies were also popular among the higher castes, even if they served only as festival patrons, mandating or paying proxies to swing for their own religious benefit and social prestige.[18]

By contrast, colonial reports show that in most parts of South India the ritual was designed for the "propitiation" of divine feminine deities (*saktis*) or village goddesses (e.g., *Mariyamman*).[19] Hook-swinging was therefore linked to notions of sacrifice rather than asceticism. Sometimes even animal sacrifices accompanied the swinging ceremony. It is important to underscore the point that in South India hook-swinging was not linked to the Sanskritic-brahmanical ritual tradition in Hinduism, but was part of popular forms of religion in villages and towns. The ritual was part of the annual temple festivals, which also featured other practices, such as walking over burning coals. Also, in contrast to the Bengali form, hook-swinging in South India was often designed as a cart procession, wherein a cart with a swinging apparatus fixed on it was dragged around the temple. This practice indicates that the communal and territorial power of the village deities was also implied by the hook-swinging ritual. While in Bengal the ritual was clearly a low-caste practice, the involvement of various castes and even Brahmans in the South Indian festivals underlines the importance of village deities as protectors of the entire community.[20] The swingers were usually men or women from lower castes, for example *Kallars* or *Pariahs*, but in some cases they were members of higher castes, and even priests.[21] As Brahmans of lower orders were sometimes also involved in the cults of *saktis* and village deities, the festivals were mostly performed under their superintendence and under the auspices of wealthier patrons of higher castes. Colonial sources often state corporate reasons for the swinging festivals—that they were intended to secure the well-being and prosperity of the entire community: "The great idea is to put the goddess into a good humor and get her to interfere in cases of outbreaks of small-pox, scarcity of rain, &c. The goddess, it is thought, likes to have as much 'tamasha' as possible during these festivals, and as 'hook-swinging' brings together a large crowd of worshippers the goddess is pleased with the practice and is likely to be angry if the custom be discontinued."[22]

Besides being a community-based ritual, there was also an individual form of hook-swinging that served as fulfillment of a vow (*neertti*) previously made to a deity; such vows were linked to pleas for healing from dangerous diseases or, in the case of women, pleas for conception of a child or even for a good match.[23] The Tamil term *neerttikkatan* includes both the act of making a vow as well as its fulfillment by performing an offering.[24] Such individual swinging rituals could be done by men as well as by women.

But one should be cautious about interpreting the ritual as simply a form of propitiation through sacrifice and entertainment—a line of thinking that follows the colonial perception, which was colored by fear of "barbaric sacrifices." One aspect that is usually omitted or understated in contemporary sources that can help us to shed light on the ritual is the role of the swinger himself—the most important actor during the ceremony. Swingers were often dressed as deities or depicted as fighters; holding a sword and shield or even a shotgun,[25] they seemed to be enacting a kind of spiritual drama. A report from Cochin in South India states that the swinger symbolized Kali in her fight against the demon Darika.[26] Some sources also indicate that swingers were temporarily divine or possessed by the deity.[27] The Tamil term *cetilaattam* that is used for hook-swinging also implies notions of divine dance and possession. In addition, the swinger distributed flowers and fruits to the spectators, who received them as gifts from the deity.

HOOK-SWINGING AS OBJECT OF THE COLONIAL DISCOURSE: "RELIGION" AND THE CONTEST OF RELIGIOUS LEGITIMATION

Considering the varieties of hook-swinging one wonders why this diversity seemed insignificant to objectors. Moreover, the colonial debate did not distinguish between different forms and contexts. Instead, critique was focused on the performative aspects of the ritual that ostensibly contradicted the morals, values, and ethical beliefs of the Victorian age.[28]

This focus reflected a shift at the beginning of the nineteenth century, when reactions ranging from moral concern to repugnance—both strengthened by the Evangelical Revival—came to dominate British attitudes toward Indian religions.[29] The debate about hook-swinging, which became an object of colonial interest from the 1830s onwards, was part of the larger discourse about religious and social reform in colonial India triggered by the prohibition of *sati* in 1829 as a symbol of the "backwardness" of Indian civilization.[30] Like hook-swinging, *sati* and female infanticide had been targeted by missionary and colonial critique largely because all such practices were seen to contradict the rational and educational impetus of colonial rule as well as the bourgeois morality of Europe.[31] Colonial officials and missionaries such as the Reverend Morris condemned hook-swinging as "barbarism" in the name of Indian religion and tradition and thus not only contradictory to the civilizing efforts of British colonial rule but also a danger to public morality and decency. Missionaries especially objected to these practices as "cruel," "barbarous," and "inhuman," reflecting the widespread preconception that hook-swinging was a degraded form of human sacrifice; hence the swingers were conceived of as "victims" or "wretches," with neither a will of their own nor any ritual agency.[32] As Nicholas Dirks has pointed out, the central question about the relation of agency to tradition paralleled the *sati* debate.[33] In fact, the Bengal origin of the hook-swinging debate indicates that it was a direct sequel to the *sati* debate and inherited many of the same concerns and cultural preoccupations.

Calcutta, capital of the Bengal presidency, was the first field of dispute in the 1830s, when the debate was initiated by missionaries and the emerging Hindu reformist movement. It is revealing to take a closer look at the genealogy of this discourse because the refutation developed there provided key arguments that subsequently figured in the hook-swinging debate in South India. The Bengal newspaper *Reformer*, edited by a disciple of the Hindu reformer Rammohan Roy, and the *Bengal Herald*, a newspaper of the reformist party, initiated the debate.[34] The agitation against hook-swinging was further pressed by the Baptist missionaries headquartered in the precincts of Calcutta, in the Danish colony of Serampore. Their leading agitator, William Ward (1769–1823), had already described practices of self-torture during the *chŭrŭkŭ* (*charak*) festival in Bengal in his comprehensive work on Hindu religion.[35] *Friend of India*, a missionary periodical edited by the Baptist Mission in Serampore, started to critique hook-swinging in 1835. Unlike other public voices, this critique was aimed at promoting government interference in terms of a general prohibition of the *Churuk pooja*, instead of only a modification of its most "cruel" parts:

> The second question is, whether Government should not interfere to prevent the churuk [*sic*] altogether. Such a procedure could be justified only on one of two grounds—either that the tortures of the churuk are no part of the Hindoo religion at all—or that they are so abhorrent to humanity and iniquitous in entailing undeserved suffering upon individuals, as to render null in respect of them the guarantee of Government to protect the Hindoos in the practice of their religion. The first ground does not seem honestly tenable. It is true the churuk is not named in any of the higher shastras. It was instituted by king Vanu in comparatively modern times; and its authority rests upon a single pooran[.] Nevertheless this pooran is numbered amongst the shastras; and the practice it sanctions has been long observed by Hindoos as part and parcel of Hindooism[.] [In a] man's religion he must have liberty to make out for himself: others have no business to tell him that he does not believe what he knows himself that he does believe. If he has a right to be protected in the exercise of his religion, it is according to the view that his own conscience takes of it: else the right is a nonentity.[36]

Interestingly, the author was still careful not to exclude hook-swinging from the sphere of Hindu religion, observing that this practice did in fact have scriptural legitimization and thus appealing to the individual agency of each believer to "make out" his religion for himself. But as religious liberty without a firm scriptural basis was an impracticality in the eyes of Western Christians, this liberty could not be upheld for the benefit of Hindus. In an article published in *Friend of India* on April 30, 1835, the author retracts his previous statement, preferring scriptural legitimization to religious liberty. The article indicates that in the meantime the argument regarding scriptural legitimization was being openly debated in letters to the editor as well as in other Bengal newspapers. The author thus concluded:

> The Reformer has argued with no little force that we were wrong in stating that the pooja was authorized by even a single pooran: and on reviewing the subject we are inclined to think he is right. All that the pooran appears to afford is, a first example of very limited extent, which has been taken from as a precedent to authorize all the self-tortures which the whim or fanaticism of devotees could invent. A few degraded brahmhuns assist the sunyasees in previous acts of worship to *Siva*; but at the churuk itself, their aid, we believe, is not required. At any rate we should [be] putting ourselves in a false and odious position, were we to undertake against a Hindoo to prove that such an abomination is sanctioned by his shastras; unless we meant thereby to bring the religion which was capable of such an appendage into contempt and abhorrence: which we might do with a very good will, although it is not our present purpose. We will rather take the Reformer's argument to be perfectly just, and allow all the Hindoos to be mistaken who think their religion sanctions the Churuk poojah. . . . We are happy to find by conversation with a very orthodox Hindoo, that, contrary to our expectation, the party to which he is attached are very indifferent to the maintenance of the pooja, or, its prevention by Government. On whatever principle, therefore, such a prevention may be grounded, it gives us much pleasure to be able to think, that its actual occurrence would give no serious offence.[37]

This argumentative turn indicates the direction the discourse about hook-swinging would take: at stake was the issue of religious legitimization of popular religious rituals such as hook-swinging. The frequent interference of missionaries at festivals took the debate from the newspapers to the streets, as missionaries attempting to put an end to hook-swinging performances simultaneously used these occasions for street preaching and proselytizing. This in turn often led to violent reactions and excited discussions in the press, as in the case of the missionary Thomas Boaz,[38] whose efforts to stop a ceremony in Calcutta in 1839 ended in a fray. Boaz was apparently defeated by the local executives, and he appealed to the *Calcutta Christian Observer* to print his correspondence with another newspaper, the *Bengal Hurkaru*, to restore his renown. The following report from the *Bengal Hurkaru* offers a glimpse of local Indian reactions to missionary agitation in Calcutta. In this case, a festive procession that had preceded the hook-swinging was styled as a ritual imitation of a Christian funeral procession, poking fun at the Christian missions: "The Hindus, improving with the march of intellect, had their mummers dressed in quite novel costumes, and perhaps, in retaliation for the attacks made by the Missionaries on their religious prejudices, the mummery of a Christian burial train, coffin, clergyman, bible, pall-bearers and mourners, was paraded through the streets in a most indecent manner, to the Scandal of all Christians who passed by."[39]

In addition to such provocative mockery and the frequent disruption of the Lord's Day by hook-swinging festivities, missionary aversion was heightened by the common Christian association of the suspended "victim" with the crucified Christ. Not surprisingly, the impression mounted that hook-swinging was in fact the most accurate expression of barbaric heathenism in opposition to Christianity. The fact that such an event attracted thousands of people, who were obviously immune to missionary preaching, made clear that hook-swinging ceremonies were daunting obstacles to promulgating the Gospel in India. In a letter to the *Missionary Herald* the Reverend Noyes wrote, "We preached to several audiences, but such occasions are very unfavorable to making an impression. I much prefer to see the people when they are quiet in their own villages."[40]

The call for governmental interference that had started with the Bengal debate paved the way for the discursive delegitimization of hook-swinging as a religious practice in the following decades. Missionary conferences issued petitions against hook-swinging, urging governmental action.[41] In European eyes the performance of "brutal" rites like *sati* and hook-swinging in public spaces was striking evidence of the brutalizing and coercive effect inherent in Indian culture and religion.[42] Consequently, the public debate about Indian religious practices clearly served a reformist agenda and provided an "extraordinary occasion for the re-articulation of the tradition around the designation of, and subsequent debate over, the scriptural sanction for religious practice in early colonial Hinduism."[43] Lata Mani has shown that in the case of *sati* the orientalist assumption that texts form the basis of a religion created a hegemony of religious texts over practice. Regional variations were seen "as 'peripheral' to the 'central' principle of textual hegemony."[44] Although this principle also prevailed in the case of hook-swinging, the argument of missing scriptural legitimization was used here to play religious folk practices of "lower classes of society" off brahmanical Hinduism and the "better instructed and higher orders of community."[45] Brahmanical advice and consultations with reform-oriented Indian and Hindu associations such as the Dharma Sabha were used as examples of "enlightened native opinion," thereby providing evidence against the religious legitimization of the ritual. Moreover, as the upper castes were subject to the pressure of colonial discourse and its reformist agenda as much as the lower castes, they attempted to disengage from the "uncivilized" "lower classes of society." Hence the educated upper classes readily mirrored the colonial view in their answers and responses. As Nicholas Dirks has noted, Indian elites and missionaries became "unwitting partners" in the colonial discourse, sharing more or less the same arguments about Indian public religion, the lower classes, and social reform.[46] In effect, the construction of a concept of "religion" separate from other categories was a direct outcome of this unwitting partnership. The reply of an official from Vizagapatam to the inquiry by the Madras government in 1893 thus reads like an exclusion of popular religious practices such as hook-swinging from a clear concept of "Hindu religion":

> The Chairmen of Municipal Councils have taken the opinion of local Pandits, and the Maharajah's Manager has consulted the Pandits of the Dharma Sabha of

> Vizianagram (an association to propound the doctrines of the Hindu ritual and ceremonial observances) which is maintained under the patronage of the Maharajah. There is a consensus of opinion that the practice of hook-swinging is not sanctioned by the Hindu religion and is repugnant to the feelings of the higher castes and educated Hindus. The practice is not known in this district and not been observed for more than 30 years.[47]

In essence, then, the hook-swinging controversies provided an occasion not only for the rearticulation of Indian tradition, but also for shaping the concept of Hindu religion in the colonial discourse under the predominant norms of brahmanical Hinduism. What this shift implicitly reveals is the dominance of cultural and religious paradigms in colonial discourse. For the practice of hook-swinging the effect was double-edged: in the first place, the ritual as representative of popular Hinduism was fixed as the maximum deviation from the norms of Western Christian culture;[48] in the second place, the practice was excluded from the field of "proper" Hindu religion and ritual by being degraded to a "custom" of the lower classes. The prevailing identification of social with religious hierarchy in the colonial discourse downgraded hook-swinging to a "low-caste practice" associated with Pariahs and other inferior social groups. This delegitimization of the religious dimension by pointing to a lack of scriptural evidence effectively reduced popular religious practices to irrelevance, while enhancing the status of brahmanical Hinduism to that of a bona fide religion. Therefore the suppression of hook-swinging practices was also a (discursive) de-ritualization as regards the breadth and depth of their religious meaning. In sum, the social importance of the ritual for the entire community, which derived in South India from the authority of the village deity and which also justified the participation of higher castes and Brahmans, was thus fully neglected.

Significantly, the distinction between "custom" and "religion" became the most important tool in defining what could be carried out as a proper form of religion and what counted simply as "custom." In particular, the term "custom" was used as a discursive means of denying the agency of the participants, especially that of the swingers, by symbolizing their manipulation and oppression by tradition and consequently the ritual's contradictory nature alongside (European) modernity.[49] The term "victim," which was frequently used in the accounts of hook-swinging, functioned similarly to uncover the heteronomy of the participants by "tradition." According to Dirks this semantic field indirectly marked the public domain that threatened British rule. By prohibiting hook-swinging, such forms of subaltern ritual agency were banned from the public sphere: "Colonial subjects, in cases such as those concerning sati and hook-swinging, were constructed as victims when they were subjected to some form of custom that either threatened British rule or appeared to violate its moral foundations. Only then did their subjectivity in relation to the possibility of freedom become an issue in colonial discourse. Subjectivity presented itself as an absence, it was only there if it was totally suppressed."[50]

The inclination to subsume hook-swinging under the auspices of torture in the name of religion continued in early ethnography from the late nineteenth century onward, as researchers drew parallels to similar practices in other cultural contexts, for example, those of North American Indians.[51]

"RELIGION" AND "CUSTOM": THE SHIFT FROM A RELIGIOUS TO A "SOCIAL" PRACTICE

The governmental actions that started in the middle of the nineteenth century enforced this gradual shift. The fear of popular rebellion as well as concern regarding native elites who stood to gain economic and social profits from the practice led to more tentative considerations instead of an immediate ban. Remarkably, the initial efforts to suppress the practice were all under way before the Great Rebellion in 1857–58. Although British policy in India changed afterwards to noninterference in religious affairs, the attempts to discontinue or suppress hook-swinging festivals were never relinquished, and in fact finally led to their prohibition in all three presidencies.[52] But before the prohibition in the Madras presidency was finally accomplished, events took a different turn from what went on in the other two presidencies of Bombay and Bengal.

The first steps in governmental suppression were official inquiries in all three presidencies.[53] Seeking a sufficient base for legislative enactment, government officials surveyed the dispersion of hook-swinging along with other popular rites of self-mortification such as fire-walking. These surveys probably marked the first systematic attempt in all presidencies to generate a larger body of ethnographic and administrative information about a ritual practice in India. However, this information was insufficient as a basis for legislative enactment. Despite the predominant perception of colonial magistrates that hook-swinging had nothing to do with (higher) "religion," what remained unclear was whether the interpretation of hook-swinging as a nonreligious practice was evidence enough to prohibit the ritual without provoking public disturbance. Therefore measures put in place were aimed at the suppression of the practice, and a general verdict (i.e., outright ban) was avoided. Instead, the colonial administration concentrated on exerting its influence over local elites so that they would renounce their support for the hook-swinging festivals and withdraw from their festive privileges. The governmental direction for the Madras presidency refers clearly to the distinction between proper "religion" and mere "practice" that had emerged in the discourse:

> The best method of discouraging this objectionable practice must be left to the discretion of the different magistrates, but the Right Honourable the Governor in Council feels confident, that if it be properly explained that the object of Government is not to interfere with any religious observance of its subjects but to abolish a cruel and revolting practice, the efforts of the Magistracy will be willingly seconded by the influence of the great mass of the community, and, more particularly, of the wealthy and intelligent classes who do not seem, even now, to countenance or support the Swinging ceremony.[54]

This pressure on indigenous elites forced upper castes to dissociate from hook-swinging, both in terms of active local support and in general public discourse, even if some local elites resisted abolition.[55] This distancing in turn supported the shift of hook-swinging away from a communal ritual to a low-caste practice. Colonial officials were ordered to express government disapproval to natives whenever possible. The result was that village headmen, patrons, and priests had to appear before governmental officials and grant the discontinuance of the hook-swinging rituals under their authority.[56]

This suppression through discouragement was only partly successful in the long term. In the late 1860s and in the 1890s, hook-swinging was revived in parts of the Madras presidency, and once it became obvious that the government was discouraging but not absolutely prohibiting hook-swinging, devotees reverted to their ritual practices. Some colonial sources explained this resurgence as a reaction to economic and social suffering. The German missionary Carl Ochs, for instance, reported that villagers told him the ban on hook-swinging had resulted in their severe misfortune. Unlike most missionaries Ochs went on to criticize the colonial government for suppressing low castes and privileging upper castes in the exercise of their religion.[57] A glimpse of the inauspicious effects of the ban is also provided by Thurston, who mentions petitions by farmers to revive hook-swinging. According to Thurston their reasoning was that "since this ceremony had been stopped, the rainfall had been deficient and the crops scanty; cholera had been prevalent; and in families where there were five or six children ten years ago, there were now only two or three."[58]

RITUAL AND RESISTANCE

The revivals marked a crucial point in the course of the debate.[59] Since the continuance of the ritual can be interpreted as a form of subaltern agency and resistance to colonial and social suppression, the perspectives and strategies of these revivals as they are presented in colonial sources deserve special attention. What these sources show is that ritual practitioners did not remain silent, even if the predominant discourse denied their agency. If anything, participants insisted on their right to perform the swinging ritual by sending petitions to local authorities. The festival at Sholavandan in 1891 is one of the most interesting cases of these ritual revivals. In the village of Sholavandan, one of the most active communities in the revival of hook-swinging, the ritual was performed at least annually from 1891 until 1894, when it was fully prohibited by law in the Madras presidency.[60] From the perspective of practitioners, the interruption of the ritual practice had severe consequences for the relationship between deities and worshippers. The disruption was seen as inauspicious, provoking disaster and misfortune. A petition of the Sholavandan villagers in 1894 even claimed that the village deity had appeared to possess a villager, demanding the continuance of the ritual. Divine intervention would of course support the discursive position of the subalterns; moreover, the petition depicted hook-swinging as a "proper" religious ritual through the use of Sanskrit terms. As Dirks notes, the villagers' claim was not only fortified by divine authority, but their petition showed both a clear knowledge of the discursive paradigm of hook-swinging as well as awareness of subaltern agency, by virtue of the fact that they were actively seeking to restate the religious dimension of the ritual: "Far from being paralyzed by their lack of choice under the weight of custom, these subaltern petitioners could not only speak but write."[61]

Divine intervention was also reported in other places. The revival in Cumbum (Kurnol District), for instance, offers another interesting example of how subaltern agency—in response to hegemonic suppression—was represented as divine agency in the discourse:

> Hook-swinging still exists in two villages in the Cumbum division. . . . [One village] is in a picturesque gorge on the banks of the Gundlakamma. Here just a couple of months ago two date palms are said to have exhibited the unusual phenomenon of prostrating themselves every morning and rising again gradually by midday! A third tree not far off exhibited a similar phenomenon, though not to the same extent. This was attributed by the villagers to their neglect of the worship due to Sarabheswaramma, or Kona, as it locally called, the goddess of the forest. The result was the flocking of thousands of people to the place and their worshipping the trees, followed by the hook-swinging ceremony, the victim, however only being an unfortunate goat. After the ceremony the trees stopped their eccentric behaviour, thus lending weight to the popular belief in the efficacy of such ceremonies.[62]

But the call for a revival of hook-swinging does not seem to have met with undivided consent in all places. In the case of the Valambagudi revival in 1890, the government file indicates that the reintroduction of hook-swinging ceremonies was a controversial issue even among the villagers themselves. The revival in Valambagudi (Tanjore District) prompted the Madras government to call on all magistrates to insist more carefully on the prevention of hook-swinging. T. E. Thomas, superintendent of police in Tanjore, reported that the "Pariahs" who were in charge of swinging, but had an inferior social status, wanted to stop the ceremony, but for fear of the dominant "Kullar" caste did not enforce their claim.[63] It seems that the conflict had already split the villagers into factions in previous years; the division magistrate had even interfered in favor of a continuance of the festival: "In 1888 the villagers were split into two factions, and one of them put in an application to the Division Magistrate and District Magistrate praying for an injunction to discontinue the practice. The Prayer was not granted and serious breach of the peace was apprehended, but averted by the presence of the Inspector and Sub-Magistrate."[64]

It remains unclear whether a second petition followed some time after, but finally the submagistrate was ordered to prevent the further continuance of the festival, even though this suppression does not seem to have been successful for long; by 1890 the ceremony was taking place again. As it is evident from the case of Valambagudi, a side effect of the colonial hook-swinging policy was the provision of new opportunities for the emancipation of lower castes that were contesting the social and ritual dominance of the upper castes.

But the contestation of hook-swinging was not put to an end by the final prohibition in the Madras presidency in 1894. Even after this date the ritual did not fully disappear; rather, its practice grew more varied. Instead of humans, for instance, a wide variety of alternative objects were used in the swinging ceremonies as proxies; among them puppets, painted images, animals, and vegetables are frequently mentioned.[65] According to Wilber T. Elmore, when the swinging of animals by hooks was also prohibited at a later date, the animals were simply tied to the pole with ropes.[66] Other techniques of swinging, such as using ropes instead of hooks or big baskets for the swingers to sit in, were also in use. Not surprisingly, other practices of self-torture not subject to the new law increased, as if to compensate for the suppression of hook-swinging. Such practices included the ever-popular fire-walking and body-piercing with skewers and small hooks to which some kind of toy car could be attached by ropes and then dragged around the temple.[67]

CONCLUSION

In my introduction I argue that rituals can be conceptualized as discursive formations, consisting of both ritual action and its discursive context. This argument now deserves more consideration in order to shed light on the question of how rituals contribute to the negotiation of identity within a society, especially as a form of resistance and subversion.

My analysis of hook-swinging from a historical point of view is intended to reconstruct the shape and mechanisms of the colonial discourse that determined to a large extent what could be considered as "hook-swinging." It shows that the colonial discourse had developed a kind of typified notion of the ritual that served as a unified representation of all the varieties of hook-swinging practices, which in turn affected the socio-religious setting of the ritual. This interface reveals several ways in which hook-swinging became a concerted form of resistance within the colonial discourse: (1) as a public ritual it contested the colonial hegemony of public space and its underlying moral and ethical concepts; (2) as a ritual revival it contested the power of colonial order; and (3) when challenged by the dominant discourse the ritual provided opportunities to articulate resistance against social and ritual dominance within Indian society. In this respect the debate about hook-swinging reveals not only the hegemonic structure but also the disruptions and hybridity of colonial discourse in general. It is precisely at such discursive fissures that both the need and the opportunity to negotiate identities arises—a critical move that draws from the multiple meanings and intractability of ritual actions in their discursive contexts.

Notes

1. For an overview of ritual theories, see Kreinath, Stausberg, and Snoek, *Theorizing Rituals;* Rao, "Ritual als Performanz"; Belliger and Krieger, *Ritualtheorien.*

2. See the editors' introduction to this volume for a critical discussion of this classic approach to rituals.

3. Comaroff, *Body of Power,* 198.

4. Hüsken, *When Rituals Go Wrong* and Keyes, Kendall, and Hardacre, *Asian Visions of Authority* provide insightful essays about rituals and their discursive contexts.

5. See the editors' discussion of different notions of "negotiation" in the introduction to this volume.

6. I refer here to Dirks's understanding of colonialism both as a cultural project of control and production of cultural knowledge (*Colonialism and Culture,* 3ff.), drawing on Foucault's concept of discourse; the latter has been widely discussed in the field of postcolonial studies and cultural theory. See Foucault, *Die Ordnung des Diskurses.* It should be noted here, however, that the term "colonial discourse" in the field of Indian (post)colonial studies is not unequivocal. In this paper the term is used to denote all forms of speech and action that were part of the colonial project.

7. For studies of the transformation of South Indian society under colonial rule, see, for example, Dirks, *The Hollow Crown;* Washbrook, "South India 1770–1840"; Irschick, *Dialogue and History;* Bergunder, Frese and Schröder, *Ritual, Caste, and Religion in Colonial South India*; Ludden, *Peasant History in South India;* Appadurai, *Worship and Conflict under Colonial Rule;* Brimnes, *Constructing the Colonial Encounter;* Bayly, *Saints, Goddesses and Kings.*

8. Theoretical approaches to colonial history in the field of Subaltern Studies have analyzed the meaning and role of subaltern resistance under colonial rule. See Guha and Spivak, *Selected Subaltern Studies.* The project of the Subaltern Studies Group has received strong criticism from outside of as well as from within postcolonial theory; see, for example, Spivak's own critical assessment, "Can the Subaltern Speak?" It is not straightforward to make a claim for a subaltern agency; its trajectories are still much debated within postcolonial theory. As Rosalind O'Hanlon has critically noted, the recovery of subaltern agency in the historiography of colonial India tends to invoke the liberal notions of (Western) subjectivity. Thus, it runs the risk of being an "authoritarian exercise" to keep control over people and their pasts: "We must examine . . . not only the consequences of such an identification for understanding power and resistance, but whether the strategy itself is the best way to restore the subaltern to history. There is undoubtedly an enormous dilemma here, precisely because of our difficulty in envisaging any other form which such a presence might take except the virile figure of the subject-agent, and in the resulting temptation to appropriate the categories of dominant discourse, in the form of a distinctive subaltern self and tradition." ("Recovering the Subject," 210). The problem whereby reconstructions of subaltern subject-positions turn out to be mere historiographical representations of such positions does not mean that such approaches are entirely illegitimate. Moreover, the relation between subaltern pasts and the rational narrative of conventional historiography has to be discussed; see Chakrabarty, "Minority Histories, Subaltern Pasts." Gyan Prakash has maintained that the aim of Subaltern Studies is not to "invoke 'real' subalterns, prior to discourse, in framing their critique" ("Subaltern Studies as Postcolonial Criticism," 1482). Instead, it is important to acknowledge that the recovery of subaltern positions is "entangled in the analysis of how subalternity was constituted by dominant discourses" (1480). Therefore, in my view, the question for historiographical analysis has to be how

subaltern positions emerged as a discursive effect of subordination within the field of colonial discourse. This discourse was, as Homi Bhabha has emphasized, a highly ambivalent and hybrid endeavor (see "Of Mimicry and Man"; see also his seminal essay about the role of the Bible in colonial India, "Signs Taken for Wonders"). Reading records against their grain, as I do here, intends to recover this hybridity and equivocality within the colonial archive itself.

9. For the term "discursive formation" see Foucault, *The Archeology of Knowledge.*

10. As Andreas Nehring has pointed out, it is important not only to acknowledge the role of performance or agency in colonial power structures, but to raise this as a theoretical question about the performative role of speech and, consequently, action, in theories of discourse. Following Judith Butler's theory of speech-acts, he argues that it is the citational character of performative acts that preserves their subversive potential, as well as their conformity, in predominant hegemonic structures. If one combines his insights with a critical assessment of the discourse on hook-swinging in the nineteenth century, it can be seen that it was precisely this character of ritual performances that was at stake. (See "Performing the Revival," 23ff.)

11. Letter dated September 27, 1858, cited in Dirks, "The Policing of Tradition," 190.

12. Nehring, *Orientalismus und Mission,* 291.

13. Geoffrey Oddie has written extensively about local and regional variations of hook-swinging reflected in colonial and missionary sources. For the following discussion see Oddie, "Hook-Swinging and Popular Religion in South India During the Nineteenth Century," "Regional and Other Variations in Popular Religion in India," and *Popular Religion, Elites and Reforms,* 29ff.

14. For a history of the colonial and orientalist encounter with Indian religions see van der Veer, *Imperial Encounters;* Trautmann, *Aryans and British India.*

15. See Morgan, "Report, October 1841," 526; Ward, *A View of the History, Literature and Mythology of the Hindoos,* 1:24–25.

16. See for example the accounts of the Bengali form of the ritual in "The Cherek Puja"; Sen, "A Short Account of the Charak Puja Ceremonies." Further accounts can be found in "Notices Regarding Hindu Festivals Occurring in Different Months"; Ward, *A View of the History,* 24–25; Weitbrecht, *Die protestantischen Missionen in Indien mit besonderer Rücksicht auf Bengalen,* 104–9; "Cruel Practices of the Hindus at the Charak Pújá," 132–33. The derivation of the Bengali word *charak* from the Sanskrit *cakra* is noted in various accounts; however, the term is more likely a corruption of the Persian word *charkh,* facilitated by the nearness of the Sanskrit word *cakra.* See Yule, Burnell, and Crooke, *Hobson-Jobson,* 220.

17. See Mateer, *The Land of Charity,* 185–86. For a critical approach to the missionary descriptions, see the next paragraph.

18. The swinging of proxies or mandated persons was frequently taken as a reason for the colonial concern with the question of the swingers' agency and free will. The suspicion that participants were subject to compulsion and financial inducement by higher castes, seducement by priests, and even intoxication with drugs and alcohol is suggested by many reports. See, for example, Sen, "A Short Account of the Charak Puja Ceremonies"; "Notices Regarding Hindu Festivals"; Fox, *Chapters on Missions in South India,* 76-82; Knowles, "The Hook-Swinging Ceremony as I Saw It." Knowles noted contemptuously, "sacrifice by deputy, in fact" (586). For a discussion of the colonial view of "agency," see the next paragraph.

19. The collection of reports from the two surveys in the Madras presidency in 1854 (Government of Madras, *Reports on the Swinging Festival*) and in 1893 (IOR P/4409) shows how widespread hook-swinging was throughout South India in the second half of the nineteenth

century. According to the reports of 1854, the only place in the Madras presidency where the ritual did not occur at all was the Malabar District (*Reports on the Swinging Festival,* 11).

20. Modern anthropological research into village Hinduism in South India provides analyses of the role and importance of village deities as protectors of their communities. See Masilamani-Meyer, *Guardians of Tamilnadu;* Mines, *Fierce Gods;* and the older accounts of Whitehead, *The Village of Gods of South India* and Elmore, *Dravidian Gods in Modern Hinduism.* Although it is problematic to apply contemporary findings to a historical case, it seems reasonable to assume that this relationship with local deities was also the case in nineteenth-century South India.

21. The social status and origin of the swingers seem to have been much more varied than is suggested by the discursive labeling of hook-swinging as a "low-caste ritual." The reports in *Reports on the Swinging Festival* and in IOR P/4409 show how diverse the social status of the swingers in South India actually was.

22. Statement of E. Turner, district magistrate of Madura, in IOR P/4409, 59. Various reports gathered during the inquiry in 1853–54 indicate the same (see *Reports on the Swinging Festival*). For further accounts see Ochs and Genzken, *Nachrichten aus und über Ostindien,* vol. 3, no. 118 p. 119, *Madras Mail,* October 23, 1891. In "The Revival of Hook-Swinging in India," John S. Chandler wrote, "[Mariyamman] is believed to have the power to send or withhold rain; and hook-swinging is thought to be a means of propitiating her, so as to influence her to send rain in abundance" (8).

23. See the account in Barbosa, *The Book of Duarte Barbosa,* 2:220ff.

24. See University of Madras, *Tamil Lexikon,* 4:2357; Baumann, "Selbstkasteiungen und Gelübde," 169–88.

25. See Hoole, *Madras, Mysore, and the South of India,* 358, and the account of Caspero Balbi, written in 1582: "Make him play with a weapon which he carrieth in his hands while he is drawing up" (cited in Powell, "Hook-Swinging in India," 156). See also the depictions in Wyss-Giacosa, *Religionsbilder der frühen Aufklärung,* 270–75. Other accounts mention flowers, fruits, toys, and birds: Weitbrecht, *Die protestantischen Missionen in Indien*, 107; Barbosa, *The Book of Duarte Barbosa*, 2:220ff., Hoole, *Madras, Mysore, and the South of India*, 358.

26. Krishna Iyer, *The Cochin Tribes and Castes,* 324.

27. Reverend Noyes, "Letter, June 30, 1868"; Knowles, "The Hook-Swinging Ceremony as I Saw It." See also Oddie, *Popular Religion, Elites and Reforms,* 53–54. Dirks notes that the signs of possession were frequently misunderstood by European spectators as signs of intoxication—a view that prevails in most of the colonial sources ("The Policing of Tradition," 188). The other Tamil term for hook-swinging that occurs frequently is *cetilkuttu.*

28. See Nehring, *Orientalismus und Mission*, 290.

29. See Oddie, *Popular Religion, Elites and Reforms*, 8. See also Davidson, *Evangelicals and Attitudes to India.*

30. For the colonial debate on *sati* and its prohibition, see Mani, *Contentious Traditions;* Mani, "Debate on Sati"; Major, *Pious Flames.*

31. Dirks, "The Policing of Tradition," 195.

32. See, for example, the accounts of Hoole, *Madras, Mysore, and the South of India*, 357ff., and Fox, *Chapters on Missions*, 76ff. This view is echoed by many writers and even by later ethnographers such as Edgar Thurston, *Ethnographic Notes in Southern India,* 2:487ff.

33. Dirks, *Castes of Mind,* 151.

34. Oddie, *Popular Religion, Elites and Reforms*, 117ff.

35. See Ward, *A View of the History*, 1:24ff.

36. *Friend of India*, April 16, 1835.

37. *Friend of India*, April 30, 1835.

38. See T. Boaz, "Discussion Concerning the Propriety of the Presence and Interference of Missionaries at the Charkh Puja"; E. Boaz, *The Mission Pastor.* In 1842 Thomas Boaz was again involved in a violent quarrel with upper-caste Hindus who supported hook-swinging festivals in Calcutta. The case was even submitted to a local court and the native opponent was convicted and fined. See T. Boaz, "Assault on a Missionary by a Wealthy Native." Missionary interference was not restricted to Bengal; South India is mentioned by Noyes, "Letter, June 30, 1868," Chandler, "The Revival of Hook-Swinging in India," and Knowles, "The Hook-Swinging Ceremony as I Saw It." In Masulipatam, South India, the missionary Henry Fox was thwarted by the locals in his attempt to stop the festival; they argued that the collector in charge financially supported the festival, an arrangement that had hitherto been understood as constituting official approval of the East India Company (Fox, *Chapters on Missions*, 78–79).

39. Cited in T. Boaz, "Discussion," 289.

40. Noyes, "Letter, June 30, 1868," 409.

41. Examples are the petition of the Calcutta Missionary Conference in 1857 ("Memorials to the Legislative Council") and the memorial of the Madras Missionary Conference in 1893 in IOR P/4409, 95–96. The Madras Missionary Conference was of the opinion "that this practice is barbarous and revolting, and that its public exhibition must inevitably tend to degrade and brutalize the community among which it takes place."

42. See Dirks, "The Policing of Tradition," 190.

43. Ibid., 183.

44. Mani, "Contentious Traditions," 96.

45. This opposition is frequently used, for example, in the "Letter of the British Indian Association to the Government of Bengal," February 4, 1865, reprinted in Oddie, *Popular Religion, Elites and Reforms*, appendix 5.

46. Dirks, "The Policing of Tradition," 191.

47. IOR P/4409, 75. Interestingly, in 1853 the magistrate of Vizagapatam had stated that hook-swinging was prevalent in all areas of Vizagapatam and had promised efforts to suppress the practice (*Reports on the Swinging Festival,* 8).

48. Knowles reflects this view when he says that hook-swinging was the most extraordinary of the "superstitious and cruel ceremonies" in India ("The Hook-Swinging Ceremony as I Saw It," 585).

49. See Dirks, *Castes of Mind,* 161ff.

50. Dirks, "The Policing of Tradition," 183.

51. See Thurston, *Ethnographic Notes;* Powell, "Hook-Swinging in India."

52. In the Bombay presidency the practice was already prohibited in 1856. In the Bengal presidency hook-swinging was prohibited in 1865, in the Madras presidency in 1894. Finally, hook-swinging was banned as a criminal act under section 144 of the Code of Criminal Procedure, which prohibited all acts of obstruction, annoyance, and injury (IOR P/4621).

53. Madras presidency (1853), Bombay presidency (1855) and Bengal presidency (1859). For a detailed analysis see Oddie, *Popular Religion, Elites and Reforms*, 82ff.

54. Statement of H. C. Montgomery, chief secretary of Madras presidency, in *Reports on the Swinging Festival,* 2.

55. In the Bengal presidency, the British Indian Association helped to persuade the local patrons and concluded that "the reports received from several districts shewed that the movement had been generally received in good spirit, and that many of those who used formerly to patronize the degrading social practices under comment have of their own accord

discontinued them" (British Indian Association, *Proceedings,* 8). Resistance of native elites to the ban, as was the case in the Bengal presidency, came mostly from hook-swinging patrons and priests who feared losing their local influence and renown (see Oddie, *Popular Religion, Elites and Reforms*, 118ff.). The report of C. H. Mounsey, district magistrate of Cuddapah, cites, for example, the opinions of two Brahmans who were opposed to the prevailing view (IOR P/4409, 64–65). It should not be overlooked that even the official reports contained disparate views of the questions of religious legitimization and governmental action regarding hook-swinging, although a consensus on the general view analyzed here did dominate. The debate on hook-swinging was of course much more hybrid and varied than I can present here; this essay concentrates only on the main discursive developments.

56. This sometimes even happened in advance of official orders. See the collection in *Reports on the Swinging Festival,* especially the reports of the magistrates of Coimbatore and Tanjore.

57. Ochs and Genzken, *Nachrichten aus und über Ostindien*, 3:119.

58. Thurston, *Ethnographic Notes*, 2:498.

59. Instances of revivals were, for example, reported from Kambam, Madura District (1868); Valambagudi, Tanjore District (1890); Sholavandan, Madura District (1891–94); Bheemanaickenpoliem, Trichinopoly District (1892–93); several other villages in the Trichinopoly District; Nallamaram, Madura District (1891–92). The survey in 1893 (IOR P/4409) also mentions a number of other instances. In the native states of Pudukottai and Travancore hook-swinging persisted due to a lesser degree of suppression. Cases of swinging are reported from Cunniore (Pudukottai) and Kollangodu (Travancore). See IOR P/3784, IOR P/4409, 95–96, IOR P/4247, IOR P/4621; Chandler, "The Revival of Hook-Swinging in India"; Knowles, "The Hook-Swinging Ceremony as I Saw It"; Krishna Iyer, *Cochin Tribes and Castes,* 322ff.; Chandler, *Seventy-Five Years in the Madura Mission,* 16.

60. The Sholavandan case is extensively documented in a number of sources: IOR P/4247; Chandler, "The Revival of Hook-Swinging in India"; *Madras Mail,* October 23, 1891 and October 30, 1891; *The Hindu,* June 11, 1894; Knowles, "The Hook-Swinging Ceremony as I Saw It." See also the analysis of the Sholavandan revival in Dirks, "The Policing of Tradition," 197ff.

61. Dirks, "The Policing of Tradition," 198. I refer here to Dirks's analysis of the 1894 petition as I was unable to see the related file.

62. IOR P/4409, 66–67.

63. See IOR P/3784.

64. IOR P/3784, 145.

65. See the reports in IOR P/4409; Thurston, *Ethnographic Notes*, 500–501; Knowles, "The Hook-Swinging Ceremony as I Saw It."

66. Elmore, *Dravidian Gods in Modern Hinduism*, 31–32.

67. See IOR P/4409, 56.

Bibliography

Sources from the India Office Records, British Library London

IOR P/3784 (G.O. 1418), Madras Judicial Proceedings, August 27, 1890.

IOR P/4247 (G.O. 930), Madras Judicial Proceedings, May 17, 1892.

IOR P/4409 (G.O. 2662/2663), Madras Judicial Proceedings, December 21, 1893.

IOR P/4621 (G.O. 2314), Madras Judicial Proceedings, September 24, 1894.

Government of Madras, ed., *Reports on the Swinging Festival, and the Ceremony of Walking through Fire*. Selections from the Records of the Madras Government. Vol. 7. Madras: Fort St. George Press, 1854.

Newspaper Articles

"Cruel Practices of the Hindus at the Charak Pújá." *Calcutta Christian Observer* 6 (April 1837): 182–83.

"Notices Regarding Hindu Festivals Occurring in Different Months. No. 4: April." *Calcutta Christian Observer* 5 (April 1836): 195–98.

"The Churuk Pooja." *Friend of India*, April 16, 1835.

"The Churuk Pooja." *Friend of India*, April 30, 1835.

The Hindu, June 11, 1894.

"Hook-Swinging for Rain." *Madras Mail*, October 23, 1891.

"The Hook-Swinging at Sholavandan." *Madras Mail*, October 30, 1891.

Other Primary Sources

Barbosa, Duarte. *The Book of Duarte Barbosa: An Account of the Countries Bordering on the Indian Ocean and Their Inhabitants, Written by Duarte Barbosa, and Completed About the Year 1518 A.D.* 2 vols. London: Hakluyt Society, 1918–21.

Boaz, Eliza. *The Mission Pastor: Memorials of the Rev. Thomas Boaz, Twenty-Four Years Missionary in Calcutta*. London: Snow, 1862.

Boaz, Thomas. "Assault on a Missionary by a Wealthy Native, His Trial, Conviction and Punishment." *Calcutta Christian Observer* 11 (1842): 359–66.

———. "Discussion Concerning the Propriety of the Presence and Interference of Missionaries at the Charkh Puja." *Calcutta Christian Observer* 8 (1839): 297–304.

British Indian Association, ed. *Proceedings at the Fourteenth Annual General Meeting of the Association, etc. Feb. 14, 1866*. Calcutta, 1866.

Calcutta Missionary Conference. "Memorials to the Legislative Council." *Calcutta Christian Observer* 19 (November 1858): 480–83.

Chandler, John S. "The Revival of Hook-Swinging in India." *Missionary Herald* 88 (January 1892): 7–10.

———. *Seventy-Five Years in the Madura Mission*. Madura, 1912.

"The Cherek Puja." *Asiatic Journal* 25 (January 1828): 32–35.

Elmore, Wilber T. *Dravidian Gods in Modern Hinduism*. Reprint, New Delhi: Asian Educational Services, 1984.

Fox, Henry Watson. *Chapters on Missions in South India*. London: Thames Ditton, 1848.

Hoole, Elijah. *Madras, Mysore, and the South of India, or a Personal Narrative of a Mission to Those Countries*. 2d ed. London: Longman, 1844.

Knowles, Joshua. "The Hook-Swinging Ceremony as I Saw It." *Wide World Magazine* 3 (April–September 1899): 585–91.

Krishna Iyer, L. K. Anantha. *The Cochin Tribes and Castes*. Madras: Higginbotham, 1909.

Mateer, Samuel. *The Land of Charity: A Descriptive Account of Travancore and Its People*. London: Snow, 1871.

Morgan, T. "Report, October 1841." *Baptist Magazine* 33 (1841): 524–26.

Noyes, Reverend. "Letter, June 30, 1868: Kambam, Madura Mission." *Missionary Herald* 64 (1868): 408–9.

Ochs, Carl, and Ernst Genzken, eds. *Nachrichten aus und über Ostindien: Für Freunde der Mission*. Dresden: Blochmann, 1857–67.

Powell, J. H. "Hook-Swinging In India." *Folklore* 25 (1914): 147–97.

Sen, Ramkamal. "A Short Account of the Charak Puja Ceremonies, and a Description of the Implements Used." In *Popular Religion, Elites and Reforms: Hook-Swinging and Its Prohibition in Colonial India, 1800–1894*, ed. Geoffrey A. Oddie, 151–56. New Delhi: Manohar, 1995.

Thurston, Edgar. *Ethnographic Notes in Southern India*. 2 vols. Madras: Government Press, 1906.

Ward, William. *A View of the History, Literature and Mythology of the Hindoos: Including a Minute Description of Their Manners and Customs and Translations from Their Principal Works*. 3d ed. London, 1817–22.

Weitbrecht, Johann Jacob. *Die protestantischen Missionen in Indien mit besonderer Rücksicht auf Bengalen*. Trans. W. Hoffmann. Heidelberg: Karl Winter, 1844.

Whitehead, Henry. *The Village of Gods of South India*. 2d ed. Calcutta: Association Press, 1921.

Yule, Henry, Arthur C. Burnell, and William Crooke. *Hobson-Jobson: A Glossary of Colloquial Anglo-Indian Words and Phrases*. London: Murray, 1903.

Secondary Literature

Appadurai, Arjun. *Worship and Conflict under Colonial Rule: A South Indian Case*. Cambridge: Cambridge University Press, 1981.

Baumann, Martin. "Selbstkasteiungen und Gelübde: Traditionswahrung durch religiöse Praktik." In *Tempel und Tamilen in zweiter Heimat: Hindus aus Sri Lanka im deutschsprachigen und skandinavischen Raum*, ed. Martin Baumann, Brigitte Luchesi, and Annette Wilke, 169–88. Würzburg: Ergon, 2003.

Bayly, Susan. *Saints, Goddesses and Kings: Muslims and Christians in South Indian Society, 1700–1900*. Cambridge: Cambridge University Press, 2003.

Belliger, Andréa, and David J. Krieger, eds. *Ritualtheorien: Ein einführendes Handbuch*. 3d ed. Wiesbaden: Verlag für Sozialwissenschaften, 2006.

Bergunder, Michael, Heiko Frese, and Ulrike Schröder, eds. *Ritual, Caste, and Religion in Colonial South India*. Halle (Saale): Verlag der Franckeschen Stiftungen, 2010.

Bhabha, Homi K. "Of Mimicry and Man: The Ambivalence of Colonial Discourse." In *Tensions of Empire: Colonial Cultures in a Bourgeois World*, ed. Frederick Cooper and Ann Laura Stoler, 152–60. Berkeley: University of California Press, 1997.

———. "Signs Taken for Wonders: Questions of Ambivalence and Authority under a Tree outside Delhi, May 1817." *Critical Inquiry* 12, no. 1 (1985): 144–65.

Brimnes, Niels. *Constructing the Colonial Encounter: Right and Left Hand Castes in Early Colonial South India*. Richmond, Va.: Curzon, 1999.

Comaroff, Jean. *Body of Power, Spirit of Resistance: The Culture and History of a South African People*. Chicago: University of Chicago Press, 1985.

Davidson, Allan K. *Evangelicals and Attitudes to India 1786–1813: Missionary Publicity and Claudius Buchanan*. Appleford, UK: Sutton Courtenay Press, 1990.

Chakrabarty, Dipesh. "Minority Histories, Subaltern Pasts." In *Postcolonial Passages: Contemporary History-Writing on India*, ed. Saurabh Dube, 229–42. New Delhi: Oxford University Press, 2004.

Dirks, Nicholas B. *Castes of Mind: Colonialism and the Making of Modern India.* Princeton: Princeton University Press, 2001.

———. ed. *Colonialism and Culture*. Ann Arbor: University of Michigan Press. 1992.

———. *The Hollow Crown: Ethnohistory of an Indian Kingdom*. Cambridge: Cambridge University Press, 1987.

———. "The Policing of Tradition: Colonialism and Anthropology in Southern India." *Comparative Studies in Society and History* 39, no. 1 (1997): 182–212.

Foucault, Michel. *The Archeology of Knowledge (L' archéologie du Savoir)* London: Routledge, 2002.

———. *Die Ordnung des Diskurses (L' Ordre du Discours)*. Frankfurt am Main: Fischer, 1993.

Guha, Ranajit, and Gayatri C. Spivak, eds. *Selected Subaltern Studies*. New York: Oxford University Press, 1988.

Hüsken, Ute, ed. *When Rituals Go Wrong: Mistakes, Failure, and the Dynamics of Ritual*. Leiden: Brill, 2007.

Irschick, Eugene F. *Dialogue and History: Constructing South India, 1795–1895*. Berkeley: University of California Press, 1994.

Keyes, Charles F., Laurel Kendall, and Helen Hardacre, eds. *Asian Visions of Authority: Religion and the Modern States of East and Southeast Asia*. Honolulu: University of Hawaii Press, 1994.

Kreinath, Jens, Michael Stausberg, and Jan Snoek, eds. *Theorizing Rituals*. Vol. 1: *Issues, Topics, Approaches, Concepts*. Leiden: Brill, 2006.

Ludden, David. *Peasant History in South India*, Princeton: Princeton University Press, 1985.

Major, Andrea. *Pious Flames: European Encounters with Sati, 1500–1830*. New Delhi: Oxford University Press, 2006.

Mani, Lata. *Contentious Traditions: The Debate on Sati in Colonial India*. Berkeley: University of California Press, 1998.

———. "Contentious Traditions: The Debate on Sati in Colonial India." In *Recasting Women*, ed. Kumkum Sangari and Sudesh Vaid, 88–126. New Delhi: Zubaan, 2006.

Masilamani-Meyer, Eveline. *Guardians of Tamilnadu: Folk Deities, Folk Religion, Hindu Themes*. Halle: Verlag der Franckeschen Stiftungen zu Halle, 2004.

Mines, Diane P. *Fierce Gods: Inequality, Ritual, and the Politics of Dignity in a South Indian Village*. Bloomington: Indiana University Press, 2005.

Nehring, Andreas. *Orientalismus und Mission: Die Repräsentation der tamilischen Gesellschaft und Religion durch Leipziger Missionare 1840–1940*. Wiesbaden: Harrassowitz, 2003.

———. "Performing the Revival: Performance and Performativity in a Colonial Discourse in South India." In *Ritual, Caste, and Religion in Colonial South India*, ed. Michael Bergunder, Heiko Frese, and Ulrike Schröder, 12–29. Halle (Saale): Verlag der Franckeschen Stiftungen, 2010.

Oddie, Geoffrey A. "Hook-Swinging and Popular Religion in South India During the Nineteenth Century." *Indian Economic and Social History Review* 23, no. 1 (1986): 93–106.

———. *Popular Religion, Elites and Reforms: Hook-Swinging and Its Prohibition in Colonial India, 1800–1894*. New Delhi: Manohar, 1995.

———. "Regional and Other Variations in Popular Religion in India: Hook-Swinging in Bengal and Madras in the Nineteenth Century." *South Asia: Journal of South Asian Studies* 10, no. 1 (1987): 1–10.

O'Hanlon, Rosalind. "Recovering the Subject: Subaltern Studies and Histories of Resistance in Colonial South Asia." *Modern Asian Studies* 22, no. 1 (1988): 189–224.

Prakash, Gyan. "Subaltern Studies as Postcolonial Criticism." *American Historical Review* 99, no. 5 (1994): 1475–91.

Rao, Ursula. "Ritual als Performanz: Zur Charakterisierung eines Paradigmenwechsels." *Zeitschrift für Religions- und Geistesgeschichte* 59 (2007): 351–70.

Spivak, Gayatri C. "Can the Subaltern Speak?" In *Marxism and the Interpretation of Culture*, ed. Cary Nelson and Lawrence Grossberg, 271–313. Basingstoke, UK: Macmillan Education, 1988.

Trautmann, Thomas R. *Aryans and British India*. New Delhi: Yoda Press, 2006.

University of Madras, ed. *Tamil Lexicon*. Vol. 4. Madras: University of Madras, 1982.

van der Veer, Peter. *Imperial Encounters: Religion and Modernity in India and Britain*, Princeton: Princeton University Press, 2001.

Washbrook, David A. "South India 1770–1840: The Colonial Transition." *Modern Asian Studies* 38, no. 3 (2004): 479–516.

Wyss-Giacosa, Paola. *Religionsbilder der frühen Aufklärung: Bernard Picarts Tafeln für die Cérémonies et Coutumes Religieuses de Tous les Peuples du Monde*. Wabern: Benteli, 2006.

12

Meaning and Enactment in a Buddhist Ritual

Patricia Q. Campbell

IN TORONTO'S HIGH PARK DISTRICT, in a large Victorian house overlooking the park, is the Chandrakirti Buddhist Centre.[1] Associated with the New Kadampa Tradition (NKT), an international organization based in England, the dharma center's membership comprises Western Buddhist practitioners, that is, people from non-Buddhist familial and cultural backgrounds. Twice each month the Chandrakirti Centre offers a special *pūjā*, or devotional service, called the Offering to the Spiritual Guide, a service based on a prayer that originated in seventeenth-century Tibet, where it is called *Lama Chopa*. Donald S. Lopez, who published a commentary and translation of the prayer, calls it "A Prayer to the Lama."[2] The Chandrakirti Centre uses an English-language translation by NKT's founder, Geshe Kelsang Gyatso. Composed by the first Panchen Lama, advisor to the Great Fifth Dalai Lama, the prayer serves as a means of establishing a bond between a practitioner and his or her guru or spiritual teacher.[3] At the Chandrakirti Centre the primary spiritual guide or guru-deity is the founder of the Geluk school of Tibetan Buddhism, Tsong Khapa, known to Chandrakirti members as Je Tsongkhapa.

This chapter, based on a field study of the Offering to the Spiritual Guide, explores how a ritual originating in the religious and cultural traditions of Tibet is being practiced and understood by Western practitioners in Toronto.[4] I conducted my research via participant observation and interviews with several participants at the service. Interviewees cited here are Dorje, a monk in his forties who was head teacher at the Chandrakirti Centre; Susan, the center's education program coordinator, who was in her thirties; Justin, a regular member in his twenties; Margaret, an occasional attendee in her forties; and Anne, a nun and teacher who was in her fifties.[5]

Participants use several different terms to refer to the Offering to the Spiritual Guide. "Prayer" refers to its written text, which they also call the *sadhāna*, and to the chanting of that text. Regular performances of the prayer are called services. Some members call the service a *pūjā*, the traditional term from Indo-Tibetan religion. While some practitioners are uncomfortable with the term "ritual," primarily due to its popular connotation as repetitive or meaningless, most Chandrakirti members nonetheless recognize the service as a ritual.

A ritual, as I use the term here, is a performance with a range of common performance characteristics; for example, it is formal, structured, repetitive, symbolic, religious, traditional, and communal. The greater the number of these qualities present, the more ritualized the performance.[6] The Offering to the Spiritual Guide, with its repetitive performances, formalized timing and structure, and traditional religious origins, bears all of these characteristics.

The Offering to the Spiritual Guide involves a Tantric practice called Guru Yoga, in which participants visualize themselves as a divine, Buddha-like being; consultants referred to this visualization as "self-generating as the guru-deity." Prayers and offerings are then made to the guru-deity or spiritual guide. Other elements of the service involve enacting a presence of the divine in the ritual space. At any one performance, however, there may be participants who are not familiar with Tantric practices and who know little about the official meanings of the service. As a result a variety of meanings and purposes are attributed to the service by a variety of practitioners.

As noted in the introduction to this book, negotiation is here defined as "any process of interaction in which differing positions and concepts are explicitly or implicitly acted out and/or debated." In the Offering to the Spiritual Guide the cultural and religious worldviews underlying the traditional prayer and those of Western-born participants represent different positions. Westerners are frequently attracted to Buddhism under the impression that it is nontheistic, not concerned with ritual, and/or not actually a religion at all.[7] In this service, however, they find highly ritualized practices and religious elements that involve blessings and offerings to spiritual beings. In order to develop an affinity with and acceptance of the ritual, participants must therefore find a balance, perhaps a compromise, between their own cultural or religious worldviews and those of the service. In this sense participants are constantly negotiating the meanings of the rite by acting out (performing the rite) and debating (in their own minds and with other practitioners) those differences. Through repeated performances of the rite, new positions are established and new meanings created.

Chandrakirti members and teachers are openly receptive to the presence of many differing interpretations of the service. Those participating in the service may be newcomers to the center, or they may be members involved at one of the center's three education programs: the introductory-level General Program, the intermediate Foundation Program, and the advanced Teacher Training Program. The first teaches meditation and ethics; the latter two involve intensive study of doctrinal commentaries; and the last introduces practitioners to higher level Tantric practice. Members of any of these programs are welcome to attend the Offering to the Spiritual Guide, as are members of the general public. This opportunity plays out in a plurality of interpretations of the meanings and purposes of the ritual. Plurality is, of course, the case for most ritual performances: different practitioners attach different meanings to the same rite. As is often the case, the enactment or performance of the rite becomes the means by which such differences are downplayed. At the Chandrakirti Centre participation in the service and the standardization of its performance are emphasized over and above the understanding of its meanings.

PERFORMANCE THEORY

Because performance is emphasized over meaning and understanding, an ideal approach to examining the rite is performance theory.[8] The following framework is useful in part because it highlights elements of ritual that parallel those of aesthetic performances. To list a few:

Elements of Performance	*Elements of Ritual*
Actors	Ritualists (those engaged in enacting ritual)
Audience	Witnesses or other ritual performers
Acting	Ritual action
Setting	Ritual space
Props	Ritual objects
Roles	Ritual identity
Script	Text (in this case, the *sadhāna*)
Timing	Ritual time

These categories, among others, provide a useful map for studying ritual in the field.[9] While all are important aspects of the Offering to the Spiritual Guide, I focus on ritual identity and ritual action in this essay. Because some elements of the service, such as the visualizations, are silent, mental enactments, I will apply, as well as test, performance theory.

Performance theory is not merely an extended analogy of ritual.[10] The categories listed above are performative in their own right; that is, they are parts of formalized events that are "done to be seen." Those who engage in the enactment of a rite are necessarily performers: they "show what they are doing."[11] This is not performance in the sense of pretense; it is enacting or bringing something into being. Language used in the performance of a rite makes something happen. Words are deeds: they enact something rather than simply conveying meanings.[12] Meanings may even become secondary; what is often most important is that the right words are performed at the right time in the right circumstances. In the case of the Offering to the Spiritual Guide, where different participants understand the practice in very different ways, the act of performing the chanted prayers becomes the unifying element, more so than the meaning of the prayers.

The Offering to the Spiritual Guide is complex: the text includes more than eighty short prayers, some spoken, most sung. Broadly these prayers include traditional Buddhist practices such as taking refuge in the Three Jewels of Buddha, Dharma, and Sangha; generating the motivation to achieve enlightenment (*bodhicitta*); purification; making offerings; perfecting virtues (*pāramitās*); and dedication of merit to others. The main activity is the chanting of the ritual text. Participants chant for approximately ninety minutes of the two-hour service. Many offerings made to the spiritual guide are performed verbally in the chanted prayers, without accompanying actions or ritual objects. Some actions and gestures accompany the chanted prayers, but the chanting itself is the primary means by which the practices or events that take place in the service are enacted. The service also includes meditative practices. The all-important self-generation as the guru-deity takes place in stillness and silence as practitioners visualize themselves as living buddhas.[13]

THE OFFERING TO THE SPIRITUAL GUIDE SERVICE

The service is held in the main ritual space at the Chandrakirti Centre, the meditation hall. Three long rows of chairs and one row of mats and cushions face the shrines. A large alcove to one side of the room contains three shrines, each bearing three gold-colored statues and seven offering bowls. Figures represented include the Buddha, the Bodhisattvas of wisdom and compassion, the guru Je Tsongkhapa, and the Tantric goddess Green Tara. In the center of the U-shaped shrine alcove is the teacher's seat, a wooden riser bearing a meditation mat and cushion. To the right of the main shrine area sits a table on which the food offerings, or *tsog*, are placed for the Offering to the Spiritual Guide. Food offerings are set out on several attractively arranged plates, the most elaborate of which is offered to the spiritual guide during the service.

A small table sits next to one of the chairs in the front row. On the table are a bell, a hand-held drum called a *damaru*, and a *vajra*, the palm-sized "diamond scepter" prevalent in Tibetan Buddhist ritual. The person who leads the service, either an ordained or senior lay member of the center, plays the instruments at various times during the service. A CD recording of the chanted prayers is also played, and participants sing along with the CD. At the start of the service a senior member assigns various duties to participants, including making and serving tea, reading a dedication, making the *tsog* and spirit offerings, and operating the CD player. In this democratic atmosphere anyone might be asked to take on one of these roles, and the roles are not strongly differentiated from those of the secondary performers or those who do not assume any role at all. Ritual identities are thus reassigned to different people each time the service is held.

Because chanting is accompanied by a CD of the service, the content and structure of the chanted prayers are currently nonnegotiable. At one time, however, the service was chanted in Tibetan without the use of a recording. I have spoken to older members who miss the use of the traditional language, and to others who appreciate the English prayers and the chance to know what they are singing. Since the advent of the CD, which was produced at the NKT headquarters in England, there is less opportunity for participants at Chandrakirti to change or restructure the elements of the service. Its formalized and invariant structure, however, stands in contrast to the informality of the typically relaxed demeanor of participants, the last-minute assigning of various roles at the beginning, and the fact that there is a very casual tea break in the middle of the service.

The first time I participated in the service I was just able to keep up with the chanting, following along in the booklets and turning to the pages indicated. Not all of the prayers appear in the same booklet, and the switch from one booklet to another is not usually announced. By the end I was able to recall only a few of the many elements of the service. As time went on I began to learn more and more about the prayers, what their objectives seemed to be, and why they appeared in a particular order. This gradual development of familiarity and understanding is in fact intended. For most participants, attendance at the service almost always precedes understanding of its meanings and purposes.

Traditionally Lama Chopa was a ritual performed in higher levels of yoga tantra, and as such would not be available to practitioners who had not taken the appropriate initiations.[14] Initiates would be skilled at creating strong visualizations of the spiritual guide, thereby embodying his presence. This embodiment is crucial if the subsequent prayers and offerings are to be regarded as efficacious. But at Chandrakirti newcomers and those with little or no Tantric training are welcome at the Offering to the Spiritual Guide. Dorje, Chandrakirti's head teacher, described how this openness to a variety of different participants affected the functioning of the service in both practical and spiritual terms:

> Many people are attracted to chanted prayers, even though they may have little or no familiarity with the meaning of the various rituals, but I think they just have some affinity for chanted prayers. So they join us, and we help them follow along in the prayer books and they enjoy it. They receive blessings from it, even though maybe intellectually they don't understand everything that's going on. And that's fine. Some people from the very beginning find it very calming and powerful to be present for chanted prayers, even though they may have no experience in this life.

I asked Dorje if the success of the service depended on the awareness of the audience. If a participant is unable to participate fully, does that invalidate the service? He replied:

> My experience has been that when people walk into the meditation room with an open mind they immediately feel peaceful. Even if they know nothing about the images or what we do, or about the tradition, if they just have an open mind

> about it, we do sense positive energy on the subtle level when we're there. And many people say when they just walk into the room they feel instantly more peaceful. So I think the accumulation of practice that has gone on in this building, in this room over the years, we can say it makes it a holy place. People have a feeling for that when they walk in, even if they know nothing about the actual practice.

Although one purpose of the service is to create a special atmosphere or ritual space in which a "field of merit" is created and the presence of the spiritual guide enacted, fully informed participation of everyone present is not necessary for the ritual's success. The service evidently has other significant effects than the creation of the field of merit or the embodiment of the guru-deity. Some participants might experience feelings of peace, compassion, or sacredness. According to Dorje, these experiences are beneficial, and for some participants they are sufficient; in other words, different participants understand what they are doing in very different ways from one another. Some are unaware that the service is intended to create a relationship between practitioners and the transcendent; some understand this relationship differently each time they participate. But in Dorje's view, the existence of different experiences and interpretations of the service is perfectly acceptable.[15]

Dorje was speaking in general terms about people who attend the Offering to the Spiritual Guide. Interview consultants offered more direct evidence of the negotiation of meaning through their own interpretations of the service. Justin, for example, commented on his developing understandings of the service when speaking about the *Migtsema* prayer. This is a nine-line verse, sung repeatedly in the Offering to the Spiritual Guide, in which Je Tsongkhapa is identified with several Buddhas and Bodhisattvas, including Avalokiteśvara, Bodhisattva of "unobservable compassion," and Manjuśri, Bodhisattva of "supreme stainless wisdom." Justin described how he understood the prayer when he sang it:

> Sometimes I try to say it [the prayer] as a connection to Je Tsongkhapa, but other times I try to see it as a reminder of the different ways that the idea of the Buddha can manifest. For example, compassion, Avalokiteśvara: it's not like Avalokiteśvara is a person, even though he has this physical embodiment. I just think of unobservable compassion. I find that beautiful, ever since I first heard that: compassion that is not outward, people don't know about it, you're just doing it for the sake of doing it. And I think that is this force that we all have access to. And this is a way of accessing the Buddha's mind. If we're accessing this energy and using it then we're one and the same. And Je Tsongkhapa is the embodiment of all these wonderful qualities like Manjuśri the supreme wisdom, the perfect realization of emptiness.

Justin regarded Avalokiteśvara, the Bodhisattva of compassion, not as a person, but as an aspect of Tsongkhapa, the Spiritual Guide. He mentioned that the Bodhisattva did have "this physical embodiment," a reference to Tsongkhapa. According to the traditional Tantric worldview described by Lopez, we live in a degenerate age in which individuals cannot achieve enlightenment on their own. A prayer such as this would make the necessary connection to a divine being like Avalokiteśvara through the spiritual guide, Tsongkhapa.[16] In Justin's view, however, the Bodhisattva is not necessarily a divine being, but a reminder of the quality of compassion. In his interpretation of the prayer, all enlightened beings share in the same kind of divine energy, and through *it* one can become enlightened. Justin's understanding of the prayer, therefore, differed from the traditional worldview, a difference of which Justin was aware. His comments also indicate that he explored different meanings of the prayer each time he sang it.

The *Migtsema* prayer is one means of relating to the divine in the service, but for those with some experience at the Chandrakirti Centre, the most important is self-generation as the guru-deity. This visualization takes place near the beginning of the service, following certain preparatory prayers. In a brief period of meditation (timed by silence on the CD) practitioners imagine themselves embodying the presence of the spiritual guide in the form of a Buddha, thereby enacting his presence in the ritual space. The ritual identity of the practitioner shifts, and he or she takes on the body, speech, and mind of the guru. Later in the service, when participants consume tea and *tsog* offerings, it is understood that the spiritual guide himself is taking the offerings.

Justin said that he had not undertaken advanced teacher training, nor had he done an empowerment (taken an initiation) on the Offering to the Spiritual Guide. He therefore had had no training in generating as the guru-deity. When asked what he did at this point in the service, he laughed and said that he was trying to catch up.

> Seriously, I'm only half kidding. Often with this, I'm not following along exactly with what's going on. I can't so quickly go from the refuge, to bodhicitta, to [other elements of the service]. I'm just trying to feel like I would like to be able to help all living beings in every way. And I would like to strengthen my practice and gain the tools to be able to help them, and actually develop this wish, as deep down as I can. That's sort of the beginning of every practice.
>
> When it comes to the guru deity, it comes up a lot throughout the entire thing. And, having not had instruction on it, I just think I'll become the guru or the Buddha, feeling like this is possible, this is something I can achieve and this is my true nature and this is as possible for anyone as it is for me. To arise as this is a feeling of great bliss and joy. It's like being turned inside out. You're just helping others, you have no self and no needs for yourself. But I don't know what you're supposed to be doing. I feel that that is the essence of it for me. Because it does come up a lot. There are a lot of tantric practices in here, but I know that they invite everyone to do this practice, so I feel that in doing that there must be some room for interpretation.

Despite lacking formal training on the self-generation as the guru-deity, Justin did understand what is meant to be done at this time in the service, likely because he has participated many times. It is interesting to note, however, that Justin's own perspective is that there is "room for interpretation" in the context of the ritual.

Following the embodiment of the guru-deity is a section entitled Visualizing the Field of Merit. This practice, which has both verbal and mental elements, is essentially a recitation describing a religious painting, or *thangka,* that appears at the beginning of the main booklet for the service. In the *thangka* the spiritual guide is seated on a lotus throne atop a large tree, surrounded by numerous divine beings and teachers from the Geluk-pa lineage. The chanted prayers describe the *thangka* in some detail. At this point the chanting becomes a verbal enactment of this richly detailed "field of merit." When asked why the painting is chanted in this way, another interview participant, Susan, replied that both the *thangka* and the words of the chant are only representations of the visualization that participants undertake at this moment in the service. The visualization is intended to be a mental construction of the presence of the divine beings depicted in the painting. Susan said:

> We try to generate a mental picture as well. So we try to feel that it's in front of us. What we're instructed to start with is just the feeling. So maybe we're not all visual artists, so it's difficult maybe to recall with our eyes closed something visual. But we should feel that there are beings there. So we try and bring the *thangka* to life so to speak. And apparently this is really, really important. We're making a connection with enlightenment beings, and enlightened beings aren't statues and they aren't paintings, they're living beings. They move, they appear, they have bodies of light or whatever. You try to feel that they are there.

Susan's language indicates a need to balance the official meanings of the service with her own perspectives; in the practice she debates and enacts different ways of understanding her connection to enlightenment beings. According to Anne, an ordained Chandrakirti member, these beings are believed to be present at all times, but ordinary people are not enlightened enough to see them. So by visualizing the field of merit and its divine occupants in this way, participants are creating in themselves a condition of enlightenment, namely the ability to see the ordinarily invisible divine beings. Vocalizing the visualization through the chanted prayers helps participants perform the mental action: creating a powerful visualization of, and consequently a connection to, the divine beings. This is the official understanding of the practice as taught to experienced members in higher level courses.

Susan described her own perspectives on visualizing and realizing the presence of the beings within the field of merit:

> You try to feel like you're getting to know them [the enlightenment beings]. You are making friends with them. And you become familiar with what they look like, and what *mudras* [hand postures] they are doing and what they are holding and who is in their retinue, so that you can turn to them. If your mind is familiar with something like that, it's like you have a good friend that you rely on and you always go out with them, and you tell them your problems and you have a

> relationship with them: when something comes up, then you think of that friend and you get on the phone with them. It's just like this: we try to feel that you have a relationship and they can help you in some way.

In Susan's view, the connection to these beings was not necessarily the sole means to enlightenment. She viewed the beings as more generally helpful, like friends she could turn to when she was in need. Her view differed from the more traditional reliance on holy beings in a degenerate age. Susan did not attend the service because she believed she must rely on the spiritual guide to attain enlightenment. Participating in the service helped her develop a familiarity with the practice, and that practice was the means of attaining her spiritual goals. Mental processes such as meditative visualizations therefore can act much like physical performance—with practice they train the mind, just as physical activity trains the body. Susan in fact expressed this in her own words:

> Well, a lot of it for me is very pragmatic because when you chant through it, it describes the entire path that we're following. It's like studying in a sense. It's like going over it: "All right, this is what I'm doing"; listen to the point I'm trying to memorize; this is where I'm heading. So a lot of it is like building something. You know, you create your own enlightenment. So you sketch out what it's going to be like. You start filling in the details. Maybe at this point I feel like I'm engaged in that on some level so that when I go to this practice, I'm working on that idea of enlightenment, and every aspect of it: even my faith in whether it's possible. That is something to be worked at. You go in and you do the practice and you come away and you remember stuff: "Oh, yeah, I meant to practice patience more." So it gives you that kind of boost.
>
> You become more and more familiar with the ideas. I mean, the first time I went to a class, "nirvana" was a band [i.e., the rock band Nirvana], you know. Reincarnation was kind of flaky. These ideas were completely unfamiliar to my mind. So, going to classes and going to chanted prayers, because everything's in context you start to gain understanding what the different things mean. Of course, it's a subjective experience, it's being taught. But one aspect of the practice is reprogramming your mind: the repetition and familiarity with the ideas.

For Susan, then, the service itself was a teaching tool. With each performance she reinforced and recalled the steps involved in the spiritual path. In her view, "you create your own enlightenment" by participating in the service and becoming more and more familiar with the practices. *Practice* was important; less important were some of the more religious or transcendent meanings. For instance, Susan was uncomfortable with the notion of receiving blessings and generating merit:

> Now, there's also the idea that you're receiving blessings from the Spiritual Guide, and I'm not as comfortable talking about that, because it's kind of magical. I tend to be pretty practical.

> [Regarding merit:] I have a bit of an aversion to that. It's like the idea that if you're a good girl you'll get something good, and if you're not you'll be punished. I'm not interested in that. I do understand, from the point of view of karma, if I do things, there are certain consequences to my actions. But for so many years, being brought up with this idea of an external punishing force, I just want to stay away from that. So the idea of receiving blessings or increasing my merit, it sort of has that tinge to it. It doesn't appeal as much as the idea of just practically becoming more familiar with ideas. But I still keep an open mind to it and I play with that. And I do generate special feelings and I try to feel blessings or imagine what that's like. But really, and I don't know if maybe it's a cultural thing, it's like "the emperor has no clothes." I don't want to start saying I'm getting blessings, because I can't prove it, or because it sounds kind of "out there."

Susan, unlike Justin, had taken some teacher training with the NKT. Despite this, her perspectives on some parts of the Offering to the Spiritual Guide differ from the meanings indicated in the prayer booklet and in the official commentary, *Great Treasury of Merit*, by Geshe Kelsang Gyatso.[17] This line-by-line commentary of the service, which explains the practice and its Tantric elements, emphasizes that relying on the spiritual guide for blessings is necessary for progress along the spiritual path. Some of Susan's reactions to the commentary were responses to her earlier (presumably religious) experiences: the idea that blessings constitute magic and the notion of deity as "an external punishing force." This may indicate why she preferred to view enlightenment as something she can pursue on her own as she develops a deeper familiarity with the practice. Despite this, Susan was keeping an open mind: she allowed for the possibility of the blessings and the transference of merit, but did not want to claim their definite occurrence.

While there is some openness to a variety of interpretations of the service, there is also some indication of an official line regarding the true objective of the Offering to the Spiritual Guide.[18] The third time I attended the service, for instance, one of the senior members approached another newcomer and me during the break to offer some advice for participating in the service. He said that it was important not to have the attitude that the service is long or that one is uncomfortable. He seemed concerned that we not become bored; he encouraged the two of us to listen to the chanting and feel the positive energies developed in the service. His recommendation was a clear attempt to guide our participation in and perceptions of the service, even though we might not know what was going on.

Because a wide variety of different interpretations among practitioners is accepted and even welcomed at the Offering to the Spiritual Guide, conformity of belief is therefore not crucial. What is more important is that members participate. According to some practitioners, simply participating in the Offering to the Spiritual Guide can create the conditions for meaning to arise, for beliefs to be influenced, and for participants to become more involved and knowledgeable over time. This conviction relates to the notion of karma: participation in the service is believed to create a kind of spiritual merit that can draw participants back again and again; while participants may initially come for the peaceful or sacred atmosphere, with time they will find the service increasingly meaningful. Thus repeated participation in the ritual may itself establish agreeable meanings and purposes for individual practitioners.

The anthropologist and ritual scholar Roy Rappaport asserts that the performance of a ritual inherently indicates acceptance of the rite.[19] In this view, acceptance does not refer to private belief but to the act of public participation. Belief may or may not be a part of that acceptance. Rappaport's point is that participation is a choice: one either takes part in a rite or one does not. Participation may or may not modify the "private state" of the performer or shift a performer's views from disbelief to belief.[20] Regardless, any ambiguities surrounding belief are subordinate to the act of participation. Something similar takes place in the Offering to the Spiritual Guide. The variety of meanings, interpretations, and beliefs that exist among participants with different levels of experience—their private states—are suppressed in favor of a general state of acceptance generated through enactment of and participation in the rite.

Despite this state of acceptance, a lack of understanding of the service can be an obstacle to participation. One consultant, Margaret, attended the Offering to the Spiritual Guide only once, about two years before she was interviewed. She described her reasons for attending and her experiences at the service:

> I wanted to try it out to see what it was about. And I was feeling lonely. It was a Saturday night and I had nothing to do and I was all by myself. And I thought, well why not? I should go see what it's about and what's there. . . . [It] really was a last-minute decision on a Saturday night. And I knew it was something that happened once or twice a month and I think it just happened to fall on the Saturday night. I thought I might glean some small something, or find something that really was meaningful to me by going there. . . .
>
> Now, when I went to the spiritual offering, there were only about five people. . . . The people who were there were three of the hard-core regulars, who are there all the time for everything. And Sona [one of the nuns] was there, and I think someone else. And they said, "Oh Margaret, welcome. It's nice that you're here." They weren't going to use booklets because they were all used to doing it, and then they realized that I would need a booklet to follow along. What I thought was exceptionally kind was that Sona came and sat beside me. And she had a book and I had a book, because you know, sometimes when you follow in the book, they suddenly skip a part, and then you get totally lost. And so I felt like a shy little kid in a new class, but I felt that they were being kind to me because Sona came and sat down beside me, and people were happy to see me, which I thought was really nice.

The warm welcome and Sona's assistance, however, did not serve to overcome Margaret's discomfort. She felt distracted during the service, and her experience of it was neither as engaging nor as meaningful as she had hoped it would be.

> You follow along with the text, and thank God the text is English, but still it's very flowery and you jump parts. So, I found a point where I thought: why did I come here? This is really boring. There were things that I just didn't understand. They would say odd things. And I wanted to stop and say: what does that mean? There were several times where I came across what I thought were really odd phrases. I began to feel self-conscious, like I was a kid who needed extra help from the teacher, because Sona was sitting beside me being so charitable. But everybody was really nice about it. And the combination of trying to look like I was earnest and following along and starting to drift and wander. . . . I thought: this is so long; I could have gone to a movie. And I don't understand what they're saying.

Margaret noted that she usually attended Chandrakirti's General Program events. She therefore had had little experience in the tradition's more formal rituals and no basis of understanding for the service. In the end her lack of understanding was too great an obstacle. "This particular service didn't interest me," she said. "I wasn't engaged by it." Without some means of understanding, the service was too opaque and, she said, she was not interested in going back. Ronald Grimes identifies ritual opacity as one of several reasons why rituals can fail. He writes, "Instances of ritual 'opacity' [in] a ceremony or some element in it is experienced as meaningless; the act is unrecognizable or uninterpretable. Either it fails to communicate or it communicates such conflicting messages that someone—either participant or observer—fails to grasp its sense."[21]

The Offering to the Spiritual Guide was problematic for Margaret because she could find no meaning in it. The fact that one consultant found the Offering to the Spiritual Guide confusing or "uninterpretable," however, does not represent a failure of the ritual overall. It is important to note that I had sought out this interview participant because she had attended the service one time only. Many newcomers do attend the service, and not all are put off by it. During my research, for instance, I met another newcomer who was observably interested in the service, despite not having had any other experience with Chandrakirti's programs. It was evident that he did not fully understand the ritual, at least at first, and yet this lack of familiarity was not an obstacle for him. In fact he was present at nearly all of the services I attended during my research.

Why, then, was the Offering to the Spiritual Guide too opaque for Margaret? Her experience may have been due to her initial expectations: "I thought I might glean some small something, or find something that really was meaningful to me by going there." But as we have seen, newcomers are not expected to understand the service's meanings. This lack of pressure was evident in the instructions that a senior member gave to newcomers at one of the breaks: we were encouraged to listen and participate and experience the *performative* elements of the service rather concern ourselves with its underlying meanings.

Perhaps Margaret would have been more engaged if she had regarded the service as a performance rather than trying to grasp its meanings on that first visit. But she was not attracted to the chanting either. She noted, "There is some lovely text but you say it in a sing-songy, droney voice. I wasn't sure about the music." In Margaret's case the performative elements did not help overcome the opacity of the meanings and she was unable to develop an interest in the rite. In Rappaport's terms, the general acceptance generated in the performance of the rite did not sufficiently suppress Margaret's private processes.

Margaret's interest in Buddhism revolved around the strictly practical benefits her practice had for her day-to-day life. The Offering to the Spiritual Guide, with its transcendent referents, was not what she was looking for at that particular time: "It [the service] was very metaphysical. And it was not a good fit for what I wanted. See, I have no time nor desire, or I'm not in the state of mind currently to pursue metaphysical anything. I find things that are valuable are the ones that I can connect to my life now, that I can use in a tangible, real way. Right now it's all about me finding a path because I have a very demanding life with lots of commitments and lots of things weighing on me." Margaret preferred the General Program because it focused on meditation and coping strategies. Unlike Susan and Justin, she did not find the service to be practically applicable to her personal situation. For the most part, however, Margaret indicated that the main reason she did not go back to the service was her inability to grasp its meanings. At least in this one case the service was not accessible to a participant who lacked some degree of prior understanding.

There is some emphasis on attending the Offering to the Spiritual Guide, even for participants who are not familiar with its meanings. Susan pointed this out when I asked her if she attended the service often:

> Oh yeah, I do, whenever I'm around. Whenever I can, when it's offered at the center. I've never done a retreat on the practice or anything, but twice a month it's offered. . . . I think that it's said that if you go to every single one of these practices that is offered, all of the Offerings to the Spiritual Guide, you're guaranteed to go to the Pure Land. Making that commitment and sticking to it and making every single pūjā is supposed to have great benefit. And I know that there are students that practice that way: they give up anything to get to the practice. But that's not me. I'll go most times, yeah.

Participating in the service whenever it is performed is believed to have enormous spiritual benefit; rebirth in the Pure Land is believed to be a sure means of attaining enlightenment.

In addition to the emphasis on participation, there is also some significance to how and when the service is performed. Taking place on the same days of the month in all associated centers around the world, the service is performed twice monthly. At one time it followed the lunar calendar and was performed ten days before and ten days after the full moon. In January 2005, however, the leadership in England decided that the timing of the service should be shifted to the solar calendar. The service is now offered on the 10th and the 25th day of each month. According to members at the Chandrakirti Centre, this shift made it easier for practitioners to know when the service would be held. Structural changes are evidently made from time to time, but they are standardized throughout the NKT. The constancy of the performance of the Offering to the Spiritual Guide is, as Susan noted, a means of familiarizing participants with the practice and helping them gain greater understanding of its meanings.

USING PERFORMANCE THEORY TO INTERPRET THE SERVICE

Performance theory is a helpful means of investigating the Offering to the Spiritual Guide, partly because it highlights significant elements of the ritual, such as the performers, the ritual roles or identities, and its ritual actions. Even so there are limitations to applying this theory, particularly when it comes to identifying important activities that take place in the service. Chanting, for instance, is significant, as it is the means by which most of the practices are enacted in the service. At times gestures or physical actions are downplayed, as they are in the obeisance section of the Seven-Limbed Offering, which includes several stanzas that end with the line "O Venerable Spiritual Guide I prostrate at your lotus feet." Interestingly no prostrations are performed as these lines are sung, nor are any gestures made to symbolize the prostration. Action is, in a sense, de-emphasized. This is a moment in which words enact something. J. L. Austin argued that words do more than describe or convey meaning: words also perform certain actions.[22] In this case the words of the prayer actually stand in for physical prostrations and "perform" obeisance to the spiritual guide. When asked if the words were more important than the gesture of prostration, Susan stressed another aspect: "Well, that's not correct to say as a whole. In this practice we don't do physical prostrations other than at the very beginning. But there are three types of prostrating: mental, verbal, and physical. And all prostrating is mental. So if you're actually physically prostrating you need to also have a mind to do it." Like the self-generation as the guru-deity and the visualization of the field of merit, the prostration stanzas involve an important mental quality.

During the service a few significant actions do take place: constructing the mandala or performing the mandala *mudra*; making, serving, and drinking the tea; carrying out an offering to spirits; prostrations to the shrine during the *tsog* offering; placing the *tsog* plate on the shrine; and distributing the *tsog* plates to participants. Self-generation as the guru-deity, however, is one of the most significant parts of the service, and it is neither chanted nor physically enacted. This moment in the service has particular significance for understanding the ritual in terms of performance theory.

In his commentary on the service Geshe Kelsang Gyatso notes that self-generating as the guru-deity is done through "correct imagination" and gradually increased training in Tantric practice.[23] Self-generating involves creating an "illusory body" in the mind, one that, with practice, can become the actual body and mind of a Buddha.[24] This practice takes only a few moments, but it has considerable significance for the remainder of the service. When participants drink the tea and eat the food, when they chant the guru's reply to the offerings and requests, it is understood that they have embodied the guru, and thus it is the guru who performs these actions.

How is this practice understood in terms of performance theory? The practice is not itself performative since it is not done to be seen, as many other elements of the service are. Many participants, as we have seen, do not even know what is going on. Nevertheless the practice is a formalized, ritual action: it involves prescribed steps and its purpose is to embody the sacred or transcendent within the ritual space. Where performance theory fails to emphasize the mental aspect of ritual performance, the Offering to the Spiritual Guide demonstrates that these can be central to (at least one) understanding of this particular ritual. Self-generation as the guru-deity is not the only moment in the service when mental activities are significant. They are also involved in the visualization of the field of merit and, according to Susan, when prostrations are offered to the guru through sound and mental intention rather than gesture. Because visualizations are a definitive practice in Tantric Buddhism mental activities should not be overlooked in any study of Tibetan-based ritual practices.[25]

Performance in its more secular forms also requires a mental element; actors preparing to assume a role, for example, concentrate on mentally incorporating their character's experiences and motivations into their portrayal. Thus mental states may be included in the performance theory framework by considering meditative practices as a parallel to an actor's preparatory stages. This demonstrates a few things. First, the performance theory framework need not be limited to elements that are shown or witnessed. Second, consideration of these mental processes highlights crucial aspects of the development of a role or ritual identity. In the case of the Offering to the Spiritual Guide we gain a much deeper understanding of how and why the ritual generates a relationship—even an identity—between the practitioner and the transcendent. Without considering the mental processes, those things that are performed but not seen, we are left examining silence and stillness and may miss the embodiment of the sacred in the ritual space.

CONCLUSION

Through chanting prayers and the meditative self-generation as the guru-deity, the Offering to the Spiritual Guide forges a relationship between practitioners and the transcendent. It is clear, however, that not all participants in the rite are aware of this fact, nor are they expected to be. Furthermore, participants who are aware of this objective have a variety of interpretations of that relationship and the nature of the transcendent figures evoked. With time and repetition those interpretations change. Meaning and understanding, which are initially personal and subjective, are worked out through repeated performances of the rite. In this sense participation is necessary not only for learning the practices but also for attributing both personal and received meanings to them. The performance of the service has the effect of smoothing over any debate between different beliefs and interpretations. On a personal level participants negotiate ways to balance their existing worldviews with their understanding of the rite and the guru-deity. Chandrakirti members expect that participants will, with practice, come to understand the significance of the relationship to the guru-deity and be able to participate fully in embodying his presence.

Notes

1. At the time of writing, the Chandrakirti Centre had moved to another location, in Toronto's west end.

2. Lopez, "A Prayer to the Lama," 376–86.

3. Ibid., 376.

4. Participant-observation research at the Offering to the Spiritual Guide and ethnographic interviews with members and teachers at the Chandrakirti Centre were conducted from October 2004 to February 2005 in Toronto. Participants were personally invited to participate in interviews. I sought to explore a range of experiences; the interview participants I selected were the Chandrakirti head teacher; an experienced member; a relatively new member who attended the rite frequently; one member who had attended only once; and a nun who had participated in the rite and studied Geshe Kelsang Gyatso's commentary text on the Offering to the Spiritual Guide.

5. All names used for interview participants are pseudonyms.

6. This characterization of ritual owes a great deal to the work of Ronald L. Grimes. See his *Ritual Criticism,* 14, and *Rite Out of Place,* 163n32.

7. For a discussion of reasons why Westerners turn to Buddhism, see Patricia Q. Campbell, "Transforming Ordinary Life: Turning to Zen Buddhism in Toronto," in *Wild Geese: Studies in Buddhism in Canada,* ed. John Harding, Victor Sōgen Hori, and Alexander Soucy (McGill-Queens University Press, April 2010).

8. Performance theory, an approach to the study of ritual that explores connections between ritual and other types of cultural performance, began with collaborations between Victor W. Turner and Richard Schechner in the 1970s. For introductions to performance theory, see Richard Schechner, *Performance Studies: An Introduction* (New York: Routledge, 2003); Grimes, "Performance Theory and the Study of Ritual," 109–38; Grimes. "Performance," 379–94.

9. See Grimes, *Beginnings in Ritual Studies,* 24–39.

10. Grimes, "Performance," 392.

11. Ibid., 380.

12. Grimes, *Ritual Criticism*, 23.

13. Whereas stillness and silence, as the ritualized suppression of activity (Grimes, *Beginnings in Ritual Studies*, 43) are performative, the important mental elements of the visualization are not. An expansion thus becomes necessary to include mental practices in a performance theory framework.

14. For more details on Lama Chopa, see Lopez, "A Prayer to the Lama." On highest yoga tantra, see, for example, Daniel Cozort, *Highest Yoga Tantra: An Introduction to the Esoteric Buddhism of Tibet* (Ithaca, NY: Snow Lion, 1986).

15. This perspective is an interesting change taking place as a particular rite is being introduced to practitioners with little or no background in Buddhist tradition; traditional hierarchies, training systems, and esotericism are less attractive among North Americans, who tend to value democracy and egalitarianism. See, for example, Victor Sōgen Hori, "Japanese Zen in America: Americanizing the Face in the Mirror," in *The Faces of Buddhism in America*, ed. Charles S. Prebish and Kenneth K. Tanaka (Berkeley: University of California Press, 1998), 49–78; David L. McMahan, "Repackaging Zen for the West," in *Westward Dharma*, ed. Charles S. Prebish and Martin Baumann (Berkeley: University of California Press, 2002), 218–29. For other perspectives on the adaptation of Buddhism in North America, see James William Coleman, *The New Buddhism* (Oxford: Oxford University Press, 2001); Thomas A. Tweed, "Who Is a Buddhist? Night-Stand Buddhists and Other Creatures," in *Westward Dharma*, ed. Charles S. Prebish and Martin Baumann (Berkeley: University of California Press, 2002), 17–33.

16. Lopez, "A Prayer to the Lama," 376.

17. Gyatso, *Great Treasury of Merit*.

18. Gyatso's text on the rite, *Great Treasury of Merit,* provides the official commentary for NKT members.

19. Rappaport, *Ritual and Religion in the Making of Humanity,* 119–24.

20. Ibid., 122.

21. Grimes, *Ritual Criticism*, 202–3.

22. Austin, *How to Do Things with Words.*

23. Gyatso, *Great Treasury of Merit,* 58.

24. Ibid.

25. See Lopez, introduction to *Religions of Tibet in Practice*, 16; Powers, *Introduction to Tibetan Buddhism,* 222.

Bibliography

Austin, J. L. *How to Do Things with Words*. Cambridge: Harvard University Press, 1962.

Grimes, Ronald L. *Beginnings in Ritual Studies*. Columbia: University of South Carolina Press, 1995.

———. "Performance." In *Theorizing Rituals: Classical Topics, Theoretical Approaches, Analytical Concepts*, ed. Jent Kreinath, Jan Snoek, and Michael Strausberg, 379–94. Leiden: Brill, 2006.

———. "Performance Theory and the Study of Ritual." In *New Approaches to the Study of Religion*, ed. Peter Antes, Armin W. Geertz, and Randi Warne, 109–38. New York: Walter de Gruyter, 2004.

———. *Rite Out of Place: Ritual, Media and the Arts*. Oxford: Oxford University Press, 2006.

———. "Ritual and the Media." In *Practicing Religion in the Age of the Media: Explorations in Media, Religion and Culture*, ed. Stewart Hoover and Lynn Schofield Clark, 219–34. New York: Columbia University Press, 2002.

———. *Ritual Criticism*. Columbia: University of South Carolina Press, 1990.

Gyatso, Geshe Kelsang. *Great Treasury of Merit: A Commentary to the Practice of* Offering to the Spiritual Guide. London: Tharpa, 1992.

Lopez, Donald S., Jr. Introduction to *Religions of Tibet in Practice*, ed. Donald S. Lopez, 3–36. Princeton: Princeton University Press, 1997.

———. "A Prayer to the Lama." In *Religions of Tibet in Practice*, ed. Donald S. Lopez, 376–86. Princeton: Princeton University Press, 1997.

Powers, John. *Introduction to Tibetan Buddhism*. Ithaca, N.Y.: Snow Lion, 1995.

Rappaport, Roy A. *Ritual and Religion in the Making of Humanity*. Cambridge: Cambridge University Press, 1999.

13

Buddhist Ordination as Initiation Ritual and Legal Procedure

Ute Hüsken and Petra Kieffer-Pülz

THIS ESSAY EXPLORES the negotiations connected with a conference held in July 2007 in Hamburg, Germany. The topic of that conference was the establishment of a female ordination line in Tibetan Buddhism.[1]

While the canonical texts of all Buddhist schools narrate the story of the establishment of the nuns' order by the Buddha himself, in two of the three surviving Buddhist traditions the order of nuns ceased to exist long ago or never even reached the country. Both these traditions grapple with an increasing demand of parts of the Buddhist communities to establish or reestablish a nuns' order. The 2007 Hamburg conference served as a space where negotiations took place between the diverse agents in this process.

By "negotiation" we mean the process of interaction during which differing positions are explicitly or implicitly debated and acted out. The intention to come to a common solution thereby is a necessary part of the negotiation process (see Pott in this volume). In this case study the process is the explicit, public debate that points to more implicit issues, specifically colliding perspectives on Buddhist monastic discipline. While the monastic discipline is seen primarily as a set of legal acts applicable to this specific Buddhist monastic community by one group of actors in this process, the performance aspects of an initiation ritual are much more important for other participants involved.

An "ideal" (or "complete") Buddhist community (*saṅgha*) consists of four groups: fully ordained monks (*bhikṣu*) and nuns (*bhikṣuṇī*) and male and female laypeople (*upāsaka, upāsikā*).[2] Since its origin in the fifth or fourth century BCE, the Buddhist community has split many times.[3] Distinct schools have developed, each with its own canonical texts and its own "ideal community." But of the three surviving schools (the Theravādin, prevalent in Sri Lanka, Thailand, Burma, and Vietnam; the Dharmaguptakas, transmitted mainly in China, Taiwan, Vietnam, and Korea; and the Mūlasarvāstivāda, prevalent mainly in Tibet) only the Dharmaguptaka tradition nowadays remains an "ideal community."[4] In the Mūlasarvāstivāda and Theravāda traditions the group of fully ordained nuns has been missing since the ordination lineages of female monastics ceased to exist in these schools centuries ago.[5]

Significant steps toward the reestablishment of the order of Buddhist nuns (*bhikṣuṇī*) have taken place since the 1980s.[6] Most of the relevant discussions have revolved around questions concerning the *vinaya*, or Buddhist monastic discipline. Because the ordination procedures are regulated in detail in the Vinayas of the diverse Buddhist schools, the following question arises: If an order of *bhikṣuṇīs* is to be (re)established, which rules of the relevant monastic codes are to be applied and which rules override conflicting regulations?

We argue that the negotiations at the 2007 Hamburg conference indicate that the "legal" issue is only one of several important aspects. Using the conference as a touchstone, we focus on how notions of ritual, law, authority, and authenticity affect the diverse interpretations of whether (and if so, how) the full ordination of women into Tibetan Buddhism should be performed. As invited scholars at the conference, we were in a position to see firsthand diverse perspectives evolve. It soon became evident that women's ordination is perceived primarily as a legal act by scholars who specialize in Buddhist monastic discipline and by the Western *bhikṣuṇīs*,[7] and as a "ritual of initiation" by many Himalayan Tibetan nuns and monks.

Significantly neither view excludes the other, since ritual and law as analytical categories have many features in common. Both are based on values and norms.[8] So too a legal procedure and an initiation ritual take effect in a similar way: "All it needs in order to work is the local agreement that this is the way to do it," as Podeman Sørenson characterizes what he calls "performative efficacy."[9] He bases his argument on speech acts alone, while we argue that this mode of efficacy is also at work in other ritual action, especially in life-cycle rituals and initiations. One could even say that these specific rituals are *mainly* characterized by their performative efficacy:[10] a wedding "makes" a married couple, just as a ritual of ordination makes the concerned woman a fully ordained nun by virtue of its performance. The same holds true for legal acts. As Christoph Wulf shows on the basis of contemporary European court hearings, law processes performatively confirm and constitute law at the same time. The judgment is performative in the sense that "it makes what it says." The judgment creates a new reality based on the shared belief that the actions of the law process are necessary and valid.[11]

But while performative efficacy implies that the performance itself renders the action effective, the example discussed here clearly shows that this is not an infallible mechanism but rather depends on certain preconditions. The most important aspect, namely the local agreement that this is the way it works, encompasses several other restrictions with regard to the appropriate conditions, performers, and mode of performance. All these aspects are negotiated by the diverse agents involved in the discussion of how to (or whether to) establish an order of nuns in the Tibetan tradition. In spite of the fact that ritual and law are fundamentally related, the negotiations explored in this essay also point to important differences between these two cultural domains: if seen as a ritual of initiation, an ordination is mainly regarded as effecting transformation, whereas if the procedures are regarded as legal procedures, they are seen as primarily maintaining an existing order.

HISTORICAL BACKGROUND

Although an order of *bhikṣuṇīs* is missing, even in the countries where the Theravāda and Mūlasarvāstivāda traditions are prevalent, many women live *like* Buddhist nuns: they wear a special robe and follow many of the monastic rules, despite the fact that full ordination (*upasampadā*) is not available to them. In terms of monastic hierarchy, these women have the status of laypeople or novices, although they often perceive themselves as nuns. In the literature these nuns are often called novice nuns or "nuns" in quotation marks, or they are referred to by their respective local designations: *ani* in Tibetan; *dasa-sil-mātā* ("ten-precepts-mother,") in Sri Lanka; *sila-rhan* ("owner of good moral conduct,"), *may-sila* ("Miss Virtue,"), or *bhva sila* ("granny virtue,") in Burma; and *maechi* in Thailand.[12]

The day-to-day living conditions of these nuns are generally rather discouraging. They often have to cope with extreme poverty, low social standing, and a significant lack of education. Since the end of the nineteenth century, however, attempts have been made to improve their living conditions. In Sri Lanka nuns successfully ameliorated their situation and improved their chances for education. Since the 1980s they have received some support from the government and the monks' community (*saṅgha*) regarding education; in addition their passports now acknowledge their status as *dasa-sil-mātās*. Similar developments can be observed in Burma and Thailand.[13]

Since the late 1980s attempts have also been made to reinstitute a *bhikṣuṇī* ordination. Here the International Association of Buddhist Women, Sakyadhītā, founded in 1987 in Bodhgayā, India, is especially active.[14] Success first occurred in Sri Lanka, where the Theravāda tradition's first *bhikkhunī* ordination was performed in 1996, followed by further ordinations in 1998.[15] Since then *bhikkhunīs* have been ordained every year. In April 2007 there were four hundred *bhikkhunīs*, two thousand female novices who prepared for ordination, and three thousand *dasa-sil-mātās* in Sri Lanka.[16] The situation, however, is different in other Theravāda countries. In Burma and Thailand the new *bhikkhunī* ordination is not generally accepted, and in Sri Lanka not all of the diverse Buddhist schools (*nikāya*) accept the *bhikṣuṇī* ordination unanimously. Here too the performative efficacy of the ordination rituals is challenged because there is not yet a fully established local agreement on these ordinations.

NUNS IN THE TIBETAN TRADITION

This essay deals with recent attempts to establish full ordination for women in the Tibetan or Mūlasarvāstivāda tradition. This process is not as advanced as in Sri Lanka.

We begin by introducing the context of the negotiations: the events preceding the 2007 Hamburg conference, the diverse agents partaking in the negotiations, and the basic issues at stake as perceived by (Buddhist and non-Buddhist) specialists in the field of Buddhist monastic discipline (*vinaya*). We then focus on the International Congress on Buddhist Women's Role in the Sangha: Bhikshuni Vinaya and Ordination Lineages, held in Hamburg July 18–20, 2007, to which we were invited as participating academics.[17] During this conference a "ritual perspective" on the question of the establishment of a female ordination tradition in Tibetan Buddhism became part of the negotiations.

A central actor in the field is the religious head of Tibetan Buddhism, His Holiness (HH) the XIVth Dalai Lama, who has long emphasized the relevance of women's education, especially for Tibetan nuns of Asian origin living in the Himalayas and in Indian exile. This stance is innovative insofar as in this tradition women without full ordination are not allowed to study the entire monastic discipline (*vinaya*). This marginalized position is moreover one reason why these nuns are not among the major actors in the negotiations about establishing a *bhikṣuṇī* tradition in Tibetan Buddhism. They are *not* in a position to investigate the relevant texts themselves, but must depend on the information given to them by either the Tibetan monks or the Western *bhikṣuṇīs,* who, as fully ordained *bhikṣuṇīs,* have access to the relevant texts. But HH the Dalai Lama not only is in favor of improving the Himalayan nuns' education, he also supports establishing a female ordination lineage in Tibetan Buddhism. More to the point, he explicitly aims at creating an "ideal *saṅgha*." Concerning this missing ordination lineage, as early as the 1960s he was saying that "the four-fold Buddhist community [of *bhikṣus, bhikṣuṇīs, upāsakas*, and *upāsikās*] is incomplete in the Tibetan tradition," and in 1987 he asked "for an examination of the current Tibetan practice of non-ordinations of nuns."[18] He not only requested members of the Tibetan *saṅgha* to investigate their monastic discipline (the Mūlasarvāstivāda Vinaya) for possibilities regarding the ordination of nuns but also encouraged Western *bhikṣuṇīs* (i.e., fully ordained Dharmaguptaka nuns of Western origin) who want to be part of the Tibetan Buddhist *saṅgha* to do likewise. Specifically he asked them to carry the vision of the reestablishment of a nuns' community to Asia and in cooperation with Buddhist teachers to develop new possibilities for studies and research.[19] He again emphasized this stance in 2005, at the First European Conference on Tibetan Buddhism in Zürich, when he asked the German Bhikṣuṇī Jampa Tsedroen to move the Western *bhikṣuṇīs* to enforce their investigation of possibilities for a *bhikṣuṇī* lineage.

This role assigned to the Western *bhikṣuṇīs* is based on their access to the relevant texts and on the limited interest of Tibetan monks in establishing a female ordination line in their tradition.[20] In response to this request the Committee of Western Bhikṣuṇīs (CWB) was formed in autumn 2005.[21] The committee consists of six *bhikṣuṇīs* and two advisors.[22] The objectives of this committee are "(1) to conduct research on the procedures for ordination, bi-monthly confession ritual, and the rainy season retreat for bhikṣuṇīs, and (2) to explore the possibilities for the establishment of viable, sustainable communities for the training of bhikṣuṇīs and novice nuns."[23] The CWB met on

March 16–18, 2006, at Sravasti Abbey in Seattle to discuss the possibilities for ordination according to the texts of the Mūlasarvāstivāda tradition. Their findings were summarized in an eleven-page paper titled "Research Regarding Bhikṣuṇī Ordination: A Response to 'Necessary Research Regarding the Lineage of Bhikṣuṇī-Vinaya.'"[24] It was then that one of the CWB members, Bhikṣuṇī Jampa Tsedroen, moved that the International Conference on women's ordination be conducted in Hamburg in 2007.

While the motivation of the Western *bhikṣuṇīs* to become actively engaged in the ordination issue certainly has been spiritual and religious, their approach was primarily academic. Yet relying mainly on Western-style research into the diverse Buddhist monastic disciplines was fitting, since some of the Western *bhikṣuṇīs* also conduct academic research in this field.[25] Generally they interpreted the Vinaya as a coherent system of rules that is both authoritative and applicable. At the same time Vinaya scholars, like lawyers, may find holes in the system that allow for adjustments and changes. The Western academic perspective on Vinaya rules as guiding legal acts is evident from the commonly used translation of relevant terms: while the basic meaning of *karman*, *kamma* (Pāli), and *las* (Tibetan) is "work," these terms are usually translated as "legal acts" or "ecclesiastical acts" in the context of Vinaya studies, and *vinaya* (conduct) is rendered as "Buddhist monastic law code." From this legal perspective, there are various factors pertaining to the validity of an ordination lineage in the Buddhist tradition. Ordinations as *bhikṣus* or *bhikṣuṇīs* are fixed procedures requiring various "legal acts" to be carried out within local communities, according to the rules of the school in which the ordination takes place.[26] A legally valid ordination tradition is even seen as the precondition for the very existence of a Buddhist community. Among other things "legally valid" refers to adherence to the relevant rules. According to these rules a monk's ordination must be performed by at least ten (in border districts, five) monks. For the ordination of women a functioning *bhikṣuṇīs'* order with ten to twelve members is required. If a local community (*saṅgha*) does not consist of a sufficient number of *bhikṣus* or *bhikṣuṇīs*, no legally valid ordination can be performed—as is the case in the Mūlasarvāstivāda tradition, where a *bhikṣuṇīs'* community does not exist.[27] From this perspective, full ordination for *bhikṣuṇīs* in this tradition seems to be impossible.

Looking for loopholes in Buddhist monastic discipline, the Vinaya specialists suggest several solutions to solving this problem. For example, no Vinaya rule forbids *expressis verbis* the installation of a new *bhikṣuṇīs'* ordination tradition if that tradition has been interrupted and while an order of *bhikṣus* of the same tradition still exists. Thus the creation of a new (or renewed) monastic order of *bikṣuṇīs* is not a priori ruled out in the Vinayas. Such a situation would resemble the state of affairs in the beginning, at the time of the Buddha or shortly after,[28] when *bhikṣus* had to ordain *bhikṣuṇīs* because a *bhikṣuṇīs'* community did not yet exist. Furthermore the "four great instructions" (*mahāpadeśa*, Pāli *mahāpadesa*, Tib. *cher ston pa*) allow for deciding new cases in analogy to (and avoiding conflicts with) existing prescriptions.[29] These "great instructions" thus facilitate such context-sensitive solutions as those currently under discussion. It is crucial for members of the Buddhist community to find a unanimous solution, otherwise the establishment of the *bhikṣuṇī* ordination lineage could lead to a split in the community (*saṅghabheda*),[30] a severe transgression to be avoided by all means.

OPTIONS FOR ESTABLISHING AN ORDINATION LINEAGE

We will now present the three options that are currently under discussion with respect to the establishment of a *bhikṣuṇī* ordination lineage within the Mūlasarvāstivāda tradition.

First, a faction of monks and nuns of all Buddhist traditions prefers not to establish a *bhikṣuṇī* ordination at all. Already before 1982 the Tibetan Department of Religion and Culture (DRC) of the Tibetan Administration-in-exile in Dharamsala, India gave orders to conduct detailed research on the Vinaya texts available in Tibetan and subsequently organized several conferences to which Vinaya masters and scholars were invited to discuss the issue.[31] A number of such meetings took place, including a symposium in Dharamsala in August 1988 for Vinaya specialists from the Mūlasarvāstivāda, Dharmaguptaka, and Theravāda traditions,[32] and a meeting in Dharamsala on May 22–24, 2006. The question discussed most intensively, according to Bhikṣuṇī Jampa Tsedroen, who attended the 2006 conference, was whether or not it is even necessary to install *bhikṣuṇī* ordination. Moreover, as we shall see below, at least some of the Himalayan nuns opted for not establishing a *bhikṣuṇīsaṃgha* under any circumstances.

Second, a *bhikṣuṇī* lineage could be established by first ordaining women by Tibetan (Mūlasarvāstivāda) monks, and then transferring the task of ordaining to the *bhikṣuṇīs* as soon as the nuns have reached the minimal prescribed ordination age.[33] This was another suggestion by the DRC.[34] A *bhikṣusaṅgha* of the Mūlasarvāstivāda tradition should "bestow the vows of *brahmacharyopasthana* and *bhikshuni* to several dozen nuns through performing the *bhikshu karmavidhi* [ceremonial rites]." In other words, an ordination by the Tibetan monks' *saṅgha* alone was suggested for the first group of *bhikṣuṇīs*, using the procedure applicable for a monk's ordination.[35] Later on, when the *bhikṣuṇīs* would have attained the prescribed age of ordination, allowing them to ordain other women, the dual *saṅgha*—that is, the *saṅgha* of *bhikṣus* and *bhikṣuṇīs* of the Mūlasarvāstivāda tradition—would carry out the regular ordination of *bhikṣuṇīs* according to the Mūlasarvāstivāda tradition.

This second solution could be perceived as corresponding to the ordination of women at the beginning of the Buddhist *saṅgha*, when a *bhikṣuṇīsaṅgha* did not yet exist.[36] Here, however, the issue of what would happen to the Western *bhikṣuṇīs* is not dealt with. The Western *bhikṣuṇīs* are fully ordained in the Dharmaguptaka tradition and live according to the Tibetan tradition. Because one's position in the internal hierarchy of the *saṅgha* is determined by ordination age, this question is critical for the Western *bhikṣuṇīs*.[37] Would they have to give up their first ordination before they could be ordained a second time in accordance with the Mūlasarvāstivāda tradition? Would their time as *bhikṣuṇīs* since the first ordination in the Dharmaguptaka tradition (more than twenty years in many cases) be acknowledged, or would their ordination age be counted anew from the second, Mūlasarvāstivāda ordination?

A second suggestion by the DRC is another version of this solution, in which the Dharmaguptaka *bhikṣuṇīs* would function as witnesses. First a *bhikṣuṇī* ordination would be performed by an "assembly of dual sangha—a *bhikshu sangha* of the Mulasarvastivadin Vinaya tradition and a *bhikshuni sangha* of the Dharmaguptaka Vinaya tradition—[then] women [would be] given the vows of *brahmacharyopasthana* and *bhikshuni* in the presence of an abbot of the Mulasarvastivadin Vinaya tradition through performing the bhikshu ceremonial rites of the Mulasarvastivadin Vinaya tradition."[38] Here two *saṅghas*, a *bhikṣusaṅgha,* and a *bhikṣuṇīsaṅgha* would be present. However, as in the other solution, the performance of the ordination ritual would follow that for Mūlasarvāstivāda monks and not for nuns. From the legal point of view, this solution would constitute an ordination by the Mūlasarvāstivāda *bhikṣusaṅgha* alone because the Dharmaguptaka *bhikṣuṇīs* would not be actively involved.[39] Once the lineage of *bhikṣuṇīs* was restored in this way, "there [would be] a prospect of initiating a new method whereby the dual *sangha*—the *sangha* of *bhikshus* and *bhikshunis*—of the Mulasarvastivadin Vinaya tradition could bestow the *bhikshuni* vows," at least according to the DRC's suggestion.[40]

Third, one could perform the proceedings with the active involvement of *bhikṣuṇīs* of the Dharmaguptaka tradition.[41] This suggestion was the one most discussed at the 2007 conference.[42] However, an ordination performed by a Mūlasarvāstivāda monks' *saṅgha*, together with a Dharmaguptaka *bhikṣuṇīsaṅgha,* implies a "mix of Vinaya traditions." This poses a major problem. Over the centuries the original Buddhist community split into a large number of schools, each with its own monastic discipline that included rules for ordination. Today there is no *single* ordination procedure; rather each school has developed its own procedures, which differ in some details from the procedures of other schools.[43]

During the first ritual within the *bhikṣuṇīsaṅgha* the Mūlasarvāstivāda tradition has the female candidate ask for "the allowance to enter an ascetic life" (Skt. *brahmacaryopasthānasaṃvṛti*; Tib. *tshaṅs par spyod pa skyed pa'i sdom pa*) from the *bhikṣuṇīsaṅgha*, that is, to assume the status of a *bhikṣuṇī*.[44] This first act is not part of the ordination procedure proper, and for the female candidate in the Mūlasarvāstivāda tradition the ordination procedure has not yet begun.[45] The female candidate receives *one* ordination by a "double *saṅgha*," that is, by the *bhikṣusaṅgha* and *bhikṣuṇīsaṅgha*, simultaneously.

In contrast, in the Theravāda and Dharmaguptaka traditions, after a first ceremony in the *bhikṣuṇīsaṅgha* the female candidate is considered "ordained from one side," the "one side" being the *bhikkhunīs'* community (Pāli *ekato-upasampannā*). Then the candidates receive a second ordination from the *bhikṣusaṅgha* and are then declared to "be ordained by both *saṅghas*" (Pāli *ubhato-upasampannā*).

An important aspect of this difference between the diverse traditions is that the second formal act of a woman's ordination is performed within the monks' community (*bhikṣusaṅgha*) according to the Theravāda and Dharmaguptaka traditions, whereas this act is performed by a *bhikṣusaṅgha* together with a *bhikṣuṇīsaṅgha* according to the Mūlasarvāstivādins.[46]

Thus what is acceptable from a Dharmaguptaka or Theravāda perspective can be interpreted as not acceptable from a Mūlasarvāstivāda perspective, and vice versa.[47] While such differences seem minor to an outsider, they are essential in terms of Buddhist monastic law.

NEGOTIATIONS AT THE HAMBURG CONFERENCE

Two of these three options were also discussed at the Hamburg conference;[48] the first solution (not to establish a *bhikṣuṇī* lineage) was ruled out by the organizers right from the start. According to the statement on the conference's website, the aim of the international congress was to "lead to the requested decision or at least a supportive declaration in collaboration with worldwide expert researchers in the fields of Vinaya, religious precepts and their transmission lineages during the history of Buddhism."[49] Already the invitation letter by the Studienstiftung für Buddhismus (dated July 31, 2006) made clear that "it would be highly desirable if a declaration about a preferred procedure from the viewpoint of all Buddhist tradition could be announced." The "Background and Objectives" statement forwarded with this invitation was quite explicit regarding the expected role of HH the Dalai Lama. After an introductory paragraph in which a quotation from the Dalai Lama indicated that he might even be willing to change rules "somewhat" and that he expected the worldwide Buddhist community to agree on a right way to do so, the statement continues: "The congress is supposed to be concluded by a declaration of HH the 14th Dalai Lama, explaining the re-establishment of the full ordination of bhikshunis within the Tibetan tradition of Buddhism," based on a "worldwide consensus. . . . Ultimately, the goal is to elicit a statement from His Holiness the Dalai Lama declaring that and how the Bhikshuni lineage will be established in the Tibetan tradition."[50]

In sum the explicit goal of the conference was clearly to find "legal" ways of how—and not whether—to establish a *bhikṣuṇī* ordination tradition in Tibetan Buddhism. Consequently, there was a strong emphasis on the academic and nonsectarian perspectives: specialists from various Buddhist traditions as well as from outside the *saṅgha* were invited to participate in the negotiations.[51] These choices underscore the basic stance taken by the organizers: that the main issues—for the time being—were to open up new possibilities for women within the Tibetan monastic tradition and at the same time to find a "legally valid method" for the reintroduction of a *bhikṣuṇī* ordination and therewith also to acknowledge the status of the Western *bhikṣuṇīs*.

As earlier, when HH the Dalai Lama had asked Western *bhikṣuṇīs* to conduct research on the issue, here again members of other traditions, as well as scholars of Buddhism, were asked to suggest solutions for the Tibetan monastic tradition. While HH the Dalai Lama used this international, nonsectarian, and academic support to strengthen his position within the tradition without directly superimposing a specific solution on the Tibetan monastic community, looking for "legal solutions" as one step in a long process was not the primary goal for the Western *bhikṣuṇīs*, as we gather from the conference's explicitly stated goals.

However, very few conference papers actually focused on details of the ordination rite's performance. This oversight is significant given that the third, and preferred, suggestion (the "mix" of two Vinayas) clearly transcends the competence of the law specialists, who are not familiar with the detailed regulations in other traditions.[52] The diverse presenters' suggestions of how to perform the ritual—an installation of a *bhikṣuṇī* lineage in the Tibetan tradition with the help of the Dharmaguptaka tradition—were not based on the notion of nuns' ordination as a legal procedure alone. Clearly there were many more considerations that would determine the process of negotiation, including long-term effects, practical considerations, and the performance aspect of the rituals themselves.

In addition to the choice of presenters, a look at those groups that did not have a voice during the conference is telling. While most, if not all, the lectures were positive about introducing the *bhikṣuṇī* ordination lineage, the conference took a crucial turn in the discussion on the second day, when a small number of Himalayan nuns for the first time had a chance to publicly voice their concerns and opinions.[53] After making clear that they felt their position was not adequately represented and that in fact they were offended to learn that some conference presenters did not consider them "real nuns," the Himalayan nuns declared that they did not need full ordination under all circumstances, but that they were more keen on having access to good education (for example, the opportunity to obtain the Geshe degree, the highest Tibetan university degree). If, however, a full ordination were to be introduced, these nuns explicitly preferred that the ordination lineage stem solely from their own Tibetan tradition and be performed in Tibetan.[54]

Here it finally became evident that there was a considerable gap between the aspirations of many, if not all, Western *bhikṣuṇīs* and those of (some of) the Himalayan Tibetan nuns.[55] The latter group explicitly preferred their "own tradition" to a "mix of traditions," because only then could they be sure that the ordination would be in accordance with the Tibetan tradition. Moreover it was important to this group of nuns not to be associated with feminist aspirations. "The real reason for getting the higher ordination," one nun said, "is [for] understanding humankind and furthering the self, rather than [for] who is discriminating [against] whom and who is high and who is low."[56] Not surprisingly, in contrast to the plans the general discussion did not lead to a common memorandum.

A plenary discussion concluded the conference on the third day. On stage eight monks and nine nuns and *bhikṣuṇīs* of diverse Buddhist traditions presented their views to HH the Dalai Lama. The general tenor of these presentations was that the *bhikṣuṇī* ordination should be established in the Mūlasarvāstivāda tradition.[57] The slightly different suggestions of how to perform the ritual obviously depended on the speakers' school affiliation.[58] However, some of the statements of the monastics on the nature of the Vinaya as a set of rules clearly were based on the speakers' practical experience. Statements such as "Vinaya rules are flexible," "The rules should be considered guidelines," and "Convention is not dharma" were voiced during the stage discussion. One monk even suggested that the Tibetan monks should consider consciously breaking the rules and then taking upon oneself the required penalty, because a slightly faulty procedure would not invalidate the ordination. At the same time the importance of the internal harmony of the *saṅgha* was stressed, as was the relevance of the teacher-disciple relationship, which is established through ordination.

The conference concluded with the final statement of HH the Dalai Lama.[59] Contrary to the expectations of many, his statement did not deal with any preferred mode of installation.[60] Indeed the statement itself was dated July 18; in other words, it had been composed the day the conference began—a fact that evidently rules out any notion that he expected the conference to bring about decisive results.[61] However, because HH the Dalai Lama strongly supports the installation of a *bhikṣuṇī* lineage and had personally requested research in this direction, his inconclusive final statement was certainly not caused by indifference. If anything, his talk made clear that one of his major aims was to see that the Mūlasarvāstivāda monks acknowledge the Tibetan nuns once the lineage is established. He emphasized the importance of support from other Buddhist schools, but explicitly refused to superimpose on the *saṅgha* one solution or to "act as dictator."[62] Clearly he favors a gradual solution process. It seems fair to say, then, that HH the Dalai Lama's main objective for the conference was to make the issue known internationally, to show that representatives of various Buddhist traditions support the installation of the *bhikṣuṇī* lineage in the Tibetan tradition, and perhaps to establish a more positive climate within the Tibetan monks' order, in particular among the more conservative groups. The ritual procedure itself has to be determined by the Tibetan *saṅgha* alone, albeit taking into account both information provided by *saṅgha* members of other traditions and by scholars. In sum the Hamburg conference was not the anticipated final stage in the process of negotiation; in fact HH the Dalai Lama proposed to conduct another conference in 2008 or 2009 in India.[63]

CONCLUSION

It is evident that the differences in opinion reflect not only diverse but even conflicting agendas. Our main point is that these differences simultaneously express divergent perspectives on the process itself. Some interpret Vinaya rules mainly as norms guiding legal procedures, applicable independent of their context; others see the rules as guidelines for ritual performances, which in turn produce long-term effects in their specific settings. In the first group are the Western *bhikṣuṇīs,* who mainly refer to the discourse prevalent among Vinaya scholars, a discourse that perceives the Buddhist discipline as monastic law. From this perspective a central concern is which rules of the three relevant Vinayas (Mūlasarvāstivāda, Theravāda, Dharmaguptaka) are to be applied, and whether rules from one tradition can be transferred to another. The rules' authority (which is based on their traditional interpretation as the "word of the Buddha" that overrules every other consideration) is mainly concerned with the maintenance of the existing order, yet aims at an adaptation to contemporary needs. This debate is based on the thorough study of the relevant texts and as such is largely disconnected from the actual local, historical, and personal contexts in which the ritual is to be performed or where it takes effect. Moreover the debate is based on the consensus that the Vinaya is authoritative, irrespective of the question of practicability and irrespective of whether one personally agrees or disagrees with the consequences the application of the rules might have. Significantly this discourse is strongly rooted in Buddhist tradition; there exists a continuous Buddhist tradition of legalistic reflections on Vinaya rules and their interpretation(s), and this holds true for each of the schools that has survived to date. From this perspective the Vinaya—as law in general—is an "ought," that is, an attempt to order reality,[64] rather than an applied resource for reconnecting theory (represented in the texts) with on-the-ground practice (which is determined largely by contextual factors).

By contrast the stance of the Himalayan nuns, and to a certain degree that of the representatives of the diverse Buddhist traditions (including HH the Dalai Lama), reflects the perception that the ordination ritual is a performance that is part of their lived religion.[65] This view is evident, for example, in the strong emphasis on Tibetan as the language that should be used for the ritual. Moreover ancient reservations on the Tibetans' side about the Chinese Buddhist tradition play an important role here. In the Tibetan tradition a debate began several centuries ago as to whether an ordination lineage is valid if Chinese monks are involved in the ordination procedures.[66] Therefore ordinations performed by or with the help of Chinese monastics are a very sensitive issue. This perspective on the Chinese Buddhist tradition is not shared by the Western *bhikṣuṇīs*, some of whom evidently even favor establishing an "international *bhikṣuṇī* order," with all its members ordained in the (Chinese) Dharmaguptaka tradition.[67]

The Himalayan nuns emphasize the transformative rather than the legal aspects of the process. As rituals of initiation, ordinations enact, mark, and effect transition from the state of being a layman or laywoman to that of a monk or nun.[68] Choosing to undergo such a ritual implies a permanent change of status that can be "undone" only through another ritual.[69] These initiation rituals have a variety of critical functions: they serve to demarcate a group's identity; they mark a change in the participants' religious status; they make the concerned person a member of a specific group; they alter relations between the individual and his or her former group; and they mark the fact that the concerned person has acquired a new competence. Here ritual clearly is a mode of identity formation that de- and reconstructs a person and a group in a lived context.

Especially in a South Asian context the relation between the teacher (who confers the initiation) and the student (who receives it), which is officially marked and acknowledged by the initiation ritual, is extremely important; at times this relationship is even regarded as more important than the parent-child relationship. It might be hard, then, for the Himalayan nuns to imagine having a group of (Chinese or Taiwanese) Dharmaguptaka *bhikṣuṇīs* participate in the performance of ordination rituals, which implies that the newly ordained Himalayan women ought to live with and be dependent on the Dharmaguptaka *bhikṣuṇīs* for several years.[70] While for the Western *bhikṣuṇīs* the institution of a female ordination line in the Tibetan tradition with the Dharmaguptaka *bhikṣuṇīs'* active involvement would basically constitute a "legalization" of the status quo they already enjoy, and not make much difference, if at all, for Himalayan nuns, such an initiation ritual would imply a transformative process with ambiguous long-lasting effects.

This tension indicates another implicit aspect of the negotiations: initiation is a ritual marking a certain point in time, and initiating is a process that starts before the ritual event and continues long after the ritual has taken place. Or, as Ronald Grimes puts it, "initiating and initiation goes on all the time."[71] Moreover, as Bruce Kapferer rightly points out about rituals as transformative processes, the transformations effected by ritual are "an aspect of context and of the elements (objects, actions, symbols, identities), which compose the context." He suggests that "the analysis of ritual as form, particularly in relation to how it effects important transformations of contexts of meaning and action, cannot be satisfactorily achieved without considering the process of its performance."[72] The need to attend to ritual form *and* process is strikingly illustrated by the case at hand: the active participation of Dharmaguptaka *bhikṣuṇīs* (preferred by the Western *bhikṣuṇīs*) versus the performance of the ordination ritual by Tibetan monks alone (the preferred solution of the Himalayan nuns).[73]

Legal acts and ritual performances are closely related yet different concepts, and in the case of the Buddhist monastic discipline they are two sides of the same coin—thus a matter of perspective. From the "ritual performance perspective," the emphasis is not on the word-for-word execution of rules, but rather on agents (whether the ritual should be performed by Tibetans alone, or in collaboration with "Chinese" *bhikṣuṇīs*); local circumstances and practicability (e.g., the language question); and long-term implications of the initiations (whether the process confirms a status quo or implies a profound transformation).[74] From both the legal and the ritual points of view, the Vinaya rules facilitate and guide the ordination procedure. However, the question of how to ordain women in the Tibetan tradition is much more context-oriented when ordination is perceived as a ritual of initiation rather than a legal procedure. Here too the main authority lies with the Buddha, but in ritual performance the performing agents, as representatives of the Buddha, are also invested with the authority to deviate from the rules if necessary. Viewing the Vinaya as facilitating the performance of religion rather than as guiding legal acts is a pointed reminder that rituals are grounded in day-to-day reality, and that they are subject to the same limitations as all other expressions of religious life. Although rules are the foundational framework, they can never cover all contextual issues, unless they are adapted when and as the need arises. This becomes especially evident when rituals move through space and time, from India in 500 BCE to Europe and the United States in the beginning of the twenty-first century CE. It would be easy, if not tempting, to simply dismiss the position of the

Western *bhikṣuṇīs* as typical for the appropriation of Eastern religions by the West. However, we argue that the understanding of these conflicts over a tradition that is shared and owned by people in very different cultural settings has to move beyond this one-sided (and morally loaded) pattern of interpretation. We have to go beyond such a frame of thinking because it is neither useful nor adequate; it replaces old hierarchies with new hierarchies instead of enabling us to understand the mechanisms at work.

A ritual tradition remains alive if it is rule-governed but flexible, as McClymond's essay in this volume confirms. The ritual's performance enacts, validates, and enforces the rules; it embodies rules,[75] and therefore also places them in a concrete context. The context, and thus the agenda of the negotiating agents, makes the agents adopt different perspectives. As legal procedures the ordination of women into the Tibetan monastic community that acknowledges and confirms status is nonetheless primarily about maintaining an existing order. On the other hand, as a ritual of initiation the same procedure effects radical change, and thus is about transformation occurring in a particular context. The negotiations during the Hamburg conference thus point to the fact that the procedures under discussion are not so much a method to create a single outcome by one single performance as a field where efficacy, the participant's intentions, and the social reality that emerges from the process are all negotiated.

Notes

1. Ann Heirman published an article on this topic in *Numen;* unfortunately that article was not yet published when this paper was finalized.

2. The term *upasampadā* and the corresponding verb forms are rendered here as "full ordination" or "fully ordained" in order to distinguish them from the "lower ordination" (*pravrajyā*), which refers to the conferment of novice status. A more detailed division of the Buddhist community includes the groups of male and female novices (*śrāmaṇera, śrāmaṇerikā*) and the female "students" (*śikṣamānā*); the status of the students is in between female novices and fully ordained nuns.

3. These splits, based on differences of opinion about doctrinal and legal issues, took place when the Buddhist community became geographically dispersed; see Kieffer-Pülz, "Die buddhistische Gemeinde," 287–88.

4. The terms "Theravāda," "Mūlasarvāstivāda," and "Dharmaguptaka" refer to the Hīnayāna school in which Vinaya (monastic discipline) is authoritative. Neither regional, doctrinal, nor Hīnayāna/Mahāyāna distinctions are indicated in our essay. Because, for example, the Mūlasarvāstivāda tradition is prevalent mainly in Tibet and the adjacent Himalayan regions, the designation "Tibetan tradition" is frequently used. However, as indicated below, the question of whether the tradition is "owned" by the Buddhists of the Himalayan regions or by those Buddhists who follow the Mūlasarvāstivāda monastic code is an important implicit issue at stake in these negotiations; therefore we use the term "Mūlasarvāstivāda" when referring to the legal aspects and "Tibetan" when referring to other aspects of the discussion.

5. In the Theravāda tradition the ordination lineage was extinguished probably in the eleventh century CE. The Mūlasarvāstivāda *bhikṣuṇī* lineage existed when this school was

prominent in India, but evidently was never introduced to Tibet. See Skilling, "A Note on the History of the Bhikkhunī-saṅgha (II)," 223.

6. Unless otherwise indicated, italicized terms are Sanskrit.

7. These are European or American women who are fully ordained in the Dharmaguptaka tradition and who wish to be fully acknowledged as nuns by the Tibetan *saṅgha*. For brevity's sake, they are called "Western *bhikṣuṇīs*" here.

8. However, when there is no conflict about the values and norms in ritual, these different perspectives on the relevant process (its meanings, functions, and implications, all of which are closely connected to its performance) are usually not reflected by the practitioners.

9. Podeman Sørensen, "Efficacy," 526.

10. "Efficacy" is used here to denote the ability to produce an effect, but not only a specifically desired effect. On diverse modes of efficacy, see Moore and Myerhoff, "Secular Ritual," 10ff.; see also Hüsken, "Ritual Dynamics and Ritual Failure," 251ff.

11. See Wulf, "Recht und Ritual," 31, 39.

12. In Sri Lanka they are also called *dasa sil mātavā* or *sila mātavā*. See Lottermoser, "Buddhist Nuns in Burma." In Burma the nuns' own catalogue of rules was developed, the *Bhikkhuni Winisaya Satan*. This essay refers to all such women as nuns; the status of fully ordained nuns is designated by the terms *bhikṣuṇī* (Skt.) or *bhikkhunī* (Pāli, the language of Theravāda Buddhism).

13. For Burma, see Kawanami, "The Bhikkhunī Ordination Debate," 226–44. For Thailand, see Seeger, "The Bhikkhunī-Ordination Controversy in Thailand," 155–86.

14. Founding members of Sakyadhita are Ayyā Khemā (Germany), Bhikṣuṇī Karma Lekshe Tsomo (United States), Prof. Dr. Chatsumarn Kabilsingh (now Bhikkhunī Dhammānandā, Thailand), and Bhikṣuṇī Jampa Tsedroen (Germany). The last three were also actively involved in the 2007 conference.

15. For details regarding the revival of the Theravāda *bhikkhunī* ordinations, see Kieffer-Pülz, "Die Wiedereinrichtung des Nonnenordens in der Theravāda-Tradition," 29–41.

16. See www.dailynews.lk/2007/04/18/fea06.asp (accessed January 2008). Other sources give slightly different numbers.

17. Ute Hüsken gave the paper "The Eight Garudhammas" (July 18, 2007); Petra Kieffer-Pülz spoke on "Presuppositions for a Valid Ordination with Respect to the Restoration of the *bhikṣuṇī* Ordination in the Mūlasarvāstivāda Tradition" (July 18, 2007). Both papers discussed the Vinaya as a legal document and are published in Mohr and Jampa Tsedroen, *Dignity and Discipline*.

18. www.congress-on-buddhist-women.org/index.php?id=142, p. 1 (accessed April 24, 2008).

19. HH the Dalai Lama in *Buddhismus aktuell* I/2006, 69–70, quoted in Jampa, "Wiederbelebung der Bhikṣuṇī-Gelübde im Tibetischen Buddhismus," 141.

20. Strictly speaking, HH the Dalai Lama asked outside specialists (the Western *bhikṣuṇīs* are ordained according to the Dharmaguptaka tradition, not according to the Mūlasarvāstivāda tradition) to suggest a solution for his own tradition.

21. See Jampa Tsedroen, "Wiederbelebung der Bhikṣuṇī-Gelübde im Tibetischen Buddhismus," 141n22. Their efforts were funded with 50.000 Sfr., administered by the Studienstiftung für Buddhismus in Hamburg (Foundation for Buddhist Studies in Hamburg).

22. Bhikṣuṇī Tenzin Palmo (born Diane Perry in 1943 in London; novice ordination in 1964; full ordination in 1973 in Hong Kong), Bhikṣuṇī Pema Chodron (born Deirdre Blomfield-Brown in 1936 in New York; novice ordination in 1974; full ordination in 1981 in Hong Kong), Bhikṣuṇī

Prof. Dr. Karma Lekshe Tsomo (currently president of Sakyadhita International and assistant professor in San Diego; novice ordination in 1977; full ordination in 1982 in Korea and Taiwan), Bhikṣuṇī Thubten Chodron (born in 1950 in the United States; novice ordination in 1977; full ordination in 1986 in Taiwan), Bhikṣuṇī Dr. Jampa Tsedroen (born Carola Roloff in 1959 in Holzminden, Germany; novice ordination in 1981; full ordination in 1985 in Taiwan), and Bhikṣuṇī Ngawang Dolma (novice ordination in 1992; full ordination in 2000). The advisors are Bhikṣuṇī Prof. Dr. Heng-ching Shih (born in 1943 in Taiwan; currently professor of philosophy at Taiwan National University; full ordination in 1975 in San Francisco) and Bhikṣuṇī Wu-yin, Vinaya-master. Two of them, Jampa Tsedroen and Karma Lekshe Tsomo, are also cofounders of Sakyadhīta, see note 14.

23. Email from Jampa Tsedroen to Petra Kieffer-Pülz, January 11, 2008.

24. www.congress-on-buddhist-women.org/fileadmin/files/Establishing%20Full%20Ordination%207_dia.pdf (accessed April 29, 2008). In addition the committee looked for sources to prove the validity of the ordination lineages of the Dharmaguptaka *bhikṣus* and *bhikṣuṇīs* and sent material on the topic to the Office of HH the Dalai Lama (see www.congress-on-buddhist-women.org, letter of the Committee of Western Nuns to the office of HH the Dalai Lama, April 13, 2006; accessed April 24, 2008).

25. Karma Lekshe Tsomo published *Sisters in Solitude: Two Traditions of Buddhist Monastic Ethics for Women. A Comparative Analysis of the Chinese Dharmagupta and the Tibetan Mūlasarvāstivāda Bhikṣuṇī Prātimokṣa Sūtras* (Albany: State University of New York Press, 1996). For additional publications see http//home.sandiego.edu/~ktsomo/; Jampa Tsedroen (Carola Roloff), *A Brief Survey of the Vinaya: Its Origin, Transmission, and Arrangement from the Tibetan Point of View with Comparisons to the Theravāda and Dharmagupta Traditions* (Hamburg: Dharma-Ed. 1992); Carola Roloff, "Red mda' ba (1349–1412) und Tsong kha pa (1357–1419): Zwei zentrale Figuren des tibetischen Buddhismus und ihr wechselseitiges Lehrer-Schüler-Verhältnis," master's thesis, Hamburg, 2003; http://carolaroloff.de; see also www.transcript-verlag.de/ts1263/ts1263_1.pdf.

26. Irrespective of subdivisions within the three living Buddhist schools, all subgroups of one school follow a single Vinaya. Thus all Tibetan schools, whether Gelugpa, Karmapa, or other, are Mūlasarvāstivādins according to the ordination lineage and follow the rules for ordination given in this Vinaya. The same holds true for the Dharmaguptaka and the Theravāda traditions. As Griffith Faulk informs us, five different recensions of the Indian Vinaya were translated into Chinese, one of which was the Dharmaguptaka. The ordination procedures followed by nuns today are those of the Nanshan Vinaya school, founded by Daoxuan (Dao-hsuan), who basically combined the various Vinayas into one standard set of Chinese rules (personal communication with Griffith Foulk, February 2010).

27. Because Tibet is a borderland (compared to the middle country in India, where the Buddha lived) five *bhikṣus* and six *bhikṣuṇīs* are sufficient according to the Tibetan tradition. The question of whether or not *bhikṣuṇīs* must necessarily be present is controversial among Tibetan scholars. This, however, is not generally accepted by Tibetan monastics. In their opinion, Tibet is a "central land" of Buddhism. See, for example, the following statement by the Dalai Lama in Mohr and Jampa, *Dignity and Discipline* (see above, note 16): "Among the eighteen qualities of a precious human rebirth, one is being born in a central land. This can be defined in two ways. Geographically, Tibet is not the central land, since that just means India. Defined in terms of Buddhadharma, however, a land is central if and only if the fourfold community of disciples is complete; thus Tibet is not a central land and birth there is not a precious human rebirth. In effect, Tibetans have been saying that if bhikṣus are present, that

suffices to make it a central land, because bhikṣus are the most important of the four groups. Clearly it is a central place for the Dharma, they say. But that is just a similitude of a central land and doesn't qualify fully. The early masters should have taken this more seriously and made greater effort to ensure the bhikṣuṇī vow was introduced in Tibet."

28. See Hinüber, "The Foundation of the Bhikkhunīsaṃgha," 3–29. See also Analayo, "Theories on the Foundation of the Nuns' Order," 105–42.

29. In the Theravāda tradition this passage is given in the *Vinayapiṭaka,* ed. Hermann Oldenberg (London, 1969, first published in 1879), 1:250,31–251,6; see Isaline B. Horner, trans., *Book of the Discipline* (London, 1982, first published 1951), 4:347. In the Tibetan tradition the "four great instructions" are found in the Mātṛkā embedded in the Uttaragrantha (*Derge,* "Dul ba PA 252b3–253b4; information courtesy of Shayne Clarke).

30. For *saṅghabheda* see Bechert, "Aśokas 'Schismenedikt' und der Begriff Sanghabheda," 18–52.

31. One of those who did research on behalf of the department was Acarya Geshe Tashi Tsering (also Acharya dge bshes thub bstan byang chub or Acarya Muni Shasana Bodhi). See Tashi Tsering, *A Comparative Study of Mūlasarvāstivāda and Theravādin Vinaya*; Thub bstan byang chub, *Bod du dge slong mar bsgrubs pa'i dpyad gzhi rab gsal me long.*

32. *Concerning the Lineage of Bhikshuni Ordination* (not consulted by us).

33. According to the Mūlasarvāstivāda Vinaya, a *bhikṣuṇī* may ordain other nuns when she has been herself ordained for twelve years.

34. After the 2006 Dharamsala conference another committee was formed by the prime minister of the Tibetan government-in-exile, Prof. Samdhong Rinpoche. This committee's task was to investigate the case and to present a solution at the end of September 2006 to leading lamas and heads of monasteries. We are unaware of the contents of this solution (see Jampa, "Nonnenordination bald im tibetischen Buddhismus?," 20–23). Another committee, the Bhikshuni Lineage Research Committee, consisting of internal and external experts on Vinaya questions, was supposed to comment on suggestions made by Vinaya experts of the Tibetan community; these suggestions were presented in a letter (dated June 20, 2007) from the DRC specifically requesting comment on the proposals. We do not know how many members commented on the two proposals, and/or whether their comments had any subsequent influence.

35. Letter of the minister of the Department of Religion and Culture to the Members of Bhikshuni Lineage Research Committee, Central Tibetan Administration of HH the Dalai Lama, June, 20, 2007, p. 2. According to Jampa Tsedroen (email to Kieffer-Pülz, June 24, 2008) this was the procedure followed by Shakya Chogden (Sha-kya mChog-ldan, 1428–1507) in fifteenth-century Tibet. At that time the *bhikṣusaṅgha* used the formula for the *bhikṣuṇīsaṅgha* to give the *brahmacāryopasthāna* to the nuns, with Shakya Chogden functioning as a "female preceptor." However, Shakya Chogden was criticized because of this action, and the validity of the ordination was doubted. The suggestion, however, contains an inconsistency: the "vows of *brahmacharyopasthāna*" are regularly given to female candidates by a nun's community. If the ceremony were performed "through performing the bhikshu *karmavidhi*," that is, following the method applied in the case of monks, it would make no sense "to bestow the vows of *brahmacharyopasthāna*."

36. See Hüsken, *Die Vorschriften für die buddhistische Nonnengemeinde im Vinaya-Piṭaka der Theravādin*, 414–15.

37. The "ordination age" has implications for the *bhikṣuṇī*'s rights to ordain other women, to educate novices, and nuns, and hence for the entire life within the *bhikṣuṇī saṅgha.* To count

the ordination age anew would imply that nuns who had been ordained more than ten years ago would not be allowed to confer ordination for the next twelve years.

38. Letter of the minister of the Department of Religion and Culture to the Members of Bhikshuni Lineage Research Committee, Central Tibetan Administration of HH the Dalai Lama, June 20, 2007, p. 2. Samdhong Rinpoche remarked on the third day of the conference that according to the Mūlasarvāstivāda Vinaya a monk may leave the residence for up to seven days if a woman is to be initiated as a *śikṣamānā*. Because no *bhikṣus* are needed (at least in principle) for an initiation as *śikṣamānā*, ostensibly this passage can be interpreted as indicating that in this tradition the *śikṣamānā* initiation may be performed by monks. However, another interpretation suggests that monks were invited as guests and witnesses of *śikṣamānā* initiations and did not have any formal function in the ceremony.

39. Here again the same problem arises as in the first suggestion: How can the *brahmacaryopasthānasaṃvṛiti* ritual be carried out by a *bhikṣusaṅgha* who follows the rules for *bhikṣus*? (see notes 39 and 51).

40. This type of dual ordination could be perceived as a variant of that described in the Mūlasarvāstivāda Vinaya, according to which the *brahmacaryopasthānasaṃvṛti* has to be carried out in a *bhikṣuṇīsaṅgha*, followed by an ordination by the dual *saṅgha* according to the method for *bhikṣuṇīs* (not for *bhikṣus*). It is not clear whether these are the only variants discussed and whether there was one version preferred by the Tibetan *bhikṣusaṅgha*.

41. This may have been one of the reasons why not only members of the Tibetan *saṅgha*, but also representatives of other Buddhist traditions and scholars from various fields of research were asked for their opinions at the conference.

42. Leaving aside whatever procedures precede the actual ordination, we are concentrating on the two most important acts concluding the ordination procedure, namely that by the *bhikṣuṇīsaṅgha* and that by the *bhikṣusaṅgha*, together with the *bhikṣuṇīsaṅgha*.

43. Although there is a common thread to all ordination procedures, they deviate in detail and wording. The Mūlasarvāstivādin version especially deviates greatly from those of the other schools.

44. *Saṃvṛti*, "allowance," is rendered as *gnaṅ ba* and *sdom pa* in Tibetan texts; see Kieffer-Pülz, *Die Sīmā*, 368–69. This request is often misunderstood as asking for ordination in the nun's community, because in other Buddhist schools (e.g., Dharmaguptaka and Theravādin) the female candidate asks for ordination (Skt. *upasampad/upasampat*, Pāli *upasampadā*) within the nun's community. The position of this procedure in the succession of the legal acts (*karma*) corresponds to asking for "the allowance for ordination" (*vuṭṭhānasamuti*) in the Theravāda tradition, which precedes the ordination in the *bhikṣuṇīs*' community and formally terminates the candidate's successful status as a probationer (Skt. *śikṣamānā*, Pāli *sikkhamānā*). This probationer status is in between novice status and nunhood.

45. Nevertheless this *karman* can be considered part of the ordination procedure as a whole because the ordination proper within the *bhikṣu*- and the *bhikṣuṇīsaṅgha* has to be performed on the same day.

46. See Schmidt, "Bhikṣuṇī-Karmavācanā," 256, fols. 18b5–19a1.

47. Significantly the different monastic disciplines do not take notice of the Vinayas of the other schools. Therefore no Vinaya discusses the possibility of transferring an ordination line from another Vinaya tradition.

48. The conference was organized by the Studienstiftung für Buddhismus. The main organizers were Bhikṣuṇī Jampa Tsedroen, Hamburg, and Dr. Thea Mohr, Frankfurt, in close

cooperation with the Asia-Africa-Institute of the University of Hamburg; see www.congress-on-buddhist-women.org (accessed April 24, 2008). Dr. Thea Mohr is a religious studies scholar whose PhD thesis focused on the background and development of the Sakyadhita movement; see Thea Mohr, "Weibliche Identität und Leerheit: Eine ideengeschichtliche Rekonstruktion der buddhistischen Frauenbewegung Sakyadhita International," Frankfurt, 2002.

49. See www.congress-on-buddhist-women.org/index.php?id=3, p. 1 (accessed April 24, 2008). In contrast the invitation letter (dated August 14, 2006) from the cohost, the Asia-Africa-Institute of the University of Hamburg, reads, "The purpose of this Conference is to help to offer a neutral platform to conclude a long-term discussion on the re-establishment of the full bhikshuni ordination with the help of scholars and representatives of all Buddhist traditions."

50. This aim is presented as being based on "Buddhist theory": "Because gender discrimination conflicts with the ethic of social and spiritual equality maintained in Buddhist theory, the issue of full ordination for women has become a major concern in the contemporary international Buddhist diaspora." While it remains unclear exactly what constitutes the "international Buddhist diaspora," here the "ownership of tradition" is clearly at stake.

51. During the first two days sixty-five speakers from nineteen countries presented papers. Half of the presenters were scholars from outside the *saṅgha*; the others were monks and nuns from diverse Buddhist traditions.

52. Thus the (legally) crucial differences between the Dharmaguptaka and the Mūlasarvāstivāda rules for ordaining *bhikṣuṇīs*, as outlined above (that is, the differences between ordination and *brahmacaryopasthānasaṃvṛti,* and between a single ordination in a *bhikṣusaṇgha* and a double ordination by a *bhikṣusaṅgha* and a *bhikṣuṇīsaṅgha*), were hardly addressed.

53. Only one of these nuns gave a paper at the conference. This omission was, as far as we know, mainly due to gaps in communication beforehand.

54. Thus the situation in the Tibetan tradition seems, at least in this respect, to be similar to the situation in Burma, where the Burmese women succeeded in developing their own acknowledged status without having, or wishing they had, a full ordination lineage. See Kawanami, "The Bhikkhunī Ordination Debate," 226–44.

55. These nuns all belonged to one group, officially represented by Ven. Lobsang Dechen, vice president of the Tibetan Nuns' Project, who was the only one of this group to give a conference lecture.

56. Here the important issue of who "owns" the tradition is implicitly touched upon: Is it the Buddhists of the Himalayan regions, or those Buddhists who follow the Mūlasarvāstivāda monastic code? And what does "authenticity" refer to here? Moreover this explicit distancing from a feminist agenda is in stark contrast to the aspirations of some of the Western *bhikṣuṇīs* to establish an international *bhikṣuṇī* order in which all nuns belong to the Dharmaguptaka tradition in order to "unify and strengthen Buddhist women worldwide" (email from Bhikṣuṇī Jampa Tsedroen to Petra Kieffer-Pülz, June 24, 2008).

57. Groups or individuals who did not want to establish a nuns' ordination lineage were not represented on stage. Leaders of Buddhist groups who do not support such a reinstallment, for example, the Theravāda traditions from Thailand and Burma, did not attend the conference; their letters to the conference organizers were general well-wishing letters only.

58. The representatives of the Theravāda *saṅgha*s favored a form of ordination using a "formal act of strengthening" (Pali *da| hikamma)* common in their own tradition. Here the first ordination is "strengthened" by another ordination (in this case in a different Vinaya tradition) in

order to allow for movement between *nikāyas*. The representatives of the Dharmaguptaka tradition were not explicit about their favored procedure but clearly supported a double ordination with the active involvement of Dharmaguptaka nuns, whereas the Tibetan monks and Himalayan nuns were in favor of an ordination performed within the Mūlasarvāstivāda monks' order alone.

59. For reports on that conference, see Alexander Berzin, "A Summary Report of the 2007 International Congress," www.berzinarchives.com/web/en/archives/approaching_buddhism/world_today/summary_report_2007_international_c/part_1.html; Sister Cintamani, "Women's Role in the Sangha," www.amaravati.org/fsn/women.htm (accessed April 24, 2008); Carola Roloff, "Volle Ordination von Nonnen nur noch eine Frage der Zeit," *Tibet und Buddhismus* 83, no. 4 (2007): 12–14, www.schattenblick.de/infopool/religion/buddha/rbpre635.html (accessed April 24, 2008).

60. He invited the Western *bhikṣuṇīs* to spend the rainy season retreat in Dharamsala and to perform the *upavasatha* and the *pravāraṇā* ceremony there, using the formulas of the Dharmaguptaka school (albeit in Tibetan translation) and learning them by heart rather than reciting them from a manuscript, as is allowed in the Dharmaguptaka tradition.

61. This does not mean that the results are ignored. It may well be that they are, at least partly, to be taken into account for later research.

62. Although HH the Dalai Lama certainly has the authority to establish a new or modified ordination procedure, he is evidently very much aware of the necessity for "local consensus" in order to make the procedure effective in the long run. Moreover as a member of the *saṅgha* HH the Dalai Lama must prevent every action that might lead to a split in the community.

63. At the time of writing, we learned that a "Gelongma Meeting held by DRC on 28/29th April 2008" had taken place in Dharamsala, to which no nuns were originally invited. However, four nuns from each of the five local nunneries were permitted to attend as observers. In any case attendance was evidently confined to members of the Tibetan monastic community.

64. Schild, "Recht und Körperlichkeit," 130–33.

65. While this holds true for the Western *bhikṣuṇīs* too, the impact of an ordination on the day-to-day life is entirely different for Western *bhikṣūṇīs* and Himalayan nuns. In the end the "lived context" of both groups is entirely different, the Western *bhikṣuṇīs* being members of a globally acting and interacting Buddhist community, the Himalayan nuns being anchored first and foremost in their local monastery and local setting.

66. See Davidson, *Tibetan Renaissance*.

67. This opinion was not publicly voiced, however, and therefore not discussed at all during the 2007 Hamburg conference. Bhikṣuṇī Jampa Tsedroen's June 24, 2008, email to Petra Kieffer-Pülz states, "Usually Western bhikshunis have no reservation about the Dharmagupta lineage, while many Tibetan monks do have. The doubts they have, they have somehow 'transmitted' to a large number of their Western and Tibetan novice nuns' disciples. When talking to them, it becomes evident that this view is not well found[ed], because many even do not know what Vinaya school the Chinese, Vietnamese and Korean follow. Very often they judge from [the] outside. For example they conclude that since the monks in those countries do not wear 'proper robes' they cannot know the Vinaya. Their robes have the wrong color, wrong cut, etc. Others base their doubts on rumors that their lineage is broken." We would argue that this statement, which reflects a more general attitude of the Western *bhikṣuṇīs* toward the Himalayan nuns present at the conference, is partly grounded in interactions that took place beforehand. On the one hand, the Himalayan nuns' attitude was attributed to the influence of

their monk advisors; on the other hand, the attitude itself was dismissed on the grounds that it was not based on a thorough knowledge of the Vinaya.

68. In most traditions these initiation rituals are not seen as life-cycle rituals. However, in some countries part of men's life cycle is to become a Buddhist monk for a certain period of childhood or early adulthood. In other countries it is common to become a monk for a short period of time each year. In Sri Lanka and Tibet the decision to become a monk is supposed to be for one's entire life.

69. This act of renouncing the order is an option only for monks in most schools, not for nuns; see Hüsken, *Die Vorschriften für die buddhistische Nonnengemeinde im Vinaya-Piṭaka der Theravādin,* 2.1.3, 3.1n; Hüsken, "A Stock of Bowls Requires a Stock of Robes," 201–38. Only according to the Mūlasarvāstivāda Vinaya is it possible for nuns to leave the monastic community in the same formalized way as the monks. This difference results from the fact that Pārājika 1 for nuns contains the rule for disrobing, "having acquired the same training, without having abandoned the training, without having declared weakness with regard to the training" (T. 1443 913a19–21). This passage implies that nuns may abandon the training (however, they may not be reordained because a rule against reordination is given in the Mūlasarvāstivāda-Vinayavastu). We thank Shayne Clarke for this information, given in an email to Kieffer-Pülz, October 24, 2007.

70. For the relevant regulations in the Theravāda school, see Hüsken, *Die Vorschriften für die buddhistische Nonnengemeinde im Vinaya-Piṭaka der Theravādin,* 461.

71. Grimes, *Deeply into the Bone,* 89.

72. Kapferer, "Introduction," 3, 4.

73. However, Western *bhikṣuṇīs* also declared that they would be content with every form of ordination acceptable for the Tibetan monks.

74. It should be mentioned, however, that HH the Dalai Lama declared that "in terms of the modality of introducing Bhikshuni vows within the tradition, we have to remain within the boundaries set by the Vinaya," that is, the boundaries set by the Vinaya of the Mūlasarvāstivādin.

75. Rituals can also be regarded as the bodily dimension of law; see Wulf, "Recht und Ritual," 30.

Bibliography

Analayo, Bhikkhu. "Theories on the Foundation of the Nuns' Order—A Critical Evaluation." *Journal of the Centre for Buddhist Studies, Sri Lanka* 4 (2008): 105–42.

Bechert, Heinz. "Aśokas 'Schismenedikt' und der Begriff Sanghabheda." *Wiener Zeitschrift für die Kunde Süd- und Ostasiens* 5 (1961): 18–52.

Bikkhuni Winisaya Satan. Yangon: Ministry of Religious Affairs, 2004.

Concerning the Lineage of Bhikshuni Ordination. Proceedings of the Seminar of Mulasarvastiva [sic], *Theravada, and Dharmaguptaka Vinaya Holders, 3rd–5th August 1998 at the Noburlingka Institute, Dharamsala.* Ed. Central Tibetan Administration-in-Exile (India), Department of Religion and Culture. Dharamsala, 2002.

Davidson, Ronald M. *Tibetan Renaissance: Tantric Buddhism in the Rebirth of Tibetan Culture.* New York: Columbia University Press, 2005.

Derge. The Sde-dge Mtshal-par Bka'-'gyur. Facsimile edition of the eighteenth-century redaction of Si-Tu Chos-kyi-'byuṅ-gnas prepared under the direction of HH the 16th Rgyal-dbaṅ Karma-pa. Delhi, 1976.

Grimes, Ronald L. *Deeply into the Bone: Re-inventing Rites of Passage*. Berkeley: University of California Press, 2000.

Hinüber, Oskar von. "The Foundation of the Bhikkhunīsaṃgha: A Contribution to the Earliest History of Buddhism." In *Annual Report of the International Research Institute for Advanced Buddhology at Soka University for the Academic Year* 2007, 3–29. Tokyo, 2008.

Hüsken, Ute. "Ritual Dynamics and Ritual Failure." In *When Rituals Go Wrong: Mistakes, Failure, and the Dynamics of Ritual*, ed. Ute Hüsken, 337–66. Numen Book Series 115. Leiden: Brill, 2007.

———. "A Stock of Bowls Requires a Stock of Robes: Relations of the Rules for Nuns in the Theravāda Vinaya and the Bhikṣuṇī-Vinaya of the Mahāsāṃghika-Lokottaravādin." In *Untersuchungen zur buddhistischen Literatur II, Gustav Roth zum 80. Geburtstag gewidmet*, ed. Heinz Bechert, Sven Bretfeld, and Petra Kieffer-Pülz, 201–38. Sanskrit-Wörterbuch der buddhistischen Texte aus den Turfan-Funden, Beiheft 8. Göttingen, 2007.

———. *Die Vorschriften für die buddhistische Nonnengemeinde im Vinaya-Piṭaka der Theravādin*. Monographien zur indischen Archäologie, Kunst und Philologie 11. Berlin: Reimer, 1997.

Jampa Tsedroen. "Nonnenordination bald im tibetischen Buddhismus? Dalai Lama engagiert sich für Nonnen." *Tibet und Buddhismus* 20. Jg., 79, no. 4 (2006): 20–23.

———. "Wiederbelebung der Bhikṣuṇī-Gelübde im Tibetischen Buddhismus—Aktuelle Entwicklungen." In *Buddhismus in Geschichte und Gegenwart—Erneuerungsbewegungen. Weiterbildendes Studium Universität Hamburg*. Hamburg, 2006. (Also at http://www.buddhismuskunde.uni-hamburg.de/fileadmin/pdf/digitale_texte/Bd11-K09Roloff.pdf).

Kapferer, Bruce. "Introduction: Ritual Process and the Transformation of Context." *Social Analysis* 1 (1979): 3–19.

Kawanami, Hiroko. "The Bhikkhunī Ordination Debate: Global Aspirations, Local Concerns, with Special Emphasis on the Views of the Monastic Community in Burma." *Buddhist Studies Review* 24, no. 2 (2007): 226–44.

Kieffer-Pülz, Petra. "Die buddhistische Gemeinde." In *Der Buddhismus I: Der indische Buddhismus und seine Verzweigungen*, 278–399. Religionen der Menschheit. Stuttgart: Kohlhammer Verlag, 2000.

———. *Die Sīmā: Vorschriften zur Regelung der buddhistischen Gemeindegrenze in älteren buddhistischen Texten*. Monographien zur indischen Archäologie, Kunst und Philologie 8. Berlin: Reimer-Verlag, 1992.

———. "Die Wiedereinrichtung des Nonnenordens in der Theravāda-Tradition." In *Buddhismus in Geschichte und Gegenwart—Erneuerungsbewegungen—. Weiterbildendes Studium*, vol. 11. Universität Hamburg, 29–41. Hamburg, 2006. (Also at www.buddhismuskunde.uni-hamburg.de/fileadmin/pdf/digitale_texte/Bd11-K03KiefferPuelz.pdf; short English version: "The Restoration of the bhikkhunīsaṅgha in the Theravāda Tradition," www.congress-on-buddhist-women.org/fileadmin/files/Sri%20Lanka%20bki%20final.pdf. April 27, 2008.

Lottermoser, Friedgard. "Buddhist Nuns in Burma." *Sakyadhita Newsletter* 2, no, 2 (1991). (Also at www.enabling.org/ia/vipassana/Archive/L/Lottermoser/burmeseNunsLottermoser.html).

Mohr, Thea, and Jampa Tsedroen, eds. *Dignity and Discipline: Reviewing Full Ordination for Buddhist Nuns*. Boston: Wisdom Publications, 2007.

Moore, Sally Falk, and Barbara G. Myerhoff. "Secular Ritual: Forms and Meanings." In *Secular Ritual*, ed. Sally Falk Moore and Barbara G. Myerhoff, 3–24. Amsterdam: Van Gorcum, 1977.

Podeman Sørensen, Jørgen. "Efficacy." In *Theorizing Rituals: Classical Topics, Theoretical Approaches, Analytical Concepts, Annotated Bibliography*, ed. Jens Kreinath, Jan Snoek, and

Michael Stausberg, 523–32. Numen Book Series: Studies in the History of Religions 114–1. Leiden: Brill, 2006.

Ridding, Caroline Mary, and Louis de La Vallée Poussin. "A Fragment of the Sanskrit Vinaya, Bhikṣuṇīkarmavācanā." *Bulletin of the School of Oriental Studies* 1 (1920): 123–43.

Roloff, Carola. "Volle Ordination von Nonnen nur noch eine Frage der Zeit." *Tibet und Buddhismus* 83, no. 4 (2007): 12–14.

Schild, Wolfgang. "Recht und Körperlichkeit." In *Körper und Recht: anthropologische Dimensionen der Rechtsphilosophie*, ed. Ludger Schwarte, 130–45. München: Fink, 2003.

Schmidt, Michael. "Bhikṣuṇī-Karmavācanā. Die Handschrift Sansk. c.25® der Bodleian Library Oxford." In *Studien zur Indologie und Buddhismuskunde: Festgabe des Seminars für Indologie und Buddhismuskunde für Prof. Dr. Heinz Bechert*, ed. Reinhold Grünendahl et al., 239–88. Bonn: Indica et Tibetica 22, 1993.

Seeger, Martin. "The Bhikkhunī-Ordination Controversy in Thailand." *Journal of the International Association of Buddhist Studies* 29 (2008): 155–86.

Skilling, Peter. "A Note on the History of the Bhikkhunī-saṅgha (II)." *Pāli and Sanskrit Studies* (1993): 208–51.

Tashi Tsering, Acarya Geshe. *A Comparative Study of Mūlasarvāstivāda and Theravādin Vinaya.* Dharamsala: Central Tibetan Administration-in-Exile (India), Department of Religion and Culture, 2002.

Thub bstan byang chub, Acharya dge bshes (Acarya Muni Shasana Bodhi). *Bod du dge slong mar bsgrubs pa'i dpyad gzhi rab gsal me long* (Clear mirror: A basis of investigation regarding bhikṣuṇī ordination in Tibet). Dharamsala: Central Tibetan Administration-in-Exile (India), Department of Religion and Culture, 2000.

Wulf, Christoph. "Recht und Ritual." In *Körper und Recht: Anthropologische Dimensionen der Rechtsphilosophie*, ed. Ludger Schwarte, 30–45. München: Fink, 2003.

14

Negotiating the Social in the Ritual Theory of Victor Turner and Roy Rappaport

Grant Potts

THIS VOLUME FORWARDS the thesis that the concept of ritual is the result of a negotiation between different agents, including those who perform ritual and those who study it. The idea that concepts such as ritual are *negotiated* suggests a complementary notion that such concepts are scholarly *constructions*. Even if they adopt a term from the general lexicon of their culture, scholars invariably construct their concepts over a series of texts that in turn present intellectual negotiations as a writer articulates both what her theoretical forbears can contribute and what the subject of investigation itself has to say to the conversation. In writing anchored in fieldwork this process becomes especially apparent, as the writer negotiates between at least two fruitful zones of discourse—that of scholarship and that of the field—each of which she may be only partially familiar with as she conducts her investigation.

The introduction to the present volume identifies negations as "processes of interaction during which differing positions are debated and/or acted out." Thus a number of different positions are examined, disputed, and subverted by different actors, all with the purported goal of achieving agreement. The term "negotiation" has often been used to indicate the process of contestation and the mediation of different positions within or between fields of discourse. To have a negotiation, though, there has to be at least a pretense of a goal of reconciliation between the conflicting positions. This is not to suggest that negotiation necessarily achieves its goal of agreement, that this agreement cannot take the form of détente, that the goal of agreement is necessarily maintained if it is achieved, or that actors within a negotiation are forthright with their motives. I do not mean to substitute the word "negotiation" for a process of building consensus. Nevertheless without the goal of reconciling the different positions, there is no negotiation, there is only contestation.

Even with a clear goal of agreement, though, negotiation remains a complex process—and negotiation often takes place with very little sense of how agreement might be reached. As the process unfolds, additional sources of tension surface that require attention before one can proceed. One of the values of theoretical reflection on past scholarly work is its ability to uncover previous presuppositions that have driven inquiry and that may continue to motivate inquiry today. In shedding light on those presuppositions we gain greater understanding of the scope of the subject we are engaging, whether we decide that those presuppositions need to be retained, dismissed, or simply modified.[1] We catch the breaks within scholarly negotiation and, in the process, identify areas that may require further attention in future work.

Because the location of scholarly negotiation is by and large in texts, so it is that scholarly negotiation proceeds as much within the work of a particular writer as between different social actors. My argument is that, in the process of articulating their understandings of ritual, two twentieth-century theorists of ritual, Victor Turner and Roy Rappaport, mediate a long-standing negotiation between two notions of the social: on one hand the social as constituted within a structured, determinate whole, and on the other the social as constituted through an experience of ecstatic collectivity. Turner and Rappaport provide insightful cases for exploring such scholarly negotiation both because of their ongoing influence on contemporary understandings of ritual and because each helped articulate theories of ritual during the formative period for ritual studies in the decades following World War II.[2] For both Turner and Rappaport, ritual becomes the theoretical key to reconciling the two seemingly conflicting notions as the theorists identify ritual as a particular type of social experience that provides motivational substance to the social order. Before looking at their particular concepts of ritual, though, I offer a brief discussion of how these concepts of the social initially developed in the analysis of sacred practices by William Robertson Smith and Émile Durkheim.

EXPERIENCING THE SOCIAL: ROBERTSON SMITH AND DURKHEIM

Although both Turner and Rappaport come to an understanding of ritual through a number of sources, both theorists build that understanding out of a tradition of social thought defined by Émile Durkheim and his students. Durkheim in turn gained insight into the relationship between sacred action and the social constitution of the group through the Scottish ethnographer and churchman William Robertson Smith. Both Robertson Smith and Durkheim held that one could understand human society by first identifying its primary forms in "primitive" life, and so to understand this relationship between ritual and the social, they looked for an ideal form of that life.

The connection between Durkheim's and Robertson Smith's theories of religion is well established. Durkheim read Robertson Smith in 1895 and became convinced with that reading that religion was a particularly formative social institution.[3] Robertson Smith held that religion was a matter of practice as well as belief. He identified a primary form of religion he called natural religion, holding that in this primary form, religion is concerned with organizing the practical life of the group. Religion, then, is a type of polity, providing the basis for society through sacred tradition, thus giving structure to the institutions of social life.[4] Perhaps the most significant religious practice he focused on was that of sacrifice. As Margit Warburg points out, the "pivot of Robertson Smith's theory of Semitic sacrifice" is the idea that sacrifice is, first and foremost, a meal—an occasion to gather together for mutual nourishment.[5] Within the context of this meal is the experience of kinship with other attendees, and so as a symbolic act sacrifice accumulates the weight of that experience of communion.[6] The practical work of religion, then, was not merely in establishing a series of norms and institutions but also in providing the primary experience of collectivity that motivates those norms and institutions. Durkheim took up this two-part theory of the constitution of the social world.

The ideal form of social life sought by Robertson Smith and Durkheim was supplied by the concept of totemism. Both writers saw the sacrificial meal as originally a totemic meal in which the victim was a stand-in for the social group, a notion Durkheim extended to argue that the social group itself is the ultimate referent for sacred representations. Whereas Robertson Smith focused on the kinship of the sacrificial meal, Durkheim was more concerned with the mediation provided by the totemic animal. Durkheim postulated the totem as a kind of emblem for the group, an emblem that is infused with emotional power such that it became the focus of collective religious life.[7] To account for this power, he held that the religion of totemism eventually developed into that of a "kind of anonymous and impersonal force" that, though it could be associated with the totem, was not necessarily identical to it.[8] In his early essay "Concerning the Definition of Religious Phenomena" he identified this force as *l'esprit collectif*, but by the writing of *Elementary Forms of Religious Life* he used a Melanesian concept that Marcel Mauss and Henri Hubert had outlined in their *General Theory of Magic*, the concept of *mana*.[9] This force is rooted in a collective experience of communion in the primary sacred act. Durkheim used the metaphor of electricity to describe this experience, suggesting that the emotional intensity of gathering builds into a series of amplifications and feedback loops until it falls into a "rhythm or regularity."[10] The social group referenced in religious representations is thus a negotiation between two modes of the social: the force of emotional ecstasy and a developed series of beliefs and practices arising out of the regulated expression of that ecstasy in the life of the group.

The totemic theory of the sacrificial meal as the primary constituting social act eventually faded to the background of intellectual history. Later writers nevertheless continued the notion that religious acts performed the work of constituting the social group. Lacking the narrative of the totemic meal, though, a different understanding was needed to mediate between the ecstatic and the normative dimensions of the social. That concept was *ritual*.

RITUAL BETWEEN STRUCTURE AND COMMUNITAS: TURNER'S NEGOTIATION OF THE SOCIAL

Victor Turner's concept of ritual is notoriously untidy.[11] Ronald Grimes argues that this concept operates in at least three modes—a definition, a theory, and a sense of ritual—and that each mode in some way contradicts the others.[12] But even Grimes's assessment presents too neat a picture; Turner's work is better understood as an interacting network of concepts that emerge across a series of texts, each concept as much defined by its linkage to other ideas, texts, and reports of ethnographic experiences as by clear definition or determinate reference. This is not to suggest that, for Turner, a concept like ritual lacks substance, only that any attempt at formalizing Turner's thought will necessarily neglect to some degree the fluidity that defined his work.[13] What is clear is that he saw ritual as social, and while he did not suggest that it was necessarily the primary constituting social mode, he identified ritual as particularly fruitful for analyzing how the social is constituted.

Turner described ritual primarily through two other forms of social experience: symbols and social dramas. For Turner, ritual is a redressive activity in the process of a wider social drama. Actors use ritual to reconcile conflicting social norms to address a crisis created by a breach in the social field. Ritual's ability to address the crisis arises from its use of symbols. Turner saw symbols as intricately tied to ritual, identifying them as the "smallest unit of ritual which still retains the specific properties of ritual behavior."[14] Symbols, particularly the sacred symbols at the center of ritual, are able to mediate social crisis because they operate in a cultural field of reference defined by multivocality, association, and integration as much as by clear reference and distinction. In other words, it is the vagueness of ritual symbols that allows them to be tools to negotiate that crisis. A dominant symbol can bring together conflicting ideas, norms, or lower-level symbols because of its breadth of reference.[15] Turner further extended this reconciling function for ritual beyond the lived experience of crisis; he understood contradiction not only as something that arose in the process of the social drama, but as intrinsic to the social field itself. Thus he saw rituals as not only mediating the outbreak of crisis—as in rites of affliction, or as mediating the social norms of two stations within a life cycle, as in a rite of passage—but also as symbolically resolving tensions between conflicting normative structures that are part of the constitution of the group itself. An example of the latter was the matrilineal and verilocal principles of group affiliation that Turner identified as operational in his fieldwork among the Ndembu people.

Turner's commitment to the idea of the social as a structured and determinate whole reflects the tradition of thought in which he was trained, that of British social anthropology. While he rejected the idealistic structuralism of Claude Lévi-Strauss, his own work followed that of the tradition instantiated by A. R. Radcliffe-Brown, a tradition that validated social structure as the way of understanding the arrangements of institutions, roles, and norms in a social field.[16] Turner understood this structure as an ordered whole: even if individual social actors may not comprehend the system in its totality, that system nevertheless emerges clearly across the social field and can be diagrammed by a trained observer.[17] Yet he had to fit the concepts of this tradition of interpretation to his experience in the field, to understand and interpret the rituals he was observing among the Ndembu. His earliest field reports concentrated almost exclusively on symbolic analysis, identifying multivocal symbols as primarily responsible for bringing resolution and solidarity to the group in instances of conflict. He developed a method for examining these symbols that relied heavily on informant exegesis of particular symbols, exegesis he then analyzed to understand both how the various symbols interact and how they relate to a larger symbolic system. One of his earliest analyses of the *Chihamba* rite, for instance, displays such an approach. The rite is conducted by the Ndembu in response to a perceived affliction by the spirit of a female ancestor and further involves a natural spirit named Kavula. First publishing his report as a paper issued by the Rhodes-Livingston Institute in 1962, Turner gave a point-by-point account of the episodes of the ritual, breaking between episodes to share exegesis by the Ndembu interlocutors. He followed this account with his own discussion of the symbols in the rite, identifying primary symbols, like the whiteness associated with Kavula, as integrating many of the disparate meanings around virtue and masculinity and thus providing efficacy for the participants.[18] At this point in his thought it is structural aspects of certain symbols that mediate social conflicts.

Having both observed and participated in these rituals, though, he could not simply portray them as functioning exclusively through representation. The rituals were lived events, and to participate in ritual was to experience it. Initially he approached this experience through the idea that, through their vague, multivocal field of reference, ritual symbols allowed the participants to engage with the ritual on both a cognitive and an emotional level. In his early reports, like that of the *Chihamba* rite, he merely identified this emotional dimension but did not give it substantial elaboration.[19] As he developed his theory of ritual, though, he gave this psychological, emotional dimension more discussion. In his report on the *Nkang'a* ritual, a Ndembu rite of passage for girls, carrying them into womanhood, he followed the same style of report developed for his discussion of *Chihamba*. Continuing with his symbolic analysis, he then went into more depth on how the primary symbol of this second ritual, the *mudyi* tree, carrying associations with matrilineal descent and femininity, is placed in conflict and resolution with masculine symbols associated with verilocality. While he continued to describe symbols as accumulating a field of reference, by this point he was prepared to say that it is the experience of unity within the ritual that provides the resolution of conflict. The solidarity of the work of performance sets the conflicts within an overall context of group unity. While the *Nkang'a* ritual portrays, symbolically, common conflicts within Ndembu social life, "all the conflicts, great or small, overtly expressed or concealed under symbolic guise, are made to subserve the great aim of the ritual, to convert a girl into a fruitful married woman, fully aware of the rights and duties of her adult status."[20]

For the most part, though, Turner steered clear of trying to provide a psychological analysis of this dynamic within ritual, considering it beyond his particular expertise.

What he is remembered for is developing a sociocultural language to account for these experiences of solidarity and to position that experience as in dialectical tension with the structural components of society, as a mode of antistructure. In choosing the terminology of antistructure, though, he did not want to position these components as primarily destructive to social structure. They are positive and generative modes of the social that operate in relation to structure.[21] His initial inspiration came from his reading of Arnold von Gennep, whose concept of liminality helped Turner understand phases within rituals where social norms are suspended or inverted, thereby creating an experience of the social outside those norms.[22] Turner chose to call that experience *communitas*, where social differentiation is replaced by "homogeneity and comradeship."[23] In developing the concept of communitas he revisited his observations of the *Nkang'a* ritual regarding the emotional solidarity of ritual actors and amplified them into a state experienced by the subjects in the ritual process. Both that initial sense of ritual solidarity and the idea of a state of ecstatic emotional communion recall Durkheim's primal experience of collectivity discussed above, particularly emphasizing the connection between people that occurs in that experience. Turner transformed what is essentially a conjectured historical experience into something that is an ongoing process within the normative order of society. In the process he also gave this alternate mode of the social a theoretical form and substance it had hitherto lacked.

As Turner thought through the concept of ritual, he sought to reconcile the two contrasting notions of the social that Durkheim and Robertson Smith had identified before him, normativity and collectivity. In the earlier tradition negotiating the positions into a theoretical whole essentially positioned them as force and form. *Mana* provided force that motivated the normative form of society. Turner, in contrast, set them as two forms of the social in dialectical tension, on one hand the social as structure and on the other hand the antistructural notion of the social as an experience of human collectivity, both mediated by ritual. His ability to give this theoretical constitution to that notion of collectivity came from his own experience observing rituals, participating in them, and engaging insider accounts of the meaning of the rituals. His notion of the social incorporated not only what he learned from his participation and attention to the wider context of ritual, but the idea of experience that participation itself implies. As Bennetta Jules-Rosette notes in her examination of Turner as an ethnographer, he is one of the earliest anthropologists to include his subjects' interpretations as legitimate voices within his own account, to give a place within the negotiation of the meaning of ritual to the ritual participants themselves.[24] Thus he had to account for ritual not merely as a representation of the social, but as an experience of the social, a living experience of collectivity and its representations.

THE RHYTHM OF THE SACRED: RAPPAPORT'S NEGOTIATION OF THE SOCIAL

In contrast to Turner, Roy Rappaport was a highly formal thinker. Although he developed his concept of ritual over the course of his life—in his ethnographic report, occasional essays, and debates—he systematized his concept in a single text, *Ritual and Religion in the Making of Humanity*. Keith Hart points toward the stylistic similarities between Rappaport's argument and those of analytic philosophy, but his formality is not purely stylistic.[25] Rappaport resisted persistent labeling as a functionalist, arguing instead that his construction of ritual was primarily as a formal category, defined as a series of characteristics independent of either the content or the purpose of the ritual form.[26] But his concept of ritual is not limited to this formal definition; rather it unfolds from the definition, and in the process engages a series of other concepts borrowed from realms as disparate as evolutionary biology, phenomenology of religion, and his own ethnographic experience. Like Turner, Rappaport understood ritual to be a social concept and "*the* basic social act."[27]

Rappaport defined ritual as "the performance of more or less invariant sequences of formal acts and utterances not entirely encoded by the performers."[28] Most significant for my analysis is his emphasis on invariance, adherence to convention (formality), and the dislocation of encoding from performers. Though he avoided recourse to functionality in defining ritual, nevertheless his formal definition accounts for ritual's role in maintaining social order through the encoding of social norms, even against the continued violation of those norms in practice.[29] Ritual becomes a kind of grand engine that, because of its invariance and because it carries encoded acts and utterances that are independent of the direct intention of performers, preserves the ideas and forms necessary to maintain a coherent social whole. Rites themselves are part of a larger liturgical order that organizes life to provide the fundamental principles through which a social world is maintained. Also, because performers must accept the constraints of the liturgical order to participate in it, they must structurally accept that order, making ritual the foundation of morals.[30] Again a comparison with Turner is helpful. Turner saw ritual as fundamental to social constitution but emphasized its particular role in reconciling contradictions within the social. Although he did not dedicate substantial portions of his work to it, he acknowledged other institutions and practices, such as juridical practices, that also serve to constitute the social. For Rappaport, other such practices are derivative from ritual, as they rely on liturgical orders to maintain the premises upon which they are based. He states, "In enunciating, accepting and making conventions moral, ritual contains within itself not simply a symbolic representation of the social contract, but tacit social contract itself."[31]

The image of the social contract is an apt one, as it displays Rappaport's understanding of the social as a coherent, normative order. The social is like a civil constitution, comprising a series of top-level premises that are considered highly invariant and subject to amendment only under extreme cases. These top-level premises he terms *ultimate sacred postulates*. He claimed that these postulates have their origin in the formal structure of ritual itself, in both the relative invariance within ritual and the acceptance the actor must have of the ritual form in order to participate in it. He identified them as statements that occur repeatedly in rituals that have potentially little relevance to the intent of the performers engaging in the rituals and that carry the foundational premises out of which the moral order is built. These postulates themselves do not necessarily contain a great deal of information; rather their meaning arises in the acceptance of their certainty as postulates upon which more informational axioms can be founded.[32] Thus the normative social order is essentially an organized series of statements, the most fundamental of which primarily serve to constitute the order and are encoded in rituals. There is a curious resonance between Turner's idea of dominant symbols and Rappaport's idea of ultimate sacred postulates. Both posit an ordered system centered on entities of meaning that are able to bring together more determinate aspects of social norms precisely because of their vagueness. What is notable is that in attempting to forge a determinate notion of the social that can account for change, transformation, and supposedly lower-level variance, both theorists posited relatively indeterminate root structures.

Despite the formality of his analysis, Rappaport was not an analytic philosopher; he was an anthropologist. Thus he had to account for how his formal construct of ritual actually relates to the practice of ritual in lived experience. He had to give a theoretical account for why it is that humans engage in this kind of behavior, of what motivates them. On the most basic level he argued that ritual is a useful tool in adaptation, in maintaining groups that allow us to survive and reproduce. He developed his initial understanding of ritual as regulatory in his report on a particular group of Maring, the Tsembega. That report focused on a multiyear ritual cycle regulating warfare between groups of Maring, ultimately culminating in the *kaiko* festival, featuring the ritual sacrifice of a large proportion of the group's stock of pigs. Thus he postulated that the cycle not only regulated warfare but also relations with the local ecology, as it regularly decreased a pig population that would eventually have grown to a harmful level.[33] As he generalized his understanding of ritual's role to all of humanity, he argued that the entire system of ritual and religion arose as a response to a problem created by language. Language allows us to reference things that are not present, and therefore it allows us to lie, and so destroys the trust fundamental to group cohesion, thereby threatening human survival.[34] Liturgical orders reestablish that trust by creating foundations for certainty in our social relations.

At the center of his argument Rappaport followed Durkheim and Turner in looking for the establishment of this certainty in collective ecstatic experience. Like them, he saw this as occurring within the experience of ritual, where the normal conditions of social operation are dismissed in favor of the conditions required by the separate time defined by ritual. Whereas Turner emphasized the experience of communion that arises in this period of communitas, Rappaport emphasized the rhythmicity and loss of personal identity that occurs in the ecstatic experience, such that the ritual experience is that of belonging to a larger organism rather than being an individual actor. Actions are no longer decisions; they follow with certainty from those actions around the actor, creating an experience that exists as a whole.[35] It is out of this experience that humans regain trust in the group, grounding that trust in the postulates they encounter as part of that ritual experience. Thus in a muted form Rappaport retains the second idea of the social as an ecstatic experience of collectivity by rooting that experience in the evolutionary necessity of social trust.

While Rappaport based his early understanding of ritual on his observation of the Tsembega's *kaiko* festival, his later development of the concept of ritual was primarily as an intellectual construct. He often returns to his own account of Maring ritual life and to others' reports of rituals in constructing his theory of ritual, but after giving his report in his first book, *Pigs for the Ancestors*, he does not provide additional original interpretations of ritual. Also in contrast with Turner, while Rappaport sought to account for his subject's interpretations of their ritual life, he did not give them a voice in the negotiation of the ultimate meaning of those rituals. Instead he engaged ideas and concepts from other scholars, often directly confronting critical readings of his work, as he did in the almost 150-page epilogue appended to the second edition of *Pigs*. It is really in these later writings, negotiated in scholarly debate, that he formulates his theory of ritual in relation to these two understandings of the social. In *Pigs* the social as a normative order is assumed, though that order is almost exclusively described through ritual. Later, in part using Turner's theory of communitas, Rappaport formulated this normative order as gaining its motivation through ecstatic communion. His reconciliation of the two notions of the social seems to subordinate the experience of collectivity to the normative social order, yet it also makes that experience constitutive to the liturgical orders that provide the foundation for social order, even their very reason for existence. There is thus a dialectical relationship between trust and order beyond what his linear, evolutionary narrative might initially suggest, as both modes constitute each other—the experience of certainty providing the context for ultimate sacred postulates, which in turn provide the social context for those experiences to take place.

NEGOTIATING RITUAL, NEGOTIATING THE SOCIAL

Turner and Rappaport both examined ritual as a way to understand human social life, and so their inquiry was guided by the presupposition that ritual is foremost a type of social action, a presupposition they inherited from Durkheim and his students. This presupposition continues to guide much of ritual studies today. We look at rituals as windows into the social world, though we may debate the dimensions of the social that window will show us and the opacity of glass through which we look. Over a decade ago Ronald Grimes questioned this presupposition, arguing that the priority and emphasis that ritual studies gives to this collective dimension of ritual may neglect important research into the role of ritual as a potential process of individuation.[36] Yet even an account of individualized ritual would require an understanding of the social that the individual relates to, so the question is not so much whether ritual is truly a social act, but what is at stake and what is entailed in thinking of it as such. Even if we recognize that rituals are necessarily neither traditional nor always collective, we can nevertheless see in ritual an action that reaches between the traditional and the collective, between an immediate lived experience and a larger experience of a social world that transcends that particular moment. Turner's and Rappaport's respective negotiations of the social as both normative structure and ecstatic communion arose as an account of the relationship between the immediate experience of the social and the experience of its larger frame. The field of ritual studies has increasingly concerned itself with ritual as a creative force, and the tension and resolution around the seemingly conflicting ideas of the social suggest a location for examining that creativity. Whether it was figured as trust or comradeship, both Turner and Rappaport were able to recognize within that collective experience a force that *makes*, that forges together and channels human creativity and social experience. The negotiation of ritual is not merely between social actors, but between different representations of the social experience for those actors and for their interpreters.

Turner's and Rappaport's examinations of ritual as social action also display the multiple levels of interest that exist within theorizing about ritual. Recent analysis of ritual theory has focused on the interest of power in the development of the concept of ritual. Catherine Bell states that the concept of ritual is "the result of a drawn-out, complex, intrinsically political process of negotiating cultural differences and similarities."[37] As theorizing is, like ritual, a practice, Bell considers ritual theory as constituted in an essentially political context, conditioned by interests of cultural and material accumulation. While there is no question that raw political interest is an important dimension to any aspect of human life, it rarely takes the form of purely rational interest—whether that interest is understood as motivating rational choice in the marketplace of ideas or as occluded by ideological pressures. And there are always other interests at work. Within the practice of scholarship there are competing interests with respect to the accumulation of power and capital, not the least of which is an intellectual interest in the subject matter itself. In ritual studies the intellectual interest at stake, though, is not only that of understanding ritual, but also that of understanding the social world. Although contemporary analysis of ritual may not use as rigid an understanding of the normative social order as Rappaport or even Turner did, we must question the level at which the social is such a determinate order. If ritual arises in an experience of creative action rooted in collective life, the dynamism implicit in that action suggests that the order and the interests that motivate ritual are only partially determinate. It is telling that both Turner and Rappaport had to rely on relatively indeterminate root structures, dominant symbols and ultimate sacred postulates, as operating at the center of their respective accounts of the symbolic systems associated with ritual. It is the relative indeterminate nature of these structures that allows them to engage in the participation, subversion, and contextualization that the present volume identifies as central to negotiation.

But the interest motivating ritual theory is not solely political or intellectual. Both Turner and Rappaport identify a central role for communitas, with the experience either of companionship or of trust. Where Durkheim had to imagine the primal experience of collectivity in his hypothetical subjects, both Turner and Rappaport encountered it directly in their fieldwork. The negotiation between the social as a determinate order and as an experience of communion or trust reflects a deeper negotiation taking place between the understanding of the social as a theoretical entity and the experience of the social in human life. As ethnographers Turner and Rappaport experienced both a high degree of differentiation from their subjects and a loss of certainty about their own role, and yet both found themselves welcomed into a collectivity that was not their own, where the social structures operated in unfamiliar terms, and yet where each scholar found shelter, comradeship, and trust. Both scholars also experienced rituals, whether as observers or as participants. Positing ritual as a mediating process between two dimensions of the social world allowed them to mediate then own experience with the constructed understanding of ritual in scholarly discourse. Their examples suggest a significant role for experience both in constituting the category of ritual and in understanding the role of ritual for participants, and ritual studies would do well to more substantially explore the issue of experience, as Turner himself suggested toward the end of his life.[38] It is insufficient to simply point to the significance of experience, though. The exploration that Turner called for demands the development of a formal language for understanding the dynamics of that experience, with particular attention to the relation between the immediacy of the experience engaged in direct participation and the mediated experience of a wider frame that is engaged by contextualization.

The concept of ritual is historically constituted through the negotiation of commonsense uses of the term, academic theory-construction, and experiences of ritual by both participants and observers. This suggests that ritual is more then an arbitrary scholarly construct, but a meaningful category for understanding human experiences and expressions of their social worlds. This is not to say that we can delimit ritual as a universal category; rather ritual's historically constituted nature provides the texture of understanding that allows us to continue to examine sacred actions as modes through which the social is performed, negotiated, experienced, and understood. Having identified a particular trajectory through which different dimensions of the social are understood, and understood to be negotiated through ritual, I would suggest that it is precisely as this mediated, negotiated, multidimensional framework that social action is best situated. Turner's and Rappaport's theories of ritual, whatever their particular failings, remain compelling because they did not reduce ritual or the social to a particular, determinate entity, but rather maintained an openness that allowed those concepts to function effectively in the interpretation of ritual experience.

Notes

1. I follow Gadamer's analysis of the role of prejudice in understanding. He states that in a hermeneutical situation, sensitivity to the otherness of the subject under inquiry "involves neither 'neutrality' with respect to content nor extinction of one's self, but the foregrounding and appropriation of one's fore-meanings and prejudices" (*Truth and Method,* 271). My goal here is to foreground one particularly significant area of presupposition in the constitution of ritual as a category of experience.

2. Catherine Bell identifies both Rappaport and Turner as key figures in the development of social theories of ritual (*Ritual,* 29–30, 39–42). Although Turner's influence and relevance are

widespread, it is most evident in the work of two students of his own mentor, Max Gluckman, Don Handelman and Bruce Kapferer, and in his influence on interpretive approaches to ritual within religious studies, such as those of Ronald Grimes. Rappaport's influence has primarily been on ecological anthropology, though with the posthumous publication of his major work in 1999, he has been more substantially engaged across the field of ritual studies. For a recent example, note the use of his work in Seligman, Weller, Puett, and Simon, *Ritual and Its Consequences.*

3. See Revière, "William Robertson Smith and John Ferguson Mclennan," 301. Smith's lectures were published in 1894, but they received extensive, if critical, review in the French *Revue de l'histoire des religions* in 1890. See Strenski, *Theology and the First Theory of Sacrifice,* 109.

4. Robertson Smith, *Religion of the Semites.*

5. Warburg, "William Robertson Smith and the Study of Religion," 48.

6. Robertson Smith, *Religion of the Semites,* 269–81.

7. Durkheim, *The Elementary Forms of Religious Life*, 118.

8. Ibid., 191.

9. Durkheim, "Concerning the Definition of Religious Phenomena," 94. See also Durkheim, *Elementary Forms*, 327; Mauss and Hubert, *A General Theory of Magic*, 108–12.

10. Durkheim, *Elementary Forms*, 217–18.

11. See Grimes, *Beginnings in Ritual Studies*, 154; Handelman, "Is Victor Turner Receiving His Intellectual Due?," 122.

12. Grimes, "Victor Turner's Definition, Theory, and Sense of Ritual," 141–46.

13. Matthieu Deflem provides such a formalization, systematically outlining Turner's thought. Deflem nevertheless acknowledges many of the tensions of that thought. See "Ritual, Anti-Structure, and Religion," 1–25.

14. Turner, *The Forest of Symbols,* 19.

15. On dominant symbols, see ibid., 50; Deflem, "Ritual, Anti-Structure, and Religion," 6.

16. Turner, *Dramas, Fields and Metaphors,* 201.

17. Ibid., 36.

18. Turner, *Revelation and Divination in Ndembu Ritual,* 168–69.

19. Ibid., 175.

20. Turner, *The Drums of Affliction,* 267.

21. Ibid., 273.

22. Turner, *On the Edge of the Bush,* 7.

23. Turner, *The Ritual Process,* 96.

24. Jules-Rosette, "Decentering Ethnography," 166.

25. Rappaport, *Ritual and Religion in the Making of Humanity,* xvi.

26. Ibid., 29.

27. Rappaport, *Ecology, Meaning, and Religion,* 174; Rappaport, *Ritual and Religion*, 138, emphasis in the original.

28. Rappaport, *Ritual and Religion*, 24.

29. Ibid., 130.

30. Ibid., 133.

31. Ibid., 138.

32. Ibid., 284–86.

33. Rappaport, *Pigs for the Ancestors,* 166.

34. Rappaport, *Ritual and Religion*, 11–17.

35. Ibid., 219–30.

36. Grimes, *Reading, Writing, and Ritualizing,* 11.

37. Bell, *Ritual*, 259.

38. Turner, *Edge of the Bush*, 221–24.

Bibliography

Bell, Catherine. *Ritual: Perspectives and Dimensions*. Oxford: Oxford University Press, 1997.

Deflem, Mathieu. "Ritual, Anti-Structure, and Religion: A Discussion of Victor Turner's Processual Symbolic Analysis." *Journal for the Scientific Study of Religion* 30, no. 1 (1991): 1–25.

Durkheim, Émile. "Concerning the Definition of Religious Phenomena." In *Durkheim on Religion: A Selection of Readings with Bibliographies and Introductory Remarks*, ed. W. S. F. Pickering. London: Routledge and Kegan Paul, 1975.

———. *The Elementary Forms of Religious Life*. Trans. Karen E. Fields. New York: Free Press, 1995.

Gadamer, Hans-Georg. *Truth and Method*. New York: Continuum, 2004.

Grimes, Ronald. *Beginnings in Ritual Studies*. Revised ed. Columbia: University of South Carolina Press, 1995.

———. *Reading, Writing, and Ritualizing: Ritual in Fictive, Liturgical, and Public Places*. Washington, DC: Pastoral Press, 1993.

———. "Victor Turner's Definition, Theory, and Sense of Ritual." In *Victor Turner and the Construction of Cultural Criticism: Between Literature and Anthropology*, ed. Kathleen M. Ashley, 141–6. Bloomington: Indiana University Press, 1990.

Handelman, Don. "Is Victor Turner Receiving His Intellectual Due?" *Journal of Ritual Studies* 7, no. 2 (1993): 117–24.

Jules-Rosette, Bennetta. "Decentering Ethnography: Victor Turner's Vision of Anthropology." *Journal of Religion in Africa* 24, no. 2 (1994): 160–81.

Mauss, Marcel, and Henri Hubert. *A General Theory of Magic*. Trans. Robert Brain. London: Routledge and Kegan Paul, 1972.

Rappaport, Roy. *Ecology, Meaning, and Religion*. Richmond, CA: North Atlantic Books, 1979.

———. *Pigs for the Ancestors: Ritual in the Ecology of a New Guinea People*. 2d ed. New Haven: Yale University Press, 1984.

———. *Ritual and Religion in the Making of Humanity*. Cambridge: Cambridge University Press, 1999.

Revière, Paul. "William Robertson Smith and John Ferguson McLennan: The Aberdeen Roots of British Social Anthropology." In *William Robertson Smith: Essays in Reassessment*, ed. William Johnstone, 293–302. Sheffield, UK: Sheffield Academic Press, 1994.

Robertson Smith, William. *Religion of the Semites*. New Brunswick, NJ: Transaction, 2002.

Seligman, Adam, Robert R. Weller, Michael J. Puett, and Bennett Simon, *Ritual and Its Consequences: An Essay on the Limits of Sincerity*. Oxford: Oxford University Press, 2008.

Strenski, Ivan. *Theology and the First Theory of Sacrifice*. Leiden: Brill, 2003.

Turner, Victor. *Dramas, Fields and Metaphors*. Ithaca, NY: Cornell University Press, 1974.

———. *The Drums of Affliction: A Study of Religious Processes among the Ndembu of Zambia*. London: Oxford University Press, 1968.

———. *The Forest of Symbols: Aspects of Ndembu Ritual*. Ithaca, NY: Cornell University Press, 1967.

———. *On the Edge of the Bush: Anthropology as Experience*. Tucson: University of Arizona Press, 1985.

———. *Revelation and Divination in Ndembu Ritual*. Ithaca, NY: Cornell University Press, 1975.

———. *The Ritual Process: Structure and Anti-Structure*. New York: Aldine de Gruyter, 1995.

Warburg, Margit. "William Robertson Smith and the Study of Religion." *Religion* 19 (1989): 41–61.

INDEX